VISIONS
ACROSS THE AMERICAS

Short Essays for Composition

J. STERLING WARNER
Evergreen Valley College

JUDITH HILLIARD
San Jose State University

VINCENT PIRO
Merced College

Harcourt Brace Jovanovich College Publishers

Fort Worth   Philadelphia   San Diego   New York   Orlando   Austin   San Antonio
Toronto   Montreal   London   Sydney   Tokyo

D0153620

Publisher	Ted Buchholz
Acquisitions Editor	Michael Rosenberg
Development Editor	Christine Caperton
Design / Project Editor	Publications Development Company
Production Manager	Kathleen Ferguson
Cover Art & Design Supervisor	Vicki McAlindon Horton
Cover Design	Eva Thornton
Composition	Publications Development Company

Cover Image: Fanny Zucchiatti; 4″ × 5″ full-color transparency of cross-cultural illustration.

Requests for permission to make copies of any part of the work should be made to: Permissions Department, Harcourt Brace Jovanovich Publications, 8th Floor, Orlando, Florida 32887.

Address Editorial Correspondence to: 301 Commerce Street, Suite 3700, Fort Worth, TX 76102

Address Orders to: 6277 Sea Harbor Drive, Orlando, FL 32887
1-800-782-4479, or 1-800-433-0001. (in Florida)

Acknowledgments appear on pages 401–403

Printed in the United States of America

Library of Congress Cataloging-in-Publication Data
Visions across the Americas : short essays for composition / [compiled
   by] Sterling Warner, Judith Hilliard, Vincent Piro.
      p.   cm.
   Includes index.
   ISBN 0-03-073594-7
   1. College readers.   2. English language—Rhetoric.   I. Warner,
Sterling.   II. Hilliard, Judith.   III. Piro, Vincent.
PE1417.V56   1991
808′.0427—dc20   91-28429
                                                                          CIP

2 3 4 5   016   9 8 7 6 5 4 3 2 1

PREFACE

Visions Across the Americas, a basic-writing reader, takes an intensive look at cross-cultural issues and themes affecting the lives of Americans today as well as those in the past. Overall, the essays represented in the text offer a broad perspective of selected topics, providing an opportunity to evaluate and re-evaluate biases, prejudices, or "programmed notions" about subjects. Most importantly, the selections present good writings that act as models. Such model essays are valuable tools in generating material for writing logs and journals, for collaborative work activities, and for individual writing assignments, all of which encourage creativity and help the reader to think and write clearly and critically.

The reading selections in *Visions Across the Americas* are arranged from easiest to most difficult. Some of the readings challenge and test the reader's new abilities. To re-enforce an understanding of rhetorical modes and their purposes, a short discussion of them is included at the beginning of each chapter. The brief list of tips that follows tells how to effectively compose a particular type of essay (i.e., narration or cause/effect). Additional writing topics are included at the end of each rhetorical chapter, and a glossary of common literary and rhetorical terms appears as an appendix. This book is designed primarily to consider short essay development through rhetorical mode but does more than merely acquaint students with cause/effect, argumentation, narration, and so on. The selections also enrich students' vocabulary because clear, written expression often is a matter of good reasoning coupled with a broad command of words in the English language.

To emphasize the connection between reading and writing, we have designed specific questions and activities to engage students in the reading process. We suggest that you *first* thoroughly consider pre-reading questions and do what they suggest prior to reading the selection. *Second*, scan the composition, underline, list, and then write the definition of each unfamiliar word. *Third*, carefully read the composition and jot down in the margins of the text any notes or questions that come to mind. *Fourth*, reread the selection after looking over the post-reading questions and then write the answers to the questions found in the following sections: Content, Strategies and Structures, and Language and Vocabulary.

Many students may be unfamiliar with the reading-writing process. Therefore, apart from a discussion of reading strategies, we have included a brief overview of the writing process in Chapter One that (1) serves as a resource for students and (2) allows instructors the flexibility to teach what we offer, disregard it, and/or combine our information with that from a standard rhetoric. We have narrowed our discussion of the writing process to (a) generating writing topics, (b) organizing material for paragraphs and essays, and (c) strengthening and developing one's thesis or controlling ideas. Once students have made the connection between reading and writing, how the two go hand-in-hand, they not only will read more clearly with greater retention but also be able to respond to material critically and confidently, which will be important to their growth as writers.

This text was greatly enriched by the careful, critical responses that we received from our reviewers: Lawrence Carlson, Orange Coast College; Jeannine Edwards, Memphis State University; Margie Glazier, Merced College; Carolyn Hartnett, College of the Mainland; Shirley Kahlert, Evergreen Valley College; Regina Lebowitz, New York City Technical College; Robert Mehaffy, American River College; Margaret Murray, Temple University; and Joanne Pinkston, Daytona Beach Community College. We appreciate their thoughtful comments.

We want to thank the authors who have contributed to *Visions Across the Americas*, Carole Warner for her help with the layout of our initial manuscript, San Jose State University for its technical support, and our family, friends, and colleagues for their encouragement and patience while we were writing our text. We also want to thank those at Harcourt Brace Jovanovich, particularly: Michael Rosenberg, English Acquisitions Editor;

Christine Caperton, our Developmental Editor; Mary Pat Donlon, Marketing Manager; Kathleen Ferguson, Production Manager; and Nancy Land, Project Editor at Publications Development Company, for their time, cooperation and assistance in preparing our text. Finally, our indebtedness to Stephanie Surface, HBJ Publisher's Representative, deserves special mention; her enthusiasm, support and critical advice never wavered as she followed our text from its inception to its completion.

Sterling Warner
Judith Hilliard
Vincent Piro

RHETORICAL CONTENTS

11 ARGUMENTATION: THE LOGICAL APPEAL   308

THEMATIC CONTENTS

EDUCATION AND INTELLIGENCE

PLACES

PEOPLE

LIFESTYLES

OLD AGE

RACISM AND SEXISM

AMERICAN SOCIETY

PREJUDICES AND STEREOTYPES

WORKING IN AMERICA

TRADITION AND RITUAL

1

COMMUNICATING IS LANGUAGE AT WORK

Listening, speaking, reading, and writing all deal with communication. If you write a word, you create meaning by simply arranging letters in some sort of recognizable pattern. Words, whether spoken or written, assist people in expressing themselves, for instance, in relating a story, presenting an argument, or explaining a misunderstanding. The ability to communicate in one way or another enables one to explore ideas and issues outside of his or her realm of personal experience.

In the following essays, the authors explore many different issues about language use. Amy Tan looks at her mother's English and how it influences the way others perceive her. Peter Elbow is interested in the writing process, particularly how one can generate topics and ideas by "freewriting." Looking at his own writing habits, Donald Murray illustrates that writing takes place in several stages; it does not just "happen." Coming from the American Indian oral tradition, Frank LaPeña discusses the merits of listening to our elders as they share their knowledge, wisdom, and stories with us. In each instance, the author illustrates the power of language.

Before you begin reading, it would be helpful to review the *process* of reading—how to read carefully and correctly and how to become actively involved in the reading process. The following tips will help you to become an active reader.

Tips on Becoming an Active Reader

1. **Preview Your Reading.** Before you begin to read, preview the selection and get an idea of what to expect from the piece. Previewing means that you:

   • Read the title. Does it suggest what the article or story will be about?

   • Scan the subheadings. What do they suggest about the order of this piece?

   • Read the opening and concluding paragraphs since main ideas are often presented and summarized in these sections. Is there a thesis or controlling idea presented in the first paragraph? Is there a concluding statement in the final paragraph?

   • Read any bibliographical or biographical prefaces. Who wrote the piece? When and where was the piece written? How might this information suggest something about the essay or story?

2. **Ask Questions.** Remain active while reading by asking questions about the piece. You can start with the title; turn it into a question by using one of the journalist's six queries (who, what, where, when, why, and how). As you read, question a character's motives, the validity of an argument, or the "meaning" of the piece. Ask yourself what the author is trying to accomplish here, what is the main point of his or her argument, and what makes this an effective or ineffective composition? (You should jot these questions down in the margins.)

3. **Make Connections.** To make connections between what you have read and your own life constantly ask yourself what in your life is similar to this author's experiences or ideas. Begin by looking into: (1) your past to find connections between the reading and yourself, (2) the world around you to see what relates to your reading, (3) history

to see what in the past connects to what you are reading now, and (4) your past readings to see what you already have experienced that affirms or repudiates the ideas of this author.

4. **Recognizing Patterns That Lead to Coherence.** Try to discover a pattern of development: Is the author comparing and contrasting, moving from general to specific, showing cause and effect, or exploring a problem and solution? How do patterns of development help to establish relationships between words, clauses, and phrases leading to an understanding of the writer's ultimate purpose?

5. **Underline and Jot Down Notes.** If you are an active reader, you will write a lot, underlining things you feel are essential to an understanding of the piece: the thesis, the main ideas, important examples and images, key words, and new vocabulary. Terms that cause confusion—unknown words, confusing passages that need rereading, and unfamiliar names—are also underlined or noted in some way.

   You also will write in the margins quite a bit. Sometimes, it's as simple as noting "thesis!" or "key term." Other times, it's to help with rereading, "What does all this mean?" "Confusing." At times, notes in the margins make judgments, such as "good point—we do all need love" or "this example does not prove the point."

6. **Reread and Re-Evaluate.** Since reading is a process similar to writing, there is a rereading stage. It is necessary to go back over particularly illustrative examples or what you feel are the main points of the essay, reread confusing sections, and search the passage for a key phrase that will clarify an idea. It is particularly helpful to read a confusing passage aloud, paying careful attention to the punctuation.

7. **Write.** After reading and rereading, you may begin to write by summarizing the ideas found in the essay, writing an evaluation of the piece, or establishing connections between different readings.

8. **Share with Others.** Sharing your thoughts with others can often produce a new line of thinking and better ideas for writing. How? You can discuss what you enjoyed or disliked about a piece, what you felt the author hoped to accomplish,

what connections you made between the reading and your own experiences and observations, what passages you found confusing, what ideas you have on the subject matter, and how they either validate or reject the author's ideas.

The following excerpt from Toni Morrison's article "Writers Together" has been annotated in the same fashion that you will use to mark your own reading assignments. It further illustrates steps a writer might take to become actively involved in an article or story he or she is reading.

Writers Together
TONI MORRISON

A poet, essayist, and novelist, Toni Morrison's works include *The Bluest Eye* (1970), *Sula* (1973), *Song of Solomon* (1977), *Tar Baby* (1981), and *Beloved* (1985). In addition to writing, Morrison has worked as an editor for Random House Publishing Company.

Something is wrong. The puddle of public funds *good imagery* allocated to writers (always the least amount of all the arts) has been reduced to drops. Government support has been so blasted that it is at the moment a *strange term - why did author choose this?* gesture of nickels and dimes so humiliating, so contemptuous of writers, that one is staggered by the sheer gall.

Editors are judged by the profitability of what they acquire, not by the way they edit or the talent they nourish. Major publishers—for whom mere

solvency is death—are required to burst with
growth or attach themselves to a parent bursting
with growth. Otherwise they wither. Small presses
that do not starve hang on—hungry, feisty and always in danger of eclipse.

That this notion of the writer as toy—
manipulable toy, profitable to—jeopardizes the literature of the future is abundantly clear. But not only is
the literature of the near future endangered; so is
the literature of the recent past. This country has
had an unsurpassed literary presence in the world
for several decades now. But it will be lucky, in the
coming decade, if it can hold its own. What emerges
as the best literature of the 1980s or even the 1990s
may be written elsewhere by other people. Not because of an absence of native genius but because
something is very wrong in the writers' community.
Writers are less and less central to the idea and subject of literature. Whole schools of criticism have dis-
possessed the writer of any place whatever in the
critical value of his work: Ideas, craft, vision, meaning—all of them are just so much baggage in these
critical systems. The text itself is a mere point of
departure for philology, philosophy, psychiatry, theology, and other disciplines.

The political consequences for minority workers,
dissident writers and writers committed to social

change are devastating. For it means that there is no
way to talk about what we mean, because to mean anything is not in vogue. Just as to feel anything about
what one reads is "sentimental" and also not in vogue.
If our works are prohibited from having (overt) or
[not hidden]
(covert) meaning—if our meaning has no meaning—
[secret]
then we have no meaning either. *interesting*

The literature of the past is endangered not only
by brilliant intellectualism but also by glaring anti-
intellectualism. Apparently there are still such things
as books (already written, already loved) that are so
evil they must be burnt like witches at the stake for
fear of contaminating other books and other minds.
Censorship in new and old disguises is (rampant.) And
[unchecked, unrestrained]
contempt gives way to fear. There has been a ritual
spasm of book-snatching—rivaling that in South
Africa for (pernicious) (oppressiveness.)
[deadly] [tyranny cruelty]

I think it is our sense of that danger to both the
future and the past that has brought us here. What is
it? Does the danger really come from the (monolithic)
[large organization corporation]
publishers or are they symptoms of some larger (malady?) Is the disease really local censorship and out-
[disease]
raged illiterates, or are those also (symptomatic) of a
[characteristic of an event]
larger malady? It is perhaps the mood of a terrified,
defensive, bullying nation no longer sure of what
the point is? A nation embarrassed by its own
Bill of Rights? Burdened by its own constitutional

guarantees and promises of liberty and equal protection under the law? A country so hungry for a purely imagined past of innocence and clarity [being clear, lucid] that it is willing to subvert [to destroy] the future and, in fact, to declare that there is none, in order to wallow [luxuriate revel] in illusion? If that were the case, if the country as a whole decided to have no future—then one of its jobs would be to stifle, fetter, [to hold back, suppress] [to chain, restrict] and dismiss the artists it could not whip into market shape. Because a writer let loose on the world, uncompromised and untamed, would notice what had become of the country, and might say so.

You can't have unmarketable writers roaming around if you have opted for an improved past in exchange for no future. After all, the future is hard, even dangerous, because it may involve change and it may involve loss. And writers would say that too.

We are, some of us, significant individual writers in the cultural life of a group or of an institution, but as writers we are no longer central to the cultural life of this country. **why?**

Writer asks questions to get reader to think and analyze the problem.

Is that the reason? The mood of the country? The times we live in? Have we given over our power and our primacy [state of being first] to others? Or is there something frail in the nature of our work? Much of what we as writers do and how we do it is shaped by our belief in the sacredness [holiness, venerable] of the individual artist and his freedom. Individualism in its particularly interesting American form may be at the heart of our dilemma. The idea of the

individual in the artistic arena has its own (ambiva-

~~mutually conflicting feelings, i.e. love and hate~~

lence) and contradiction, just as it does in the political

arena: governance by many committed to preserving

the rights of a few. Ralph Ellison said: "In the begin-

ning was the Word—and its contradiction."

Constructing Responses to Readings: Paragraphs and Essays

All compositions have at least one thing in common: a need to develop a unified thought. A unified composition makes a point and does not wander as the writer develops the paragraph. The facts, examples, reasoning, and evidence used to support a topic sentence—the idea controlling the focus of a paragraph—specifically back-up what you initially say. For instance, to insure unity in a paragraph with a topic sentence such as *"The physicians at Elizabeth Scott Memorial Hospital give the medical profession a bad name,"* a writer must show how and why *the physicians* give the medical profession a bad name. Discussing the nursing staff or hospital rooms is wandering from the controlling idea—the focus—of the paragraph, confusing the reader in the process.

Another topic sentence might be *"In the late 20th century, graffiti became the artistic expression of street youth."* Here again, evidence will be required to prove the point or to justify an opinion. Your essay must include examples and reasons to illustrate how and why graffiti is more than just defacing and vandalizing public property. In other words, you will be *showing* your reader how graffiti is an art form.

Whether writing a paragraph or an essay, on paper or on a word processor, authors must first generate ideas to determine which direction they wish to take in the development of their topic. Thus, generating ideas is the first step in achieving an overall focus.

Generating Ideas and Establishing a Focus

One of the more difficult tasks a writer faces is coming up with original ideas about a topic. Original ideas don't just pop out of our heads every time we would like them to, so we must learn how to generate fresh perspectives about a topic by brainstorming in a variety of written ways such as clustering, freewriting, and listing. After generating several ideas on a topic, the author will want to focus on a specific controlling idea, either a topic sentence or a thesis statement.

Clustering words creates a visual picture of the relationships between ideas associated with a topic. To cluster thoughts, begin with a topic or stimulus word, freely associating words and ideas around the topic, and drawing connections between your responses. For example, the following cluster helped a student generate ideas and arrive at a focus on the general topic of war.

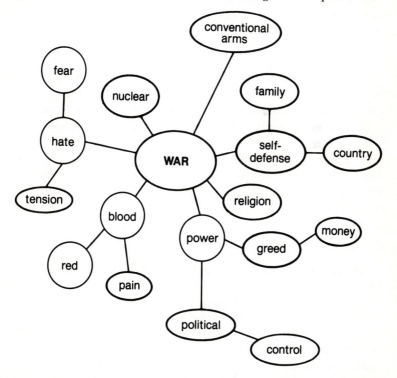

After analyzing her cluster, this student decided out of all the associations she had made with the word "war," there were three ideas that dominated her cluster—the major causes of war: hatred, power, greed, and religion. While her other information dealt with warfare, she decided to write on only the causes of war to give her paper focus. By eliminating information that did not fall into one of these four categories, the author narrowed her focus and prevented herself from wandering off the topic. Initially, the free association of thoughts allowed her to reach her controlling idea and major discussion points.

Freewriting is another popular way to brainstorm a general topic in order to arrive at a specific focus. When you freewrite, you should compose as quickly as you can, never stopping to edit. Since your goal is to freely associate ideas, you need not worry about formal essay structure, mechanics, or grammatical correctness. You are exploring your ideas by getting them into writing. For a detailed description of freewriting, see Peter Elbow's essay "Freewriting" in Chapter 1.

Listing is yet another way to examine your thoughts on a subject. Though there is no specific format for listing, most writers who make use of this technique simply write down one word or phrase and then another. Like other prewriting strategies—especially clustering—used to generate ideas, listing is based on the concept that *one thought generates another,* and for this reason, all items on a list may be important. When freely associating words, it's hard to determine which word will lead the writer to a specific focus—the ultimate objective of the activity.

Structuring Essays

Your essay is structured to support a thesis or controlling idea. Once you have arrived at a specific focus, the next step in the writing process is to organize your supporting points (topic sentences). Based on the purpose of your essay, you may want to arrange material in chronological or emphatic order. Leaving out steps in a process paper, for instance, will lead only to reader confusion. However you choose to organize your material, it should always develop your thesis logically and coherently.

Traditionally, we have three different types of paragraphs. *Introductory paragraphs* expose the reader to an idea, concept, or argument and lead to a specific thesis. *Body paragraphs* contain specific topic sentences or discussion points that support a writer's thesis. *Concluding paragraphs* draw the discussion to a close, either summarizing major points and relating them to the thesis or providing a definite sense of closure. In essence, you have a beginning, middle, and end.

Introductory paragraphs acquaint your reader with a specific topic and ultimately focus on a controlling idea or thesis

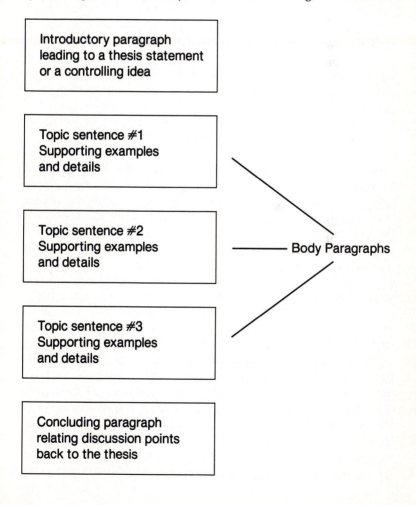

you plan to develop. Though a one-sentence introduction might inform your reader of your thesis, it seldom captures the reader's imagination or engages his or her intellect. Some of the more effective ways of leading a reader to a thesis or controlling idea include telling an illustrative story, providing startling or revealing facts or statistics, asking some provocative questions (often rhetorical questions—questions you plan to answer), or a relevant quote. All of these introductory strategies lead quite naturally to a thesis statement.

A thesis statement introduces your subject, what you have to say about a subject, and how you plan to defend your point of view. Your plan of development breaks a broad topic into manageable units—paragraphs—and suggests the structure of your composition. How many paragraphs should one include in an essay? While most people are familiar with a five-paragraph format—one introductory paragraph, three supporting paragraphs and one concluding paragraph—in reality, an essay should contain as many paragraphs as necessary to justify or develop your thesis or controlling idea.

For instance, in "Creatures That Haunt the Americas," in order to fully develop her controlling idea that *"When Africans reached the New World, the creatures [of African folktales] stepped ashore with them,"* Constance García-Barrio presents the reader with several illustrative paragraphs containing examples that support her thesis. Because her controlling idea is broad, García-Barrio must explore, explain, and support her thesis in several paragraphs in order to adequately develop it.

Body paragraphs support or develop your thesis through argument and examples. Like miniature essays, paragraphs tend to have a beginning, middle, and an end. For example, a topic sentence is usually the starting point of a paragraph. Here the author alerts the reader to the controlling idea. Supporting examples and details, often referred to as primary and secondary support, comprise the bulk of the paragraph. Such information illustrates what an author has claimed. At the end of a paragraph, an author may offer a closing or transitional statement, which either summarizes the paragraph or leads to the next discussion point.

In "Distance Learning and American Society," Mark Fissel *focuses* paragraph two with the topic sentence: *"Distance learning via interactive video instruction makes teaching student-oriented and decentralized as opposed to instructor-oriented, centralized instruction in the traditional classroom.*" The rest of Fissel's paragraph supports this claim by supplying examples and interviews. His paragraph is unified because he sticks to supporting his main point (topic sentence).

Concluding paragraphs draw the discussion to a close. In concluding paragraphs, the author strives to come up with a solution to a problem, refers to the information presented in the introductory paragraph, and makes predictions based upon the evidence presented. Just as one does not want to begin to develop an essay in an introductory paragraph, a writer will not want to develop new ideas in a conclusion. Keep in mind that the final sentence ideally should leave a lasting impression upon your reader. Once again, you may draw upon an anecdote or refer to information presented in your introduction to frame your essay as a whole.

Special Writing Activities: The Individual and Group Response

There are many ways an individual becomes an active writer and a creative thinker. Individually, a person might write notes and impressions in a journal, record responses to a reading in a reading/writing log, or create, analyze, and solve a problem in a thesis notebook. Other times, writers work together as a group, examine issues, exchange ideas, and ultimately write a composition. Whether you write alone or with others, the ultimate goals are usually the same: to generate ideas, to analyze a problem, and to structure a meaningful response to the issue or reading. The following section offers a few writing strategies to use individually or as a group that will assist you in completing some of the pre-reading and post-reading activities in this text.

Journals, Reading/Writing Logs, and Thesis Notebooks

A journal is one of the most popular resources used by writers. In a journal, the writer freely records observations (sometime in a diary format), notes events and daily activities, and jots down plans and goals. Journal entries are usually informal, and the writer concerns himself with recording ideas and observations more than grammatical or mechanical perfection. A journal should be a place to examine new ideas and re-evaluate old ones; it's a place to explore feelings and attitudes without the fear of censorship or any type of judgment or evaluation. Many techniques such as freewriting and brainstorming offer ideal strategies for writing journal entries.

Both readers and writers alike record their responses to and analysis of a book, story, poem, essay, or play in reading/writing logs. What do they write about? After reading, they jot down their emotional responses to the issues or topics discussed. They may also create a dialogue with the text, asking questions and stating opinions such as "This is seldom true!" or "Why doesn't the author support her claim?" Under "Tips for Becoming an Active Reader" in Chapter 1, you will find useful hints for keeping a reading/writing log.

Much like a journal or a reading/writing log, a thesis notebook records information. However, whereas the reading/writing log focuses on your reactions and perceptions about readings, a thesis notebook deals mostly with expository writings. In particular, the writer probes ideas to determine whether they can function as a controlling idea and be developed into an essay. During this process, the writer attempts to narrow a topic, construct a thesis, and support it. As a result, a thesis notebook often contains several drafts of writing assignments. In addition to its usefulness when structuring essays, a thesis notebook provides a place to rough out creative writings such as poems, short stories, and even plays.

In many instances, authors will combine characteristics of journals, logs, and notebooks under one cover because they all deal with the same thing: exploring and recording ideas and perceptions. A journal or notebook is seldom an end in itself but a means of working out ideas that will lead to a formal written response.

Group Activities and Collaborative Writing

Although writers often work out concepts individually, they also collaborate (work together) to generate and evaluate ideas. In the Group Activities section of this text, for instance, you will often be asked to brainstorm a topic or issue as a group, meaning you will initially share information or opinions without evaluating or judging them. Ideally, your group will have a wide range of responses to any given subject; that way, you will be able to consider a topic from as many points of view as possible before analyzing or writing about it. Group activities generate dialogue; each group member both listens and contributes to group discussion without the anxiety of being judged.

One outcome of group activities might be a collaborative composition. Here, authors work together to generate and compose an essay. To begin with, writers examine an issue in order to arrive at a specific focus and formulate a thesis. Next, after thorough discussion, they break the thesis down into sections which will serve as major points or topic sentences to structure their composition. Collaborative writers then use an essay map or outline in order to guide them as they write. Then, with one person acting as recorder/secretary, group members develop each major point (topic sentence); every individual offers his or her experiences or examples to support the group's thesis, thereby developing the rough draft. Once a draft is complete, all group members go over their collaborative effort, correcting careless errors and noting parts of the composition in need of revision or more development.

There are many variations to a collaborative writing project. Sometimes, for instance, every group member may write a rough draft of an agreed-upon thesis and then combine them into one essay. Other times, group members may be responsible for individual sections of the collaborative essay. Regardless of how you approach a collaborative writing assignment, its strength rests on cooperation with and participation by each group member.

Summary

From reading and marking textbooks to generating ideas, structuring compositions, and engaging in group (collaborative) activities, the connection between reading and writing is ever-present. As you read through the remaining essays on language in this chapter—and the essays in this book as a whole—we suggest that you review this brief section on reading and writing frequently. Doing so will enable you to keep a clear perspective on how to read and write "actively."

Sharing Tradition
FRANK LAPEÑA

Frank LaPeña is the Director of the Native American Indian Studies program at California State University, Sacramento. As suggested by the following article, LaPeña is quite interested in the arts and traditions of Native Americans.

PRE-READING QUESTIONS

1. What sort of stories did your parents tell you rather than read to you when you were a child? Did they have anything to do with your culture or society in general? Did they deal with values that transcend generations?

2. When do you tell stories and to whom? What is the purpose behind the stories you relate to others? Did you ever change the details of a story to relate to an audience or suit your purpose? How?

1   I was thinking one day about recent deaths of some of the traditional people and how difficult it is to maintain tradition. I was also thinking how important oral tradition is in helping maintain the values of culture, and how in a sense oral tradition is also an art form. As the elders pass on, the young people fill their places. Even though we know no one lives forever, no one dies if what they have gained by living is carried forward by those who follow—if we as individuals assume the responsibilities. This is easy to talk and write about, but it is hard to practice.

2   Not everyone is capable of fulfilling the roles of the elders. On one hand everyone who lives long enough automatically becomes an elder—it is something that just happens. Yet some elders have enhanced their lives by creating a special "niche," and once they have passed on, that niche is hard to fill. Religious obligations for the ceremonies and dance, for example, were reflected in their knowledge and in how those elders lived and how they affected people around them in common everyday activities as well. In fact, after the elders passed away, their knowledge of the culture and the responsibilities they had in their community had to be assumed by several individuals.

3   Because longevity is the guarantor of becoming an elder, the young don't pay too much attention to something that will happen some years down the road, but they regret it later. I have talked to individuals who were seventy years old or older, and even those forty and fifty years old, and they all expressed the feeling that they wished they had listened more, remembered more, or asked more about the things that the elders were willing to share with them.

4   The separation that exists between generations will always be with us. Each generation is faced with new technologies which replace the old; ever-growing populations make necessary new developments that replace fertile land with housing and impact on the natural resources of air and water. Part of tradition is tied to a natural world which is being destroyed. If we are not worried about the apocalypse, getting killed in the streets, or having the drug culture undercut our lives, we might wonder what kind of world it will be in the future. It is hard to live with all the stress, worry, and change that modern technology imposes on people. It is hard to maintain traditions in such circumstances. Our world is not the world of our great-grandparents.

5   So we have to remind ourselves that there are things that transcend generations, and the living force of that truth is carried by the person-to-person confidentiality of oral tradition. A lot depends upon the transmission of information from one person to another. Oral tradition is the educational tool of understanding the natural world.

6   Oral tradition is not, however, the way many people in modern society learn things. The educational process of getting degrees to show how educated we are forces people to do things

out of necessity and not necessarily out of interest, passion for the true story, or because it is good for the community. Sometimes modern researchers gathering what they think is "oral" material "in the field" are not always told the truth. I can still see the smile of my friend who used to tell people "whatever they wanted to hear. I let them figure it out later," he said. Or a person doesn't understand what has been told, so he/she corrects it by modifying the material so it makes sense. The result is that erroneous information is published and falsely validates [sic] one's research. With the printed word there is a tendency to place the author as "someone who knows" what's going on. As "experts," writers and lecturers may be put into a position where they think they must have an answer, so they answer by making something up. We need to learn to say we don't know the answer, and direct the question to someone who might know. We need to learn from the elders who sometimes say "I'll sleep on it," or who approach a problem by having everybody's input come up with an answer—which can be changed. Logistically, it is harder to correct errors in a book if it is already published.

7   A living oral tradition, as opposed to a literary tradition, accommodates corrections, because the stories are "known" by the listeners—although today a story could be someone's fantasy and it might be harder to validate. The source of one's information and how it was given affects how correct it is. Only if one is patient and gains information over a long period of time, is it possible to get a proper understanding of one's information. If a person is *one of the group* (an insider), usually the information is given correctly, because it relates to something the speaker and listener have a vested interest in or participate in. It is their life. It is worth doing right.

8   For an artist, the oral tradition has an impact on how one visualizes the stories, the characters, the designs and color for art, the atmosphere, and other information which can be useful to an artist. If I think of these elders whom I respect and love and who were my teachers, I sometimes wonder—as I extend and alter the traditions—if I am somehow not doing right by them. If an artist's work is abstract, is it true to the stories? At what time of doing one's art does the artist begin to relate conceptually instead of representationally to his source, and is

that good or bad? Ultimately being good or bad can refer to how we do our art—what's included or left out, and how true the artwork is to the "real" Native American thing. Do our modern life and new things function independently of or holistically with the old ways and symbols? Each of us has choices in the outcome of our lives.

9   As an artist, I won't try to answer these questions because the answers will be reflected in artists' works, and how they explain their work and how they understand their work. Each of us makes choices in how we work and how we live. If one knows tradition and modifies how he/she presents it, I hope it is not only for one's ego but that more independently we are also paying attention to the source of our inspiration. And if it is tradition, I hope that we honor the elders and think of the responsibility they entrusted to us by sharing the traditions with us.

POST-READING QUESTIONS

Content

1. What does LaPeña feel is the importance of the oral tradition? To what extent do you agree with his opinions and why?

2. Who are the people who "preserve" and "pass-on" the oral tradition? What is the danger of not passing on information? (Is there information about life that most likely will never be written down? Why?)

3. What is the difference between oral tradition and literary tradition?

4. How does LaPeña establish a relationship between art and the oral tradition?

Strategies and Structures

1. What is the controlling idea or thesis of this essay?

2. LaPeña develops four major problems with regard to maintaining the oral tradition. What are they and how are they used to structure the essay?

3. How do topic sentences guide the reader through the essay? What would be lost without them?

Language and Vocabulary

1. Vocabulary: *niche, obligation, longevity, guarantor, apocalypse, confidentiality, erroneous, logistically, validate, holistically.* You may not know many of the above words. Without looking at a dictionary, reread the essay and write down what you think the definitions might be; then verify your guesses by looking up the definitions.

2. Using the following words from the vocabulary list above: *obligation, longevity, apocalypse,* and *erroneous,* write a story at least three or four paragraphs in length that resembles one passed down from generation to generation in your culture.

GROUP ACTIVITIES

1. Get into groups and share the story you have created or one that you know has been passed down from generation to generation in your culture. Then, choose a story someone else from your group has told and tell it to another group while the original teller listens to your version. Then have the original story teller point out any differences in the stories and note how much it has changed.

2. LaPeña states that the oral tradition helps maintain the values of a culture. Today one might say that movies and television play the same role. Make a list of current popular movies and/or TV shows. What values are they promoting? Do you think these are the dominant values of our culture? Why or why not?

WRITING ACTIVITIES

1. Write a paragraph or two explaining your attitude toward the oral tradition of passing along information.

2. If you believe the oral tradition is important, write several paragraphs explaining how you intend to preserve it.

My Mother's English
AMY TAN

A freelance writer and author of the prize-winning book *The Joy Luck Club* (1989), Amy Tan currently lives in San Francisco with her family and is a popular lecturer. Her newest novel, *The Kitchen God's Wife*, was released in 1991. The following excerpt about her "mother's English" is from a speech Tan delivered at the CATE '90 Conference in San Francisco.

PRE-READING QUESTIONS

1. Who influenced the way you speak the most—your parents, your peers, or your teachers?

2. How do you use language when speaking with relatives, friends, teachers, and strangers? How does your language change depending on whom you are speaking to? When do you feel your verbal English accurately represents the "real you"? (Do you ever feel as if another person is doing the talking when you are speaking to others? When?)

3. When have you felt limited or particularly effective due to your inability or ability to read and write? (For example, have you ever had writer's block on an essay test?)

1   As you know, I am a writer and by that definition I am someone who has always loved language. I think that is first and foremost with almost every writer I know. I'm fascinated by language in daily life. I spend a great deal of time thinking

about the power of language—the way it can evoke an emotion, a visual image, a complex idea, or a simple truth. As a writer, language is the tool of my trade and I use them all, all the Englishes I grew up with.

2   A few months back, I was made keenly aware of the Englishes I do use. I was giving a talk to a large group of people, the same talk I had given many times before and also with notes. And the nature of the talk was about my writing, my life, and my book *The Joy Luck Club.* The talk was going along well enough until I remembered one major difference that made the whole thing seem wrong. My mother was in the room, and it was perhaps the first time she had heard me give a lengthy speech, using a kind of English I had never used with her. I was saying things like "the intersection of memory and imagination," and "there is an aspect of my fiction that relates to this and thus." A speech filled with carefully wrought grammatical sentences, burdened to me it seemed with nominalized forms, past perfect tenses, conditional phrases, all the forms of standard English that I had learned in school and through books, a form of English I did not use at home or with my mother.

3   Shortly after that I was walking down the street with my mother and my husband and I became self-conscious of the English I was using, the English that I do use with her. We were talking about the price of new and used furniture and I heard myself saying to her, "Not waste money that way." My husband was with me as well, and he didn't notice any switch in my English. And then I realized why: because over the twenty years that we've been together he's often used that English with me and I've used that with him. It is sort of the English that is our language of intimacy, the English that relates to family talk, the English that I grew up with.

4   I'd like to give you some idea what my family talk sounds like and I'll do that by quoting what my mother said during a recent conversation which I video-taped and then transcribed. During this conversation, my mother was talking about a political gangster and who had the same last name as her family, Du, and how the gangster in his early years wanted to be adopted by her family which was by comparison very rich. Later the gangster became more rich, more powerful than my mother's family and one day showed up at my mother's

wedding to pay his respects. And here's what she said about that, in part, "Du Yu Sung having business like food stand, like off the street kind; he's Du like Du Zong but not Tsung-ming Island people. The local people call him Du, from the river east side. He belong that side, local people. That man want to ask Du Zong father take him in become like own family. Du Zong father look down on him but don't take seriously until that man become big like, become a Mafia. Now important person, very hard inviting him. Chinese way: come only to show respect, don't stay for dinner. Respect for making big celebration; he shows up. Means gives lots of respect, Chinese custom. Chinese social life that way—if too important, won't have to stay too long. He come to my wedding; I didn't see it I heard it. I gone to boy's side. They have YMCA dinner; Chinese age I was nineteen."

5   You should know that my mother's expressive command of English belies how much she actually understands. She reads the *Forbes Report,* listens to *Wall Street Week,* converses daily with her stock-broker, reads all of Shirley MacLaine's books with ease, all kinds of things I can't begin to understand. Yet some of my friends tell me that they understand 50% of what my mother says. Some say maybe they understand maybe 80%. Some say they understand almost nothing at all. As a case in point, a television station recently interviewed my mother and I didn't see this program when it was first aired, but my mother did. She was telling me what happened. She said that everything she said, which was in English, was subtitled in English, as if she had been speaking in pure Chinese. She was understandably puzzled and upset. Recently a friend gave me that tape and I saw that same interview and I watched. And sure enough—subtitles—and I was puzzled because listening to that tape it seemed to me that my mother's English sounded perfectly clear and perfectly natural. Of course, I realize that my mother's English is what I grew up with. It is literally my mother tongue, not Chinese, not standard English, but my mother's English which I later found out is almost a direct translation of Chinese.

6   Her language as I hear it is vivid and direct, full of observation and imagery. That was the language that helped shape the way that I saw things, expressed things, made sense of the

world. Lately I've been giving more thought to the kind of English that my mother speaks. Like others I have described it to people as broken or fractured English, but I wince when I say that. It has always bothered me that I can think of no other way to describe it than broken, as if it were damaged or needed to be fixed, that it lacked a certain wholeness or soundness to it. I've heard other terms used, "Limited English" for example. But they seem just as bad, as if everything is limited, including people's perceptions of the Limited English speaker.

7   I know this for a fact, because when I was growing up my mother's limited English limited my perception of her. I was ashamed of her English. I believed that her English reflected the quality of what she had to say. That is, because she expressed it imperfectly, her thoughts were imperfect as well. And I had plenty of empirical evidence to support me: The fact that people in department stores, at banks, at supermarkets, at restaurants did not take her as seriously, did not give her good service, pretended not to understand her, or even acted as if they did not hear her.

8   My mother has long realized the limitations of her English as well. When I was fifteen she used to have me call people on the phone to pretend I was she. In this guise, I was forced to ask for information or oftentimes to complain and yell at people that had been rude to her. One time it was a call to her stock broker in New York. She had cashed out her small portfolio and it just so happened that we were going to New York the next week, our very first trip outside of California. I had to get on the phone and say in my adolescent voice, which was not very convincing, "This is Mrs. Tan." And my mother was in the back whispering loudly, "Why don't he send me check already? Two weeks late. So mad he lie to me, losing me money." Then I said in perfect English, "Yes I'm getting rather concerned. You had agreed to send the check two weeks ago, but it hasn't arrived." And she began to talk more loudly, "What you want—I come to New York, tell him front of his boss you cheating me?" And I was trying to calm her down, making her be quiet, while telling this stock broker, "I can't tolerate any more excuses. If I don't receive the check immediately I'm going to have to speak to your manager when I arrive in New York." And sure enough the

following week, there we were in front of this astonished stock broker. And there I was, red-faced and quiet, and my mother the real Mrs. Tan was shouting at his boss in her impeccable broken English.

9   We used a similar routine a few months ago for a situation that was actually far less humorous. My mother had gone to the hospital for an appointment to find out about a benign brain tumor a CAT scan had revealed a month ago. And she had spoken very good English she said—her best English, no mistakes. Still she said the hospital had not apologized when they said they had lost the CAT scan and she had come for nothing. She said that they did not seem to have any sympathy when she told them she was anxious to know the exact diagnosis since her husband and son and both died of brain tumors. She said they would not give her any more information until the next time; she would have to make another appointment for that, so she said she would not leave until the doctor called her daughter. She wouldn't budge, and when the doctor finally called her daughter, me, who spoke in perfect English, lo-and-behold, we had assurances the CAT scan would be found, they promised a conference call on Monday, and apologies were given for any suffering my mother had gone through for a most regrettable mistake. By the way, apart from the distress of that episode, my mother is fine.

10   But it has continued to disturb me how much my mother's English still limits people's perceptions of her. I think my mother's English almost had an effect on limiting my possibilities as well. Sociologists and linguists will probably tell you that a person's developing language skills are more influenced by peers. But I do think the language spoken by the family, especially immigrant families, which are more insular, plays a large role in shaping the language of the child . . . . [While this may be true, I always wanted, however,] to capture what language ability tests can never reveal—her intent, her passion, her imagery, the rhythms of her speech, and the nature of her thoughts. Apart from what any critic had to say about my writing, I knew I had succeeded where it counted when my mother finished reading my first book and gave me her verdict. "So easy to read."

POST-READING QUESTIONS

Content

1. What is the focus of Tan's essay? Who and what does she talk about?

2. Tan speaks of many different "Englishes." What are they?

3. How do others characterize her mother's English? How does Tan feel about her mother's English?

4. What steps does she take to hide her "broken-English"? Why does she feel it is necessary to conceal "the limitations of her English"?

Strategies and Structures

1. What is the purpose of Tan's opening paragraph? What does it establish? How does it prepare you for her discussion of her mother's English?

2. Tan says her mother's language is "full of observation and imagery." How does she support such claims throughout her essay?

3. How does the author illustrate the difficulties others have with her mother's English?

4. How does Tan illustrate the effectiveness of her mother's direct, "broken-English" in comparison to the author's use of the English language?

Language and Vocabulary

1. Vocabulary: *intersection, wrought, nominalized, transcribed, belies, empirical, portfolio, CAT Scan, linguists.* To increase your vocabulary, look up the definitions of the above words in a dictionary. Even if you think you know the meanings, look them up to confirm what you know and expand your vocabulary with additional meanings. Then write synonyms (words or word groups with similar meanings) in your writing log or journal for each word.

2. For the most part, Tan keeps her language straightforward and simple. This essay was an excerpt from a speech. Why is her style particularly appropriate to listeners as opposed to readers? What limitations does a speaker face that a writer does not?

GROUP ACTIVITIES

1. Many minorities face language discrimination. There have been several attempts by states to recognize English as the official language of American citizens. As a group, research articles debating both sides of such initiatives and then discuss the following questions: Why are some people in favor of a national language and others against it? Do you feel Tan would feel such initiatives are necessary or fair?

2. Go back through the text and note all passages where Tan's mother expresses herself. In the incident with the stockbroker, Tan claims her mother's English was more effective than Tan's own "proper" English. Compare the two Englishes and discuss why Tan would make such a claim (e.g., what was ineffective about Tan's use of the English language).

WRITING ACTIVITIES

1. Write a paragraph or so in which you discuss the differences in the language you use with your family and friends. Which is more formal? Which includes more slang? If you feel you speak to family and friends exactly alike, write a topic sentence expressing as much, and then support your controlling idea with some specific, representative examples.

2. Briefly describe a situation where you felt your use of the English language—whether it was "standard" or "broken"—played an important part in the way others perceived you.

Freewriting
PETER ELBOW

A graduate of Williams College, Peter Elbow has published numerous articles and books about the writing process, including *Writing with Power*, and *Writing without Teachers*. In the following essay, Elbow offers some suggestions on how to begin the writing process: freewrite!

PRE-READING QUESTIONS

1. Have you ever used a pre-writing exercise to generate ideas for essay topics?
2. Write nonstop for five minutes expressing everything that comes to mind when you hear the word "freewriting." Don't be concerned about grammatical or mechanical correctness at this time.

1   The most effective way I know to improve your writing is to do freewriting exercises regularly. At least three times a week. They are sometimes called "automatic writing," "babbling," or "jabbering" exercises. The idea is simply to write for ten minutes (later on, perhaps fifteen or twenty). Don't stop for anything. Go quickly without rushing. Never stop to look back, to cross something out, to wonder how to spell something, to wonder what word or thought to use, or to think about what you are doing. If you can't think of a word or a spelling, just use a squiggle or else write, "I can't think of it." Just put down something. The easiest thing is just to put down whatever is in your mind. If you get stuck it's fine to write "I can't think what to say, I can't thing what to say" as many times as you want; or repeat the last word you wrote over and over again; or anything else. The only requirement is that you *never* stop.

2   What happens to a freewriting exercise is important. It must be a piece of writing which, even if someone reads it, doesn't send any ripples back to you. It is like writing something and putting it in a bottle in the sea. The teacherless class helps

your writing my providing maximum feedback. Freewritings help you by providing no feedback at all. When I assign one, I invite the writer to let me read it. But also tell him to keep it if he prefers. I read it quickly and make no comments at all and I do not speak with him about it. The main thing is that a freewriting must never be evaluated in any way; in fact there must be no discussion or comment at all.

3   Here is an example of a fairly coherent exercise (sometimes they are very incoherent, which is fine):

> I think I'll write what's on my mind, but the only thing on my mind right now is what to write for ten minutes. I've never done this before and I'm not prepared in any way—the sky is cloudy today, how's that? now I'm afraid I won't be able to think of what to write when I get to the end of the sentence— well, here I am at the end of the sentence—here I am again, again, again, again, at least I'm still writing—Now I ask is there some reason to be happy that I'm still writing—ah yes! Here comes the question again—What am I getting out of this? What point is there in it? It's almost obscene to always ask it but I seem to question everything that way and I was gonna say something else pertaining to that but I got so busy writing down the first part that I forgot what I was leading into. This is kind of fun oh don't stop writing—cars and trucks speeding by somewhere out the window, pens clittering across peoples' papers. The sky is still cloudy—is it symbolic that I should be mentioning it? Huh? I dunno. Maybe I should try colors, blue, red, dirty words—wait a minute—no can't do that, orange, yellow, arm tired, green pink violet magenta lavender red brown black green—now that I can't think of any more colors—just about done—relief? maybe.

Freewriting may seem crazy but actually it makes simple sense. Think of the difference between speaking and writing. Writing has the advantage of permitting more editing. But that's its downfall too. Almost everybody interposes a massive and complicated series of editings between the time words start to be born into consciousness and when they finally come off the end of the pencil or typewriter onto the page. This is partly because schooling makes us obsessed with the "mistakes" we make in writing. Many people are constantly thinking about spelling and grammar as they try to write. I am always thinking about the awkwardness, wordiness, and general mushiness of my natural verbal product as I try to write down words.

4   But it's not just "mistakes" or "bad writing" we edit as we write. We also edit unacceptable thoughts and feelings, as we do in speaking. In writing there is more time to do it so the editing is heavier: when speaking, there's someone right there waiting for a reply and he'll get bored or think we're crazy if we don't come out with *something*. Most of the time in speaking, we settle for the catch-as-catch-can way in which the words tumble out. In writing, however, there's a chance to try to get them right. But the opportunity to get them right is a terrible burden: you can work for two hours trying to get a paragraph "right" and discover it's not right at all. And then give up.

5   Editing, *in itself,* is not the problem. Editing is usually necessary if we want to end up with something satisfactory. The problem is that editing goes on *at the same time* as producing. The editor is, as it were, constantly looking over the shoulder of the producer and constantly fiddling with what he's doing while he's in the middle of trying to do it. No wonder the producer gets nervous, jumpy, inhibited, and finally can't be coherent. It's an unnecessary burden to try to think of words and also worry at the same time whether they're the right words.

6   The main thing about freewriting is that it is *nonediting.* It is an exercise in bringing together the process of producing words and putting them down on the page. Practiced regularly, it undoes the ingrained habit of editing at the same time you are trying to produce. It will make writing less blocked because words will come more easily. You will use up more paper, but chew up fewer pencils.

7   Next time you write, notice how often you stop yourself from writing down something you were going to write down. Or else cross it out after it's written. "Naturally," you say, "it wasn't any good." But think for a moment about the occasions when you spoke well. Seldom was it because you first got the beginning just right. Usually it was a matter of a halting or even garbled beginning, but you kept going and your speech finally became coherent and even powerful. There is a lesson here for writing: trying to get the beginning just right is a formula for failure—and probably a secret tactic to make yourself give up writing. Make some words, whatever they are, and then grab

hold of that line and reel in as hard as you can. Afterwards you can throw away lousy beginnings and make new ones. This is the quickest way to get into good writing.

8   The habit of compulsive, premature editing doesn't just make writing hard. It also makes writing dead. Your voice is damped out by all the interruptions, changes, and hesitations between the consciousness and the page. In your natural way of producing words there is a sound, a texture, a rhythm—a voice—which is the main source of power in your writing. I don't know how it works, but this voice is the force that will make a reader listen to you, the energy that drives the meanings through his thick skull. Maybe you don't *like* your voice; maybe people have made fun of it. But it's the only voice you've got. It's your only source of power. You better get back into it, no matter what you think of it. If you keep writing in it, it may change into something you like better. But if you abandon it, you'll likely never have a voice and never be heard.

9   Freewritings are vacuums. Gradually you will begin to carry over into your regular writing some of the voice, force, and connectedness that creep into those vacuums.

POST-READING QUESTIONS

Content

1. What is freewriting? How does one begin to do it?

2. What does Elbow suggest is one of the biggest obstacles in the writing process? To what extent do you agree with him? Why?

3. How can freewriting overcome "writer's block"?

4. According to Elbow, what is the result of "compulsive, premature editing"?

Strategies and Structures

1. Why does Elbow offer such an extensive example of freewriting? What questions does it tend to answer?

2. How does the author address his reader in this essay? Does he seem to be lecturing and/or "talking down" to his audience? Explain your answer.

3. Why does Elbow devote so much time to the issue of editing? What point is he trying to make? How does he succeed or fail in his effort?

Language and Vocabulary

1. In writing this essay, Elbow was careful to avoid words that would have distracted a reader—words a reader would need to look-up in the dictionary. How does his simple word choice help to establish a reader/writer relationship? How is Elbow's own use of language and vocabulary "free" from the narrow confines of academic writing?

2. Elbow uses a simile (a comparison using like or as) to explain that freewriting "is like writing something and putting it in a bottle in a sea." After reading his entire essay, what do you think he meant by that comparison?

GROUP ACTIVITIES

1. To explore the possibilities freewriting can offer you in the way of generating ideas or focusing in on essay topics/issues, get together with two other students in class, pick an initial topic (it will serve as a starting point), and all three of you write without stopping for five minutes. Then pick a second topic and write for another five minutes, this time editing your work as you write (precisely what Elbow warns against doing). At the end of ten minutes, have other group members evaluate both pieces of writing. Which was more natural?

2. Share other methods of freewriting you have found useful with the rest of your group. Show group members how you use a particular strategy to overcome writing blocks and to generate specific, meaningful paragraph/essay topics.

WRITING ACTIVITIES

1. Write for ten minutes without stopping, putting down every word or thought that creeps into your mind, and do not worry about grammar, mechanics, or even making sense. Next, write down a specific topic of your choice at the top of a clean page, underline it, and then freewrite for ten more minutes. What sort of things did you end up saying about the topic or issue you wrote on? Pick one of them to function as the controlling idea in your thesis statement. How would you develop it?

2. Beginning today, freewrite for five minutes daily. Keep your freewritings in a bound notebook or portfolio of your choice. Like any "prewriting" technique, freewriting is bound to be a bit disorganized and at times confusing, but don't worry about it. The objective of freewriting is not to produce a finished copy of an essay. As Elbow himself said, freewriting "is an exercise in bringing together the process of producing words and putting them down on the page."

How I Write An Article — I Think
DONALD MURRAY

Donald Murray is both an experienced writer and teacher. As a journalist, he was an editor for *Time* and a columnist for the *Boston Herald*, where he won a Pulitzer Prize for editorial writing in 1954. In 1963, he joined the faculty at the University of New Hampshire where he taught journalism, established a program in Composition Studies, was director of Freshman Composition and served as English Department chairperson. Currently, he writes a column "Over Sixty" for the *Boston Globe*.

PRE-READING QUESTIONS

1. In your notebook, make a list of the steps you take when you write. What do you do first, second, third, fourth . . . ? How do you vary this pattern, if ever?

2. Do a freewriting in which you explain how you think *most* people write. What do most people do first, second, third . . . ? Do you write this way? Why or why not?

1   It is time to write when I know the answers to my questions before I ask them, when my sources tell me what I already know. I feel stuffed with information, and specific details, facts, quotations, insights, phrases, relationships rise to the surface of my mind at odd moments. These fragments try to connect with each other as if they were cells swimming towards each other and away under the eye of a microscope. I try not to think consciously about them, try not to interfere with their mating but I am intensely aware, and what I see, what I hear, what I read, what I remember, tries to relate to the pieces of information from which my article will be built.

2   I may make notes in spite of myself, record fragments of ideas, hints of a voice or a tone, scribble a phrase, but I try not to think consciously about the subject. I am simply open to the subject and when I have a moment of quiet, it rises to the surface of my mind on its own energy. The information seems to demand its own order, its own connections, its own structure and I often find myself making notes by drawing designs, or at least lines and arrows, between pieces of information.

3   Almost reluctantly I begin to write titles—as many as a hundred—at odd moments. Each helps me focus on the subject, limit it, take a point of view towards it, for each title is a quick draft which helps eliminate what doesn't belong. Then I start drafting leads—sometimes as many as fifty—working to get the first line right, the first paragraph right, sometimes even the first ten lines right. What is right? The start of a clear line through the subject and that something I sense rather than know; following it I will be surprised.

4   The lead is the beginning of the beginning, those few lines the reader may glance at in deciding to read or pass on. These

few words—fifty, forty, thirty, twenty, ten—establish the tone, the point of view, the order, the dimensions of the article. In a sense, the entire article is coiled in the first few words waiting to be released.

5   An article, perhaps even a book, can only say one thing and when the lead is found, the writer knows what is included in the article and what is left out, what must be left out. As one word is chosen for the lead another rejected, as a comma is put in and another taken away, the lead begins to feel right and the pressure builds up until it is almost impossible not to write.

6   The article is drafted as fast as possible, always without the research in front of me, occasionally with a few fragmentary notes indicating a rough sequence of ideas, never with anything as formal as an outline. Often I dictate, letting language lead me, allowing the article to shape itself instinctively. I feel both intense and relaxed at the same time; everything is concentrated on allowing the article to come out of me on its own energy, within its own evolving form.

7   Now I read the draft carelessly, the way a reader will, to hear my voice, to spot the large holes in the structure of meaning. Then I reread it half a dozen times, a dozen times, perhaps more, worrying it into shape. I have a short interest span and I work in bursts of deep concentration until I become pleased with what I have written. Then I take a break and then return to the attack. But this isn't work, it's fun. I'm making something that has not been made before.

8   I attend to the larger questions first. Do I have a subject? Must I go back and do more research, write new titles, work further on the lead, choose a different genre or form? Then I deal with matters of order and structure. I may outline now, cut and paste, insert and remove, shift chunks of copy around. Sometimes I write a paragraph a page to make this reordering easier. Once the order is firm I look to matters of evidence. Have I documented each point? Then I deal with matters of dimension. Are there parts of the piece of writing which are too long or too short in relationship to each other? Of course these questions overlap.

9   Although I cut ruthlessly, my drafts usually grow longer. I have to develop my points to make them clear to myself and then to my reader. I keep being surprised, that's what keeps me

going. I find I write what I did not expect to write; my accidents lead me on. I find out what I have to say by saying it.

10   In the earlier readings, I am not so much looking at language as exploring the subject, trying to see it clearly so I can understand it. In later drafts I look more at language, again trying to make the subject clear. At the end I cut and shape to erase myself so the reader will see what is written, not who is writing.

POST-READING QUESTIONS

Content

1. When does Murray know it is time to write? What happens to the information in his head?

2. What are the first steps in Murray's writing process? How do these first steps help him? Why do you think he does these steps first?

3. What does Murray do when he writes a first draft? Who or what does Murray suggest controls the process, Murray himself or the ideas and language as they evolve?

4. How does Murray first read his draft? How many times does he reread it? What are some of the questions he asks himself as he reads?

Strategies and Structures

1. How does Murray's title suggest what the essay will be about?

2. Murray implies his thesis here. What could be the advantage of an implied thesis? Are there any disadvantages? Explain.

3. Murray opens his essay with a metaphor (see Glossary). What is it? How does it strengthen the description of his writing process?

4. Which sentences act as topic sentences throughout Murray's essay? How does he develop each topic sentence? Does each paragraph have one controlling idea?

5. Murray is writing about a process. How does he structure his essay so that this process is clear to the reader? Why do you think he chooses a chronological strategy of development?

Vocabulary and Language

1. Vocabulary: *sources, details, quotations, phrases, voice, tone, titles, draft, leads, point of view, research, outline, dictate, sequence of ideas, structure, subject, genre, documented, "cut and paste."* Murray uses many words familiar to writers. Look over the list of above words. Which are you familiar with? Which are new to you? Make a list of the unfamiliar words and then, using your dictionary, look up the definition that is appropriate to the writing process and jot it down in your notebook. Finally, rewrite one of the answers to the Pre-Reading Questions, using as many of the words in the above list as possible.

2. Even though Murray is a professional journalist and a graduate professor who taught advanced composition, his essay is fairly easy to read. Why do you think that is so? What kind of vocabulary words does he use? Give specific examples. What does he do when there is a word or idea that he feels the reader may not understand? Give an example of this strategy.

GROUP ACTIVITIES

1. As a group, discuss your different writing processes. As you listen to others, make a list of the strategies they used which were different from yours. Then make a list of your classmates' strategies that you think might be helpful to you.

2. Murray explains how he writes; many other authors have written on the same theme. Go to your library and find an essay or interview in which an author describes the way he or she writes. (See, for example, *Writers at Work* edited by George Plimpton. Your

teacher will have many other ideas.) Then photo-copy the article, and together write an outline of the author's writing process. Be prepared to explain the author's process to the rest of the class.

WRITING ASSIGNMENTS

1. Murray writes about something he enjoys doing— writing. Write a paper in which you explain the steps in an activity you enjoy. Be sure to clearly structure your composition so that each paragraph describes a step in the activity.

2. Murray explains his writing process. Construct a paper in which you explain *your* reading process. What do you do when you read? Be very specific and detailed.

2

NARRATION

People told stories long before written languages appeared. The only way many cultures preserved their history was through stories passed down from generation to generation. In many cultures, the storyteller's position in society was second only to royalty. Chants, a form of story telling, were so important to the Hawaiians that a chanter was put to death for missing even one word of a story. Today, we still enjoy hearing and telling stories but need not fear the fate of Hawaiian chanters. Whether we're sitting around a roaring fire telling jokes or ghost stories, recalling memorable moments (good or bad), or narrating a humorous happening, we are engaged in the process of narration. We tell stories for many reasons: to inform, to entertain, or to persuade. Regardless of purpose, narration has many common elements.

Common Elements of Narration

Creating Chronological Order

Most narratives have a chronological order; that is, the events are told in the manner in which they occurred. To unify their essays and to help readers through them, authors frequently use *time transitions,* words such as: *initially, next, in addition, once, finally,* and so on. These transitional devices, often called linking words, appear in strategic places in the essay, indicating the relationship between phrases, clauses, and entire paragraphs. In "Saigon, April 1975," Nguyen Ngoc Ngan uses transitional expressions like "later," "after waiting," "the very next day," "First," and "then" in order to lead his reader through the things he did to survive when the Viet Cong took over South Vietnam.

Developing Character

In order to develop a character, you will want to use concrete nouns and active verbs whenever possible. Doing so will *show* your reader what the person is like through his or her actions. For example, in "The Origins of the Pipe," rather than telling readers the Buffalo Woman is supernatural, Black Elk shows us by writing, *"And as she sang, there came from her mouth a white cloud that was good to smell."* Similarly, Maxine Hong Kingston uses vividly descriptive words and phrases like *"Wei saw his arrow sticking in a ball of flesh entirely covered with eyes, some rolled back to show the dulling whites"* to describe a ghost. Such passages may horrify, amuse, or inform the reader, but one thing is certain; they rarely will put the reader to sleep!

Establishing Mood and Tone

Often authors use concrete details to engage the reader's imagination, establishing mood and tone; they often draw on sensory imagery. In "Journey to Nine Miles," when Alice Walker writes, *"By five o'clock, we were awake, listening to the soothing slapping of the surf and watching the sky redden over the ocean,"* she appeals to the reader's sense of sight and sound to establish a colorful sensual tone that pervades the essay.

Whether narratives are meant to inform, entertain, or persuade, they have been used by storytellers and writers for ages—and continue to be used—to engage their reader's imagination. In the process, writers have manipulated the elements of character, imagery, and plot to achieve their goals.

Tips on Writing Narrative Essays

1. Determine the purpose of your narrative. Do you plan to inform, argue an issue, define something, or simply write an amusing account for your reader?

2. Ask yourself for whom you are writing this narrative. (Your audience will determine how you will approach your topic, and what sort of language you will use.)

3. Freewrite, brainstorm, or cluster your topic using the five Ws (who, what, where, when, and why) and H (how). Once you have decided upon a particular focus or controlling idea for your composition, write the idea in the form of a thesis statement and construct your introductory paragraph.

4. Using time transitions (first, second, third, then, also) to highlight chronological order, write out your entire narrative, referring to your thesis statement to insure continuity.

5. Create mood and tone in your narrative by using concrete nouns and active verbs. During the revising stages of writing, add small descriptive details to appeal to your reader's five senses. Attempt to enable your reader to visualize everything you are recounting.

6. Before writing your final copy, have someone read your paper and tell you whether he or she felt like a participant—an observer—at the event you described. An impartial reader can often point out areas in your paper where you've assumed too much reader knowledge or sections that require additional attention.

Ghosts
MAXINE HONG KINGSTON

Maxine Hong Kingston's articles and stories have appeared in such magazines as the *New York Times*, *Ms.*, and *New West*. Her books include *China Men*, *Tripmaster Monkey* and *The Woman Warrior: Memoirs of a Girlhood Among Ghosts*, the source of the following narrative.

PRE-READING QUESTIONS

1. What does the title "Ghosts" lead you to expect in Kingston's story?
2. Brainstorm the word ghosts in small groups or as a class. Use the 5 Ws and H questions (who, what, when, where, why, and how) to generate ideas.

1   When the thermometer in our laundry reached one hundred and eleven degrees on summer afternoons, either my mother or my father would say that it was time to tell another ghost story so that we could get some good chills up our backs. My parents, my brothers, sisters, great-uncle, and "Third Aunt," who wasn't really our aunt but a fellow villager, someone else's third aunt, kept the presses crashing and hissing and shouted out the stories. Those were our successful days, when so much laundry came in, my mother did not have to pick tomatoes. For breaks we changed from pressing to sorting.

2   "One twilight," my mother began, and already the chills travelled my back and crossed my shoulders; the hair rose at the nape and the back of the legs. "I was walking home after doctoring a sick family. To get home I had to cross a footbridge. In China the bridges are nothing like the ones in Brooklyn and San Francisco. This one was made from rope, laced and knotted as if by magpies. Actually it had been built by men who had returned after harvesting sea swallow nests in Malaya. They had had to swing over the faces of the Malayan cliffs in baskets they had woven themselves. Though this bridge pitched and swayed

in the updraft, no one had ever fallen into the river, which looked like a bright scratch at the bottom of the canyon, as if the Queen of Heaven had swept her great silver hairpin across the earth as well as the sky."

3   One twilight, just as my mother stepped on the bridge, two smoky columns spiraled up taller than she. Their swaying tops hovered over her head like white cobras, one at either handrail. From stillness came a wind rushing between the smoke spindles. A high sound entered her temple bones. Through the twin whirlwinds she could see the sun and the river, the river twisting in circles, the trees upside down. The bridge moved like a ship, sickening. The earth dipped. She collapsed to the wooden slats, a ladder up the sky, her fingers so weak she could not grip the rungs. The wind dragged her hair behind her, then whipped it forward across her face. Suddenly the smoke spindles disappeared. The world righted itself, and she crossed to the other side. She looked back, but there was nothing there. She used the bridge often, but she did not encounter those ghosts again.

4   "They were Sit Dom Kuei," said Great-Uncle. "Sit Dom Kuei."

5   "Yes, of course," said my mother. "Sit Dom Kuei."

6   I keep looking in dictionaries under those syllables. "Kuei" means "ghost," but I don't find any other words that make sense. I only hear my great-uncle's river-pirate voice, the voice of a big man who had killed someone in New York or Cuba, make the sounds—"Sit Dom Kuei." How do they translate?

7   When the Communists issued their papers on techniques for combating ghosts, I looked for "Sit Dom Kuei." I have not found them described anywhere, although now I see that my mother won in ghost battle because she can eat anything—quick, pluck out the carp's eyes, one for Mother and one for Father. All heroes are bold toward food. In the research against ghost fear published by the Chinese Academy of Science is the story of a magistrate's servant, Kao Chung, a capable eater who in 1683 ate five cooked chickens and drank ten bottles of wine that belonged to the sea monster with branching teeth. The monster had arranged its food around a fire on the beach and started to feed when Kao Chung attacked. The swan-feather sword he wrested from this monster can be seen in the Wentung County Armory in Shantung today.

8   Another big eater was Chou Yi-han of Changchow, who fried a ghost. It was a meaty stick when he cut it up and cooked it. But before that it had been a woman out at night.

9   Chen Luan-feng, during the Yuan Ho era of the T'ang dynasty (A.D. 806–820), ate yellow croaker and pork together, which the thunder god had forbidden. But Chen wanted to incur thunderbolts during drought. The first time he ate, the thunder god jumped out of the sky, its legs like old trees. Chen chopped off the left one. The thunder god fell to the earth, and the villagers could see that it was a blue pig or bear with horns and fleshy wings. Chen leapt on it, prepared to chop its neck and bite its throat, but the villagers stopped him. After that, Chen lived apart as a rainmaker, neither relatives nor the monks willing to bring lightning upon themselves. He lived in a cave, and for years whenever there was drought the villagers asked him to eat yellow croaker and pork together, and he did.

10   The most fantastic eater of them all was Wei Pang, a scholar-hunter of the Ta Li era of the T'ang dynasty (A.D. 766–779). He shot and cooked rabbits and birds, but he could also eat scorpions, snakes, cockroaches, worms, slugs, beetles, and crickets. Once he spent the night in a house that had been abandoned because its inhabitants feared contamination from the dead man next door. A shining, twinkling sphere came flying through the darkness at Wei. He felled it with three true arrows—the first making the thing crackle and flame; the second dimming it; and the third putting out its lights, sputter. When his servant came running in with a lamp, Wei saw his arrows sticking in a ball of flesh entirely covered with eyes, some rolled back to show the dulling whites. He and the servant pulled out the arrows and cut up the ball into little pieces. The servant cooked the morsels in sesame oil, and the wonderful aroma made Wei laugh. They ate half, saving half to show the household, which would return now.

11   Big eaters win. When the other passers-by stepped around the bundle wrapped in white silk, the anonymous scholar of Hanchow took it home. Inside were three silver ingots and a froglike evil, which sat on the ingots. The scholar laughed at it and chased it off. That night two frogs the size of year-old babies appeared in his room. He clubbed them to death, cooked them, and ate them with white wine. The next night a dozen

frogs, together the size of a pair of year-old babies, jumped from the ceiling. He ate all twelve for dinner. The third night thirty small frogs were sitting on his mat and staring at him with their frog eyes. He ate them too. Every night for a month smaller but more numerous frogs came so that he always had the same amount to eat. Soon his floor was like the healthy banks of a pond in spring when the tadpoles, having just turned, sprang in the wet grass. "Get a hedgehog to help eat," cried his family. "I'm as good as a hedgehog," the scholar said, laughing. And at the end of the month the frogs stopped coming, leaving the scholar with the white silk and silver ingots.

POST-READING QUESTIONS

Content

1. What image(s) do you find powerful or interesting? Why?

2. What does it mean to be heroic from Kingston's cultural perspective? How does this compare or contrast with America's perspective on heroism?

3. How does she illustrate what it takes to be a ghost warrior?

4. How and why did her mother defeat the ghost? How and why did the others defeat the ghosts?

5. Why does the author bring Chinese words into the story?

Strategies and Structures

1. Where do you imagine Kingston could have obtained the information on the different ghost warriors?

2. How does Kingston illustrate what it takes to defeat a ghost?

3. How does Kingston arrange the examples of the ghost warriors?

4. What linking words does Kingston use to unify and lead the reader through the essay?

Language and Vocabulary

1. Vocabulary: *spindle, whirlwind, croaker, pluck, sputter, anonymous, ingots.* Look up these words in your dictionary and write a ten-sentence paragraph about one of the words.

2. Kingston's language is so descriptive. What "mental pictures" did or can you draw from this story? What words make her descriptions vivid?

GROUP ACTIVITIES

1. Write a collaborative ghost story. As a group, decide what the plot of your story will be. Next, have each member of the group write consecutive paragraphs. Then link your paragraphs together carefully, using transitions. Finally, proofread your essays, eliminating mechanical and grammatical errors, and as a group, read the essay, making final corrections.

2. As a group, discuss the peculiar habits of ghosts or heroes in your culture just as Kingston narrates the peculiar eating habits of ghosts in her culture.

WRITING ACTIVITIES

1. Using specific examples, write an essay wherein you illustrate your definition of a fiercely independent person at odds with the world around him or her.

2. Narrate a ghost story you remember hearing as a child.

The Offering of the Pipe
BLACK ELK

Born in 1863, Black Elk was a holyman (*wichash wakon*) of the Oglala Sioux. In *Black Elk Speaks,* the source of the following narrative, he tells his life story—which he was instructed to do in a sacred vision—to John G. Neihardt.

PRE-READING QUESTIONS

1. Black Elk, a holyman, makes offerings to nature. In your cultural tradition, who are the holy men or women who make similar offerings to *unseen* powers?
2. Freewrite in your journals about ceremonies and sacred offerings. Then read Black Elk's narrative.

1   *Black Elk Speaks:*
My friend, I am going to tell you the story of my life, as you wish; and if it were only the story of my life I think I would not tell it; for what is one man that he should make much of his winters, even when they bend him like a heavy snow? So many other men have lived and shall live that story, to be grass upon the hills.

2   It is the story of all life that is holy and is good to tell, and of us two-leggeds sharing in it with the four-leggeds and the wings of the air and all green things; for these are children of one mother and their father is one Spirit.

3   This, then, is not the tale of a great hunter or of a great warrior, or of a great traveler, although I have made much meat in my time and fought for my people both as boy and man, and have gone far and seen strange lands and men. So also have many others done, and better than I. These things I shall remember by the way, and often they may seem to be the very tale itself, as when I was living them in happiness and sorrow. But now that I can see it all as from a lonely hilltop, I know it was the story of a mighty vision given to a man too weak to use it; of a

holy tree that should have flourished in a people's heart with flowers and singing birds, and now is withered; and of a people's dream that died in bloody snow.

4   But if the vision was true and mighty, as I know, it is true and mighty yet; for such things are of the spirit, and it is in the darkness of their eyes that men get lost.

5   So I know that it is a good thing I am going to do; and because no good thing can be done by any man alone, I will first make an offering and send a voice to the Spirit of the World, that it may help me to be true. See, I fill this sacred pipe with the bark of the red willow; but before we smoke it, you must see how it is made and what it means. These four ribbons hanging here on the stem are the four quarters of the universe. The black one is for the west where the thunder beings live to send us rain; the white one for the north, whence comes the great white cleansing wind; the red one for the east, whence springs the light and where the morning star lives to give men wisdom; the yellow for the south, whence come the summer and the power to grow.

6   But these four spirits are only one Spirit after all, and this eagle feather here is for that One, which is like a father, and also it is for the thoughts of men that should rise high as eagles do. Is not the sky a father and the earth a mother, and are not all living things with feet or wings or roots their children? And this hide upon the mouthpiece here, which should be bison hide, is for the earth, from whence we came and at whose breast we suck as babies all our lives, along with all the animals and birds and trees and grasses. And because it means all this, and more than any man can understand, the pipe is holy.

7   There is a story about the way the pipe first came to us. A very long time ago, they say, two scouts were out looking for bison; and when they came to the top of a high hill and looked north, they saw something coming a long way off, and when it came closer they cried out, "It is a woman!," and it was. Then one of the scouts, being foolish, had bad thoughts and spoke them; but the other said: "That is a sacred woman; throw all bad thoughts away." When she came still closer, they saw that she wore a fine white buckskin dress, that her hair was very long and that she was young and very beautiful. And she knew their

thoughts and said in a voice that was like singing: "You do not know me, but if you want to do as you think, you may come." And the foolish one went; but just as he stood before her, there was a white cloud that came and covered them. And the beautiful young woman came out of the cloud, and when it blew away the foolish man was a skeleton covered with worms.

8   Then the woman spoke to the one who was not foolish: "You shall go home and tell your people that I am coming and that a big tepee shall be built for me in the center of the nation." And the man, who was very much afraid, went quickly and told the people, who did at once as they were told; and there around the big tepee they waited for the sacred woman. And after a while she came, very beautiful and singing, and as she went into the tepee this is what she sang:

> With visible breath I am walking.
> A voice I am sending as I walk.
> In a sacred manner I am walking.
> With visible tracks I am walking.
> In a sacred manner I walk.

And as she sang, there came from her mouth a white cloud that was good to smell. Then she gave something to the chief, and it was a pipe with a bison calf carved on one side to mean the earth that bears and feeds us, and with twelve eagle feathers hanging from the stem to mean the sky and the twelve moons, and these were tied with a grass that never breaks. "Behold!" she said. "With this you shall multiply and be a good nation. Nothing but good shall come from it. Only the hands of the good shall take care of it and the bad shall not even see it." Then she sang again and went out of the tepee; and as the people watched her going, suddenly it was a white bison galloping away and snorting, and soon it was gone.

9   This they tell, and whether it happened so or not I do not know; but if you think about it, you can see that it is true.

10   Now I light the pipe, and after I have offered it to the powers that are one Power, and sent forth a voice to them, we shall smoke together. Offering the mouthpiece first of all to the One above—so—I send a voice:

11   Hey hey! hey hey! hey hey! hey hey!

12   Grandfather, Great Spirit, you have been always, and before you no one has been. There is no other one to pray to but you. You yourself, everything that you see, everything has been made by you. The star nations all over the universe you have finished. The four quarters of the earth you have finished. The day, and in that day, everything you have finished. Grandfather, Great Spirit, lean close to the earth that you may hear the voice I send. You towards where the sun goes down, behold me; Thunder Beings, behold me! You where the White Giant lives in power, behold me! You where the sun shines continually, whence come the day-break star and the day, behold me! You where the summer lives, behold me! You in the depth of the heavens, an eagle of power, behold! And you, Mother Earth, the only Mother, you who have shown mercy to your children!

13   Hear me, four quarters of the world—a relative I am! Give me the strength to walk the soft earth, a relative to all that is! Give me the eyes to see and the strength to understand, that I may be like you. With your power only can I face the winds.

14   Great Spirit, Great Spirit, my Grandfather, all over the earth the faces of living things are all alike. With tenderness have these come up out of the ground. Look upon these faces of children without number and with children in their arms, that they may face the winds and walk the good road to the day of quiet.

15   This is my prayer; hear me! The voice I have sent is weak, yet with earnestness I have sent it. Hear me!

16   It is finished. Hetchetu aloh!

17   Now, my friend, let us smoke together so that there may be only good between us.

POST-READING QUESTIONS

Content

1. In this essay, what is the purpose of smoking the sacred pipe?

2. What is the significance of the four ribbons on Black Elk's pipe?

3. Who is the young woman in the white buckskin dress? Why does she come to Black Elk's people?

4. Whom does Black Elk pray to and why? What other spirits does he mention and why?

Strategies and Structures

1. In paragraph 7, why does Black Elk digress from his main narrative? What purpose does the story of the Buffalo Woman serve?

2. How does Black Elk explain the origins of the sacred pipe?

3. Why does Black Elk begin and conclude this narrative with the same ceremony? What effect does this have on the reader?

Language and Vocabulary

1. Vocabulary: *withered, cleansing, bison, skeleton, tepee, earnestness.* Check your dictionary for the meanings of these words, and write two or three paragraphs in which you first make up and then narrate an event in the life of a Native-American using each of the following words from the list above—withered, bison, and tepee—at least twice.

2. What context clues suggest the meaning of *hetchetu aloh*?

GROUP ACTIVITIES

1. In groups of four, pair off and take turns interviewing each other. Then write a brief profile of each member in your group.

2. Compare your freewritings on ceremonies and sacred offerings with others in your group. What did your freewritings have in common? How did they differ? Overall, how does your group assess the importance of ritual in modern life in America?

WRITING ACTIVITIES

1. Write a story explaining your origins. Who were your ancestors? What significant events can you recall during different stages of growing up?

2. Write a narrative essay wherein you start with some sort of ceremony, digress, and then conclude with the initial ceremony.

=========

Journey to Nine Miles
ALICE WALKER

In 1944, Alice Walker was born in Eatonton, Georgia—the eighth child of African-American sharecroppers. Her works include *The Third Life of Grange Copeland* (1970), *Revolutionary Petunias* (1973), *Meridian* (1976), *You Can't Keep a Good Woman Down* (1981), and *The Color Purple*, for which she won the Pulitzer Prize for Fiction (1983).

PRE-READING QUESTIONS

1. In your culture, is there a tradition of visiting the grave sites of ancestors or respected persons? Why do you go? What purpose(s) does it serve?

2. What sorts of preparations do you make for such visitations?

1   By five o'clock we were awake, listening to the soothing slapping of the surf and watching the sky redden over the ocean. By six we were dressed and knocking on my daughter's door. She and her friend Kevin were going with us (Robert and me) to visit Nine Miles, the birthplace of someone we all loved, Bob Marley. It was Christmas Day, bright, sunny, and very warm, and the traditional day of thanksgiving for the birth of someone sacred.

2   I missed Bob Marley when his body was alive, and I have often wondered how that could possibly be. It happened, though, because when he was singing all over the world, I was living in Mississippi being political, digging into my own his/her story, writing books, having a baby—and listening to local music, B. B. King, and the Beatles. I liked dreadlocks, but only because I am an Aquarian; I was unwilling to look beyond the sexism of Rastafarianism. The music stayed outside my consciousness. It didn't help either that the most political and spiritual of reggae music was suppressed in the United States, so that "Stir It Up" and not "Natty Dread" or "Lively Up Yourself" or "Exodus" was what one heard. And then, of course, there *was* disco, a music so blatantly soulless as to be frightening, and impossible to do anything to but exercise.

3   I first really *heard* Bob Marley when I was writing a draft of the screenplay for *The Color Purple*. Each Monday I drove up to my studio in the country, a taxing three-hour drive, worked steadily until Friday, drove back to the city, and tried to be two parents to my daughter on weekends. We kept in touch by phone during the week, and I had the impression that she was late for school everyday and living on chocolates.

4   My friends Jan and Chris, a white couple nearby, seeing my stress, offered their help, which I accepted in the form of dinner at their house every night after a day's work on the script. One night, after yet another sumptuous meal, we pushed back the table and, in our frustration at the pain that rides on the seat next to joy in life (cancer, pollution, invasions, the bomb, etc.), began dancing to reggae records: UB-40, Black Uhuru . . . Bob Marley. I was transfixed. It was hard to believe the beauty of the soul I heard in "No Woman No Cry," "Coming In from the Cold," "Could You Be Loved," "Three Little Birds," and "Redemption Song." Here was a man who loved his roots (even after he'd been nearly assassinated in his own country) and knew they extended to the ends of the earth. Here was a soul who loved Jamaica and loved Jamaicans and loved *being* a Jamaican (nobody got more pleasure out of the history, myths, traditions, and language of Jamaica than Bob Marley), but who knew it was not meant to limit itself (or even could) to an island of any sort. Here was the radical peasant-class, working-class consciousness that fearlessly denounced the *wasichu* (the greedy

and destructive) and did it with such grace you could dance to it. Here was a man of extraordinary sensitivity, political acumen, spiritual power, and sexual wildness; a free spirit if ever there was one. Here, I felt, was my brother. It was as if there had been a great and gorgeous light on all over the world, and somehow I'd missed it. Every night for the next two months I listened to Bob Marley. I danced with his spirit—so much more alive still than many people walking around. I felt my own dreadlocks begin to grow.

5   Over time, the draft of the script I was writing was finished. My evenings with my friends came to an end. My love of Marley spread easily over my family, and it was as neophyte Rastas (having decided that *Rasta* for us meant a commitment to a religion of attentiveness and joy) that we appeared when we visited Jamaica in 1984.

6   What we saw was a ravaged land, a place where people, often Rastas, eat out of garbage cans and where, one afternoon in a beach cafe during a rainstorm, I overheard a 13-year-old boy offer his 11-year-old sister (whose grown-up earrings looked larger, almost, than her face) to a large hirsute American white man (who blushingly declined) along with some Jamaican pot.

7   The car we rented (from a harried, hostile dealer who didn't even seem to want to tell us where to buy gas) had already had two flats. On the way to Nine Miles it had three more. Eventually, however, after an agonizing seven hours from Negril, where we were staying, blessing the car at every bump in the road to encourage it to live through the trip, we arrived.

8   Nine Miles (because it is nine miles from the nearest village of any size) is one of the most still and isolated spots on the face of the earth. It is only several houses, spread out around the top of a hill. There are small, poor farms, with bananas appearing to be the predominant crop.

9   Several men and many children come down the hill to meet our car. They know we've come to visit Bob. They walk with us up the hill where Bob Marley's body is entombed in a small mausoleum with stained-glass windows: the nicest building in Nine Miles. Next to it is a small one-room house where Bob and his wife, Rita, lived briefly during their marriage. I think of how

much energy Bob Marley had to generate to project himself into the world beyond this materially impoverished place; and of how exhausted, in so many of his later photographs, he looked. On the other hand, it is easy to understand—listening to the deep stillness that makes a jet soaring overhead sound like the buzzing of a fly—why he wanted to be brought back to his home village, back to Nine Miles, to rest. We see the tomb from a distance of about 50 feet, because we cannot pass through (or climb over) an immense chain link fence that has recently been erected to keep the too eager (and apparently destructive and kleptomaniacal) tourists at bay. One thing that I like very much; built into the hill facing Bob's tomb is a permanent stage. On his birthday, February 6, someone tells us, people from all over the world come to Nine Miles to sing to him.

10   The villagers around us are obviously sorry about the fence. (Perhaps we were not the ones intended to be kept out?) Their faces seem to say as much. They are all men and boys. No women or girls among them. On a front porch below the hill I see some women and girls, studiously avoiding us.

11   One young man, the caretaker, tells us that though we can't come in, there is a way we can get closer to Bob. (I almost tell him I could hardly be any closer to Bob and still be alive, but I don't want to try to explain.) He points out a path that climbs the side of the hill and we—assisted by half a dozen of the more agile villagers—take it. It passes through bananas and weeds, flowers, past goats tethered out of the sun, past chickens. Past the home, one says, of Bob Marley's cousin, a broken but gallant-looking man in his 50s, nearly toothless, with a gentle and generous smile. He sits in his tiny, nearly bare house and watches us, his face radiant with the pride of relationship.

12   From within the compound now we hear singing. Bob's songs come from the lips of the caretaker, who says he and Bob were friends. That he loved Bob. Loved his music. He sings terribly. But perhaps this is only because he is, though about the age Bob would have been now, early 40s, lacking his front teeth. He is very dark and quite handsome, teeth or no. And it is his humble, terrible singing—as he moves proprietarily about the yard where his friend is enshrined—that makes him so. It is as if he sings Bob's songs *for* Bob, in an attempt to animate the tomb. The little children are all about us, nearly underfoot. Beautiful

children. One little boy is right beside me. He is about six, of
browner skin than the rest—who are nearer to black—with
curlier hair. He looks like Bob.

13   I ask his name. He tells me. I have since forgotten it. As we
linger by the fence, our fingers touch. For a while we hold
hands. I notice that over the door to the tomb someone has
plastered a bumper sticker with the name of Rita Marley's
latest album. It reads: "Good Girl's Culture." I am offended by
it; there are so many possible meanings. For a moment I try to
imagine the sticker plastered across Bob's forehead. It drops
off immediately, washed away by his sweat (as he sings and
dances in the shamanistic trance I so love) and his spirit's inability to be possessed by anyone other than itself (and Jah).
The caretaker says Rita erected the fence. I understand the
necessity.

14   Soon it is time to go. We clamber back down the hill to the
car. On the way down the little boy who looks like Bob asks for
money. Thinking of our hands together and how he is so like
Bob must have been at his age, I don't want to give him money.
But what else can I give him, I wonder.

15   I consult "the elders," the little band of adults who've gathered about us.

16   "The children are asking for money," I say. "What should
we do?"

17   "You should give it," is the prompt reply. So swift and un-
studied is the answer, in fact, that suddenly the question seems
absurd.

18   "They ask because they have none. There is nothing here."

19   "Would Bob approve?" I ask. Then I think, "Probably. The
man has had himself planted here to feed the village."

20   "Yes," is the reply. "Because he would understand."

21   Starting with the children, but by no means stopping there
(because the grown-ups look as expectant as they), we part with
some of our "tourist" dollars, realizing that tourism is a dead
thing, a thing of the past; that no one can be a tourist anymore,
and that, like Bob, all of us can find our deepest rest and most
meaningful service at home.

22   It is a long hot anxious drive that we have ahead of us. We
make our usual supplications to our little tin car and its four
shiny tires. But even when we have another flat, bringing us to

our fourth for the trip, it hardly touches us. Jamaica is a poor country reduced to selling its living and its dead while much of the world thinks of it as "real estate" and a great place to lie in the sun; but Jamaicans as a people have been seen in all their imperfections and beauty by one of their own, and fiercely sung, even from the grave, and loved. There is no poverty, only richness in this. We sing "Redemption Song" as we change the tire; feeling very Jamaica, very Bob, very Rasta, very *no woman no cry*.

POST-READING QUESTIONS

Content

1. Why did Walker "miss" Marley's music at first? What event put her in touch with it?

2. Where does her appreciation of Marley lead her and her family? What does she find at the end of her journey?

3. What does Walker learn about the Jamaican people and "Rasta" culture?

4. Walker claims that "Jamaica is a poor country reduced to selling its living and its dead. . . ." Is this much different than America or any other country? How? Why? Explain.

Strategies and Structures

1. Walker uses a "journey motif" to structure her essay. Why does she choose to use this motif? What does this symbolize?

2. What sorts of linking devices does Walker use? How do they allow the reader to follow her on the journey to Marley's grave?

3. What images or descriptions create a definite mood in this essay?

4. How does the tone at the end of Walker's essay (when she is changing her car tire for the *fourth* time) compare with the beginning?

Language and Vocabulary

1. Vocabulary: *Aquarian, acumen, sumptuous, neophyte, hirsute, kleptomaniac, shamanistic, expectant.* Find the definitions of these words and be prepared to discuss how Walker uses them as she moves through her essay. Since you may not have seen many of these words, choose three or four of them and write at least three sentences for each, making sure to use the word correctly.

2. How is the title of his essay, "Journey to Nine Miles," significant?

GROUP ACTIVITIES

1. Go to the library and find the lyrics to a Bob Marley song. How does he use words? (Pay particular attention to syntax.) Then, as a group, rewrite (paraphrase) his song lyrics using a complete paragraph for each word group. What do his lyrics lose in translation?

2. As a group, visit a rest home for elderly people, and after your visit, write a collaborative narrative detailing your group's reaction to what you see. Did the visit depress you, or did you leave with a renewed outlook on life?

WRITING ACTIVITIES

1. Narrate a journey you took to fulfill some significant purpose. How did it begin? What obstacle(s) did you have to overcome before reaching your ultimate destination?

2. Write about a nonphysical journey—mental or spiritual—which has greatly changed your way of thinking. Consider what you were like prior to your journey as well as after it.

Saigon, April 1975
NGUYEN NGOC NGAN

Now living in Toronto, Canada, Nguyen Ngoc Ngan, a refugee from South Vietnam, wrote a book called *The Will of Heaven* which detailed his experiences from the fall of South Vietnam to his escape to the free world. The following piece was excerpted from the prologue to the book.

PRE-READING QUESTIONS

1. What unavoidable conflict have you ever faced? Have you ever been powerless to do what you wanted or thought was best for others? How did you react?

2. What do you know about Saigon or Vietnam? Read the first two paragraphs and then, based upon your own knowledge of Vietnam and what you read, make a list in which you guess (speculate) what will happen next.

1   Early in the morning of April 29, 1975, I sat bolt upright in bed, awakened by the sudden explosions shaking predawn Saigon. I glanced with concern at my wife, Tuyet Lan, asleep beside me, and my one-year-old son, Tran, lying peacefully in his crib by the window. Then I raced to the roof.

2   Reddish glows pulsated in the darkness to the west, accompanied by the deep rumbling of artillery. The glows seemed to be coming from the general direction of Tan Son Nhut airport. I shuddered, for there I knew that thousands of Vietnamese had assembled for the American airlift. That throbbing brilliance seemed the final incinerating flash of an almost endless war. From it could come only the blackened cinder of my country's defeat.

3   I stared at the scene with an aching heart. Who would have thought that all our agonizing years of death and sacrifice would finally be reduced to simply a reddish glow in the darkened western sky? I turned, and with leaden steps descended the stairs.

4   When I returned to the bedroom, my wife was sitting on the edge of our bed.

5   "Where have you been? When I woke up from the noise and found you gone, I was frightened." She stared up at me, her dark eyes large and fearful.

6   "I've just been up on the roof, checking. Those shells are falling miles away," I tried to reassure her. "You might as well try to get some more rest. It's only twenty past four."

7   "No, Ngan," she said, shaking her head. "Let's talk, be honest with me now, don't treat me like a child. I have to know! It's almost over, isn't it? They're not going to negotiate, are they? The Viet Cong are going to come right in with their tanks and soldiers. There'll be fighting in the streets." Then there was stark fear in her voice. "They'll do the same thing here that they did at Hue."

8   Tuyet Lan was referring to the Hue horror of Tet, 1968. She had had relatives among the more than two thousand civilians in the Northern city of Hue who were forced to dig shallow trenches, then were lined up in front of them and shot in cold blood. That grisly recollection now filled her with terror. She clung to me, her body trembling with sobs.

9   I brushed the tears from Tuyet Lan's eyes and tried to comfort her. She stared up at me, her gentle eyes full of fear.

10   "Isn't it possible," she finally asked tremulously, "that we could get on one of the flights out of Tan Son Nhut? I know there are many leaving who don't have proper credentials."

11   "There are no more flights out of Tan Son Nhut, Tuyet Lan," I said gently. "That's where they're shelling now."

12   Tuyet Lan paled, "But there must be boats," she persisted. "Yes, we must try to get on a boat down at the harbor. There'll be some American ships out there somewhere. They'll pick us up."

13   I was surprised to hear these words. Only two days before when I had asked her whether we should leave the country she had had entirely different views. But at that time there had been much talk about a negotiated peace and that General Duong Van ("Big") Minh, appointed president only the day before, was the one person who could achieve it. Then Tuyet Lan had said, "The war has kept you away from me so much, Ngan! Now that peace is coming, why not stay here and enjoy our life

together for a change? Certainly, there's no better place to be than in our own homeland."

14   I recalled those words now as my wife stood before me, pale and tense.

15   "There'll be plenty of American ships out there, Ngan," she repeated, looking up at me imploringly.

16   I gathered her again in a gentle embrace. "We can try, Tuyet Lan," I said softly. "We can try."

17   So later that morning Tuyet Lan and I said good-bye to our parents and soon, with Tran, became part of the seething mass of humanity we found milling around the waterfront. It seemed hopeless. Thousands and thousands of people were there ahead of us, trying to get aboard the few boats. After waiting for two hours and still finding ourselves on only the periphery of the crowd, we edged our way out of the growing throng and set out again on the motor scooter for the American Embassy. We had heard that helicopter flights were beginning to leave from there.

18   As we approached the embassy, we saw its fortress like walls surrounded by a boundless sea of people. Coming closer, we could see no evidence of any helicopters, and, upon inquiring, learned that the flights had not yet begun. Reluctantly I admitted to myself that it would require a miracle for the three of us ever to get past the huge, grim-faced Marines at the gates, and finally we headed back home.

19   As we passed now-deserted American installations, we saw Vietnamese leaving the buildings, bending under the heavy burdens of boxes of food and cases of beer and soft drinks. At long last, it seemed, American aid was finally reaching the people.

20   That night I lay sleepless, twisting the radio dial, trying to pick up the BBC or the Voice of America broadcasts. Lately I had begun to lose faith in the BBC because of their consistently premature announcements of the fall of cities to the north, which added to the general panic prevailing there. Now they were saying that the Viet Cong would occupy Saigon tomorrow. With the night alive with the stammering clatter of machine-gun fire and the crash of distant shells, the BBC pronouncement was very believable indeed.

21   The very next day, April 30, 1975, the North Vietnamese Army, with disarming cries of *hoa binh* ("peace"), swept triumphantly into Saigon. The world as I had known it for twenty-eight years ended abruptly.

22   I rose apprehensively at six-fifteen and opened the side window of the living room. It was still a bit dark, but I was able to discern some figures lying in our small yard near the cassia shrub. I called out, "Who's there?"

23   "Please excuse us for trespassing," came a woman's polite voice out of the semidarkness, "but the grass looked so inviting. We're from Hoc Mon. The Viet Cong are already there. In fact, they are here in Saigon. We have been running from the fighting but there's no place now to run."

24   A few minutes later I heard a heavy rumble that seemed to be getting closer to the house. I ran out into the street and looked up and down in the hazy morning light. In the distance I could see a tank approaching, loaded with ARVN (our Army of the Republic of Vietnam) soldiers.

25   From the other direction I could hear the ominous roar of several approaching tanks and blasts from other guns. Russian T-54's! There was going to be a battle right on our street, I thought, running back inside. The refugees were right. The Viet Cong were here and in strength. I roused Tuyet Lan and Tran and a few minutes later we were on my motor scooter, fleeing the scene of probable confrontation.

26   Frantically hopeful, we once again approached the Saigon harbor, which had become a scene of chaos. Cars, motorcycles, and people were hopelessly snarled as thousands fought to get aboard the few boats. Ahead of us at the waterfront we could see a boat pulling out, loaded almost to sinking. The crowd surged forward, fighting to be first on the next boat, and there was a wild melee to get aboard. This scene repeated itself several times until there were no more boats.

27   A few people had begun to drift sadly away when the shelling began. There was screaming. Everyone panicked and ran wildly for cover, blindly trampling the fallen. I clutched Tuyet Lan tightly by the hand and fled with Tran in my arms, looking helplessly for a building that would afford some protection. We passed the Saigon market and the sprawled bodies of some shelling victims. Finally I came upon a school building,

and, thrusting Tuyet Lan ahead of me, went inside. It was packed. We all huddled fearfully there, waiting for the roof to crash down on us. At least it would take a direct hit to kill us; we were safe from random shell fragments.

28   It was in that building, over a tiny radio, that we heard our president of three days, General Duong Van Minh, offer his unconditional surrender and order a cease-fire. Some people heaved sighs of relief; others wept. A few sat staring silently into space. Someone near me commented that, earlier that morning, Minh had appealed to his army to put an end to all hostilities, and had implored "our brothers of the provisional government" to do likewise.

29   "They're our 'brothers' now," said my neighbor, smiling bitterly. "They're no longer the 'murdering Viet Cong.'"

30   Tuyet Lan and I sat in stunned silence as the building began to empty. It had all happened so quickly, but still, I was filled with self-recrimination for having been so indecisive during the last few days. I should have been firmer with Tuyet Lan, I thought. We could probably have gotten on one of those flights out of Tan Son Nhut. And instead of giving up so easily yesterday and going home, we should have tried the port at Nha Be. Boats most surely were leaving from there. I had just not planned properly; I had waited too long. Even though I had anticipated this inevitable moment for the past few days, some small part of me had hoped right up to the end that somehow the United States would ultimately come to our rescue. How could they do otherwise? Who would have thought that after all these years they would let this happen?

31   With a start I suddenly realized that everyone had left the building. Tuyet Lan and I were sitting there alone. We got up and headed for home through streets now filled with a palpable sorrow. We passed gruesomely mutilated shell victims sprawled on the streets. People hurried by them with averted eyes.

32   "How terrible it is to die like that at the last moment of the war," I said. "Just as peace comes."

33   Tuyet Lan made no answer. She held tightly to my hand as we hurried along the saddened street. A soft, warm rain was falling. Once Tuyet Lan stumbled slightly, and as I reached out to steady her, I saw that her eyes were blinded by tears.

34   Discarded weapons—M-16 rifles, Colt .45 automatics, grenades, bayonets, cartridge clips—were scattered where our soldiers had dropped them in their rush to acquire the anonymity of civilian attire. More than the words I had just heard on the radio, they brought home to me the full realization that now the war was completely lost.

35   When we arrived at home about three-thirty that afternoon, my father anxiously met us at the door. "You didn't make it!" he exclaimed sadly. "You didn't get away."

36   There were tears in his eyes, and despite his words, I could tell that he was glad to see us back. Now he would not be lonely. His shoulders sagged and his deeply lined face was haggard. In just the past few days he'd grown much older than his sixty years. I asked him about the tank battle that had seemed imminent when we had fled early that morning. He said he thought that a small flurry of fighting had taken place a considerable distance down the street, but it had not amounted to much.

37   "*Troi oi* [Good heavens], Ngan!" he then said impatiently. "Everybody's burning things—you'd better get busy! Burn everything that might be incriminating. They'll be here soon with their questions, making their eternal lists."

38   I spent that evening collecting and burning anything that would connect me or my family with active support of the fallen regime. This may perhaps seem to be a less than courageous thing to do by some who have never had their own instincts for survival put to a severe test. But the vivid recollections of Hue in 1968, and entire families of military officers and civil servants being put to death, gave impetus to all our actions now.

39   First I burned all my uniforms. Then I searched through Tuyet Lan's photograph albums for pictures of me in uniform. What a flood of memories that brought forth. I stared in amused disbelief at the very first photograph I found. It was of me standing alone in front of the barracks at the Infantry Officer Training Academy in Thu Duc in 1970. How raw and youthful I looked in my ill-fitting uniform and short military-style haircut! And how naive I actually was, then, of the war and the political situation. Except for the Tet Offensive I had been virtually untouched by the war. There was another photograph

of me with Tuyet Lan, snapped by one of my fellow cadets. I had to smile, seeing how skinny and solemn I looked. But how lovely and innocent was Tuyet Lan. I came to another that had been enlarged and put on display on the table in the living room. It showed me, looking very fierce and proud, receiving my officer's commission from the academy deputy commandant, a colonel who was later murdered by the Viet Cong when he answered his doorbell one evening in Thu Duc. I stared at these photographs of only a few years ago as though they belonged to another age, and then slowly dropped them into the flames.

POST-READING QUESTIONS

Content

1. What does the author describe in his narrative account? What unavoidable conflict is he forced to face? Why?

2. Why was the author angry with the BBC network? Explain why his anger was or was not justified, logical, and fair.

3. Why did the author say, "The world as I had known it for 28 years ended abruptly"? What did he mean?

Strategies and Structures

1. How does the author's firsthand experience of the U.S. pullout of Vietnam strengthen this narrative?

2. What is the tone or mood in Ngan's passage? What events foreshadow his impending sense of doom?

3. Go through the text and underline specific words and phrases you believe the author uses to state a general point in a powerful, memorable manner. Include derogatory terms that force a reaction like shock or indignance in a reader.

4. What makes Ngan's descriptions vivid and clear? What sort of details can you recall after reading this essay?

Language and Vocabulary

1. Vocabulary: *imminent, haggard, melee, palpable, incriminating, impetus, ominous, self-recrimination, triumphantly, disarming, provisional.* Most of these vocabulary words suggest power or powerlessness in one way or another. Which words indicate futility and which words describe the impending military takeover, the source of panic among the South Vietnamese?

2. Go back through the essay and locate instances where the author uses images that suggest sadness. Using the author's images and your own, write a paragraph about a time in your life that was particularly sad.

GROUP ACTIVITIES

1. War is usually not what one thinks it will be like. During a war, people are given a license to kill other human beings, ideally clear of conscience because of their noble cause. However, once a war ends, the same people are expected to act humanely towards each other. As a group activity, discuss the problems that you would expect people to have when they are *ordered* to make friends with their enemies. What is the difference between being told to become friends and having the right to choose your own?

2. How does your image of Vietnam, possibly influenced by the news media and movies like *Apocalypse Now, Platoon,* and *Good Morning, Vietnam,* differ from the picture Ngan draws of Americans pulling out of Saigon and the Viet Cong moving into what would become Ho Chi Minh City? It may be a good idea to select a group leader for this exercise so that everyone has an opportunity to talk, question, and respond to each other in the time allotted for this activity.

WRITING ACTIVITIES

1. Write an essay wherein you rationalize or reason how the instinct to survive would allow you to do things you usually would consider cowardly, dishonest, degrading, or immoral.

2. Has there ever been a time in your life when you figuratively or literally destroyed symbols of your past hopes or beliefs in order to pursue a realistic future? Limit your focus and write about the event.

Additional Topics and Issues for Narrative Essays

1. Write a short narrative essay about the culture shock you encountered after moving from one neighborhood or country to another.

2. Compose an essay about a time in your life when you gave in to peer pressure rather than sticking to your personal convictions.

3. As closely as you can remember, narrate a story one of your parents used to tell you about his or her life. To frame your composition, provide your reader with the reasons or occasions your mother or father would tell you the story. Then, relate the story, and conclude with your present perceptions about such moments with your parent(s).

4. Write a narrative about a person you met on a bus, plane, train, elevator, etc., who began to talk to you like an intimate friend. What was the person like? How did you react to him or her? Did you try to ignore the person? What was his or her response to what you did or said? What conclusions can you draw about such people?

5. Discuss a situation or event that taught you a valuable lesson about life or survival in America in general.

6. Write a personal narrative recounting a typical holiday meal with your family. What takes place before, during, and

after the meal? It may be helpful to narrow your focus to a specific holiday like Thanksgiving, New Year's, Hanukkah, or Christmas.

7. Compose a narrative essay based on a social function or a sporting event you participated in during the past year. Make sure you mention what your expectations were prior to the event as well as your feelings following it.

8. Write a humorous account of a recent concert, play, night club act, or sporting event you attended. Your humor should reflect your attitude towards your subject matter (the event).

3

DESCRIPTION

While many college readers include description in their narration chapter, we feel the rhetorical strategy of description is worthy of consideration in its own right. To be sure, there is frequently a narrative element in descriptive compositions. One need only read Maya Angelou's "Champion of the World" to realize how narration and description tend to overlap, producing a visual picture of an event (Joe Louis defending his heavyweight title).

Details: Appealing to the Five Senses

What makes an essay memorable? How do specific details engage one's imagination and enable writers to vividly convey a setting, a person, an object, or situation in general? One of the most effective strategies authors employ to accomplish such ends is to appeal to the five senses: sight, sound, taste, touch, and smell. Barry Lopez illustrates the rich variety of the desert in "Perimeter" by appealing to our sense of sight in such passages as *"inside the mountains are old creeks that run in circles over the floors of low-ceilinged caves. The fish in these waters are white and translucent; you can see a pink haze of organs beneath the skin . . . ,"* and *"On the walls are white spiders like tight buttons of surgical cotton suspended on long hairy legs. "* In "Notes from a Son to His Father,"

Russell C. Leong's vivid description of his father's culinary (cooking) skills appeal to our senses of taste and smell in addition to sight in phrases like "the hardest, fibrous vegetables to be cooked first in a dash of oil, and then the more delicately flavored ones, with purple and orange-tipped spears of heat sizzling them in the heart."

Appealing to our sense of hearing, Toshio Mori writes, "*She says silence is the most beautiful symphony, . . .*" and "*. . . the Southern Pacific trains rumble by and the vehicles whiz with speed. . . .*" In "Old Before Her Time," Katherine Barrett combines sight, sound, and touch when she writes, "*She saw only a blur of sneakers and blue jeans, heard the sounds of mocking laughter, felt the fist pummeling her —on her back, her legs, her breast, her stomach.*" Capitalizing on our natural ability to see, to smell, to hear, to feel, and to taste when we compose an essay allows us to write more creatively and make what we say easy to picture.

Figurative Language: Appealing to the Imagination

While literal language can convey specific information and facts, occasionally you'll find the figurative use of language quite effective because it stimulates the imagination. Since figurative language tends to use strong imagery, it can often make abstract concepts come to life. In doing so, your material will become more accurate and precise. Of all the figurative devices, *similes* and *metaphors* are the most frequently used.

When you make a comparison between two unlike objects using the words "like" or "as," you are using a simile. For example, Russell C. Leong writes that his father arranges the bitter melons so that they "*come out in even green crescents, like perfect waves of a green sea.*" Likewise, when Barry Lopez writes, "*At night, the wind lies in a trough at the base of the red mountains, sprawled asleep over the white sand dunes like a caterpillar,*" he is making his reference to the wind more real by comparing its appearance to something we are familiar with: a caterpillar.

A metaphor compares one thing to another by stating that one thing is another. It is a device many authors in this chapter use at least once. Toshio Mori compares a room to a depot. For

Maya Angelou, when Joe Louis falls in the boxing ring, she compares it to "*our people falling . . . another lynching . . . One more woman ambushed and raped.*"

Dialogue: Revealing Characters Through Speech

In addition to using details to describe their characters, authors often employ dialogue that refines them, giving us a glimpse of their characters' actual personalities. In "Champion of the World" for example, Maya Angelou uses colloquial language (slang/every-day speech) when one of her characters says, "*I ain't worried 'bout this fight. Joe's gonna whip that cracker like it's open season.*" Also, an occasional use of dialogue adds variety and interest to a descriptive narrative. In the line, "*It's been a long time since anyone hugged me,*" for instance, Katherine Barrett reveals the loneliness of old age effectively *without* directly telling the reader that she is lonely.

Tips on Writing Descriptive Essays

1. Ask yourself questions such as: What is the purpose of my essay? How will description further advance my purpose?

2. Write sentences that appeal to the five senses: sight, sound, touch, taste, and smell. Add dialogue to provide variety.

3. Use adjectives (descriptive words) to further modify an object. For instance, when the word house is mentioned, each of us, undoubtedly, has a different mental image. When we use adjectives, however, each of us will have similar mental images, (e.g., The little, red, ramshackle, two-story house is surrounded by knee-high, withered grass and a broken-down, unpainted wooden fence.)

4. Adverbs also are used to modify words—verbs, adjectives, and other adverbs. For example, The track star raced *half-heartedly* to the finish line. The word half-heartedly is an adverb modifying the verb raced. An example of an adverb modifying an adjective is: The *extremely* over-dressed girl

felt out of place at the barbeque. The adverb extremely modifies the adjective over-dressed. In the sentence the crippled train inched *very* slowly up the mountain, the adverb very is modifying the other adverb slowly. Try using more adverbs in your writing to aid in description.

5. Employ figurative language such as metaphors and similes in order to stimulate the imagination and leave a lasting impression on your reader.

The Woman Who Makes Swell Doughnuts
TOSHIO MORI

A former professional baseball player, Mori started writing extensively in his late teens. He wrote mostly about the Japanese-American experience, trying to capture the way his people spoke in the 1930s and 1940s. His works have appeared in several anthologies and magazines, including *New Directions, Best American Short Stories of 1943, Common Ground,* and *Writer's Forum.* His books include *Yokohama, California* (1949), *The Chauvinist and Other Stories* (1979), and *The Woman from Hiroshima* (1979).

PRE-READING QUESTIONS

1. What elderly person have you admired? Who? Why?
2. Using the 5 Ws and H (who, what, where, when, why, and how) make the title of this essay into questions. For example, "Who is the lady making swell doughnuts?"

1   There is nothing I like to do better than to go to her house and knock on the door and when she opens the door, to go in. It is one of the experiences I will long remember—perhaps the

only immortality that I will ever be lucky to meet in my short life—and when I say experience I do not mean the actual movement, the motor of our lives. I mean by experience the dancing of emotions before our eyes and inside of us, the dance that is still but is the roar and the force capable of stirring the earth and the people.

2   Of course, she, the woman I visit, is old and of her youthful beauty there is little left. Her face of today is coarse with hard water and there is no question that she has lived her life: given birth to six children, worked side by side with her man for forty years, working in the fields, working in the house, caring for the grandchildren, facing the summers and winters and also the springs and autumns, running the household that is completely her little world. And when I came on the scene, when I discovered her in her little house on Seventh Street, all of her life was behind, all of her task in this world was tabbed, looked into, thoroughly attended, and all that is before her in life and the world, all that could be before her now was to sit and be served; duty done, work done, time clock punched; old-age pension or old-age security; easy chair; soft serene hours till death take her. But this was not of her, not the least bit of her.

3   When I visit her she takes me to the coziest chair in the living room, where are her magazines and books in Japanese and English. "Sit down," she says. "Make yourself comfortable. I will come back with some hot doughnuts just out of oil."

4   And before I can turn a page of a magazine she is back with a plateful of hot doughnuts. There is nothing I can do to describe her doughnut; it is in a class by itself, without words, without demonstration. It is a doughnut, just a plain doughnut just out of oil but it is different, unique. Perhaps when I am eating her doughnuts I am really eating her; I have this foolish notion in my head many times and whenever I catch myself doing so I say, that is not so, that is not true, Her doughnuts really taste swell, she is the best cook I have ever known, Oriental dishes or American dishes.

5   I bow humbly that such a room, such a house exists in my neighborhood so I may dash in and out when my spirit wanes, when hell is loose. I sing gratefully that such a simple and common experience becomes an event, an event of necessity and growth. It is an event that is a part of me, an addition to the

elements of the earth, water, fire, and air, and I seek the day when it will become a part of everyone.

6   All her friends, old and young, call her Mama. Everybody calls her Mama. That is not new, it is logical. I suppose there is in every block of every city in America a woman who can be called Mama by her friends and the strangers meeting her. This is commonplace, it is not new and the old sentimentality may be the undoing of the moniker. But what of a woman who isn't a mama but is, and instead of priding in the expansion of her little world, takes her little circle, living out her days in the little circle, perhaps never to be exploited in a biography or on everybody's tongue, but enclosed, shut, excluded from world news and newsreels; just sitting, just moving, just alive, planting the plants in the fields, caring for the children and the grandchildren and baking the tastiest doughnuts this side of the next world.

7   When I sit with her I do not need to ask deep questions, I do not need to know Plato or The Sacred Books of the East or dancing. I do not need to be on guard. But I am on guard and foot-loose because the room is alive.

8   "Where are the grandchildren?" I say. "Where are Mickey, Tadao, and Yaeko?"

9   "They are out in the yard," she says. "I say to them, play, play hard, go out there and play hard. You will be glad later for everything you have done with all your might."

10   Sometimes we sit many minutes in silence. Silence does not bother her. She says silence is the most beautiful symphony, she says the air breathed in silence is sweeter and sadder. That is about all we talk of. Sometimes I sit and gaze out the window and watch the Southern Pacific trains rumble by and the vehicles whizz with speed. And sometimes she catches me doing this and she nods her head and I know she understands that I think the silence in the room is great, and also the roar and the dust of the outside is great, and when she is nodding I understand that she is saying that this, her little room, her little circle, is a depot, a pause, for the weary traveler, but outside, outside of her little world there is dissonance, hugeness of another kind, and the travel to do. So she has her little house, she bakes the grandest doughnuts, and inside of her she houses a little depot.

11   Most stories would end with her death, would wait till she is peacefully dead and peacefully at rest but I cannot wait that long. I think she will grow, and her hot doughnuts just out of the oil will grow with softness and touch. And I think it would be a shame to talk of her doughnuts after she is dead, after she is formless.

12   Instead I take today to talk of her and her wonderful doughnuts when the earth is something to her, when the people from all parts of the earth may drop in and taste the flavor, her flavor, which is everyone's and all flavor; talk to her, sit with her, and also taste the silence of her room and the silence that is herself; and finally go away to hope and keep alive what is alive in her, on earth and in men, expressly myself.

POST-READING QUESTIONS

Content

1. What image(s) in Mori's essay do you find powerful or interesting? Why?

2. Why does Mori respect the woman who makes swell doughnuts?

3. How does Mori suggest the "woman who makes swell doughnuts" is a person who has had varied experiences during her long life?

4. What do the doughnuts symbolize to Mori? If they are a symbol for the woman and her way of life, what do they symbolize about her and her lifestyle?

Strategies and Structures

1. For different paragraphs in the essay, Mori uses different controlling metaphors or images. What is the controlling image of paragraph 6? What is the controlling image of paragraph 10? What does each paragraph suggest about the old woman?

2. How does Mori illustrate different aspects of the old woman in paragraph 2? How does the description of events in her life show what kind of woman she is?

3. Mori uses dialogue only a few times. Why do you think he uses it when he does? Why do you imagine he doesn't use dialogue more often?

4. Why does Mori write about her before she dies instead of after her death?

Language and Vocabulary

1. Vocabulary: *immortality, tabbed, pension, serene, coziest, wanes, monkier, depot.* Reread Mori's essay noting where these vocabulary words appear. Which words do you feel need further definition, and which words are easy to understand because of their context (see glossary)? What other words or descriptions make the vocabulary words easy to comprehend?

2. Mori's language is very descriptive. What mental pictures did or can you draw from this story; what words make his descriptions vivid?

3. Mori uses many active verbs in this story. What are a few of them and how do they make the story more descriptive?

GROUP ACTIVITIES

1. As a group, create a list of words that describes "the woman who makes swell doughnuts." Then, take quotes from the essay that illustrate each point. Be prepared to explain your choices to the rest of the class.

2. As a group, discuss some of the qualities you associate with old age. How do you imagine elderly people live? What concerns, hopes, and desires do they have? What do they participate in, what activities, hobbies, or events? Does your picture of an elderly person's life correspond with the picture of the life described by Mori?

WRITING ACTIVITIES

1. Write a portrait of someone you know. Include details from his or her life that best illustrate the type of person he or she is. Pick several key images and words to describe the person as you develop your paragraphs.
2. Interview an elderly person and then write a description of him or her based on your notes. First you'll want to make up a list of questions to take to the interview. Then you'll want to make an appointment with a person. (*Hint:* During the interview, you may want to use a tape recorder.)

Perimeter
BARRY LOPEZ

Author Barry Lopez has written extensively about humanity's relationship with nature in magazines, such as *Harper's, National Geographic,* and the *North American Review* as well as in his several books. Among his works are *Desert Notes: Reflections in the Eye of a Raven* (1976), the best-selling *Of Wolves and Men* (1979) and *Arctic Dreams,* which won the National Book Award in 1986.

PRE-READING QUESTIONS

1. This essay comes from a book entitled *Desert Notes: Reflections in the Eye of a Raven.* Cluster the words desert and perimeter, jotting down images and details that come to mind.
2. Write your own brief description of a desert—even though you may never have been to one. Use your imagination and creativity to compose a vivid picture.

I.

1   In the west, in the blue mountains, there are creeks of grey water. They angle out of the canyons, come across the brown scratched earth to the edge of the desert and run into nothing. When these creeks are running they make a terrific noise.

2   No one to my knowledge has ever counted the number, but I think there are more than twenty; it is difficult to be precise. For example, some of the creeks have been given names that, over the years, have had to be given up because a creek has run three or four times and then the channel has been abandoned.

3   You can easily find the old beds, where the dust has been washed out to reveal a level of rock rubble—cinnabar laced with mercury, fool's gold, clear quartz powder, and fire opal; but it is another thing to find one of the creeks, even when they are full. I have had some success by going at night and listening for the noise.

4   There is some vegetation in this area; it does not seem to depend on water. The rattlesnakes live here along with the rabbits. When there is any thunder it is coming from this direction. During the day the wind is here. The smells include the hellebore, vallo weed and punchen; each plant puts out its own smell and together they make a sort of pillow that floats a few feet off the ground where they are not as likely to be torn up by the wind.

II.

5   To the north the blue mountains go white and the creeks become more dependable though there are fewer of them. There is a sort of swamp here at the edge of the desert where the creeks pool and where grasses and sedges grow and the water takes a considerable time to evaporate and seep into the earth. There are some ducks here, but I do not know where they come from or where they go when the swamp dries up in the summer. I have never seen them flying. They are always hiding, slipping away; you will see their tail feathers disappearing in the screens of wire grass. They never quack.

6   There are four cottonwood trees here and two black locusts. The cottonwoods smell of balsam, send out seeds airborne in a mesh of exceedingly fine white hair, and produce a

glue which the bees use to cement their honeycombs. Only one of the cottonwoods, the oldest one, is a female. The leaf stem meets the leaf at right angles and this allows the leaves to twitter and flash in the slightest breeze. The underside of the leaf is a silver green. I enjoy watching this windflash of leaves in strong moonlight.

7 The black locusts are smaller, younger trees and grow off by themselves a little. They were planted by immigrants and bear sweet smelling pea-like flowers with short, rose-like thorns at the leaf nodes. There are a few chokecherry bushes and also a juniper tree. You can get out of the sun here at noon and sleep. The wind runs down the sides of the cottonwoods like water and cools you.

8 An old tawny long-haired dog lives here. Sometimes you will see him, walking along and always leaning to one side. There is also part of a cabin made with finished lumber lying on its back; the dark brown boards are dotted with red and yellow lichen and dry as sun-baked, long forgotten shoes.

III.

9 To the east the white mountains drop off and there is a flat place on the horizon and then the red mountains start. There is almost nothing growing in these mountains, just a little sagebrush. At the base, where they come to the desert, there are dunes, white like gypsum.

10 Inside the mountains are old creeks that run in circles over the floors of low-ceilinged caves. The fish in these waters are white and translucent; you can see a pink haze of organs beneath the skin. Where there should be eyes there are grey bulges that do not move. On the walls are white spiders like tight buttons of surgical cotton suspended on long hairy legs. There are white beetles, too, scurrying through the hills of black bat dung.

11 I have always been suspicious of these caves because the walls crumble easily under your fingertips; there is no moisture in the air and it smells like balloons. The water smells like oranges but has no taste. Nothing you do here makes any sound.

12 You have to squeeze through these red mountains to get around them; you can't walk over them. You have to wedge

yourself in somewhere at the base and go in. There is always a moment of panic before you slip in when you are stuck. Your eyes are pinched shut and the heels of your shoes wedge and make you feel foolish.

13   At night the wind lies in a trough at the base of the red mountains, sprawled asleep over the white sand dunes like a caterpillar. The edge of the desert is most indistinct in this place where the white sand and the alkaline dust blow back and forth in eddies of the wind's breath while it sleeps.

IV.

14   In the south the red mountains fall away and yellow mountains rise up, full of silver and turquoise rock. There are plenty of rabbits here, a little rain in the middle of the summer, fine clouds tethered on the highest peaks. If you are out in the middle of the desert, this is the way you always end up facing.

15   In the south twelve buckskin horses are living along the edge of the yellow mountains. The creeks here are weak; the horses have to go off somewhere for water but they always come back. There is a little grass but the horses do not seem to eat it. They seem to be waiting, or finished. Ten miles away you can hear the clack of their hooves against the rocks. In the afternoon they are motionless, with their heads staring down at the ground, at the little stones.

16   At night they go into the canyons to sleep standing up.

17   From the middle of the desert even on a dark night you can look out at the mountains and perceive the differences in direction. From the middle of the desert you can see everything well, even in the black dark of a new moon. You know where everything is coming from.

POST-READING QUESTIONS

Content

1. What is the dominant image of section I? Why do you feel Lopez starts his description of the desert with this image?

2. What kinds of wildlife, vegetation, and geography does Lopez find in his journey through the desert?

3. What are the primary images of section II? Are these the types of images you expect to find in a description of a desert? Why or why not? Considering what Lopez describes, why is "Perimeter" a good title for this essay?

4. Why does Lopez fear the caves described in section III? How does he create this sense of fear?

5. In section IV, Lopez describes what the desert looks like when facing south. Why does he claim that, "If you are out in the middle of desert, this is the way you always end up facing?"

Strategies and Structures

1. How does Lopez arrange his description? How does the use of similar phrases at the beginning of each section help unify and structure the essay?

2. In sections I, II, III, and IV how many of the five senses does Lopez appeal to in his description? Which images appeal to which senses?

3. Several times, Lopez alludes to the history of humanity in this location. Where does he tell us about humanity's relationship to the area? How does the author use these historical allusions to create an argumentative edge in his essay?

4. What dominant images does the author employ to conclude this essay, and why are they appropriate?

Language and Vocabulary

1. Vocabulary: *Hellebore, vallo weed, punchen, sedges, wire grass, cottonwoods, black locust, lichen, sagebrush* —all of these words are names of plants, trees, or vegetation. Look up the definitions of any of the words you do not know. Then pair the words and write a sentence in which you contrast the two plants. (For example, "While the daisy is a yellow flower, moss is green fungus that clings to trees and rocks.")

2. Which colors appear in Lopez's essay? What does the use of colors add to the specific items being described and to the essay as a whole? Do these colors appear as adjectives (descriptive words) or nouns (names of things)?

GROUP ACTIVITIES

1. As a group, meet at a local park. First as a group, take notes on all the plants you see. Then take notes on all the animals there. Next take notes on all the geographical features, such as creeks, hills, and mountains. Make your notes as descriptive as possible.

2. Write a collaborative essay of an imaginative landscape. Be as creative as you like, referring to unique and fantastic plants, animals, and geographical features. As Lopez does, use the five senses so that your reader can vividly imagine the place. You may first want to brainstorm in order to arrive at what one would see, hear, taste, touch, and smell there.

WRITING ACTIVITIES

1. Describe an area considered hostile to life which you know well from personal experience and that you feel has been given an unfair reputation. What is it about this area that most people do not realize but you are aware of?

2. Compose an essay in which you describe some place familiar to most of your classmates; however, do not mention the name of the place. Instead make your description so vivid that they will be able to guess what place you are describing.

Champion of the World
MAYA ANGELOU

Born Marguerita Johnson in 1928, Maya Angelou spent her youth encountering one personal tragedy after another. Angelou's talents are many; she has acted in the television Mini-series "Roots," produced a series about Africa for PBS-TV, and written several volumes of poetry. A recipient of several honorary doctorates, Angelou is best known for her autobiography *I Know Why the Caged Bird Sings* (1970). More recent works include *All God's Children Need Traveling Shoes* (1986).

PRE-READING QUESTIONS

1. The following piece is an excerpt from Angelou's *I Know Why the Caged Bird Sings*. Without worrying about accuracy, explain the meaning behind the title of her autobiography in your journal or writing log.

2. Think about the title of this descriptive narrative, "Champion of the World," a title taken directly from a phrase in the book. Then turn to the person sitting next to you and brainstorm the word *champion*. What qualities do you associate with a champion?

1   The last inch of space was filled, yet people continued to wedge themselves along the walls of the Store. Uncle Willie had turned the radio up to its last notch so that youngsters on the porch wouldn't miss a word. Women sat on kitchen chairs, dining-room chairs, stools and upturned wooden boxes. Small children and babies perched on every lap available and men leaned on the shelves or on each other.

2   The apprehensive mood was shot through with shafts of gaiety, as a black sky is streaked with lightning.

3   "I ain't worried 'bout this fight. Joe's gonna whip that cracker like it's open season."

4   "He gone whip him till that white boy call him Momma."

5   At last the talking finished and the string-along songs about razor blades were over and the fight began.

6   "A quick jab to the head." In the Store the crowd grunted. "A left to the head and a right and another left." One of the listeners cackled like a hen and was quieted.

7   "They're in a clinch, Louis is trying to fight his way out."

8   Some bitter comedian on the porch said, "That white man don't mind hugging that niggah now, I betcha."

9   "The referee is moving in to break them up, but Louis finally pushed the contender away and it's an uppercut to the chin. The contender is hanging on, now he's backing away. Louis catches him with a short left to the jaw."

10   A tide of murmuring assent poured out the door and into the yard.

11   "Another left and another left. Louis is saving that mighty right . . ." The mutter in the Store had grown into a baby roar and it was pierced by the clang of a bell and the announcer's "That's the bell for round three, ladies and gentlemen."

12   As I pushed my way into the Store I wondered if the announcer gave any thought to the fact that he was addressing as "ladies and gentlemen" all the Negroes around the world who sat sweating and praying, glued to their "master's voice."

13   There were only a few calls for R. C. Colas, Dr. Peppers, and Hires root beer. The real festivities would begin after the fight. Then even the old Christian ladies who taught their children and tried themselves to practice turning the other cheek would buy soft drinks, and if the Brown Bomber's victory was a particularly bloody one they would order peanut patties and Baby Ruths also.

14   Bailey and I laid the coins on top of the cash register. Uncle Willie didn't allow us to ring up sales during a fight. It was too noisy and might shake up the atmosphere. When the gong rang for the next round we pushed through the near-sacred quiet to the herd of children outside.

15   "He's got Louis against the ropes and now it's a left to the body and a right to the ribs. Another right to the body, it looks like it was low . . . Yes, ladies and gentlemen, the referee is signaling but the contender keeps raining the blows on Louis. It's another to the body, and it looks like Louis is going down."

16   My race groaned. It was our people falling. It was another lynching, yet another Black man hanging on a tree. One more woman ambushed and raped. A Black boy whipped and maimed. It was hounds on the trail of a man running through slimy swamps. It was a white woman slapping her maid for being forgetful.

17   The men in the Store stood away from the walls and at attention. Women greedily clutched the babes on their laps while on the porch the shufflings and smiles, flirtings and pinching of a few minutes before were gone. This might be the end of the world. If Joe lost we were back in slavery and beyond help. It would all be true, the accusations that we were lower types of human beings. Only a little higher than apes. True that we were stupid and ugly and lazy and dirty and, unlucky and worst of all, that God Himself hated us and ordained us to be hewers of wood and drawers of water, forever and ever, world without end.

18   We didn't breathe. We didn't hope. We waited.

19   "He's off the ropes, ladies and gentlemen. He's moving towards the center of the ring." There was no time to be relieved. The worst might still happen.

20   "And now it looks like Joe is mad. He's caught Carnera with a left hook to the head and a right to the head. It's a left jab to the body and another left to the head. There's a left cross and a right to the head. The contender's right eye is bleeding and he can't seem to keep his block up. Louis is penetrating every block. The referee is moving in, but Louis sends a left to the body and it's an uppercut to the chin and the contender is dropping. He's on the canvas, ladies and gentlemen."

21   Babies slid to the floor as women stood up and men leaned toward the radio.

22   "Here's the referee. He's young. One, two, three, four, five, six, seven . . . Is the contender trying to get up again?"

23   All the men in the store shouted, "NO."

24   "—eight, nine, ten." There were a few sounds from the audience, but they seemed to be holding themselves in against tremendous pressure.

25   "The fight is all over, ladies and gentlemen. Let's get the microphone over to the referee . . . Here he is. He's got the Brown Bomber's hand, he's holding it up . . . Here he is . . ."

26   Then the voice, husky and familiar, came to wash over us—
"The winnah, and still heavyweight champeen of the world
. . . Joe Louis."

27   Champion of the world. A Black boy. Some Black mother's
son. He was the strongest man in the world. People drank Coca-
Colas like ambrosia and ate candy bars like Christmas. Some of
the men went behind the Store and poured white lightning in
their soft-drink bottles, and a few of the bigger boys followed
them. Those who were not chased away came back blowing
their breath in front of themselves like proud smokers.

28   It would take an hour or more before the people would
leave the Store and head for home. Those who lived too far had
made arrangements to stay in town. It wouldn't do for a Black
man and his family to be caught on a lonely country road on a
night when Joe Louis had proved that we were the strongest
people in the world.

POST-READING QUESTIONS

Content

1. Why were so many people gathered at Uncle Willie's
   store at night? What did they all have in common,
   "even the old Christian ladies"?

2. Why did the people who lived far away from Uncle
   Willie's store make arrangements to stay "in town"
   for the night?

3. While we know he is literally defending his heavyweight boxing title, Joe Louis is figuratively defending something else. What is it? (see paragraphs 16
   and 17)

4. How did the radio announcer's description of the
   fight affect the people in Willie's store?

5. How did people at Uncle Willie's store celebrate the
   outcome of the fight?

Strategies and Structures

1. When and where is dialogue used in this narrative?
   What is its purpose? What would this narrative

account lose if no dialogue had been included? Why?

2. What type of sentence pattern helps Angelou build suspense in this narrative? In what way do observations of those around her echo the author's own feelings? How do we know for sure?

3. What sort of details does Angelou offer her readers so they can visualize the scene she describes? Without rereading the narrative, jot down as many details as you can remember.

4. What images in the opening paragraph create an atmosphere of suspense and anticipation?

Language and Vocabulary

1. Vocabulary: Go through this descriptive narrative and locate any unfamiliar words. Write them down on a piece of paper, along with their dictionary definitions. Continue to add to your personal vocabulary list throughout the semester.

2. What instances of nonstandard English did you notice in this essay? What purpose did such language serve?

GROUP ACTIVITIES

1. Go back through the essay and select four or five descriptive phrases. When you assemble in groups, share three of the phrases you wrote down on a separate piece of paper, stating the descriptive phrase you liked best and why. Using complete sentences, imitate each group member's favorite descriptive phrase twice (a separate sentence for each phrase imitation).

2. Spend five minutes or so discussing what you think Uncle Willie's store looks like based upon the concrete details provided by Angelou (refer to your response to question 3 under strategies and structures). Next, locate a video copy of *I Know Why the*

Caged Bird Sings, a television movie, in your college's audiovisual center, and watch the film. Pay particular attention to the sequence where everybody gets together at Uncle Willie's store to listen to the Joe Louis fight on the radio. Finally compare and contrast the way your group pictured the occasion based upon Angelou's written description to the way the film presented (1) the store, and (2) the gathering of people on the night of the Joe Louis fight. (*Note:* Though Maya Angelou adapted *I Know Why the Caged Bird Sings* to television, she was not the set designer.)

WRITING ACTIVITIES

1. Describe an incident that gave you a feeling of pride in your family, culture, nation, religious group, political group, or gender.

2. Construct a thesis that says something about afterthoughts, the things we think about after saying or not saying something. Then, develop your thesis by describing a recent argument or two you've had with another person, noting what you did *not* say or think about until after the argument (perhaps you wish you had said something but neglected to do so). Include dialogue in your descriptive essay to show rather than just tell your reader what you said and did.

Notes from a Son to His Father
RUSSELL C. LEONG

A fourth-generation Chinese-American, Russell C. Leong writes poetry and fiction as well as expository essays. His work has appeared in such anthologies as *Aiiieeeee!: An Anthology of Asian American Writers.* Leong is currently the editor of *Amerasia Journal* at the Asian American Studies Center, U.C.L.A.

PRE-READING QUESTIONS

1. Cluster the word father. What images, emotions, and ideas do you associate with the word?
2. Write a letter to your father. Explain memories and feelings about the past. Describe the image you had of him when you were young.

1   There is nothing good about being a son. I know; I am a son. When you have to admit that you have a father, allowing people to think that you are a father and son, as if any relation existed between those two terms, when there is really nothing to say.

2   And yet I usually find myself talking about my father, telling my friends and any strangers what he does and where he has been, trying to describe with exactness his activities, trying to grasp his life through what little information I have of him. Doing this, I feel like a small child pressing a string of hard beads to my chest, a rosary of sorts, chanting the same phrases and images a thousand times in order to derive an order, a strength out of them. But the polished beads do not yield a thing: it is a repetition of uselessness. Nothing comes out of them.

3   I know my father like this. I see him working in his white apron, flashing and sharpening his cleaver on the back rim of a white Chinese pottery bowl. Zhap zhap zhap, the gray steel cleaver on the sturdy bowl. After arranging different vegetables on the table, I see him grasping the handle of the cleaver

firmly, then nudging the jade bitter melon under the blade, at a slant, so that the pieces come out in even green crescents, like perfect waves of a green sea, at the same angle, and then the carrots, in thin narrow ovals, cut and dropped to boil lightly in a pot a while, and then the green bell peppers, the seeds and pale green mulch scooped out with a spoon, then cut in quarters and sliced. Then all the vegetables are arranged in neat piles on a large plate, ready to be cooked; the hardest, fibrous vegetables to be cooked first in a dash of oil, and then the more delicately flavored ones, with purple and orange-tipped spears of heat, sizzling them in the heart, while all along the rice is boiling on another part of the stove, each white grain destined to be firm and separate from his brother.

4   My father's hands were always busy preparing food and papers, writing and touching inanimate and ultimately useful things such as pencils and knives. Yet I do not know the real strength of my father's arm, I have never been lifted on his hand, brought up to see any life outside of my own. As a child I dreamed of my father.

5   Was this true, could he see his father dancing, away from the stiff and solemn pace of himself as father, provider, and businessman? Was it true, his father strong and bare, bravely dancing, using the wind as rope to catch all the worlds, flinging his arms and legs?

6   No, that is not him at all; his motions are never quick or free, but formal, stern, and placid for every emotion except rage.

7   At the door to my room, my father is glittering in anger, a knife poised in his hand. His face is pulsing pink, the once pale cauliflower flesh tinged with color and rage, and he is on one side of the room, about to throw the knife into me. I am just standing there, cringing; how can I defend myself against this violence, this dark pearl which I have struck? So this is what is beneath my father's calmness, his layered dispassion, his view of my foolishness and ignorance and youth, it is this seething fury, not really his, but an inherited bitterness from some vague source, from a life not his, a frustration that has finally found its point in a knife, a silver gleaming tooth that will draw blood from my chest. My father, I screamed inside, but outside I tried

to remain calm and rather disinterested in any personal aspect of the situation, as if his piercing my body was an event apart from the two of us, beyond any relation of father and son, as if my death or any son's death could happen like this, if the son did not observe and obey the rules—the correct way of doing things. During these moments I appeared calm, waiting for the blade to fall, and I despised him even more when his arm suddenly dropped down and the knife fell to the floor; he was not strong enough to go through with his convictions—he could not even kill his own son. I had heard the story about Abraham and Isaac, how Abraham would have killed his own son for God, because of his trust in God, but my father was not as good as that, because he does not believe in God in the first place. He will just kill me for no god at all.

8   At a later age, when one is a little older, one begins to strike back against his father with a vengeance, with a force akin to hatred or love, with the urge utterly to destroy all images of men or seek all images of them wherever and whenever possible.

9   Because one is a son himself he must realize his peculiar tendency to be i.e. manly and so he searches. I went out into the streets to look for this, this peculiar stuff of which pictures, pride, and parades are made of. Now I am in the middle of it, sunk into it. With love to the Father and to the Son.

POST-READING QUESTIONS

Content

1. Why do you feel Leong says, *"There is nothing good about being a son"*? Does he clearly explain this statement or must you imply its meaning from the context of the opening paragraphs? Could we also say there is nothing good about being a daughter?

2. What frustrations does Leong feel when he attempts to describe his father? How does he try to recall the image of his father?

3. What are the two primary images Leong has of his father? What do these two descriptions suggest about his father's character?

4. What does Leong suggest a son must do when he is older? Why must a son do this? Is this a natural stage in a parent-and-child relationship? Explain your opinion.

Strategies and Structures

1. What is the purpose of Leong's opening paragraphs? How do they introduce the topic of this descriptive essay and imply some of its themes?

2. Where does Leong create a vivid description of his father cooking? What images create this vivid description? Which of the five senses does he appeal to? Which images appeal to which senses?

3. What images in paragraph 7 create a vivid description of the scene in Leong's childhood bedroom? How does he combine a physical description of the scene with an emotional description as well? What is the effect on the reader of combining the two?

4. Leong unifies the essay by using similar images in both descriptions. What are they? What mood do they create? What images in paragraph 3 foreshadow the mood of paragraph 7?

5. Which images appear in the last paragraph that appear in the earlier descriptions of Leong's father? What themes are repeated?

Language and Vocabulary

1. Vocabulary: *fibrous, delicately, inanimate, pulsing, dispassion, seething, disinterested, despised, vengeance.* *In-* and *dis-* both mean "not." How would the elimination of such prefixes change the meaning of the sentence in which they appear? Could you change the meaning of any of the other vocabulary words by adding *in-* or *dis-* to them? What prefixes can you think of that could change the meanings of the other vocabulary words?

2. Leong vividly describes action. Imitate the following sentences describing an action with which you are familiar:

a. *"I see him working in his white apron, flashing and sharpening his cleaver on the back rim of a white Chinese pottery bowl."*

b. *"After arranging different vegetables on the table, I see him grasping the handle of the cleaver firmly, then nudging the jade bitter melon under the blade, at a slant. . . ."*

c. *"My father's hands were always busy preparing food and papers, writing and touching inanimate and ultimately useful things such as pencils and knives."*

d. *"During these moments I appeared calm, waiting for the blade to fall. . . ."*

GROUP ACTIVITIES

1. Discuss the impact of the allusion to Abraham and Isaac. Where does this allusion come from? What is the complete story of Abraham and Isaac? And what does it suggest about the relationship between fathers and sons? What does his comment, *"He will just kill me for no God at all,"* suggest about his father's character, in particular, and the relationship between Leong and his father, in general?

2. Leong makes his narrative exposition come alive through the use of descriptive words and vivid language. Pick a paragraph from this essay and rewrite it without the use of any descriptive language. What is lost in doing so? Next give your rewritten paragraph to another group and have it rewrite the paragraph, making your group's initial rewrite vivid and descriptive once again. (Use your own descriptions, not Leong's.)

WRITING ACTIVITIES

1. Write a clear description of a relative, describing the performance of an action which you associate with him or her. For example, you may describe your father gardening or your aunt cleaning. Use vivid

images and sentence patterns that will aid you in describing the action. As Leong does in paragraph 3, use the five senses as much as possible to heighten your description.

2. Relate a conflict you had with your parent(s). How was it resolved: Physically? Intellectually? How did you grow or learn from the situation? Did the conflict change your relationship with your parents? How? Why?

Old Before Her Time
KATHERINE BARRETT

Katherine Barrett specializes in human interest stories. She is a contributing editor to *The Ladies' Home Journal* and a regular writer for *Finance World*. Barrett's following highly biographical essay originally appeared in the August 1983 issue of *The Ladies' Home Journal*.

PRE-READING QUESTIONS

1. What do you think when you see old people on the street? Do you talk with them or ignore them? Why? Would the way elderly people dress (e.g., well, modest) influence your willingness to talk to them?

2. When an old person is on the bus, do you offer him or her your seat? Do you open doors for elderly people? Do you make fun of them? Do you ever think about what it will be like when you grow old—or do you think you'll never age?

1   This is the story of an extraordinary voyage in time, and of a young woman who devoted three years to a singular

experiment. In 1979, Patty Moore—then aged twenty-six—transformed herself for the first of many times into an eighty-five-year-old woman. Her object was to discover firsthand the problems, joys and frustrations of the elderly. She wanted to know for herself what it's like to live in a culture of youth and beauty when your hair is gray, your skin is wrinkled and no men turn their heads as you pass.

2   Her time machine was a makeup kit. Barbara Kelly, a friend and professional makeup artist, helped Patty pick out a wardrobe and showed her how to use latex to create wrinkles, and wrap Ace bandages to give the impression of stiff joints. "It was peculiar," Patty recalls, as she relaxes in her New York City apartment. "Even the first few times I went out I realized that I wouldn't have to *act* that much. The more I was perceived as elderly by others, the more 'elderly' I actually became . . . I imagine that's just what happens to people who really are old."

3   What motivated Patty to make her strange journey? Partly her career—as an industrial designer, Patty often focuses on the needs of the elderly. But the roots of her interest are also deeply personal. Extremely close to her own grandparents—particularly her maternal grandfather, now ninety—and raised in a part of Buffalo, New York, where there was a large elderly population, Patty always drew comfort and support from the older people around her. When her own marriage ended in 1979 and her life seemed to be falling apart, she dove into her "project" with all her soul. In all, she donned her costume more than two hundred times in fourteen different states. Here is the remarkable story of what she found.

4   **Columbus, Ohio, May 1979.** Leaning heavily on her cane, Pat Moore stood alone in the middle of a crowd of young professionals. They were all attending a gerontology conference, and the room was filled with animated chatter. But no one was talking to Pat. In a throng of men and women who devoted their working lives to the elderly, she began to feel like a total nonentity. "I'll get us all some coffee," a young man told a group of women next to her. "What about me?" thought Pat. "If I were young, they would be offering me coffee, too." It was a bitter thought at the end of a disappointing day—a day that marked Patty's first appearance as "the old woman." She had planned to attend the gerontology conference anyway, and almost as a lark

decided to see how professionals would react to an old person in their midst.

5   Now, she was angry. All day she had been ignored . . . counted out in a way she had never experienced before. She didn't understand. Why didn't people help her when they saw her struggling to open a heavy door? Why didn't they include her in conversations? Why did the other participants seem almost embarrassed by her presence at the conference—as if it were somehow inappropriate that an old person should be professionally active?

6   And so, eighty-five-year-old Pat Moore learned her first lesson: The old are often ignored. "I discovered that people really do judge a book by its cover," Patty says today. "Just because I looked different, people either condescended or they totally dismissed me. Later, in stores, I'd get the same reaction. A clerk would turn to someone younger and wait on her first. It was as if he assumed that I—the older woman—could wait because I didn't have anything better to do."

7   **New York City, October 1979.** Bent over her cane, Pat walked slowly toward the edge of the park. She had spent the day sitting on a bench with friends, but now dusk was falling and her friends had all gone home. She looked around nervously at the deserted area and tried to move faster, but her joints were stiff. It was then that she heard the barely audible sound of sneakered feet approaching and the kids' voices. "Grab her, man." "Get her purse." Suddenly an arm was around her throat and she was dragged back, knocked off her feet.

8   She saw only a blur of sneakers and blue jeans, heard the sounds of mocking laughter, felt fists pummeling her—on her back, her legs, her breasts, her stomach. "Oh, God," she thought, using her arms to protect her head and curling herself into a ball. "They're going to kill me. I'm going to die. . . ."

9   Then, as suddenly as the boys attacked, they were gone. And Patty was left alone, struggling to rise. The boys' punches had broken the latex makeup on her face, the fall had disarranged her wig, and her whole body ached. (Later she would learn that she had fractured her left wrist, an injury that took two years to heal completely.) Sobbing, she left the park and hailed a cab to return home. Again the thought struck her:

What if I really lived in the gray ghetto . . . what if I couldn't escape to my nice safe home . . . ?

10　　Lesson number two: The fear of crime is paralyzing. "I really understand now why the elderly become homebound," the young woman says as she recalls her ordeal today. "When something like this happens, the fear just doesn't go away. I guess it wasn't so bad for me. I could distance myself from what happened . . . and I was strong enough to get up and walk away. But what about someone who is really too weak to run or fight back or protect herself in any way? And the elderly often can't afford to move if the area in which they live deteriorates, becomes unsafe. I met people like this and they were imprisoned by their fear. That's when the bolts go on the door. That's when people starve themselves because they're afraid to go to the grocery store."

11　　**New York City, February 1980.** It was a slushy, gray day and Pat had laboriously descended four flights of stairs from her apartment to go shopping. Once outside, she struggled to hold her threadbare coat closed with one hand and manipulate her cane with the other. Splotches of snow made the street difficult for anyone to navigate, but for someone hunched over, as she was, it was almost impossible. The curb was another obstacle. The slush looked ankle-deep—and what was she to do? Jump over it? Slowly, she worked her way around to a drier spot, but the crowds were impatient to move. A woman with packages jostled her as she rushed past, causing Pat to nearly lose her balance. If I really were old, I would have fallen, she thought. Maybe broken something. On another day, a woman had practically knocked her over by letting go of a heavy door as Pat tried to enter a coffee shop. Then there were the revolving doors. How could you push them without strength? And how could you get up and down stairs, on and off a bus, without risking a terrible fall?

12　　Lesson number three: If small, thoughtless deficiencies in design were corrected, life would be so much easier for older people. It was no surprise to Patty that the "built" environment is often inflexible. But even she didn't realize the extent of the problems, she admits. "It was a terrible feeling. I never realized how difficult it is to get off a curb if your knees don't bend easily. Or the helpless feeling you get if your upper arms aren't strong enough to open a door. You know, I just felt so vulnerable—as if I was at the mercy of every barrier or rude person I encountered."

13   **Ft. Lauderdale, Florida, May 1980.** Pat met a new friend while shopping and they decided to continue their conversation over a sundae at a nearby coffee shop. The woman was in her late seventies, "younger" than Pat, but she was obviously reaching out for help. Slowly, her story unfolded. "My husband moved out of our bedroom," the woman said softly, fiddling with her coffee cup and fighting back tears. "He won't touch me anymore. And when he gets angry at me for being stupid, he'll even sometimes. . . ." The woman looked down, embarrassed to go on. Pat took her hand. "He hits me . . . he gets so mean." "Can't you tell anyone?" Pat asked. "Can't you tell your son?" "Oh, no!" the woman almost gasped. "I would never tell the children; they absolutely adore him."

14   Lesson number four: Even a fifty-year-old marriage isn't necessarily a good one. While Pat met many loving and devoted elderly couples, she was stunned to find others who had stayed together unhappily—because divorce was still an anathema in their middle years. "I met women who secretly wished their husbands dead, because after so many years they just ended up full of hatred. One woman in Chicago even admitted that she deliberately angered her husband because she knew it would make his blood pressure rise. Of course, that was pretty extreme. . . ."

15   Patty pauses thoughtfully and continues. "I guess what really made an impression on me, the real eye-opener, was that so many of these older women had the same problems as women twenty, thirty or forty. Problems with men . . . problems with the different roles that are expected of them. As a 'young woman' I, too, had just been through a relationship where I spent a lot of time protecting someone by covering up his problems from family and friends. Then I heard this woman in Florida saying that she wouldn't tell her children their father beat her because she didn't want to disillusion them. These issues aren't age-related. They affect everyone."

16   **Clearwater, Florida, January 1981.** She heard the children laughing, but she didn't realize at first that they were laughing at her. On this day, as on several others, Pat had shed the

clothes of a middle-income woman for the rags of a bag lady. She wanted to see the extremes of the human condition, what it was like to be old and poor, and outside traditional society as well. Now, tottering down the sidewalk, she was most concerned with the cold, since her layers of ragged clothing did little to ease the chill. She had spent the afternoon rummaging through garbage cans, loading her shopping bags with bits of debris, and she was stiff and tired. Suddenly, she saw that four little boys, five or six years old, were moving up on her. And then she felt the sting of the pebbles they were throwing. She quickened her pace to escape, but another handful of gravel hit her and the laughter continued. They're using me as a target, she thought, horror-stricken. They don't even think of me as a person.

17   Lesson number five: Social class affects every aspect of an older person's existence. "I found out that class is a very important factor when you're old," says Patty. "It was interesting. That same day, I went back to my hotel and got dressed as a wealthy woman, another role that I occasionally took. Outside the hotel, a little boy of about seven asked if I would go shelling with him. We walked along the beach, and he reached out to hold my hand. I knew he must have a grandmother who walked with a cane, because he was so concerned about me and my footing. 'Don't put your cane there, the sand's wet,' he'd say. He really took responsibility for my welfare. The contrast between him and those children was really incredible. The little ones who were throwing the pebbles at me because they didn't see me as human. And then the seven-year-old taking care of me. I think he would have responded to me the same way even if I had been dressed as the middle-income woman. There's no question that money does make life easier for older people, not only because it gives them a more comfortable life-style, but because it makes others treat them with greater respect."

18   **New York City, May 1981.** Pat always enjoyed the time she spent sitting on the benches in Central Park. She'd let the whole day pass by, watching young children play, feeding the pigeons and chatting. One spring day she found herself sitting with three women, all widows, and the conversation turned to the few available men around. "It's been a long time since anyone hugged me," one woman complained. Another agreed. "Isn't

that the truth. I need a hug, too." It was a favorite topic, Pat found—the lack of touching left in these women's lives, the lack of hugging, the lack of men.

19   In the last two years, she had found out herself how it felt to walk down Fifth Avenue and know that no men were turning to look after her. Or how it felt to look at models in magazines or store mannequins and *know* that those gorgeous clothes were just not made for her. She hadn't realized before just how much casual attention was paid to her because she was young and pretty. She hadn't realized it until it stopped.

20   Lesson number six: You never grow old emotionally. You always need to feel loved. "It's not surprising that everyone needs love and touching and holding," says Patty. "But I think some people feel that you reach a point in your life when you accept that those intimate feelings are in the past. That's wrong. These women were still interested in sex. But more than that, they—like everyone—needed to be hugged and touched. I'd watch two women greeting each other on the street and just holding onto each other's hands, neither wanting to let go. Yet, I also saw that there are people who are afraid to touch an old person . . . they were afraid to touch me. It's as if they think old age is a disease and it's catching. They think that something might rub off on them."

21   **New York City, September 1981.** He was a thin man, rather nattily dressed, with a hat that he graciously tipped at Pat as he approached the bench where she sat. "Might I join you?" he asked jauntily. Pat told him he would be welcome and he offered her one of the dietetic hard candies that he carried in a crumpled paper bag. As the afternoon passed, they got to talking . . . about the beautiful buds on the trees and the world around them and the past. "Life's for the living, my wife used to tell me," he said. "When she took sick she made me promise her that I wouldn't waste a moment. But the first year after she died, I just sat in the apartment. I didn't want to see anyone, talk to anyone or go anywhere. I missed her so much." He took a handkerchief from his pocket and wiped his eyes, and they sat in silence. Then he slapped his leg to break the mood and change the subject. He asked Pat about herself, and described his life alone. He belonged to a "senior center" now, and went on trips and had lots of friends. Life did go on. They arranged

to meet again the following week on the same park bench. He brought lunch—chicken salad sandwiches and decaffeinated peppermint tea in a thermos—and wore a carnation in his lapel. It was the first date Patty had had since her marriage ended.

22   Lesson number seven: Life does go on . . . as long as you're flexible and open to change. "That man really meant a lot to me, even though I never saw him again," says Patty, her eyes wandering toward the gray wig that now sits on a wig-stand on the top shelf of her bookcase. "He was a real old-fashioned gentleman, yet not afraid to show his feelings—as so many men my age are. It's funny, but at that point I had been through months of self-imposed seclusion. Even though I was in a different role, that encounter kind of broke the ice for getting my life together as a single woman."

23   In fact, while Patty was living her life as the old woman, some of her young friends had been worried about her. After several years, it seemed as if the lines of identity had begun to blur. Even when she wasn't in makeup, she was wearing unusually conservative clothing, she spent most of her time with older people and she seemed almost to revel in her role—sometimes finding it easier to be in costume than to be a single New Yorker.

24   But as Patty continued her experiment, she was also learning a great deal from the older people she observed. Yes, society often did treat the elderly abysmally . . . they were sometimes ignored, sometimes victimized, sometimes poor and frightened, but so many of them were survivors. They had lived through two world wars, the Depression and into the computer age. "If there was one lesson to learn, one lesson that I'll take with me into *my* old age, it's that you've got to be flexible," Patty says. "I saw my friend in the park, managing after the loss of his wife, and I met countless other people who picked themselves up after something bad—or even something catastrophic— happened. I'm not worried about them. I'm worried about the others who shut themselves away. It's funny, but seeing these two extremes helped me recover from the trauma in my own life, to pull *my* life together."

25   Today, Patty is back to living the life of a single thirty-year-old, and she rarely dons her costumes anymore. "I must admit, though, I do still think a lot about aging," she says. "I look in the

mirror and I begin to see wrinkles, and then I realize that I won't be able to wash *those* wrinkles off." Is she afraid of growing older? "No. In a way, I'm kind of looking forward to it," she smiles. "I *know* it will be different from my experiment. I *know* I'll probably even look different. When they aged Orson Welles in *Citizen Kane* he didn't resemble at all the Orson Welles of today."

26   But Patty also knows that in one way she really did manage to capture the feeling of being old. With her bandages and her stopped posture, she turned her body into a kind of prison. Yet, inside she didn't change at all. "It's funny, but that's exactly how older people always say they feel," says Patty. "Their bodies age, but inside they are really no different than when they were young."

POST-READING QUESTIONS

Content

1. What is the controlling idea of this essay?

2. How many times did Moore dress as an elderly woman? In how many different states did she pull her charade?

3. Why did Patty Moore want to "transform herself" into an "eighty-five-year-old woman"?

4. How did Moore's relationships with elderly people help her to pull the pieces of her life together?

Strategies and Structures

1. What are the seven lessons about life Patty Moore learned, and how did Barrett use them to unify the content of her essay?

2. Why do the first few words in some sentences appear in bold-face-type? What do they signal to the reader?

3. In your opinion, how well does Barrett's narrative of Patty Moore's experiences illustrate the broader theme of her essay?

4. What strategies does Barrett use to keep her readers interested in her rather long essay?

Language and Vocabulary

1. Vocabulary: *condescending, audible, deteriorate, disillusion, revel, abysmal.* Use the following suffixes to change the above words from one word form to another: ly, ment, tion. (For example, one could change friend, a noun, to friendly, an adjective.) Use both word forms in a sentence.

2. A lot of the dialogue in this essay is not really addressed to a particular person; rather, it's like a person talking out loud. Analyze how the author's use of dialogue is appropriate to the theme of her essay.

GROUP ACTIVITIES

1. Role-playing: Assume a role that definitely is not you or any member of your group. For example, you could dress as a street person or a business executive. Make sure you notice how people judge and treat you. Then dress exactly the opposite and notice if people react differently towards you. Afterward, meet with your group and discuss the different reactions.

2. *Semester Project:* Keep a running journal account of role-playing you have done for the duration of this class, making sure to record the lessons you've learned, much as Katherine Barrett did in this essay. After condensing your material, construct a unified composition in which you use the lessons you've learned to guide you in proving your thesis.

WRITING ACTIVITIES

1. Take one of the lessons in life (the issue or moral it offers) Moore experienced and use it as an essay topic. Take a definite position on the issue and

argue/describe why it is true or incorrect, using specific detail drawn from personal experience.

2. Describe a situation where you learned something by role-playing (acting like another person, talking like another person, thinking like another person). Lead your reader through a sequence of narrated events to help the person understand how role-playing in itself taught you a lesson.

Additional Topics and
Issues for Descriptive Essays

1. Describe a place or thing that you fear. What is it that you fear, and when do you fear it most? What sorts of steps do you take to try and overcome your fear?

2. Write a description of your favorite place. Use specific details to make your essay vivid. You may want to answer some of the following questions. Where is this place? What kinds of things are there? Why do you like this place? When do you go there? How did you find this place? Who else goes there?

3. Write a visual portrait of what you perceive to be the youth of America. What or who are they? How do they dress, eat, and think? What sort of music do they listen and dance to? Try to avoid stereotypes when dealing with this subject.

4. Describe your favorite or ideal meal. Use adjectives and adverbs to help your reader smell, taste, and visualize the meal spread before him or her.

5. Compose an essay describing a place usually considered undesirable to visit; for example, you may want to write about a trip to the local garbage dump, slaughterhouse, or cannery. Make sure to include all the unpleasant sights, sounds, and smells. After all, the purpose for using description in this sort of essay is to enable the reader to share in your experience.

6. Describe a sporting or social event which you attended and felt was quite significant in one way or another. Be sure to

include the sounds, the sights, and any other sensual imagery that impressed you.

7. Using figurative language, describe two unlike objects, showing how they can be compared with each other by using similes and/or metaphors. (You may wish to review the chapter introduction, particularly if you intend to use an extended metaphor.)

8. Describe a meeting that you have had with a particularly colorful character, integrating dialogue exchanged between the two of you to add variety and interest to your essay.

4

ILLUSTRATION
AND EXAMPLE

Supporting a statement through the use of specific examples is essential to good, clear expository and argumentative writing. We illustrate what we claim with personal experiences, observations, and readings. Citing statistics can also support our examples. When we omit information that will help our reader to visualize our observations, we reduce our arguments to generalizations or simply reinforce stereotypes. In essence, writers use illustrations and examples like an artist uses brushes and paint; authors paint pictures with words for their readers.

Developing Your Thesis

After writing the thesis paragraph, writers then offer the reader detailed evidence to explain and support material. Where do writers gather their examples? Many authors illustrate their points using personal experience. For instance, in the essay "My Own Style," Nikki Giovanni states that she likes "useful things" like candles and then explains (illustrates) why by using reasoning and examples: She keeps candles around the house just in case it "gets hit by lightning" and her electrical power is lost; with candles she'll have a sure source of light.

Observations, like personal experiences, can also vividly explain a point in an essay or other form of literature. By watching and listening to what others do and say, we can gather a valuable reserve of material, material we can use in everyday conversations as well as essays. (This is one reason many writers keep diaries or journals of what they see.) A fine example of supporting a point with observations is Philip K. Chiu's mention of Chinese stereotypes in "The Myth of the Model Minority." Chiu illustrates a Chinese stereotype by referring to a film character, "the insidious villain" Fu Manchu, followed by a positive—but nonetheless inaccurate—Chinese stereotype: Charlie Chan. His specific examples illustrate general points.

Alluding to what other writers have observed (readings) is yet another way to illustrate what you claim. If you are writing an essay about the future capabilities of computers, you might quote information from R. Colin Johnson's essay from the "Artificial Intelligence" section of *Omni*, a science magazine. In fact, referring to books, articles, or reports (especially for statistics) written by authorities in a given field can make your examples more convincing than if you rely solely on your own experience to illustrate a theory or point. Initially citing an authoritative study on *why* more Americans are involved in some sort of physical fitness program today than 30 years ago, for instance, supports what *you may believe* with verifiable evidence.

Creating Vivid Examples

Simply supplying examples to support your points will not be enough to actively engage your reader's imagination, however. To hook your reader's interest and spark his or her imagination, you should make your examples specific and detailed, using concrete nouns and active verbs. Nouns are concrete when they create unmistakable images. Nouns like *things* and *stuff* are vague, imprecise words and may mislead or confuse your reader. Therefore, rather than writing, "Place your *things* on the counter," you would replace the vague word *thing* with a word like *clothes, tools,* or *books* —a concrete noun!

Using active verbs will also keep your reader involved in your essay. Often overlooked by the inexperienced writer, verbs can be the most powerful tool an author has for showing us what is happening as opposed to telling us. One way of making your essay vivid is to replace verbs that merely link ideas with verbs that indicate action. *Robert is angry at us* would be more effective written as *Robert scowled at us.* Why? The linking verb *is* links the subject, Robert, with the adjective, angry. The verb *scowl* shows the reader Robert's mood instead of just telling us what he is: angry.

Tips on Writing Illustration and Example Essays

1. The best use of illustration and example occurs when a writer has a clear idea of *what* he or she is trying to explain to the reader. To arrive at this point, you may want to freewrite, cluster, or use any method you find effective in generating ideas and limiting your thesis.

2. After you select a topic to write on, determine what sort of illustrations or examples would help to clarify your points and support them. Draw your examples from personal experiences, observations, and readings.

3. Whenever possible, use specific, concrete nouns so your reader will be able to vividly picture what you intend.

4. Complement your use of concrete nouns with verbs expressing action and mood. Again, this will enable you to *show* rather than simply *tell* your reader about your topic.

5. As in most compositions, transitional words and phrases that indicate relationships between words, clauses, and entire paragraphs will help lead your reader from one idea to the next, unifying the sections of your essay. To introduce an example in an illustration essay, use transitions such as *for instance* or *for example.*

My Own Style
NIKKI GIOVANNI

Nikki Giovanni, who lives in Cincinnati and teaches at Ohio State University, is not only a fine essayist, but also a prolific poet. Her works include *Black Talk, Black Feeling, Black Judgment* (1968), *The Women and the Men* (1973), and *Those Who Ride in the Night Winds* (1983). In the following essay from *Sacred Cows . . . and Other Edibles* (1988), she explains her style of doing things.

PRE-READING QUESTIONS

1. What is style? How does style influence actions or reactions?
2. What do you associate with uniformity? How might you conform to a uniform way of doing things while developing individual style? Is it possible?

1   I want to be a modern woman. I still have a nostalgic Afro, though it's stylishly short. I apologize to the hair industry, but frankly, I like both my kinks and my gray strands. Plus, being a sixties person, glowing in the dark carries negative implications for me. Most of my friends do wear base, pancake, powder, eye makeup, lipstick and always keep their nails in perfectly ovaled shapes with base, color, sealer and oil for the cuticles. Do I use these things? No. But neither do I put them down nor try to make my friends feel guilty for not being natural. There is something to be said for improvement. I've been known to comment: "Wow, you look really good. Who does your nails?" Why, I even have a dear friend who is a few months younger than I and uses a night cream to guard against wrinkles. Do I laugh? No, ma'am. I say: "Well, your face is very, very smooth," which (1) makes her feel good about her efforts and (2) keeps the friendship intact.

2   My major contribution to cosmetics is soap. I love soap . . .
in pretty colors . . . hand milled . . . in interesting shapes
. . . with the names of good perfumers on them . . . preferably
French. I use it to bathe, of course, but it's also so pretty on my
open shelves. Plus it smells good and when properly arranged,
is more or less sculpture. No one in my immediate family, and
few who have ever used my bathroom, ever wonders what to
give me for my birthday, Christmas, Valentine's Day, Mother's
Day, the Fourth of July, Labor Day, Martin Luther King Jr.'s
Birthday or Lincoln Heights Day. The way I figure, ask for
what you want.

3   I really like useful things. You never know. Take candles. I
really like a candle. I'm a Democrat, so I have a donkey. I'm a
Delta, so I have an elephant. I'm a woman, so I have an apple.
(Well, maybe I don't have to justify that.) I also have candle
candles. Just tall, pretty candles in little holders. If the house
gets hit by lightning, I'm ready. Like all modern women, I like
to be ready.

4   Without raising a hair on my chinny-chin-chin I can turn
three cans of anything and a quarter cup of dry white wine into
a gourmet meal in 15 minutes flat. Give me an ounce of cognac
and I really raise hell. I've been known to make the most
wicked bean soup with warm croutons and garlic zwieback (the
secret is a dabble of sherry) the world has known. People say:
"How can you be a full-time mother, full-time professional, and
still cook like this?" I smile sweetly, indicating that perhaps the
very best is yet to come. Or as the old folks liked to say: "It ain't
what you do; it's the way you do it."

5   In observing the younger women, that seems to be the one
thing that they are missing: the ability to take nothing and make
everybody think that something is there. Know what I mean?
The younger women like to brag that they can't cook, as if that
makes them modern. What is really modern is that you can
throw it together from cans and frozen food and pretend that it
was easy. Half of life is not avoiding what you don't like but
doing it with no sweat.

6   I must congratulate the twentieth-century woman on her
internationalism. You go into practically any house these days
and they have Nigerian art, Egyptian cotton throws, French
water, Hawaiian fruit, Japanese televisions, California wines,

Polish crystal, Haitian lace curtains, Lesothoan rugs and Dutch flowers sitting on grandmother's handmade quilts draped across an Early American table. I remember when you could go by the apartment of any guy and find stale beer in the refrigerator. Nowadays even *their* places are perking up. Everybody wants to make a statement.

7   Oh sure, I've heard all the jokes about BUMP's (Black Upwardly Mobile Professionals), but I like a BUMP. Hell, I am one. The modern woman is a BUMP who is not a grind. And we could use a little ambition in our community. Every time somebody wants to trade their Toyota for a BMW, it means they have to have more people to supervise, a bigger budget to spend. If they're in business for themselves, they have to sell more, do more, 'cause everybody knows you don't get big in business by saving; you get big by spending, by expansion.

8   We are only 15 years away from the twenty-first century! The Black community is 40 percent teenage unemployed, social security froze, Medicaid stopped, unwed, underemployed, unpromoted and generally a not-appreciated-at-all community in America. Who we gonna call—Honkeybusters? No! We're gonna climb out on the BUMP's. We can do it 'cause we've done everything else. And hey, even though my body will be old, sitting on a porch in some home (unless I can convince my son, now 15, to let me live with him), I'll be surrounded by the good feeling that I am a modern woman, 'cause even if I'm old, I'm sure to be positive—and that's our ace in the hole.

POST-READING QUESTIONS

Content

1. What does Giovanni observe about younger professional women? Why does the author "congratulate" them? Do they deserve her congratulations? Why or why not?

2. How is the author different from other professional women?

3. In paragraph 8, Giovanni states "We gonna climb out on those BUMP's." What is she referring to here?

Strategies and Structures

1. Why does Giovanni spend the first paragraph establishing differences between herself and many other "modern women?"

2. Throughout the essay, the author shows the reader that she never sacrificed individual identity or style to get ahead in the world. How do her illustrations and examples reinforce her controlling idea—captured by the essay's title?

3. How does the tone of this essay suit Giovanni's ultimate purpose?

Language and Vocabulary

1. Vocabulary: *implications, croutons, honkey, zwieback.* Giovanni's use of language is rather simple. The style of her prose is appropriate for the general audience she is writing for. Write a paragraph or so in your notebook reflecting on what you presently consider your writing style. How does your style of writing change when you write for different people? Why?

2. Cite two instances in Giovanni's essay where she uses acronyms (see Glossary). Also, write down as many acronyms in your notebook that you can. What do the acronyms represent? Translate them.

GROUP ACTIVITIES

1. Have a ten-minute panel discussion wherein you examine Giovanni's reference to "Honkeybusters." The preceding phrase, "Who you gonna call?" came from a movie called *Ghostbusters* which involved four men who claimed to be specialists in getting rid of ghosts. How might the allusion to *Ghostbusters* suit Giovanni's purpose in her essay? What is she trying to accomplish?

2. As a group, carefully go over Giovanni's essay, and discuss it regarding her style of communication.

What do you find particularly effective about her prose and the essay? How do the particular qualities that you have found work together to make up an identifiable style? What is the role of humor in this essay? Why does she use so many clichés (see Glossary) and trendy phrases?

WRITING ACTIVITIES

1. Giovanni says that *"Everyone wants to make a statement."* Based on personal observation and experience, write an essay proving or disproving what she states. Extensive use of examples will be essential to build a strong expository essay.

2. After summing up and illustrating how *most* people would approach or perform a task, meet new people, or visit new places, write an expository essay— making ample use of illustration and example— examining how your individual style is responsible for the way in which you do things.

The Myth of the Model Minority
PHILIP K. CHIU

A Chinese-American writer, Philip K. Chiu's works have appeared in many publications in the United States, including *U.S. News and World Report* where this essay originally appeared.

PRE-READING QUESTIONS

1. What Chinese-American stereotypes are you familiar with? Make a list of the qualities you associate with people of Chinese ancestry.

2. How does the word *myth* affect the meaning of the essay title? What does it suggest about Chinese-Americans being *the Model Minority?*

1   For years, Chinese Americans have been labeled a model minority. We read in the newspapers how diligently they have worked and saved. We see on television how quietly they obey the laws and how conscientiously they stay clear of crime. We learn in magazines how they climb the economic ladder and how much better than the Caucasian kids their children do in school.

2   But of late, we have been reading about a different side of Chinese American life. In January, *U.S. News* reported on Chinese gangs and their criminal activities. Not long afterward, a gun battle in the quiet streets of Pasadena, Calif., left two federal drug agents and two Chinese drug dealers dead. Now, the press is reporting on rising Chinese organized crime on the West Coast and citing the Pasadena incident as the latest manifestation.

3   What has happened to that law-abiding, humble Chinese American we have heard so much about? Have the media been wrong all these years? The answer is a complex one.

4   About 60 years ago, the silver screen gave us the insidious Fu Manchu and the ever inscrutable Charlie Chan. We heard about the dim opium dens and the filthy gambling halls. We saw slant-eyed, ever obedient little men toiling about with their pigtails freshly cut off. And we wondered just what kind of expression was "long time no see."

5   Then came World War II, and the Chinese became our allies. The pictures of a smiling, beautiful Madame Chiang Kai-Shek appeared in every newspaper. And we read about clean, amiable, upright and industrious Chinese Americans who, nearly a century before, had contributed to winning the American West by working day and night in the mines, on the farms and on the railroads.

6   The Korean War brought a picture of ferocious Chinese hordes marching to conquer Asia. And we learned that the Chinese spoke with forked tongues. They felt no pain when you stuck a needle in their tummies. They ate from their rice bowls

with disgusting noises and giggled with delight when they stabbed you in the back.

7   The 1972 Nixon visit to China ushered in an era of high praise for anything Chinese. The newly discovered extraordinary accomplishments of Chinese Americans in the face of prejudice sent social scholars scrambling for answers. And it was in the late '70s and the early '80s that the scholars told the world that the Chinese Americans were the model minority.

8   Is the wind changing its direction again in 1988? I don't know for sure, but I do know that as a Chinese American I am glad to see reporting on the underside of Chinese American life. In part, I am tired of hearing how miraculously the wellbehaved Chinese Americans have been doing, and I'm sick of reading about those bespectacled teenage bookworms who have contributed to exceptionally low juvenile-delinquency rates among Chinese American kids. But mostly I am fed up with being stereotyped as either a subhuman or superhuman creature.

9   Certainly, I am proud of the academic and economic successes of Chinese Americans and proud that many of us have excelled in science, the arts, law, medicine, business, sports and other endeavors. But it's important for people to realize that there is another side.

10   A few Chinese Americans steal when they are desperate; a few rape when nature overwhelms them; a few sell drugs when they see an easy way to make a buck; a few embezzle when instant fortunes blind them; a few murder when passions overtake them, and a few commit crimes simply because they are wicked.

11   It is about time for the media to report on Chinese Americans the way they are. Some are superachievers, most are average citizens, and a few are criminals. They are only human—no more and no less.

POST-READING QUESTIONS

Content

1. Why were Chinese-Americans labeled the *model minority* in the late 1970s and the early 1980s? Who or what was responsible for furthering this stereotype?

2. What are some of the stereotypes Chinese-Americans have been labeled with over the last 60 years?

3. Why does Chiu feel it is important for people "to realize that there is another side" to Chinese-Americans, a side not associated with a model human being?

4. What does Chiu request that the media do? Why?

Strategies and Structures

1. Chiu begins and concludes his essay with references to the media. How does this frame his essay as a whole?

2. How successfully does Chiu illustrate the superhuman and the subhuman character traits of the Chinese? Why is a discussion of the two extremes of strategic importance to his essay's concluding paragraph?

3. Chiu provides a brief history of the stereotypes— including the model minority—placed on Chinese people by other members of American society, prior to answering the rhetorical question, "Have the media been wrong all these years?" What is the purpose of the history? What does it show the reader?

Language and Vocabulary

1. Vocabulary: *diligently, conscientiously, Caucasian, manifestation, insidious, inscrutable, opium, amiable, bespectacled, embezzle, endeavors.* Once you have looked up the meanings of these words, decide which of them fit your definition of a model minority. What makes these words positive in your opinion? The remaining words should be looked over carefully. Why didn't you choose them? Do they have a negative meaning to you, or are they merely part of each human's reality?

2. Does Philip Chiu's word usage reflect what we would expect of a writer from the model minority? What effect does Chiu's casual reference to crimes such as rape, robbery, drug use/sales, embezzlement, and

murder—and the motivation behind each crime— have on a reader? Explain your position on Chiu's word use thoroughly.

GROUP ACTIVITIES

1. Write a collaborative essay showing how the dominant stereotypes attributed to an ethnic group may never have been more than myths. Begin by brainstorming to come up with specific ethnic or gender stereotypes. Next, have each group member research a stereotype from a specific time period like the 1940s, share his or her findings, and assemble the group essay.

2. Briefly share your knowledge about people like Charlie Chan, Fu Manchu, Madame Chiang Kai-Shek, as well as events like the Chinese Cultural Revolution, the Korean War, and the Vietnam War. After your initial discussion, list other Chinese people who personify stereotypes of a given era. Also, try to think of one or two events involving people of Chinese origin in the last century, events which have prejudiced or typecast our perception of them.

WRITING ACTIVITIES

1. This article was written several years ago. At the time, Chiu asked, "Is the wind changing its direction again in 1988?" Here he was referring to the numerous stereotypes placed on the Chinese during the last 60 years. Write an essay in which you devise a thesis that answers Chiu's question. Use illustrations and examples to support what you say.

2. Is there a model social, political, or religious minority in the United States today? What is it? Compose an original thesis on this issue and demonstrate the truth of it through the use of illustration and example.

A Young Polish American Speaks Up: The Myth of the Melting Pot
BARBARA MIKULSKI

Barbara Mikulski has been actively involved in urban issues for the past two decades. She has served on MUD and is currently a U.S. Senator. The following essay was taken from a speech which Mikulski delivered in 1979 at the Task Force on Urban Problems of the United States Catholic Conference.

PRE-READING QUESTIONS

1. What is meant by "the melting pot" in America? Who makes up this melting pot? How is this melting pot formed?

2. What do you consider some of the common problems facing people from different ethnic backgrounds in America? Do you feel all ethnic minorities have an equal chance to succeed in America? Why/why not?

3. What does it mean to be a member of the working class? Based on your own experience and observation, what problems do you feel the working class faces?

1   America is not a melting pot. It is a sizzling cauldron for the ethnic American who feels that he has been politically extorted by both government and private enterprise. The ethnic American is sick of being stereotyped as a racist and dullard by phoney white liberals, pseudo black militants and patronizing bureaucrats. He pays the bill for every major government program and gets nothing or little in the way of return. Tricked by the political rhetoric of the illusionary funding for black-oriented social programs, he turns his anger to race—when he himself is the victim of class prejudice. He has worked hard all of his life to become a "good American;" he and his sons have

fought on every battlefield—then he is made fun of because he likes the flag.

2   The ethnic American is overtaxed and underserved at every level of government. He does not have fancy lawyers or expensive lobbyists getting him tax breaks on his income. Being a home owner he shoulders the rising property taxes—the major revenue source for the municipalities in which he lives. Yet he enjoys very little from these unfair and burdensome levies. Because of restrictive eligibility requirements linked either to income or "target areas," he gets no help from Federal programs. If he wants to buy in the "old neighborhood" he cannot get an FHA loan. One major illness in his family will wipe him out. When he needs a nursing home for an elderly parent, he finds that there are none that he can afford nor is he eligible for any financial assistance. His children tend to go to parochial schools which receive little in the way of government aid and for which he carries an extra burden. There is a general decline of community services for his neighborhood, e.g., zoning, libraries, recreation programs, sanitation, etc.

3   His income of $5,000 to $10,000 per year makes him "near poor." He is the guy that is hurt by layoffs, tight money that chokes him with high interest rates for installment buying and home improvements. Manufacturers with their price fixing, shoddy merchandise and exorbitant repair bills are gouging him to death. When he complains about costs, he is told that it is the "high cost of labor" that is to blame. Yet he knows he is the "labor" and that in terms of real dollars he is going backwards.

4   The ethnic American also feels unappreciated for the contribution he makes to society. He resents the way the working-class is looked down upon. In many instances he is treated like the machine he operates or the pencil he pushes. He is tired of being treated like an object of production. The public and private institutions have made him frustrated by their lack of response to his needs. At present he feels powerless in his daily dealings with and efforts to change them.

5   Unfortunately, because of old prejudices and new fears, anger is generated against other minority groups rather than those who have power. What is needed is an alliance of white and black; white collar, blue collar, and no collar based on mutual need, interdependence and respect, an alliance to develop

the strategy for a new kind of community organization and political participation.

POST-READING QUESTIONS

Content

1. What is the author's opinion about "the melting pot" theory in America?

2. How is the ethnic American taken advantage of by all levels of government in the United States, which supposedly serves the needs of its citizens?

3. What are some of the specific problems faced by ethnic Americans caught in the "sizzling cauldron" of the melting pot?

4. Why does the ethnic American feel "looked down upon" by the rest of society?

Strategies and Structures

1. What makes the first two sentences in this essay an effective thesis statement? How do they limit the topic, establish the controlling idea, and suggest the structure of an essay?

2. How does Mikulski structure her composition? What is the *implicit* controlling idea (topic sentence) for each paragraph?

3. How does Mikulski support her claims? What specific types of examples does she use to illustrate her points?

4. How is Mikulski's conclusion more than just a summary? What does she hope to achieve?

Language and Vocabulary

1. Vocabulary: *cauldron, pseudo, dullard, patronizing, bureaucrats, rhetoric, municipality, white-collar, blue-collar, interdependence, mutual, exorbitant, shoddy.* Write synonyms (see Glossary) for each vocabulary word. Then choose three or four of these vocabulary

words, and write a unified paragraph, using them and their synonyms *at least* two times each.

2. Which words in paragraph 3 deal specifically with money? In what way do these key words unify the paragraph and create continuity? Write your own paragraph about work and leisure using key words of similar meaning to unify your theme.

GROUP ACTIVITIES

1. After assembling in groups, examine your perspectives on how the working class has changed over the years. Since this essay was written in 1970, what blue-collar and white-collar jobs have been created? Which jobs have decreased? Ultimately, how have the changes in the work force affected ethnic minorities in the United States?

2. Mikulski contends that ethnic Americans have had labor problems over the years. Representing different segments of our multi-ethnic population (e.g., Hispanic, African-American, Chinese-American, Polish-American), break up in small groups, and research the most recent problems your ethnic group has had to face, and how your ethnic group dealt with its problems. Take notes during your group discussion which you can refer to when you do one of the writing activities.

WRITING ACTIVITIES

1. Write an essay tracing the work history of your mother/grandmother *or* father/grandfather, relating the problems they had and the ways they solved them. Then tell your reader what you intend to do with your work life. Conclude by showing your audience how your work life will differ from those of your ancestors.

2. Using the information collected from group activity 1, trace the work history of ethnic Americans, and illustrate what steps they have made to resolve problems.

Artificial Intelligence
R. COLIN JOHNSON

R. Colin Johnson, the author of *Cognizers: Neural Networks and Machines That Think,* is the advanced-technology editor of *Electronic Engineering Times* and editor of his own industry report, *Technology Reviews.* The following article on artificial intelligence is from the February 1990 issue of *Omni.*

PRE-READING QUESTIONS

1. What is your definition of a computer and is it a vital part of your life? Why/why not?
2. Do you believe that computers ever will be able to think as humans do?
3. Would you trust a computer with your safety and/or life?

1   "You've got to make sure they get at least eight hours of sleep each day," Carlos Tapang says to the first employee of Syntonics Systems. "Whatever you do, don't pull their plugs—you'll kill them."

2   Someday Tapang, the founder of the Oregon-based company, will probably offer that advice about his cognizers, modeled after human cognition.

3   Computer simulations of the brain's more basic functions—artificial neural networks—already exist. Banks use them to read the handwritten amounts on checks, brokerage firms employ them to predict the movement of stock prices, and the military trusts them to distinguish friend from foe on the hightech battlefield. But the next generation of machine intelligence—cognizers—will not be mere artificial imitators of human perceptual abilities: rather they will have genuine cognitive faculties, albeit ones cast in synthetic materials.

4   Such a technological advance is not far off. In the near future, Tapang hopes to market cognizer microchips able to

bestow genuine intelligence upon any computer in which they are installed.

5   The chips will be smarter in large measure because they contain a new approach to the vexing problem of data storage— thanks to a device called a capacitor. This remembers what "happens" to the chip, much the way the brain itself maintains a record of an individual's experience. The cognizer will even lose its memory if deactivated. Thus once Tapang's cognizer is turned on, it should never be turned off. "When it is first turned on, it is like being born; it starts to observe and learn about its environment immediately . . . But if you turn it off, it is like killing a person," Tapang says. Having to leave the cognizer running all the time, however, is a small price to pay: By using hardware, not elaborate software, to keep track of the past, these devices will be able to solve some of the trickiest problems faced by today's AI programs—such as mimicking the process of human visual perception.

6   Though you can't unplug cognizers, you do have to bid them good night. "They must sleep," Tapang explains. "My chips are modeled after humans: They can stay awake for eighteen to twenty-four hours, but then they need about eight hours of rest to get refreshed." He puts them to sleep by closing their "eyes" and other senses, that is, by letting them run with no input from the outside world.

7   Cognizers also need to dream during each of their "nights." During these sleep periods a special circuit on the chips senses the need to dream and triggers a mode that Tapang has, in the past, compared to REM (rapid eye movement) sleep in people. "I don't like to stress the analogy with REM," he says, "because my circuits are so much simpler than real neural networks in the brain."

8   An age-old philosophical problem has been whether a human remains the same person throughout life—despite amnesia, close brushes with death, and the like. For humans this puzzle has spawned myriad theories, none of which has proved the definitive answer. But for Tapang such problems are easy. "We are our memories," he asserts. Thus his cognizer's self is the same as long as the power has not been interrupted.

9   These devices may someday usher in the sort of machines that have heretofore been the stuff that science-fiction dreams

are made of: voice typewriters that discuss your writing with you; robots that, without human help, can design and build their successors; airplanes that can change their course in response to emergencies; and cars that drive themselves. Our electronic offspring will then become alive in the truest sense: able to cope with novelty by changing their internal representations of the world to match changing circumstances. And we, by learning to mimic this technique, will gain not only a fundamentally useful technology but also a greater understanding of ourselves.

POST-READING QUESTIONS

Content

1. What is artificial intelligence?
2. Why will computer chips be "smarter" in the near future?
3. What is unusual about a "cognizer?"
4. Did your definition of a computer change after reading this article? Why or why not?

Strategies and Structures

1. How does the essay's title prepare you for the composition that follows? What expectations did you have and were they satisfied?
2. Why does Johnson compare the machine to a living person? What is he trying to impress upon the reader?
3. One way to "lead-in" to an essay and capture your reader's interest and attention is to open with a quote. In your opinion why was or wasn't Johnson's lead-in effective? What other lead-ins might have been used here to achieve the same purpose?
4. Why could this computer of the future be considered practically human?

Language and Vocabulary

1. Vocabulary: *cognition, simulation, neural, albeit, microchip, analogy, capacitor, hardware, software, myriad.* Look up these words in the dictionary and decide which of them are associated with human beings and which are associated with machines.

2. Why is the use of a metaphor (see Glossary) an effective way to introduce some computer terminology and establish similarities between artificial and human intelligence?

GROUP ACTIVITIES

1. Divide into two groups, one of which will watch and analyze human interaction with computers in the movie *2001: A Space Odyssey* and the other will watch the movie *2010.* As your group watches the film, it should note the characteristics of the computer named Hal. Bring this list to class and discuss: (1) how Hal seems to have changed, and (2) the way Dr. Chandler relates to Hal in the latter movie.

2. Have your group create its own idea of artificial intelligence (you need not even mention computers or high technology). Key questions to address include: What does it mean to be artificial? Is artificial necessarily superficial? For another perspective, see Isaac Asimov's essay "What Is Intelligence, Anyway," (p. 130).

WRITING ACTIVITIES

1. Write a paper in which you develop your own definition of intelligence and argue whether cognizers can truly be considered intelligent. Make sure you show your reader how and why your point of view is valid.

2. Devise an original thesis, and use specific examples and logical reasoning to compare and contrast your concept of artificial intelligence with human

intelligence. Be sure you have enough supporting material to justify your conclusions.

Additional Topics and Issues for Illustration and Example Essays

1. Painters or sketchers often are called illustrators. Find a painting or drawing, either in a museum or a book, and in an essay describe what the artist is attempting to illustrate.

2. Attend a meeting of the student government body on your campus or a city council meeting where you live and, through illustration and example, write a composition showing what issues were discussed and how they were resolved. Show how the interactions among the members of the council contributed to the resolutions.

3. Illustrate what it is like (or what you believe it would be like) to work in a fast-food restaurant. Remember your objective: you want to paint a vivid picture using words so your reader will be able to visualize what you are saying.

4. More and more frequently, people do not want to go out at night since they are afraid of being attacked. To what extent is this fear justified? Using examples and observations drawn from personal experience, develop a thesis supporting your point of view on this issue.

5. Illustrate the differences between what we refer to as "civilized" societies and those which are "underdeveloped" or "primitive." In order to avoid stereotyping, support every general point with at least two specific examples.

6. Construct an essay wherein you illustrate the benefits of using animals, instead of humans, to test the effects of new drugs, wonder cures, and cosmetics. If you believe such a practice is inhumane, illustrate the negative side of this issue. Make sure you illustrate what you believe using specific examples; do not just tell your reader what you think.

5

DEFINITION

Definition plays an important part in the development of most expository essays. Why? Without a clear definition of terms, a reader will have only a vague idea of what you are writing about. Specifically defining whom and what you are explaining will help you, the writer, focus on your goals, giving you less opportunity to digress and wander.

Often writers define a problem, group or subgroup, a concept, a place, another person, or themselves. By defining these things, writers may wish to call certain problems or concepts to the reader's attention or to dispel a currently popular definition and supplement his or her own definition. For example, Jo Goodwin Parker defines "poverty" in order to call the reader's attention to the problems of the poor: hunger, dirt, and despair. On the other hand, Isaac Asimov writes his essay "What Is Intelligence, Anyway?" to dispel the myth that all intelligence can be measured and evaluated in an academic setting. To Asimov, a person's intelligence is based on the situation (e.g., the author is intelligent at the university but not at the auto repair shop).

For whatever reasons you define something, you should be careful and concerned about how you define. For example, people often define themselves cautiously so as to be perceived in positive ways. In the 1987 campaign for the presidency, George Bush did not originally want to use the lines "Read my lips" because no previous U.S. president had ever mentioned parts of the human body in a debate or campaign speech. Because of this, he did not want to be defined as peculiar or immoral.

Writers have many techniques available to them when they create a definition; that is, they can arrange and develop their definitions in a variety of ways. However, all good writers realize that definition essays require them to do a considerable amount of prewriting and research before they can even begin to organize their thoughts in a coherent fashion. Once the preliminary steps have been completed, the writer is ready to organize his or her major discussion points: supporting material that helps define the topic or issue. Some of the most common techniques writers use when they create definitions are discussed next.

Definition by Example

Often authors will offer a definition of a term, issue, or topic by giving examples and descriptions. For example, Jo Goodwin Parker in her essay "What Is Poverty" explains poverty to us by offering examples of her own poverty-stricken life. *"Let me explain housekeeping with no money. For breakfast I give my children grits with no oleo or cornbread without eggs or oleo. This does not use many dishes. What dishes there are, I wash in cold water with no soap. . . . Look at my hands so cracked and red."* These examples solidify the definition of poverty in a graphic way for the reader.

Definition by History

Another technique that will aid in creating a definition is to offer the history of the term, issue, or topic being defined. By creating a historical context, the writer establishes where a term, issue, or topic has come from and how it has developed, what has been its uses through out history, and how it has evolved. For instance, Woody Allen in his satirical essay "Slang Origins" gives the reader the history of the slang phrases he is defining. He tells when the expression "to eat humble pie" first came into usage and how it has evolved to its current meaning. *"Jumbo pie soon became jumble pie and 'to eat a jumble pie' referred to any kind of humiliating act. When the Spanish seamen heard the word 'jumble,' they pronounced it 'humble,' although many preferred to say nothing and simply grin."*

Definition by Comparison or Contrast

It is often useful to define an unknown term, issue, or concept by comparing or contrasting it with a known term, issue, or concept. The writer will take advantage of what the audience knows already in order to create a clear definition of what it may not know. Guillermo Gómez-Peña in his essay "Documented/Undocumented," contrasts his definition of himself and his culture with the definitions found in other cultures. *"I am Mexican but I am also Chicano and Latin American. At the border, they call me chillango or mexiquillo. In Mexico City, its pocho or norteno; and in Europe its sudacca. The Anglos call me 'Hispanic' or 'Latino'. . . ."*

In whatever way you decide to develop your definition, remember that definitions are a way to clarify your ideas, concepts, and issues. Writers often use definition to call the reader's attention to a problem or to offer a counter-definition to a popular notion.

Tips on Writing Definition Essays

1. First, ask yourself questions to limit your topic. What do you want to define? Why do you want to define it? Freewrite about your topic or issue in order to focus on what you want to define. Remember an unfocused topic or issue will lead to a vague or unclear definition.

2. Next, gather information from a variety of sources that will aid in the development of your definition.

3. Organize your definition paper so that it has a clear pattern. If the reader must guess at what you are attempting to define and how you will define it, he or she may become confused or misinterpret your purpose.

4. Fully develop your definition with examples and specifics. You may find the strategies for development listed above useful.

5. As you proofread your essay prior to writing the final copy, ask yourself "What is my purpose for writing this paper? Do my examples clearly illustrate the term, concept, or issue that I am defining? Where would additional examples strengthen my definition?"

6. Keep in mind that you are writing for a reader who may not be familiar with the term, topic, or issue. Your development with examples will create concrete meaning for the reader.

What Is Intelligence, Anyway?
ISAAC ASIMOV

Born in the Soviet Union, Isaac Asimov immigrated with his parents to the United States in 1923. A PhD. from Columbia University and a well-respected writer on general science, Asimov has published numerous books and is one of the most prolific science fiction writers of the 20th century. His books include *I. Robot* (1950), *The Foundation Trilogy* (1951–53), *The Stars in Their Courses* (1976), and *The Gods Themselves* (1977) just to name a few.

PRE-READING QUESTIONS

1. What qualities do you associate with intelligence? If you have trouble thinking of specific things, free-write or cluster the word.

2. What is a fair test of intelligence? Should people who work in different occupations take different tests to measure their knowledge?

1   What is intelligence, anyway? When I was in the army I received a kind of aptitude test that all soldiers took and,

against a normal of 100, scored 160. No one at the base had ever seen a figure like that, and for two hours they made a big fuss over me. (It didn't mean anything. The next day I was still a buck private with KP as my highest duty.)

2   All my life I've been registering scores like that, so that I have the complacent feeling that I'm highly intelligent, and I expect other people to think so, too. Actually, though, don't such scores simply mean that I am very good at answering the type of academic questions that are considered worthy of answers by the people who make up the intelligence tests—people with intellectual bents similar to mine?

3   For instance, I had an auto-repair man once, who, on these intelligence tests, could not possibly have scored more than 80, by my estimate. I always took it for granted that I was far more intelligent than he was. Yet, when anything went wrong with my car I hastened to him with it, watched him anxiously as he explored its vitals, and listened to his pronouncements as though they were divine oracles—and he always fixed my car.

4   Well, then, suppose my auto-repair man devised questions for an intelligence test. Or suppose a carpenter did, or a farmer, or, indeed, almost anyone but an academician. By every one of those tests, I'd prove myself a moron. And I'd *be* a moron, too. In a world where I could not use my academic training and my verbal talents but had to do something intricate or hard, working with my hands, I would do poorly. My intelligence, then, is not absolute but is a function of the society I live in and of the fact that a small subsection of that society has managed to foist itself on the rest as an arbiter of such matters.

5   Consider my auto-repair man, again. He had a habit of telling me jokes whenever he saw me. One time he raised his head from under the automobile hood to say: "Doc, a deaf-and-dumb guy went into a hardware store to ask for some nails. He put two fingers together on the counter and made hammering motions with the other hand. The clerk brought him a hammer. He shook his head and pointed to the two fingers he was hammering. The clerk brought him nails. He picked out the sizes he wanted, and left. Well, doc, the next guy who came in was a blind man. He wanted scissors. How do you suppose he asked for them?"

6   Indulgently, I lifted my right hand and made scissoring motions with my first two fingers. Whereupon my auto-repair man laughed raucously and said, "Why, you dumb jerk, he used his voice and asked for them." Then he said, smugly, "I've been trying that on all my customers today." "Did you catch many?" I asked. "Quite a few," he said, "but I knew for sure I'd catch you." "Why is that?" I asked. "Because you're so goddamned educated, doc, I *knew* you couldn't be very smart."

7   And I have an uneasy feeling he had something there.

POST-READING QUESTIONS

Content

1. According to Asimov, what is intelligence?

2. What sort of intelligence does Asimov, an academic, have? Is it any better than the intelligence of the auto mechanic or blue collar worker? Why?

3. How did Asimov value I.Q. tests at the start of this essay, and what made him reconsider his position?

Strategies and Structures

1. Why does Asimov include several short episodes in this paper (e.g., time in the army, a trip to an automobile mechanic)? How do they assist him in defining *intelligence*?

2. What would happen if Asimov placed his trip to the automobile mechanic prior to his discussion of his performance on I.Q. tests? Why do you think he arranged his material as he did?

3. What might have been Asimov's strategic purpose for concluding his essay with a one-sentence paragraph?

Language and Vocabulary

1. Vocabulary: *KP, complacent, indulgently.* Outside of KP (kitchen police), the other two vocabulary words

deal with qualities associated with someone who is lacking intelligence. What other characteristics do you associate with an unintelligent person? Write a list of them, and, through repeated usage for at least three days, make them a part of your everyday speech.

2. How many of Asimov's words *sound* intelligent? Make some sort of chart of important sounding or scholastic words (be sure you know their definitions), and spend a day consciously using them whenever you have an opportunity. How did others react to your use of words? Did using *big* words make you feel more or less intelligent? Why?

GROUP ACTIVITIES

1. In groups of two, in much the same way as Asimov reported his conversations with his mechanic, visit a person who runs a business neither of you knows anything about and, together, write a summation of this person's intelligence. In what areas do you feel superior to this person, and in what ways is his or her intelligence inferior to your own?

2. After the class has been divided into four or five groups, have each group member write down three things he or she knows little about as well as three things he or she knows much about. Compare notes and find a common element of expertise in your group (e.g., math, "street smarts," science, philosophy). Next, make up an intelligence quiz based on questions from your group's area of expertise (ten questions), and make copies of it for the rest of the class. Finally, with the exception of your own, take each group's intelligence quiz, correct them all as a class, and graph the results for each test. What do the results infer about intelligence tests? Did the outcome of the class exercise confirm Asimov's conclusions about I.Q. tests? How?

WRITING ACTIVITIES

1. Write an essay defining your own conception of intelligence. As Asimov has done, cite some specific instances that demonstrate how and why your definition is valid.

2. Make up a list of the qualities you associate with stupidity, lunacy, or another human characteristic. Focus on a recurring theme from your list, and use it as the controlling idea in an essay defining your topic.

What Is Poverty?
JO GOODWIN PARKER

When Jo Goodwin Parker originally published this article, she preferred that the editor present no by-line. In keeping with the spirit of its initial publication, we have decided to reprint Parker's article without any biographical data about its author.

PRE-READING QUESTIONS

1. Write a three-sentence definition of poverty. Who are the poor? Why are they poor? Where do the poor usually live? What problems must poor people overcome?

2. What are your feelings about poor people? Do you feel superior to them? Do they make you feel angry? Do they make you feel despair? Do you try to help them? If so, why? If not, why not?

1   You ask me what is poverty? Listen to me. Here I am, dirty, smelly, and with no "proper" underwear on and with the stench of my rotting teeth near you. I will tell you. Listen to

me. Listen without pity. I cannot use your pity. Listen with understanding. Put yourself in my dirty, worn out, ill-fitting shoes, and hear me.

2   Poverty is getting up every morning from a dirt- and illness-stained mattress. The sheets have long since been used for diapers. Poverty is living in a smell that never leaves. This is a smell of urine, sour milk, and spoiling food sometimes joined with the strong smell of long-cooked onions. Onions are cheap. If you have smelled this smell, you did not know how it came. It is the smell of the outdoor privy. It is the smell of young children who cannot walk the long dark way in the night. It is the smell of the mattresses where years of "accidents" have happened. It is the smell of the milk which has gone sour because the refrigerator long has not worked, and it costs money to get it fixed. It is the smell of rotting garbage. I could bury it, but where is the shovel? Shovels cost money.

3   Poverty is being tired. I have always been tired. They told me at the hospital when the last baby came that I had chronic anemia caused from poor diet, a bad case of worms, and that I needed a corrective operation. I listened politely—the poor are always polite. The poor always listen. They don't say that there is no money for iron pills, or better food, or worm medicine. The idea of an operation is frightening and costs so much that, if I had dared, I would have laughed. Who takes care of my children? Recovery from an operation takes a long time. I have three children. When I left them with "Granny" the last time I had a job, I came home to find the baby covered with fly specks, and a diaper that had not been changed since I left. When the dried diaper came off, bits of my baby's flesh came with it. My other child was playing with a sharp bit of broken glass, and my oldest was playing alone at the edge of a lake. I made twenty-two dollars a week, and a good nursery school costs twenty dollars a week for three children. I quit my job.

4   Poverty is dirt. You can say in your clean clothes coming from your clean house, "Anybody can be clean." Let me explain about housekeeping with no money. For breakfast I give my children grits with no oleo or cornbread without eggs and oleo. This does not use up many dishes. What dishes there are, I wash in cold water and with no soap. Even the cheapest soap has to be saved for the baby's diapers. Look at my hands, so cracked and

red. Once I saved for two months to buy a jar of Vaseline for my hands and the baby's diaper rash. When I had saved enough, I went to buy it and the price had gone up two cents. The baby and I suffered on. I have to decide every day if I can bear to put my cracked sore hands into the cold water and strong soap. But you ask, why not hot water? Fuel costs money. If you have a wood fire it costs money. If you burn electricity, it costs money. Hot water is a luxury. I do not have luxuries. I know you will be surprised when I tell you how young I am. I look so much older. My back has been bent over the wash tubs every day for so long, I cannot remember when I ever did anything else. Every night I wash every stitch my school age child has on and just hope her clothes will be dry by morning.

5   Poverty is staying up all night on cold nights to watch the fire knowing one spark on the newspaper covering the walls means your sleeping child dies in flames. In summer poverty is watching gnats and flies devour your baby's tears when he cries. The screens are torn and you pay so little rent you know they will never be fixed. Poverty means insects in your food, in your nose, in your eyes, and crawling over you when you sleep. Poverty is hoping it never rains because diapers won't dry when it rains and soon you are using newspapers. Poverty is seeing your children forever with runny noses. Paper handkerchiefs cost money and all your rags you need for other things. Even more costly are antihistamines. Poverty is cooking without food and cleaning without soap.

6   Poverty is asking for help. Have you ever had to ask for help, knowing your children will suffer unless you get it? Think about asking for a loan from a relative, if this is the only way you can imagine asking for help. I will tell you how it feels. You find out where the office is that you are supposed to visit. You circle that block four or five times. Thinking of your children, you go in. Everyone is very busy. Finally, someone comes out and you tell her that you need help. That never is the person you need to see. You go see another person, and after spilling the whole shame of your poverty all over the desk between you, you find that this isn't the right office after all—you must repeat the whole process, and it never is any easier at the next place.

7   You have asked for help, and after all it has a cost. You are again told to wait. You are told why, but you don't really hear

because of the red cloud of shame and the rising cloud of despair.

8   Poverty is remembering. It is remembering quitting school in junior high because "nice" children had been so cruel about my clothes and my smell. The attendance officer came. My mother told him I was pregnant. I wasn't, but she thought that I could get a job and help out. I had jobs off and on, but never long enough to learn anything. Mostly I remember being married. I was so young then. I am still young. For a time, we had all the things you have. There was a little house in another town, with hot water and everything. Then my husband lost his job. There was unemployment insurance for a while and what few jobs I could get. Soon, all our nice things were repossessed and we moved back here. I was pregnant then. This house didn't look so bad when we first moved in. Every week it gets worse. Nothing is ever fixed. We now had no money. There were a few odd jobs for my husband, but everything went for food then, as it does now. I don't know how we lived through three years and three babies, but we did. I'll tell you something, after the last baby I destroyed my marriage. It had been a good one, but could you keep on bringing children in this dirt? Did you ever think how much it costs for any kind of birth control? I knew my husband was leaving the day he left, but there were no good-bys between us. I hope he has been able to climb out of this mess somewhere. He never could hope with us to drag him down.

9   That's when I asked for help. When I got it, you know how much it was? It was, and is, seventy-eight dollars a month for the four of us; that is all I ever can get. Now you know why there is no soap, no needles and thread, no hot water, no aspirin, no worm medicine, no hand cream, no shampoo. None of these things forever and ever and ever. So that you can see clearly, I pay twenty dollars a month rent, and most of the rest goes for food. For grits and cornmeal, and rice and milk and beans. I try my best to use only the minimum electricity. If I use more, there is that much less for food.

10   Poverty is looking into a black future. Your children won't play with my boys. They will turn to other boys who steal to get what they want. I can already see them behind the bars of their prison instead of behind the bars of my poverty. Or they will turn to the freedom of alcohol or drugs, and find themselves

enslaved. And my daughter? At best, there is for her a life like mine.

11   But you say to me, there are schools. Yes, there are schools. My children have no extra books, no magazines, no extra pencils, or crayons, or paper and most important of all, they do not have health. They have worms, they have infections, they have pink-eye all summer. They do not sleep well on the floor, or with me in my one bed. They do not suffer from hunger, my seventy-eight dollars keeps us alive, but they do suffer from malnutrition. Oh yes, I do remember what I was taught about health in school. It doesn't do much good. In some places there is a surplus commodities program. Not here. The country said it cost too much. There is a school lunch program. But I have two children who will already be damaged by the time they get to school.

12   But, you say to me, there are health clinics. Yes, there are health clinics and they are in the towns. I live out here eight miles from town. I can walk that far (even if it is sixteen miles both ways), but can my little children? My neighbor will take me when he goes; but he expects to get paid, *one way or another.* I bet you know my neighbor. He is that large man who spends his time at the gas station, the barbershop, and the corner store complaining about the government spending money on the immoral mothers of illegitimate children.

13   Poverty is an acid that drips on pride until all pride is worn away. Poverty is a chisel that chips on honor until honor is worn away. Some of you say that you would do *something* in my situation, and maybe you would, for the first week or the first month, but for year after year after year?

14   Even the poor can dream. A dream of a time when there is money. Money for the right kinds of food, for worm medicine, for iron pills, for toothbrushes, for hand cream, for a hammer and nails and a bit of screening, for a shovel, for a bit of paint, for some sheeting, for needles and thread. Money to pay *in money* for a trip to town. And, oh, money for hot water and money for soap. A dream of when asking for help does not eat away the last bit of pride. When the office you visit is as nice as the offices of other governmental agencies, when there are enough workers to help you quickly, when workers do not quit

in defeat and despair. When you have to tell your story to only one person, and that person can send you for other help and you don't have to prove your poverty over and over and over again.

15   I have come out of my despair to tell you this. Remember I did not come from another place or another time. Others like me are all around you. Look at us with an angry heart, anger that will help you help me. Anger that will let you tell of me. The poor are always silent. Can you be silent too?

POST-READING QUESTIONS

Content

1. What does Parker claim poverty is? Look at the beginning of each paragraph for some specific definitions. Next, jot down her definitions of poverty and compare them to the list you wrote as a pre-reading activity.

2. How is poverty difficult on Parker's children? List some specific examples.

3. In what ways does Parker try to obtain help, and what problems does she encounter?

4. Why are people's opinions and prejudices her greatest obstacles?

Strategies and Structures

1. What writing strategy does the author use at the beginning of most paragraphs? Do you notice a recurring pattern? What is it?

2. How does Parker develop each paragraph? What details make each paragraph memorable?

3. How does Parker defend her inability to get help? How does she discount the usual solution society has for poverty (e.g., welfare, education, and health clinics)? In the final paragraph, how does the author use questions to involve the reader in the issue of poverty?

Language and Vocabulary

1. Vocabulary: *chronic, immoral, illegitimate, antihista-mines, enslaved.* Which of these words tend to produce a negative feeling in you? Why? Pick one of the negative words and cluster the feelings the word evokes in you. Save your list.

2. Note the author's use of adjectives to describe the subhuman conditions in which they live. For instance, instead of writing "poverty is looking into a future," she writes, "Poverty is looking into a black future." How many other such adjectives can you find?

GROUP ACTIVITIES

1. In small groups, go to one of the charity or social-welfare organizations in town and interview a social worker about the life of the poor. After this, determine whether Parker was exaggerating the problem.

2. As a group, create a realistic list of possible solutions to Parker's problem: poverty. Consider the possible role of government programs, charity organizations, and individual participation in your solution.

WRITING ACTIVITIES

1. Define a social problem (homelessness, sexism, racism) imitating Parker's style, beginning several of your paragraphs with "*your topic* . . . is" to define your topic or issue.

2. Using adjectives to highlight the futility of the situation, write a short definition essay on *Growing up in Poverty.*

Documented/Undocumented
GUILLERMO GÓMEZ-PEÑA

Besides writing, Guillermo Gómez-Peña works as a visual artist. The following essay which initially appeared in the *L.A. Weekly*, 1988, was translated by Ruben Martinez.

PRE-READING QUESTIONS

1. What images of Mexican-Americans do we find on television and in the newspapers? Who are they? Where are they from? What is their history? When did they become a part of American history? How are they perceived by the rest of society? As a class, share your perceptions of this culture. Remember these are only perceptions and not hard-and-fast definitions.

2. In the essay you are about to read, Gómez-Peña defines himself as "a border-crosser." What do you think—without reading the essay—are the characteristics of a border-crosser?

1   I live smack in the fissure between two worlds, in the infected wound: half a block from the end of Western Civilization and four miles from the start of the Mexican-American border, the northernmost point of Latin America. In my fractured reality, but a reality nonetheless, there cohabit two histories, languages, cosmologies, artistic traditions, and political systems which are drastically counterposed. Many "deterritorialized" Latin American artists in Europe and the U.S. have opted for "internationalism" (a cultural identity based upon the "most advanced" of the ideas originating out of New York or Paris). I, on the other hand, opt for "borderness" and assume my role: My generation, the *chilangos* [slang term for a Mexico City native], who came to "el norte" fleeing the imminent ecological

and social catastrophe of Mexico City, gradually integrated itself into otherness, in search of that other Mexico grafted onto
the entrails of the et cetera . . . became Chicano-ized. We de-
Mexicanized ourselves to Mexi-understand ourselves, some
without wanting to, others on purpose. And one day, the border became our house, laboratory, and ministry of culture (or
counterculture).

2   Today, eight years after my departure (from Mexico), when
they ask me for my nationality or ethnic identity, I can't re-
spond with one word, since my "identity" now possesses multi-
ple repertories: I am Mexican but I am also Chicano and Latin
American. At the border they call me *chilango* or *mexi-quillo;* in
Mexico City it's *pocho* or *norteno;* and in Europe it's *sudaca.* The
Anglos call me "Hispanic" or "Latino," and the Germans have,
on more than one occasion, confused me with Turks or Italians.
My wife Emilia is Anglo-Italian, but speaks Spanish with an
Argentine accent, and together we walk amid the rubble of the
Tower of Babel of our American post-modernity.

3   The recapitulation of my personal and collective topography has become my cultural obsession since I arrived in the
United States. I look for the traces of my generation, whose
distance stretches not only from Mexico City to California, but
also from the past to the future, from pre-Columbian America
to high technology and from Spanish to English, passing
through "Spanglish."

4   As a result of this process I have become a cultural topographer, border-crosser, and hunter of myths. And it doesn't matter where I find myself, in Califas or Mexico City, in Barcelona
or West Berlin; I always have the sensation that I belong to the
same species; the migrant tribe of the fiery pupils.

POST-READING QUESTIONS

Content

1. What does Gómez-Peña mean when he begins his
   essay by writing, *"I live smack in the fissure between two
   worlds, in the infected wound?"* How might this explain
   his sense of "fractured reality?" What do the words
   "fractured reality" suggest?

2. What is the history of *chilangos?* Where are they originally from and where did they flee? Finally, why did they flee?

3. What names do others use when defining Gómez-Peña? What does he use when defining himself?

4. How does Gómez-Peña's definition of himself explain why he has *"become a cultural topographer, border-crosser, and hunter of myths?"*

Strategies and Structures

1. How does the opening sentence set the theme of the essay? What tension does it create? How does it limit the scope of the essay?

2. Gómez-Peña defines his "self" in two ways. What are they? How does he organize the essay around these two ways of defining one's self?

3. How does the title of Gómez-Peña's essay define his topic as a whole?

Language and Vocabulary

1. Vocabulary: *fissure, cohabit, cosmologies, counterposed, deterritorialized, ecological, post-modernity, recapitulation, topography.* After looking up the definitions in the dictionary, reread the essay. Does the topic take on a new meaning for you? Explain.

2. Using the word *topography,* make an essay map (see Glossary) of your own cultural background.

GROUP ACTIVITIES

1. As a group, research one culture or social segment in the United States. What is its history? How have others used names to define this group? What names have members of this group used to define themselves? Be prepared to present your findings to the rest of the class.

2. Create a collage that defines your group. Use magazine photos, newspaper headlines, etc. Finally, translate (define) your visual collage into the written language.

WRITING ACTIVITIES

1. Write a short essay in which you define yourself by providing the history of your family and by stating the perceptions others have of you. Here you might mention names and categories others use to label you.

2. Compose an essay in which you explain what you feel it means to grow up caught between two cultures, two realities.

Slang Origins
WOODY ALLEN

Woody Allen, a comedian, actor, screenwriter, and essayist, was born in Brooklyn, New York, in 1935 and began writing jokes when he was a high school student. Early in his career, he wrote for several television programs, including *The Tonight Show*. Among the many films Allen has written and directed are *Bananas* (1970), *Play it Again Sam* (1972), Academy Award winning *Annie Hall* (1975), and *Manhattan* (1979). His books and collections of essays include *Getting Even* (1971), *Without Feathers* (1975), and *Side Effects* (1980).

PRE-READING QUESTIONS

1. Based on the title of this essay, "Slang Origins," and your knowledge of the author, what do you expect this essay to be about? (Do not read it before thinking about an answer for this question.)

2. In the essay you're about to read, Woody Allen gives some unorthodox definitions of slang. Explain the word origins of the following: "eat humble pie," "take it on the lam," and "to look down one's nose." Do not consult a dictionary. Make up your definitions using your imagination and common sense. (Feel free to use humor.)

1   How many of you have ever wondered where certain slang expressions come from? Like "She's the cat's pajamas," or to "take it on the lam." Neither have I. And yet for those who are interested in this sort of thing I have provided a brief guide to a few of the more interesting origins.

2   Unfortunately, time did not permit consulting any of the established works on the subject, and I was forced to either obtain the information from friends or fill in certain gaps by using my own common sense.

3   Take, for instance, the expression "to eat humble pie." During the reign of Louis the Fat, the culinary arts flourished in France to a degree unequaled anywhere. So obese was the French monarch that he had to be lowered onto the throne with a winch and packed into the seat itself with a large spatula. A typical dinner (according to DeRochet) consisted of a thin crêpe appetizer, some parsley, an ox, and custard. Food became the court obsession, and no other subject could be discussed under penalty of death. Members of a decadent aristocracy consumed incredible meals and even dressed as foods. DeRochet tells us that M. Monsant showed up at the coronation as a wiener, and Étienne Tisserant received papal dispensation to wed his favorite codfish. Desserts grew more and more elaborate and pies grew larger until the minister of justice suffocated trying to eat a seven-foot "Jumbo Pie." *Jumbo* pie soon became *jumble* pie and "to eat a jumble pie" referred to any kind of humiliating act. When the Spanish seamen heard the word *jumble,* they pronounced it "humble," although many preferred to say nothing and simply grin.

4   Now, while "humble pie" goes back to the French, "take it on the lam" is English in origin. Years ago, in England, "lamming" was a game played with dice and a large tube of

ointment. Each player in turn threw dice and then skipped around the room until he hemorrhaged. If a person threw a seven or under he would say the word "quintz" and proceed to twirl in a frenzy. If he threw over seven, he was forced to give every player a portion of his feathers and was given a good "lamming." Three "lammings" and a player was "kwirled" or declared a moral bankrupt. Gradually any game with feathers was called "lamming" and feathers became "lams." To "take it on the lam" meant to put on feathers and later, to escape, although the transition in unclear.

5   Incidentally, if two players disagreed on rules, we might say they "got into a beef." This term goes back to the Renaissance when a man would court a woman by stroking the side of her head with a slab of meat. If she pulled away, it meant she was spoken for. If, however, she assisted by clamping the meat to her face and pushing it all over her head, it meant she would marry him. The meat was kept by the bride's parents and worn as a hat on special occasions. If, however, the husband took another lover, the wife could dissolve the marriage by running with the meat to the town square and yelling. "With thine own beef, I do reject thee. Aroo! Aroo!" If a couple "took to the beef" or "had a beef" it meant they were quarreling.

6   Another marital custom gives us that eloquent and colorful expression of disdain, "to look down one's nose." In Persia it was considered a mark of great beauty for a woman to have a long nose. In fact, the longer the nose, the more desirable the female, up to a certain point. Then it became funny. When a man proposed to a beautiful woman he awaited her decision on bended knee as she "looked down her nose at him." If her nostrils twitched, he was accepted, but if she sharpened her nose with pumice and began pecking him on the neck and shoulders, it meant she loved another.

7   Now, we all know when someone is very dressed up, we say he looks "spiffy." The term owes its origin to Sir Oswald Spiffy, perhaps the most renowned fop of Victorian England. Heir to treacle millions, Spiffy squandered his money on clothes. It was said that at one time he owned enough handkerchiefs for all the men, women and children in Asia to blow their noses for seven years without stopping. Spiffy's sartorial innovations were legend, and he was the first man ever to wear gloves on his head.

Because of extra-sensitive skin, Spiffy's underwear had to be made of the finest Nova Scotia salmon, carefully sliced by one particular tailor. His libertine attitudes involved him in several notorious scandals, and he eventually sued the government over the right to wear earmuffs while fondling a dwarf. In the end Spiffy died a broken man in Chichester, his total wardrobe reduced to kneepads and a sombrero.

8   Looking "spiffy," then, is quite a compliment, and one who does is liable to be dressed "to beat the band," a turn-of-the-century expression that originated from the custom of attacking with clubs any symphony orchestra whose conductor smiled during Berlioz. "Beating the band" soon became a popular evening out, and people dressed up in their finest clothes, carrying with them sticks and rocks. The practice was finally abandoned, during a performance of the *Symphonic fantastique* in New York when the entire string section suddenly stopped playing and exchanged gunfire with the first ten rows. Police ended the melee but not before a relative of J. P. Morgan's was wounded in the soft palate. After that, for a while at least, nobody dressed "to beat the band."

9   If you think some of the above derivations questionable, you might throw up your hands and say, "Fiddlesticks." This marvelous expression originated in Austria many years ago. Whenever a man in the banking profession announced his marriage to a circus pinhead, it was the custom for friends to present him with a bellows and a three-year supply of wax fruit. Legend has it that when Leo Rothschild made known his betrothal, a box of cello bows was delivered to him by mistake. When it was opened and found not to contain the traditional gift, he exclaimed, "What are these? Where are my bellows and fruit? Eh? All I rate is fiddlesticks!" The term "fiddlesticks" became a joke overnight in the taverns amongst the lower classes, who hated Leo Rothschild for never removing the comb from his hair after combing it. Eventually "fiddlesticks" meant any foolishness.

10   Well, I hope you've enjoyed some of these slang origins and that they stimulate you to investigate some of your own. And in case you were wondering about the term used to open this study, "the cat's pajamas," it goes back to an old burlesque routine of Chase and Rowe's, the two nutsy German professors.

Dressed in oversized tails, Bill Rowe stole some poor victim's pajamas. Dave Chase, who got great mileage out of his "hard of hearing" specialty, would ask him:

>*Chase:* Ach. Herr Professor. Vot is dot bulge under your pocket?
>
>*Rowe:* Dot? Dot's de chap's pajamas.
>
>*Chase:* The cat's pajamas? Ut mein Gott?

11   Audiences were convulsed by this sort of repartee and only a premature death of the team by strangulation kept them from stardom.

POST-READING QUESTIONS

Content

1. In the first paragraph, Woody Allen explains the purpose of his essay. What is that purpose? Why would Woody Allen provide a guide to more interesting slang origins if he is not interested in them?

2. How did the expression "to eat humble pie" develop? What was its original meaning, and how did it change? Does Allen's explanation seem reasonable?

3. What two sayings derived from marital customs does Allen define? What do his explanations suggest about the relationship between the sexes through the ages?

Strategies and Structures

1. How does beginning and concluding his essay discussing "She's the cat's pajamas" provide a framing device for this essay?

2. What pattern does Allen follow in each paragraph?

3. What techniques does Allen use to make his essay humorous? Do you find the use of humor disturbing or distracting? Why or why not? What is the purpose of the humor in this essay? Whom is he making fun of?

Language and Vocabulary

1. What linking devices does Allen use to lead the reader through the essay?

2. Vocabulary words: *frenzy, culinary, winch, decadent, hemorrhaged, wiener, ointment, treacle, libertine, brothel, & burlesque.* Using five related words from this list, write a sentence for each, based on a common theme. Once you have written your five sentences, combine them into a unified paragraph. Use additional sentences to provide coherence where necessary.

GROUP ACTIVITIES

1. Make a list of five slang terms that you use every day. Look up their origins and dictionary definitions. (Such books as *Hog on Ice* or *Who Put the Butter in Butterfly?* may be helpful.) Write down the real definitions and make up your own definitions. Present both definitions to the class without telling the students which is the true meaning, and let the class vote on which is the real definition.

2. Make a glossary of slang terms you hear others using but feel uncomfortable using yourself.

WRITING ACTIVITIES

1. After doing some preliminary research, write your own definition essay explaining the slang words or phrases used by a particular group, for example, sports slang, business jargon, and cultural expressions.

2. Write a humorous essay explaining the origins of some of your own *original* slang expressions. Certain humorous devices that you may find helpful are: exaggeration, absurdity, sarcasm, and irony. (You may want to consult the Glossary for definitions of these devices.)

Additional Topics and Issues for Definition Essays

1. Write an essay in which you compare and contrast Asimov's definition of human intelligence with Johnson's definition of artificial intelligence (see Chapter 4).

2. Write an essay in which you define one of the following: love, hate, peace, or happiness. Since such qualities are difficult to measure, you'll want to provide several representative examples to win your reader over to your viewpoint.

3. Define "elevator music." What is it? Where is it heard most? Need a person be in an elevator to experience such music? After your initial definition, illustrate the effects of this music on people who, unwillingly, are subjected to it.

4. What does it mean to be an independent or a dependent person? Compose an essay in which you define yourself as one of the above, supporting your ideas with examples drawn from personal experience.

5. Define the concepts of liberalism and conservatism. Which is better? Do you consider yourself a liberal or a conservative? Why? Attempt to integrate information from recent news articles which justifies the concept you have chosen.

6

PROCESS ANALYSIS

What is process analysis? In contrast to narration which relates *what* happens or cause and effect which explains *why* something occurs, process analysis addresses the question of *how*. Of crucial importance in explaining how is carefully organizing materials and marking them with time transitions (first, second, third). Such linking devices help a reader follow a process from start to finish. When do we use process analysis? Usually, process analysis explains one of two things: *how* to do something (directive process analysis) or *how* something is or was done (informative process analysis).

Directive Process Papers: How to Do Something

Like most expository strategies, process analysis explains. We are all familiar with the process of explaining how to do something; if we aren't explaining how to do something to others, then others may be explaining how to do something to us. Think for a moment about the last time you gave another person directions on how to get somewhere. What did you do? Undoubtedly, you told the person which direction to go and where and when to make left or right turns. In doing so, you were actively involved with a process; you were analyzing the possibilities and determining what a person had to do in order to reach a desired destination.

The "how to" essay is deceptively simple. That is, while an author may have no trouble explaining how to read a book, how to mow a lawn, or how to ride a bike, he or she may find it difficult to "hook" the interest of the intended audience. Why? The topics sound rather dull and will be just as dull as their titles promise when fully written unless the writer creates a reason—real or contrived—such a topic is relevant and therefore *meaningful* to its reader. In "How to Write a Personal Letter," Garrison Keillor begins his essay with: "We shy persons need to write a letter now and then, or else we'll dry up and blow away." Here the author has identified his intended audience, shy people, points out that he himself is a shy person, and proceeds to explain how writing letters will fulfill an important void in the lives of shy people. By the end of the introductory paragraph, Keillor has established a reason why the reader, shy or aggressive, should be interested in learning how to write a personal letter: a letter is better than a telephone call.

In a similar manner, through a light-hearted poke at what he refers to as *"America's most treasured art form, loafing,"* Sam Negri captures his reader's attention in "Loafing Made Easy." To suggest that "doing nothing" has the elevated status of an art form sparks the curiosity of readers, and whether they are novices or professional loafers themselves, they want to read more about Negri's directions on how to loaf with the least amount of effort.

Informational Process Essays: How Something Is/Was Done

Process analysis can also be an effective way of informing someone on how a process occurs. Informative process analysis explains topics like how a tree grows, how a gas engine runs, or how a worm regenerates itself. Such information is usually expressed in some sort of logical sequence process. Alexander Pertrunkevitch, for instance, informs his readers of the odd relationship between certain tarantulas and the Pepsis wasp in his process essay, "The Spider and the Wasp." Pertrunkevitch begins with a brief overview of each insect, and then step by step, he explains what the Digger (Pepsis) Wasp does to perpetuate its species, showing how certain tarantulas are crucial to the Digger Wasp's method of regeneration.

Informative process analysis is not limited to the natural sciences, of course. Rather than explain a natural relationship, Malcolm X discusses the strategy (process) he used to increase his "word base" in "Homemade Education." Like Pertrunkevitch, Malcolm X uses process analysis to inform us rather than direct us (tell us how to do something). Granted, it is possible to imitate what another person did in hopes of achieving the same results; we see this in the acting world and political arena daily. Nonetheless, there is an unmistakable difference between imitating to achieve an end (informative process analysis) and following directions to accomplish a task (directive process analysis).

Tips on Writing Process Analysis Essays

1. Have a clear sense of the process, whether it is informative or directive, you plan to explain. When in doubt, check a reliable source; don't try to bluff your way through an introduction and assume your reader will perceive the controlling idea of your composition.

2. Use transitional and linking devices indicating *time* in order to lead your reader from step to step, point to point.

3. Bear in mind that like any expository essay, your goal in writing is to *explain how* to do something (directive process analysis) or how something is or was done (informative process analysis). Avoid getting sidetracked on issues that would only confuse your reader.

4. Make sure to use key words and specific references. These will help your reader remain focused on the controlling idea or purpose of your essay.

5. Go over your rough draft and carefully check your work for omitted steps in a process, adding them as necessary. Sometimes it is helpful to continuously ask yourself Who? What? When? Where? Why? and, of course, How?

How to Write a Personal Letter
GARRISON KEILLOR

Born in 1942, writer/humorist Garrison Keillor began his successful writing and broadcasting career after graduating from the University of Minnesota. Keillor received nationwide attention for his radio program, *Prairie Home Companion,* which was broadcast on National Public Radio every Saturday evening from 1974 until 1987. His printed works include *Happy to Be Here* (1982), *Lake Wobegon Days* (1985), and *Leaving Home: A Collection of Lake Wobegon Stories* (1987). Keillor wrote the following process essay as an advertisement for the International Paper Company.

PRE-READING QUESTIONS

1. How often do you write a personal letter to family or friends? Do you think you should write more often? Why or why not?

2. What do you consider *personal?* What do you find *impersonal?* After briefly considering these questions, freewrite for ten minutes and attempt to answer each with as many examples as you can think of.

1   We shy persons need to write a letter now and then, or else we'll dry up and blow away. It's true. And I speak as one who loves to reach for the phone, dial the number, and talk. I say, "Big Bopper here—what's shakin', babes?" The telephone is to shyness what Hawaii is to February, it's a way out of the woods, *and yet:* a letter is better.

2   Such a sweet gift—a piece of handmade writing, in an envelope that is not a bill, sitting in our friend's path when she trudges home from a long day spent among wahoos and savages, a day our words will help repair. They don't need to be immortal, just sincere. She can read them twice and again tomorrow: *You're someone I care about, Corinne, and think of often and every time I do you make me smile.*

3   We need to write, otherwise nobody will know who we are. They will have only a vague impression of us as A Nice Person, because frankly, we don't shine at conversation, we lack the confidence to thrust our faces forward and say, "Hi, I'm Heather Hooten, let me tell you about my week." Mostly we say "Uh-huh" and "Oh really." People smile and look over our shoulder, looking for someone else to talk to.

4   So a shy person sits down and writes a letter. To be known by another person—to meet and talk freely on the page—to be close despite distance. To escape from anonymity and be our own sweet selves and express the music of our souls.

5   Same thing that moves a giant rock star to sing his heart out in front of 123,000 people moves us to take ballpoint in hand and write a few lines to our dear Aunt Eleanor. *We want to be known.* We want her to know that we have fallen in love, that we quit our job, and we're moving to New York, and we want to say a few things that might not get said in casual conversation: *thank you for what you've meant to me, I am very happy right now.*

6   The first step in writing letters is to get over the guilt of *not* writing. You don't "owe" anybody a letter. Letters are a gift. The burning shame you feel when you see unanswered mail makes it harder to pick up a pen and makes for a cheerless letter when you finally do. *I feel bad about not writing, but I've been so busy,* etc. Skip this. Few letters are obligatory, and they are *Thanks for the wonderful gift* and *I am terribly sorry to hear about George's death* and *Yes, you're welcome to stay with us next month,* and not many more than that. Write those promptly if you want to keep your friends. Don't worry about the others, except love letters, of course. When your true love writes *Dear Light of My Life, Joy of My Heart, O Lovely Pulsating Core of My Sensate Life,* some response is called for.

7   Some of the best letters are tossed off in a burst of inspiration, so keep your writing stuff in one place where you can sit down for a few minutes and *Dear Roy, I am in the middle of an essay for International Paper but thought I'd drop you a line. Hi to your sweetie too* dash off a note to a pal. Envelopes, stamps, address book, everything in a drawer so you can write fast when the pen is hot.

8   A blank 8″ × 11″ sheet can look as big as Montana if the pen's not so hot—try a smaller page and write boldly. Or use a note card with a piece of fine art on the front; if your letter ain't good, at least they get the Matisse. Get a pen that makes a sensuous line, get a comfortable typewriter, a friendly word processor—whichever feels easy to the hand.

9   Sit for few minutes with the blank sheet in front of you, and meditate on the person you will write to, let your friend come to mind until you can almost see her or him in the room with you. Remember the last time you saw each other and how your friend looked and what you said and what perhaps was unsaid between you, and when your friend becomes real to you, start to write.

10   Write the salutation—*Dear You*—and take a deep breath and plunge in. A simple declarative sentence will do, followed by another and another and another. Tell us what you're doing and tell it like you were talking to us. Don't think about grammar, don't think about lit'ry style, don't try to write dramatically, just give us your news. Where did you go, who did you see, what did they say, what do you think?

11   If you don't know where to begin, start with the present moment: *I'm sitting at the kitchen table on a rainy Saturday morning. Everyone is gone and the house is quiet.* Let your simple description of the present moment lead to something else, let the letter drift gently along.

12   The toughest letter to crank out is one that is meant to impress, as we all know from writing job applications; if it's hard work to slip off a letter to a friend, maybe you're trying too hard to be terrific. A letter is only a report to someone who already likes you for reasons other than your brilliance. Take it easy.

13   Don't worry about form. It's not a term paper. When you come to the end of one episode, just start a new paragraph. You can go from a few lines about the sad state of rock'n roll to the fight with your mother to your fond memories of Mexico to your cat's urinary tract infection to a few thoughts on personal indebtedness to the kitchen sink and what's in it. The more you write, the easier it gets, and when you have a True True Friend to write to, a *compadre,* a soul sibling, then it's like driving a car down a country road, you just get behind the keyboard and press on the gas.

14   Don't tear up the page and start over when you write a bad line—try to write your way out of it. Make mistakes and plunge on. Let the letter cook along and let yourself be bold. Outrage, confusion, love—whatever is in your mind, let it find a way to the page. Writing is a means of discovery, always, and when you come to the end and write *Yours ever* or *Hugs and Kisses,* you'll know something you didn't when you wrote *Dear Pal.*

15   Probably your friend will put your letter away, and it'll be read again a few years from now—and it will improve with age. And forty years from now, your friend's grandkids will dig it out of the attic and read it, a sweet and precious relic of the ancient Eighties that gives them a sudden clear glimpse of you and her and the world we old-timers knew. You will then have created an object of art. Your simple lines about where you went, who you saw, what they said, will speak to those children and they will feel in their hearts the humanity of our times.

16   You can't pick up a phone and call the future and tell them about our times. You have to pick up a piece of paper.

POST-READING QUESTIONS

Content

1. Why does Keillor say people should write personal letters once in a while? As a means of communication, what advantages do letters have over phone calls?

2. According to Keillor, when are the best letters written? Why?

3. How does Keillor recommend you *prepare* to write a personal letter?

4. Once you begin to write, what special advice does he offer regarding the format of your letter? Explain his reasoning.

Strategies and Structures

1. In your opinion, why does the author spend five paragraphs leading up to his directions on *how* to write a personal letter? What does he achieve?

2. How does referring to a personal letter as a gift clearly indicate the author's attitude towards his subject in this essay?

3. Why does Keillor spend more time explaining ways to avoid the common problems people encounter when they write letters than leading the reader through the writing process step by step?

4. In paragraph 15, Keillor makes some predictions about the future of letters you write. How does this paragraph directly relate to the opening paragraph and reinforce the controlling idea of the essay?

Language and Vocabulary

1. Vocabulary: Outside of wahoos (any of various American trees or shrubs), *obligatory* (legally, ethically or morally binding), and *anonymity* (the state of having or giving no name), how and why does Keillor's simple choice of vocabulary words suit the purpose of his essay?

2. To create a clear, down-to-earth tone, Keillor often uses slang words and informal language. List at least five instances of informal language in his essay and explain how they reinforce the idea that a writer uses for personal letters. Then go back over your list; what *formal* words or phrases would express the same information? How is each use of language (informal and formal) appropriate to a different audience?

GROUP ACTIVITIES

1. Write a collaborative personal letter to your college president or local government officials using informative process analysis to explain how to solve a current problem. While you will want to ultimately type (and have everyone sign) the letter, you'll want to avoid extremely formal language in order to personalize what you say.

2. Personality can often be expressed through language (words and phrases) and the following exercise demonstrates: (1) the power of personality (word choice) in writing and (2) the ways we can use process analysis to explain how something is done. In small groups, go somewhere on campus to observe how something is done (e.g., how books are collected, sorted, and reshelved in the library). Take notes and, individually, write short *personal* (informal) essays explaining the process your group observed. Next, have members share: (1) their definitions and examples of what is personal and what is impersonal and (2) their informally written observations. How well did group members personalize their writing?

WRITING ACTIVITIES

1. Write an *informative* process analysis paper explaining the origin or demise or subcultures or counter cultures in America, (e.g., surfers, red-necks, and/or punk rockers).

2. Compose an essay which provides *directions* on how to eat a formal dinner served at a very refined restaurant.

Loafing Made Easy
SAM NEGRI

In "Loafing Made Easy," Sam Negri uses *directive* process analysis to explain the procedure to follow to become a successful loafer. Note how writing strategies like process analysis are as useful in developing light-hearted essays as they are in developing serious, more profound topics.

PRE-READING QUESTIONS

1. We constantly hear about programs and plans designed to increase our work productivity; how well do you know how to relax and enjoy yourself?

2. How could loafing be easier than it is? What could possibly be difficult about doing nothing? Briefly jot down some thoughts on this matter in your notebook.

1   The fabled season of the sun is upon us and it is once again time to hook our thumbs in our suspenders and talk about American's most treasured art form, loafing.

2   The purest form of loafing is practiced in Arizona, where summertime temperatures will often exceed 110 degrees. If we regard the Arizona loafer as a natural resource, as I've been doing for the last eight years, we will see that the art form has applications that go far beyond the business of surviving in hot weather.

3   When I came to Arizona, I was a mediocre loafer, displaying a definite need for a degree of mental reconditioning. I'd moved here from Connecticut, where people relax by putting aside their copy of Gray's "Anatomy" and picking up a novel by Dostoevsky. In Arizona, this is referred to as insanity.

4   Here is a better method:

5   To begin with, shut the damper on your fireplace, if you have one, and turn on your air-conditioner, if you have one. Otherwise, hang a wet sheet in the window and pray for a breeze.

6   Now you are ready to memorize a handful of important and useful phrases. Try these: "I don't know"; "I don't care"; "no"; and the old standby, "well . . ."

7   These phrases are extremely valuable when your jaws are sagging like deflated bicycle tubes and your mind has turned to wax.

8   For example, it is 106 degrees in the shade and your son comes racing in the house, shouting, "Hey, you seen those long-handled pliers anywhere?" With a minimum of effort you are free to say, "no."

9   His anger may mount and he'll insist: "But you were using them yesterday! Where'd you leave 'em?"

10   If you haven't passed out from the strain of this conversation, you can then reply, "I don't know."

11   "But I need those pliers to fix my skateboard," he will cry. Then you break out the ultimate weapon in the loafer's lexicon. Without any inflection whatsoever, you declare, "Well . . ."

12   You can now get back to some serious loafing, which means that you will try to prove that Benjamin Franklin was correct when he observed: "It is hard for an empty sack to stand upright." In short, empty your mind. Learn to ask questions like these: "Mail come yet?" and "Anything doin'?" The response to these questions usually involve one word, and often they aren't debilitating.

13   There are a few additional rules to keep in mind for successful loafing.

14   First, never loaf near a pool or a lake because you might be tempted to go for a swim. Swimming frequently leaves a body feeling refreshed and may lead to a desire to do something.

15   Second, under no circumstances should you allow anyone to coax you into a camping trip in the mountains. Mountains tend to be lush, green and cool, and next thing you know you'll be wanting to split logs for a fire, go for a hike, or pump up your Coleman stove. Resist. "Patience is a necessary ingredient of genius," said Disraeli. If you want to be a fine loafer you have to make enemies.

16   Of course, it is impossible to get by in life if you don't do something, even in the summer. Household jobs are the easiest for a loafer to contend with, if he is selective and deliberate.

17   One satisfying and undemanding job involves a ball of twine. Find a ball of twine that a cat has unraveled so badly that you can't find the end. Get scissors and slowly cut it into small pieces, scrunch it into a smaller ball, and throw it away. Now look at all the extra space you have in your junk drawer.

18   Another relatively simple and useful job for summertime loafing centers on light bulbs. Limp through your house or apartment, removing the light bulbs from every lamp. Coast the very bottom of each bulb with petroleum jelly and put it back in the lampsocket. This will clean some of the crud *off* the contact point and solve the problems with flickering lightbulbs. For variety you can take the bulb that was in a livingroom lamp and put it in a bedroom lamp. It helps to sigh and

gaze wistfully at the base of the lightbulb as you are performing this function.

19   Last, if you have a dog, sit in your most comfortable chair and stare at your dog's eyes for five of 10 minutes. Every so often, mutter something incomprehensible. Your dog is certain to understand, and your family will not come near you for the rest of the afternoon.

POST-READING QUESTIONS

Content

1. Why did Negri have to wait until he moved to Arizona before he became more than just a "mediocre loafer?"

2. When and where does the author establish his attitude towards his topic: loafing? How does the reader know the author isn't entirely serious?

3. What initial advice does Negri offer the novice loafer? What additional rules does Negri ask the reader to keep in mind in order to become a successful loafer? (paragraphs 13–19).

4. Negri refers to other authors like Gray, Dostoevsky, Franklin, and Disraeli. Does a reader really need firsthand experience reading these authors to understand what Negri has to say about them? Why? Why not?

Strategies and Structures

1. In describing how to loaf with the least effort in paragraphs 5–12, why is it so important that Negri presents his process in chronological order?

2. How does Negri strategically use dialogue? What does it accomplish?

3. In paragraph 19, the author suggests sitting in a comfortable chair and staring at your dog's eyes and mumbling for 10 minutes. Then he says, *"Your dog is certain to understand, and your family will not come near*

you for the rest of the afternoon." How could this final piece of advice be the easiest method of loafing? Why?

Language and Vocabulary

1. Vocabulary: *mediocre, damper, lexicon, debilitating, coax, lush.* At first glance, these six vocabulary words seem to have nothing to do with loafing. Mediocre means ordinary, and a damper is a fireplace valve; however, to put a damper on something also suggests to smother it. Lexicon is a dictionary and also can be a word list, debilitating is a weakening of something, coax means to encourage by flattery, and lush has two meanings: green, covered with growth, and also a drunkard. Go over these words and their meanings once more, and see if you can't discover ways in which they all relate to some aspect of loafing.

2. Negri claims that loafing is "America's most treasured art form." What is the usual definition for "art form?" How is such a phrase in keeping with the mood of the rest of his essay? What does it reveal about the author and the subject?

GROUP ACTIVITIES

1. Have group members relate their fondest memories of loafing. Are there some members who never have been able to loaf or who won't admit it? What are the necessary characteristics for a loafer? What type of weather might inspire loafing? In what way? Try to get your group to reach an agreement on all of the above.

2. Get into small groups and review how a person can use the strategy of process analysis to either inform (a "how does/did" essay) or to direct (a "how to" essay). Present your understanding of both through original examples where using process analysis would be the most natural, effective means of explaining your topic or issue.

WRITING ACTIVITIES

1. Using *directive* process analysis as Sam Negri does, write an essay entitled "Loafing Made Difficult." Your essay may be similar to Negri's (light-hearted or humorous), but your use of process analysis, a rhetorical strategy, should be taken seriously.

2. Write an original *directive* process analysis paper explaining how to thoroughly relax after work or school, how to make other people miserable and remain happy yourself, or how to enjoy living in poverty. Your paper may have either a serious or humorous tone.

A Homemade Education
MALCOLM X

Born in Omaha, Nebraska, in 1925, Malcolm X, the son of a black separatist preacher, spent his early childhood in middle America. When his father died, Malcolm X became involved with life on the streets which ultimately led to his imprisonment for burglary. It was in prison that he began his correspondence with Elijah Muhammad, leader of the Black Muslims. This relationship led Malcolm X to further his education and to become a militant leader of the Black Revolution. Ironically, he was preaching the brotherhood of man when assassinated in 1965. The following excerpt is from *The Autobiography of Malcolm X.*

PRE-READING QUESTIONS

1. What are the denotations and connotations (see Glossary) of the word "homemade?" How would you personally relate the word "homemade" to the educational process?

2. List the steps you would take if your education were left entirely up to you, without the aid of teachers or

parents. What would you do to build your vocabulary, how would you empower yourself as a writer, and how would you develop a thorough knowledge of the world around you?

1   It was because of my letters that I happened to stumble upon starting to acquire some kind of homemade education.

2   I became increasingly frustrated at not being able to express what I wanted to convey in letters that I wrote, especially those to Mr. Elijah Muhammad. In the street, I had been the most articulate hustler out there—I had commanded attention when I said something. But now, trying to write simple English, I not only wasn't articulate, I wasn't even functional. How would I sound writing in slang, the way I would *say* it, something such as, "Look, daddy, let me pull your coat about a cat, Elijah Muhammad—"

3   Many who today hear me somewhere in person, or on television, or those who read something I've said, will think I went to school far beyond the eighth grade. This impression is due entirely to my prison studies.

4   It had really begun back in Charlestown Prison, when Bimbi first made me feel envy of his stock of knowledge. Bimbi had always taken charge of any conversation he was in, and I had tried to emulate him. But every book I picked up had few sentences which didn't contain anywhere from one to nearly all of the words that might as well have been in Chinese. When I just skipped those words, of course, I really ended up with little idea of what the book said. So I had come to the Norfolk Prison Colony still going through only book-reading motions. Pretty soon, I would have quit even these motions unless I had received the motivation that I did.

5   I saw that the best thing I could do was get hold of a dictionary—to study to learn some words. I was lucky enough to reason also that I should try to improve my penmanship. It was sad. I couldn't even write in a straight line. It was both ideas together that moved me to request a dictionary along with some tablets and pencils from the Norfolk Prison Colony school.

6   I spent two days just riffling uncertainly through the dictionary's pages. I'd never realized so many words existed! I

didn't know *which* words I needed to learn. Finally, just to start some kind of action, I began copying.

7   In my slow, painstaking, ragged handwriting, I copied into my tablet everything printed on that first page, down to the punctuation marks.

8   I believe it took me a day. Then, aloud, I read back, to myself, everything I'd written on the tablet. Over and over, aloud, to myself, I read my own handwriting.

9   I woke up the next morning, thinking about those words—immensely proud to realize that not only had I written so much at one time, but I'd written words that I never knew were in the world. Moreover, with a little effort, I also could remember what many of these words meant. I reviewed the words whose meanings I didn't remember. Funny thing, from the dictionary first page right now, that "aardvark" springs to my mind. The dictionary had a picture of it, a long-tailed, long-eared, burrowing African mammal, which lives off termites caught by sticking out its tongue as an anteater does for ants.

10   I was so fascinated that I went on—I copied the dictionary's next page. And the same experience came when I studied that. With every succeeding page, I also learned of people and places and events from history. Actually the dictionary is like a miniature encyclopedia. Finally the dictionary's A section had filled a whole tablet—and I went on into the B's. That was the way I started copying what eventually became the entire dictionary. It went a lot faster after so much practice helped me to pick up handwriting speed. Between what I wrote in my tablet, and writing letters, during the rest of my time in prison I would guess I wrote a million words.

11   I suppose it was inevitable that as my word-base broadened. I could for the first time pick up a book and read and now begin to understand what the book was saying. Anyone who has read a great deal can imagine the new world that opened. Let me tell you something: from then until I left that prison, in every free moment I had, if I was not reading in the library, I was reading on my bunk. You couldn't have gotten me out of books with a wedge. Between Mr. Muhammad's teachings, my correspondence, my visitors—usually Ella and Reginald—and my reading of books, months passed without my even thinking about being

imprisoned. In fact, up to then, I had never been so truly free in my life.

POST-READING QUESTIONS

Content

1. What led Malcolm X to improve his vocabulary? That is, what were the initial problems that he had with reading, and how did these lead to his desire to build his vocabulary?

2. What steps did Malcolm X take to build his vocabulary?

3. What were his emotional responses after he copied the first page of the dictionary?

4. How did reading affect Malcolm X's outlook on life?

Strategies and Structures

1. Malcolm X starts many of his paragraphs with the first person pronoun "I." What effect does this have on the essay, and what does it suggest about the results of education?

2. Malcolm X concludes paragraph 11 by writing *"In fact, up to then, I never had been so truly free in my life,"* referring to his ability to read. How does this concluding statement sum up the value of a homemade, personally tailored education as opposed to the rigid learning methods often used in schools?

3. What transitions lead the reader from one step in Malcolm X's educational process to the next?

4. What phrases does Malcolm X use to keep his writing conversational? Which phrases does he use to suggest he is educated? What is the effect of balancing these two styles? What does it suggest about the author's personality?

Language and Vocabulary

1. Vocabulary: *articulate, hustler, emulate, riffling, inevitable, bunk.* As Malcolm X did, write down the entire dictionary definitions of the aforementioned words and bring them with you to your group activity.

2. In paragraph 2, Malcolm X suggests that slang cannot be written. Brainstorm a list of your own slang. Why is slang more effective on the streets or among your peers than it is in an academic setting?

GROUP ACTIVITIES

1. Devise some homemade, as opposed to traditional, methods for learning the above vocabulary words. Also devise some homemade study techniques that you can use in your other classes.

2. Today there is much debate over the education of prisoners. How do you feel about this issue? Should prisoners be educated or simply be punished? In groups, prepare to debate both sides of this issue in a seminar situation.

WRITING ACTIVITIES

1. Write a process essay wherein you explain how to acquire and use common sense to resolve the majority of the problems you encounter in daily life. Make sure you present your material in clear, sequential steps.

2. Research a current educational program in a local prison. Describe the program in detail, answering such questions as who is involved, what are the benefits and problems, where does the program take place, when is a prisoner or instructor eligible for such a program, why is such a program in place, and how does the program work? Your job is to inform your readers about this program. (Your local research librarian can help you find out where to get such information.)

The Spider and the Wasp
ALEXANDER PETRUNKEVITCH

A Russian-born zoologist who came to the United States in his late twenties, Alexander Petrunkevitch became a renowned authority on spiders. In addition to translating Pushkin, a Russian poet, into English, he translated Byron, the English poet, into Russian. His other works include *Index Catalogue of Spiders of North, Central and South America* (1911), *Choice and Responsibility* (1947), and *Principles of Classification* (1952). In the following essay, Petrunkevitch uses *informational* process analysis to explain a natural process in nature.

PRE-READING QUESTIONS

1. Cluster the word spider. What do you associate with them? How much of what you believe about spiders is based on fact?

2. Freewrite for five minutes, jotting down anything the word wasp brings to mind. Are the associations you make with wasps more positive than spiders? Why/Why not?

1   To hold its own in the struggle for existence, every species of animal must have a regular source of food, and if it happens to live on other animals, its survival may be very delicately balanced. The hunter cannot exist without the hunted; if the latter should perish from the earth, the former would, too. When the hunted also prey on some of the hunters, the matter may become complicated.

2   This is nowhere better illustrated than in the insect world. Think of the complexity of a situation such as the following: There is a certain wasp, *Pimpla inquisitor,* whose larvae feed on the larvae of the tussock moth. *Pimpla* larvae in turn serve as food for the larvae of a second wasp, and the latter in their turn nourish still a third wasp. What subtle balance between fertility and mortality must exist in the case of each of these four species

to prevent the extinction of all of them! An excess of mortality over fertility in a single member of the group would ultimately wipe out all four.

3　This is not a unique case. The two great orders of insects, Hymenoptera and Diptera, are full of such examples of interrelationship. And the spiders (which are not insects but members of a separate order of arthropods) also are killers and victims of insects.

4　The picture is complicated by the fact that those species which are carnivorous in the larval stage have to be provided with animal food by a vegetarian mother. The survival of the young depends on the mother's correct choice of a food which she does not eat herself.

5　In the feeding and safeguarding of their progeny the insects and spiders exhibit some interesting analogies to reasoning and some crass examples of blind instinct. The case I propose to describe here is that of the tarantula spiders and their arch-enemy, the digger wasps of the genus *Pepsis*. It is a classic example of what looks like intelligence pitted against instinct—a strange situation in which the victim, though fully able to defend itself, submits unwittingly to its destruction.

6　Most tarantulas live in the Tropics, but several species occur in the temperate zone and a few are common in the southern U.S. Some varieties are large and have powerful fangs with which they can inflict a deep wound. These formidable-looking spiders do not, however, attack man; you can hold one in your hand, if you are gentle, without being bitten. Their bite is dangerous only to insects and small mammals such as mice; for a man it is no worse than a hornet's sting.

7　Tarantulas customarily live in deep cylindrical burrows, from which they emerge at dusk and into which they retire at dawn. Mature males wander about after dark in search of females and occasionally stray into houses. After mating, the male dies in a few weeks, but a female lives much longer and can mate several years in succession. In a Paris museum is a tropical specimen which is said to have been living in captivity for 25 years.

8　A fertilized female tarantula lays from 200 to 400 eggs at a time; thus it is possible for a single tarantula to produce several thousand young. She takes no care of them beyond weaving a cocoon of silk to enclose the eggs. After they hatch, the young walk away, find convenient places in which to dig their burrows and spend the rest of their lives in solitude. Tarantulas feed mostly on insects and millipedes. Once their appetite is appeased, they digest the food for several days before eating again. Their sight is poor, being limited to sensing a change in the intensity of light and to the perception of moving objects. They apparently have little or no sense of hearing, for a hungry tarantula will pay no attention to a loudly chirping cricket placed in its cage unless the insect happens to touch one of its legs.

9   But all spiders, and especially hairy ones, have an extremely delicate sense of touch. Laboratory experiments prove that tarantulas can distinguish three types of touch: pressure against the body wall, stroking of the body hair, and riffling of certain very fine hairs on the legs called trichobothria. Pressure against the body, by a finger or the end of a pencil, causes the tarantula to move off slowly for a short distance. The touch excites no defensive response unless the approach is from above, where the spider can see the motion, in which case it rises on its hind legs, lifts its front legs, opens its fangs and holds this threatening posture as long as the object continues to move. When the motion stops, the spider drops back to the ground, remains quiet for a few seconds, and then moves slowly away.

10   The entire body of a tarantula, especially its legs, is thickly clothed with hair. Some of it is short and woolly, some long and stiff. Touching this body hair produces one of two distinct reactions. When the spider is hungry, it responds with an immediate and swift attack. At the touch of a cricket's antennae the tarantula seizes the insect so swiftly that a motion picture taken at the rate of 64 frames per second shows only the result not the process of capture. But when the spider is not hungry, the stimulation of its hair merely causes it to shake the touched limb. An insect can walk under its hairy belly unharmed.

11   The trichobothria, very fine hairs growing from dislike membranes of the legs, were once thought to be the spider's hearing organs, but we now know that they have nothing to do with sound. They are sensitive only to air movement. A light breeze makes them vibrate slowly without disturbing the common hair. When one blows gently on the trichobothria, the tarantula reacts with a quick jerk of its four front legs. If

the front and hind legs are stimulated at the same time, the spider makes a sudden jump. This reaction is quite independent of the state of its appetite.

12   These three tactile responses—to pressure on the body wall, to moving of the common hair, and to flexing of the trichobothria—are so different from one another that there is no possibility of confusing them. They serve the tarantula adequately for most of its needs and enable it to avoid most annoyances and dangers. But they fail the spider completely when it meets its deadly enemy, the digger wasp *Pepsis*.

13   These solitary wasps are beautiful and formidable creatures. Most species are either a deep shiny blue all over, or deep blue with rusty wings. The largest have a wing span of about four inches. They live on nectar. When excited, they give off a pungent odor—a warning that they are ready to attack. The sting is much worse than that of a bee or common wasp, and the pain and swelling last longer. In the adult stage the wasp lives only a few months. The female produces but a few eggs, one at a time at intervals of two or three days. For each egg the mother must provide one adult tarantula, alive but paralyzed. The tarantula must be of the correct species to nourish the larva. The mother wasp attaches the egg to the paralyzed spider's abdomen. Upon hatching from the egg, the larva is many hundreds of times smaller than its living but helpless victim. It eats no other food and drinks no water. By the time it has finished its single gargantuan meal and become ready for wasphood, nothing remains of the tarantula but its indigestible chitinous skeleton.

14   The mother wasp goes tarantula-hunting when the egg in her ovary is almost ready to be laid. Flying low over the ground late on a sunny afternoon, the wasp looks for its victim or for the mouth of a tarantula burrow, a round hole edged by a bit of silk. The sex of the spider makes no difference, but the mother is highly discriminating as to species. Each species of *Pepsis* requires a certain species of tarantula, and the wasp will not attack the wrong species. In a cage with a tarantula which is not its normal prey the wasp avoids the spider, and is usually killed by it in the night.

15   Yet when a wasp finds the correct species, it is the other way about. To identify the species the wasp apparently must explore

the spider with her antennae. The tarantula shows an amazing tolerance to this exploration. The wasp crawls under it and walks over it without evoking any hostile response. The molestation is so great and so persistent that the tarantula often rises on all eight legs, as if it were on stilts. It may stand this way for several minutes. Meanwhile the wasp, having satisfied itself that the victim is of the right species, moves off a few inches to dig the spider's grave. Working vigorously with legs and jaws, it excavates a hole 8 to 10 inches deep with a diameter slightly larger than the spider's girth. Now and again the wasp pops out of the hole to make sure that the spider is still there.

16   When the grave is finished, the wasp returns to the tarantula to complete her ghastly enterprise. First she feels it all over once more with her antennae. Then her behavior becomes more aggressive. She bends her abdomen, protruding her sting, and searches for the soft membrane at the point where the spider's leg joins its body—the only spot where she can penetrate the horny skeleton. From time to time, as the exasperated spider slowly shifts ground, the wasp turns on her back and slides along with the aid of her wings, trying to get under the tarantula for a shot at the vital spot. During all this maneuvering, which can last for several minutes, the tarantula makes no move to save itself. Finally the wasp corners it against some obstruction and grasps one of its legs in her powerful jaws. Now at last the harassed spider tries a desperate but vain defense. The two contestants roll over and over on the ground. It is a terrifying sight and the outcome is always the same. The wasp finally manages to thrust her sting into the soft spot and holds it there for a few seconds while she pumps in the poison. Almost immediately the tarantula falls paralyzed on its back. Its legs stop twitching; its heart stops beating. Yet it is not dead, as is shown by the fact that if taken from the wasp it can be restored to some sensitivity by being kept in a moist chamber for several months.

17   After paralyzing the tarantula, the wasp cleans herself by dragging her body along the ground and rubbing her feet, sucks the drop of blood oozing from the wound in the spider's abdomen, then grabs a leg of the flabby, helpless animal in her jaws and drags it down to the bottom of the grave. She stays there for many minutes, sometimes for several hours, and what

she does all that time in the dark we do not know. Eventually she lays her egg and attaches it to the side of the spider's abdomen with a sticky secretion. Then she emerges, fills the grave with soil carried bit by bit in her jaws, and finally tramples the ground all around to hide any trace of the grave from prowlers. Then she flies away, leaving her descendant safely started in life.

18   In all this the behavior of the wasp evidently is qualitatively different from that of the spider. The wasp acts like an intelligent animal. This is not to say that instinct plays no part or that she reasons as man does. But her actions are to the point; they are not automatic and can be modified to fit the situation. We do not know for certain how she identifies the tarantula—probably it is by some olfactory or chemo-tactile sense—but she does it purposefully and does not blindly tackle a wrong species.

19   On the other hand, the tarantula's behavior shows only confusion. Evidently the wasp's pawing gives it no pleasure, for it tries to move away. That the wasp is not simulating sexual stimulation is certain, because male and female tarantulas react in the same way to its advances. That the spider is not anesthetized by some odorless secretion is easily shown by blowing lightly at the tarantula and making it jump suddenly. What, then, makes the tarantula behave as stupidly as it does?

20   No clear, simple answer is available. Possibly the stimulation by the wasp's antennae is masked by a heavier pressure on the spider's body, so that it reacts as when prodded by a pencil. But the explanation may be much more complex. Initiative in attack is not in the nature of tarantulas; most species fight only when cornered so that escape is impossible. Their inherited patterns of behavior apparently prompt them to avoid problems rather than attack them. For example, spiders always weave their webs in three dimensions, and when a spider finds that there is insufficient space to attach certain threads in the third dimension, it leaves the place and seeks another, instead of finishing the web in a single plane. This urge to escape seems to arise under all circumstances, in all phases of life, and to take the place of reasoning. For a spider to change the pattern of its web is as impossible as for an inexperienced man to build a bridge across a chasm obstructing his way.

21   In a way the instinctive urge to escape is not only easier but more efficient than reasoning. The tarantula does exactly what is most efficient in all cases except in an encounter with a ruthless and determined attacker dependent for the existence of her own species on killing as many tarantulas as she can lay eggs. Perhaps in this case the spider follows its usual pattern of trying to escape, instead of seizing and killing the wasp, because it is not aware of its danger. In any case, the survival of the tarantula species as a whole is protected by the fact that the spider is much more fertile than the wasp.

POST-READING QUESTIONS

Content

1. Where do most tarantulas live? How long do some of them live?

2. What particular quality do all spiders, *especially* hairy ones, have in common?

3. Why do spiders always weave their webs in three dimensions? What happens when a spider finds it cannot complete its web in three dimensions?

4. Why is it important for the *Pepsis* wasp to explore the tarantula with its antennae? Why do you imagine the tarantula seems to allow the wasp's molestation?

Strategies and Structures

1. How does Petrunkevitch get the reader involved in this essay? How does he make his material understandable to readers without an extensive science background?

2. The first few paragraphs describe the living patterns and habits of tarantulas, including the number of eggs a female usually lays. What purpose does this serve?

3. What strategy does Petrunkevitch's discussion of how the tarantula has "*three tactile responses —to pressure on*

the body wall, to moving of the common hair, and to flexing of the trichobothria —" serve?

4. How do Petrunkevitch's examples vividly illustrate the natural process he is describing? Which examples did you find particularly memorable? Why?

Language and Vocabulary

1. Vocabulary: *progeny, archenemy, formidable, cylindrical, burrows, trichobothria, antennae, membranes, tactile, Gargantuan, chitinous, abdomen, molestation, penetrate, exasperated, maneuvering, secretion, prowlers, descendant, qualitatively, olfactory, chemo-tactile, simulating, anesthetized, chasm, instinctive.* Many of these words are scientific, but the others can be used in everyday conversation or writing. Make a list of the words that fall into each category. Several of these words also suggest aggression. Which words are they? Compose one or two paragraphs about an aggressive act using each of the words you chose at least twice.

2. Petrunkevitch relates the process of the *Pepsis* wasp killing a tarantula in a detached, matter-of-fact manner. Why is this method of relating information particularly appropriate for this *informational* process analysis?

GROUP ACTIVITIES

1. Get into groups and brainstorm: What parallels can you make between the fate of the tarantula in the jaws of the *Pepsis* wasp and people whose lives are in the hands of other people in the world today? Be prepared to share your findings with the rest of the class.

2. Pair off with another class member. One of you assume the role of the wasp (the tormenter) and the other the tarantula (the victim), but translate this to human terms. Create a life-and-death situation where one acts contrary to natural instinct (the tarantula)

and the other acts as intelligence dictates (the wasp). Remember to react just as the insect would.

WRITING ACTIVITIES

1. Using nontechnical language, write an essay describing a natural process you have read about or witnessed (e.g., how a volcano is formed or how a bee hive is made).

2. After listening to the many parallels your classmates made between the *Pepsis* wasp/tarantula relationship and different people (social, economic, or ethnic groups), select one in particular and write a process essay showing how one group—surprising as it is— submits to the other's mistreatment.

Additional Topics and Issues for Process Analysis Essays

1. Compose a process paper explaining how to make work easier. Begin by limiting your focus a bit so your reader has a pretty good idea of what you mean by work (e.g., physical labor or mental labor). Then explain your "how to" process, illustrating each step with specific examples.

2. Write an informative process analysis explaining how you would raise a child compared with how you were raised. What would be the advantages to your method of child rearing? Why do you think your parents raised you the way they did?

3. Making sure that you develop each discussion point, write an essay explaining one of the following:

(a.) How to enjoy studying and still be popular

(b.) How to earn A's without studying

(c.) How to embarrass your friends in public and still maintain your dignity

(d.) How to research your family roots or chart a family tree

4. Write a *directive* process analysis explaining how you would overhaul our present educational system (either high school or college). What can parents, teachers, and students do?

5. What sorts of things have you witnessed in your life that you consider meaningful and important? Select one particular incident, such as your graduation from high school or wedding day, and trace the process you went through from start to finish.

6. Write a paper explaining how you learned to sing, dance, or play a musical instrument or tell someone else how to do it.

7

COMPARISON AND CONTRAST

We compare and contrast every day of our lives, so much so that some psychologists believe that it is our most elemental thinking strategy. When we compare, we look at the similarities between two or more things. When we contrast, we look at the differences between them. Think about a trip to the grocery store. What types of things do we compare and contrast as we shop? We may contrast the prices of two items. We may compare and contrast the quality of items. We may compare the usefulness of items. When we write, we often compare and contrast also. In school, we may compare and contrast two different points of view on a topic. At work, we may write a report comparing and contrasting two competitors.

Successful writers know that when we compare and contrast, the most important step is gathering as much information as possible about the two items or ideas being compared and contrasted. Many of the prewriting strategies mentioned in the opening chapter on writing can help you gather the necessary information. One way that is most effective is to make a similarities list and a differences list: First, list all the similarities between the two items or ideas; next, list all the differences between them.

After a writer has gathered enough information and begins to write, he or she will often clearly introduce the items or ideas to be analyzed in the opening paragraph. For example, Suzanne Britt in "Neat People vs. Sloppy People," introduces her topic in the opening sentence of her essay, *"I've finally figured out the difference between neat people and sloppy people."*

Many writers chose to use thesis statements. For instance, in Michael Meyer's essay "The Myth of German Unity," he states his thesis at the end of the first paragraph: *"The new Germany will be one nation, but two peoples."* Such a statement creates a framework for the reader—a specific focus—and unifies the ideas that follow.

Developing Essays Using Comparison and Contrast

How one structures a comparison/contrast essay depends on the intended audience (reader), the subject matter, and an author's purpose for writing. There are two basic methods for organizing comparison and contrast essays: the *point-by-point method* and the *block method.*

In the point-by-point method, the author considers one point of comparison or contrast at a time, analyzing the two subjects in alternate sentences or paragraphs. In "The Tapestry of Friendship," Ellen Goodman frequently uses sentence by sentence comparison/contrast: *"Well, she thought, on the whole, men had buddies, while women had friends. Buddies bonded, but friends loved. Buddies faced adversity together, but friends faced each other."* On the other hand, Nassery uses the point-by-point method to compare specific items or issues in alternating paragraphs. An outline of the body of M. Daud Nassery's essay "Afghan and American Education" would look like this:

1. School Subjects
   a. Afghan subjects
   b. American subjects
2. Examinations
   a. American exams
   b. Afghan exams

3. Grades and rewards
   a. American system
   b. Afghan system

In the block method, the author first analyzes one item or idea completely and then analyzes the second item or idea, being sure to compare and contrast the same points in the same order as the first. If we were to rearrange Nassery's essay into the block method, it would look like this:

1. Afghan Education
   a. subjects
   b. exams
   c. grades and rewards
2. American Education
   a. subjects
   b. exams
   c. grades and rewards

Many, if not most, essays do not strictly follow either of these patterns. An author may mix and blend strategies as he or she feels necessary to give the reader a clear explanation of the topics. For example, notice how Andrew Lam mixes both methods in "They Shut My Grandmother's Room Door" where the first part of his composition is primarily block and the latter part tends to develop his material using the point-by-point method. Regardless of what strategy you use, remember that comparing and contrasting people, places, and things is a means to an end (proving or supporting a thesis)—not an end in itself.

Tips on Writing Comparison and Contrast Essays

1. Select topics that offer a clear basis for comparison and contrast. That is, make sure your items for comparison are closely enough related to make a meaningful analysis. (Avoid comparing *apples with oranges.*)

2. Use an effective prewriting activity to gather as much information as possible, keeping in mind that you are looking for similarities and differences.

3. Write a thesis statement that clearly explains whether you will be analyzing differences and/or similarities and that introduces the two items or ideas of your essay.

4. Decide on a clear organizational pattern for your essay, either the point-by-point method, the block method, or a blend of the two patterns.

5. As you edit, be sure that you compared and contrasted the same points for each item or idea, preferably in the same order.

They Shut My Grandmother's Room Door
ANDREW LAM

A Vietnamese immigrant who currently resides in San Francisco, writer Andrew Lam is the associate editor for the Pacific News Service. His articles have appeared in *Nation, Mother Jones,* and *The Washington Post.*

PRE-READING QUESTIONS

1. What holidays, customs, or rituals do you associate with death?

2. Answer this question before reading the following essay: Where do you imagine you'll end up in your old age? (Write your answer in your notebook.)

1   When someone died in the convalescent home where my grandmother lives, the nurses rush to close all the patients' doors. Though as a policy death is not to be seen at the home,

she can always tell when it visits. The series of doors being slammed shut remind her of the firecrackers during Tet.

2   The nurses' efforts to shield death are more comical to my grandmother than reassuring. "Those old ladies die so often," she quips in Vietnamese, "everyday's like new year."

3   Still, it is lonely to die in such a place. I imagine some wasted old body under a white sheet being carted silently through the empty corridor on its way to the morgue. While in America a person may be born surrounded by loved ones, in old age one is often left to take the last leg of life's journey alone.

4   Perhaps that is why my grandmother talks now mainly of her hometown, Bac-Lieu; its river and green rich rice fields. Having lost everything during the war, she can now offer me only her distant memories: Life was not disjointed back home; one lived in a gentle rhythm with the land; people died in their homes surrounded by neighbors and relatives. And no one shut your door.

5   So it goes. The once gentle, connected world of the past is but the language of dreams. In this fast-paced society of disjointed lives, we are swept along and have little time left for spiritual comfort. Instead of relying on neighbors and relatives, on the river and land, we deal with the language of materialism: overtime, escrow, stress, down payment, credit cards, tax shelter. Instead of going to the temple to pray for good health we pay life and health insurance religiously.

6   My grandmother's children and grandchildren share a certain pang of guilt. After a stroke which paralyzed her, we could no longer keep her at home. And although we visit her regularly, we are not living up to the filial piety standard expected of us in the old country. My father silently grieves and my mother suffers from headaches. (Does she see herself in such a home in a decade or two?)

7   Once, a long time ago, living in Vietnam we used to stare death in the face. The war in many ways had heightened our sensibilities toward living and dying. I can still hear the wails of widows and grieving mothers. Though the fear of death and dying is a universal one, the Vietnamese did not hide from it. Instead we dwelt in its tragedy. Death pervaded our poems, novels, fairy tales and songs.

8   But if agony and pain are part of Vietnamese culture, pleasure is at the center of America's culture. While Vietnamese

holidays are based on death anniversaries, birthdays are celebrated here. American popular culture translates death with something like nauseating humor. People laugh and scream at blood and guts movies. The wealthy freeze their dead relatives in liquid nitrogen. Cemeteries are places of big business, complete with colorful brochures. I hear there are even drive-by funerals where you don't have to get out of your own car to pay your respects to the deceased.

9   That America relies upon the pleasure principle and happy endings in its entertainments does not, however, assist us in evading suffering. The reality of the suffering of old age is apparent in the convalescent home. There is an old man, once an accomplished concert pianist, now rendered helpless by arthritis. Every morning he sits staring at the piano. One feeble woman who outlived her children keeps repeating, "My son will take me home." Then there are those mindless, bedridden bodies kept alive through a series of tubes and pulsating machines.

10   But despair is not newsworthy. Death itself must be embellished or satirized or deep-frozen in order to catch the public's attention.

11   Last week on her 82 birthday I went to see my grandmother. She smiled her sweet sad smile.

12   "Where will you end up in your old age?" she asked me, her mind as sharp as ever.

13   The memories of monsoon rain and tropical sun and relatives and friends came to mind. Not here, not here, I wanted to tell her. But the soft moaning of a patient next door and the smell of alcohol wafting from the sterile corridor brought me back to reality.

14   "Anywhere is fine," I told her instead, trying to keep up with her courageous spirit. "All I am asking for is that they don't shut my door."

POST-READING QUESTIONS

Content

1. What does the door symbolize in Lam's essay?
2. How is *the grandmother's* life in America different than in Vietnam? Why?

3. What are the most striking differences between American and Vietnamese culture presented in this essay?

4. How do people deal with their fear of death?

Strategies and Structures

1. In what way do Lam's first and last paragraphs "frame" the real point of this composition? What image appears in both paragraphs and how does it function as a unifying device?

2. Where does Lam gather information to illustrate his essay?

3. Reread this article omitting the initial sentence in each paragraph. How does the essay's clarity and meaning change? What does this suggest to us about the importance of opening sentences?

4. What specific examples does the author provide to illustrate his ideas? How is the comparison and contrast strengthened by his use of specific examples? What is the overall effect?

Language and Vocabulary

1. Vocabulary: *convalescent, morgue, disjointed, pang, filial, pervaded, liquid nitrogen, arthritis, monsoon.* Many of the words in this list deal with suffering and death. Using the antonyms (see glossary) to those words, write a short paragraph or two dealing with Lam's subject. Does the meaning change? What does this suggest to you about proper word selection for your essays?

2. Lam frequently makes use of alliteration (see glossary) in this composition. Why might a writer use alliteration? What is the effect of such phrases as "last leg of life's journey," "rich rice fields," and "wails of widows"? What other examples of alliteration can you find in his essay?

GROUP ACTIVITIES

1. Get into groups and compare and contrast your responses to the prereading question: "Where are you going to be when you are old?" Has reading this essay changed your response? In what way did reading this essay sharpen your focus on where you want to be when you are old?

2. Brainstorm different ways that one can take care of an elderly relative. What are the advantages and disadvantages to each solution? What are the benefits and problems of each solution?

WRITING ACTIVITIES

1. Compare and contrast how you plan to take care of your parents as opposed to Lam's description of American practices today. Comparison and contrast should be used here as the means of explaining your points as effectively as possible. Be sure to use specific examples.

2. Model an essay after Lam's composition, using the introductory and closing paragraphs as a framing device. Write a comparative paper for or against placing elderly people in rest homes. As you compare, you should make sure that your position on the issue is clear; however, make sure that you carefully consider both sides of the issue prior to making your conclusion.

Neat People vs. Sloppy People
SUZANNE BRITT

A journalist and essayist, Suzanne Britt's articles have appeared in a wide range of news magazines, journals, and papers: the *Dickens Dispatch, Newsweek,* the Des Moines *Register* and *Tribune,* the *Baltimore Sun, Newsday,* and the *New York Times.* Her books include *Skinny People Are Dull and Crunchy Like Carrots* (1982) and *Show and Tell* (1983). As Britt said in the preface to *A Writer's Rhetoric* (1988), "Competent writers are imitators; compelling writers are original." The following essay illustrates how one's natural voice can be a "compelling" rhetorical tool.

PRE-READING QUESTIONS

1. What negative things do you associate with neatness?
2. What are some positive qualities you associate with sloppiness?

1   I've finally figured out the difference between neat people and sloppy people. The distinction is, as always, moral. Neat people are lazier and meaner than sloppy people.

2   Sloppy people, you see, are not really sloppy. Their sloppiness is merely the unfortunate consequence of their extreme moral rectitude. Sloppy people carry in their mind's eye a heavenly vision, a precise plan, that is so stupendous, so perfect, it can't be achieved in this world or the next.

3   Sloppy people live in Never-Never Land. Someday is their métier. Someday they are planning to alphabetize all their books and set up home catalogues. Someday they will go through their wardrobes and mark certain items for tentative mending and certain items for passing on to relatives of similar shape and size. Someday sloppy people will make family scrapbooks into which they will put newspaper clippings, postcards, locks of hair, and the fried corsage from their senior prom. Someday they will file everything on the surface of their desks, including the cash receipts from coffee purchases at the

snack shop. Someday they will sit down and read all the back issues of *The New Yorker*.

4   For all these noble reasons and more, sloppy people never get neat. They aim too high and wide. They save everything, planning someday to file, order, and straighten out the world. But while these ambitious plans take clearer and clearer shape in their heads, the books spill from the shelves onto the floor, the clothes pile up in the hamper and closet, the family mementos accumulate in every drawer, the surface of the desk is buried under mounds of paper and the unread magazines threaten to reach the ceiling.

5   Sloppy people can't bear to part with anything. They give loving attention to every detail. When sloppy people say they're going to tackle the surface of the desk, they really mean it. Not a paper will go unturned; not a rubber band will go unboxed. Four hours or two weeks into the excavation, the desk looks exactly the same, primarily because the sloppy person is meticulously creating new piles of papers with new headings and scrupulously stopping to read all the old book catalogs before he throws them away. A neat person would just bulldoze the desk.

6   Neat people are bums and clods at heart. They have cavalier attitudes toward possessions, including family heirlooms. Everything is just another dust-catcher to them. If anything collects dust, it's got to go and that's that. Neat people will toy with the idea of throwing the children out of the house just to cut down on the clutter.

7   Neat people don't care about process. They like results. What they want to do is get the whole thing over with so they can sit down and watch the rasslin' on TV. Neat people operate on two unvarying principles: Never handle any item twice, and throw everything away.

8   The only thing messy in a neat person's house is the trash can. The minute something comes to a neat person's hand, he will look at it, try to decide if it has immediate use and, finding none, throw it in the trash.

9   Neat people are especially vicious with mail. They never go through their mail unless they are standing directly over a trash can. If the trash can is beside the mailbox, even better. All ads, catalogs, pleas for charitable contributions, church bulletins

and money-saving coupons go straight into the trash can without being opened. All letters from home, postcards from Europe, bills and paychecks are opened, immediately responded
to, then dropped in the trash can. Neat people keep their receipts only for tax purposes. That's it. No sentimental salvaging
of birthday cards or the last letter a dying relative ever wrote.
Into the trash it goes.

10   Neat people place neatness above everything, even economics. They are incredibly wasteful. Neat people throw away
several toys every time they walk through the den. I knew a
neat person once who threw away a perfectly good dish
drainer because it had mold on it. The drainer was too much
trouble to wash. And neat people sell their furniture when
they move. They will sell a La-Z-Boy recliner while you are
reclining in it.

11   Neat people are no good to borrow from. Neat people buy
everything in expensive little single portions. They get their
flour and sugar in two-pound bags. They wouldn't consider
clipping a coupon, saving a leftover, reusing plastic non-dairy
whipped cream containers or rinsing off tin foil and draping it
over the unmoldy dish drainer. You can never borrow a neat
person's newspaper to see what's playing at the movies. Neat
people have the paper all wadded up and in the trash by 7:05
A.M.

12   Neat people cut a clean swath through the organic as well as
the inorganic world. People, animals, and things are all one to
them. They are so insensitive. After they've finished with the
pantry, the medicine cabinet, and the attic, they will throw out
the red geranium (too many leaves), sell the dog (too many fleas),
and send the children off to boarding school (too many scuff-
marks on the hardwood floors).

POST-READING QUESTIONS

Content

1. What is the point of this essay? Upon what do you
   base your conclusions?
2. Why does Britt compare neat people with sloppy
   people?

3. What group of people does Britt identify with? How do you know for sure?

4. Why are neat people poor people from whom to borrow things?

5. What impact do Britt's generalizations have on her essay as a whole? Why does she dwell on extreme notions of neatness and sloppiness?

Strategies and Structures

1. What is the tone or mood of Britt's essay, and what is the function of humor?

2. Explain the effect of opening several consecutive paragraphs with the same phrase?

3. How could such liberal use of generalizations be deadly in the hands of an inexperienced writer? Do generalizations undermine the quality of Britt's essay? Justify your opinion.

4. Why does Britt focus on contrasts—differences—rather than mention things that neat and sloppy people have in common?

Language and Vocabulary

1. Vocabulary: *rectitude, distinction, stupendous, metier, mementos, excavation, meticulously, scrupulously, organic.* Write down a synonym—a word that has the same (or nearly the same) meaning as another word—for as many of the vocabulary words as you can. When you are finished or can't think of any more words, find a synonym for the unknown words by asking your classmates; likewise, share your work with others.

2. When Britt writes about people, places, or things that are opposite in nature, she often reinforces this sense of opposition through her word choice. Go back over the essay and make a list of words

associated with neatness and words associated with sloppiness.

GROUP ACTIVITIES

1. Rent the Neil Simon film, *The Odd Couple,* and watch it in a relaxing environment (there is no need to take notes). After the film, discuss the extent to which Oscar Madison (the sloppy character) and Felix Unger (the neat character) illustrate the theme of Britt's essay. Also, talk about the parts of the film you could refer to if you were using it to exemplify a point about neat and sloppy people. In part, this activity is an exercise in learning how to use your observations to your best advantage when you write. What you see can be valuable information!

2. For a group project, locate a copy of one of Britt's best known essays, "That Lean and Hungry Look." Compare the techniques she employs in this essay when contrasting fat and thin people to those used when she contrasts neat and sloppy people in "Neat People vs. Sloppy People." What patterns exist in her writing style? How are they identifiable?

WRITING ACTIVITIES

1. Using a mixture of humor and seriousness similar to Suzanne Britt's, write an essay comparing and contrasting two people, places or things to demonstrate the stupidity and/or reliability of stereotypes.

2. Write an essay in which you try to rigidly categorize two types of people, (e.g., young/old, rich/poor, coordinated/awkward), and thereby illustrate a controlling idea or thesis on the nature of stereotypes.

The Tapestry of Friendship
ELLEN GOODMAN

Ellen Goodman is a popular syndicated columnist for such newspapers as the *Washington Post* and *Boston Globe*. A collection of her best essays *appears* in the best-selling *Close to Home* (1979). Other works include *At Large* (1981), and *Keeping in Touch* (1985). Besides writing, Goodman has been a commentator for the NBC *Today Show*.

PRE-READING QUESTIONS

1. Answer the following questions before reading the essay: Who do you feel make better friends—men or women? Why? What are the differences between men as friends and women as friends?

2. Cluster the word *friend*. What associations, images, or emotions do you attach to the word? Cluster the word *buddy*. What associations, images, or emotions do you attach to the word? Write a short paragraph in which you compare/contrast the two words.

1   It was, in many ways, a slight movie. Nothing actually happened. There was no big-budget chase scene, no bloody shootout. The story ended without any cosmic conclusions.

2   Yet she found Claudia Weill's film *Girlfriends* gentle and affecting. Slowly, it panned across the tapestry of friendship— showing its fragility, its resiliency, its role as the connecting tissue between the lives of two young women.

3   When it was over, she thought about the movies she'd seen this year—*Julia, The Turning Point* and now *Girlfriends*. It seemed that the peculiar eye, the social lens of the cinema, had drastically shifted its focus. Suddenly the Male Buddy movies had been replaced by the Female Friendship flicks.

4   This wasn't just another binge of trendiness, but a kind of *cinéma vérité*. For once the movies were reflecting a shift, not

just from men to women but from one definition of friendship to another.

5   Across millions of miles of celluloid, the ideal of friendship had always been male—a world of sidekicks and "pardners," of Butch Cassidys and Sundance Kids. There had been something almost atavistic about these visions of attachments—as if producers culled their plots from some pop anthropology book on male bonding. Movies portrayed the idea that only men, those direct descendants of hunters and Hemingways, inherited a primal capacity for friendship. In contrast, they portrayed women picking on each other, the way they once picked berries.

6   Well, that duality must have been mortally wounded in some shootout at the You're OK, I'm OK Corral. Now, on the screen, they were at least aware of the subtle distinction between men and women as buddies and friends.

7   About 150 years ago, Coleridge had written, "A woman's friendship borders more closely on love than man's. Men affect each other in the reflection of noble or friendly acts, whilst women ask fewer proofs and more signs and expressions of attachment."

8   Well, she thought, on the whole, men had buddies, while women had friends. Buddies bonded, but friends loved. Buddies faced adversity together, but friends faced each other. There was something palpably different in the way they spent their time. Buddies seemed to "do" things together; friends simply "were" together.

9   Buddies came linked, like accessories, to one activity or another. People have golf buddies and business buddies, college buddies and club buddies. Men often keep their buddies in these categories, while women keep a special category for friends.

10   A man once told her that men weren't real buddies until they'd been "through the wars" together—corporate or athletic or military. They had to soldier together, he said. Women, on the other hand, didn't count themselves as friends until they'd shared three loathsome confidences.

11   Buddies hang tough together; friends hang onto each other.

12   It probably had something to do with pride. You don't show off to a friend; you show need. Buddies try to keep the worst from each other; friends confess it.

13   A friend of hers once telephoned her lover, just to find out if he were home. She hung up without a hello when he picked up the phone. Later, wretched with embarrassment, the friend moaned, "Can you believe me? A thirty-five-year-old lawyer, making a chicken call?" Together they laughed and made it better.

14   Buddies seek approval. But friends seek acceptance.

15   She knew so many men who had been trained in restraint, afraid of each other's judgment or awkward with each other's affection. She wasn't sure which. Like buddies in the movies, they would die for each other, but never hug each other.

16   She'd reread *Babbitt* recently, that extraordinary catalogue of male grievances. The only relationship that gave meaning to the claustrophobic life of George Babbitt had been with Paul Riesling. But not once in the tragedy of their lives had one been able to say to the other: You make a difference.

17   Even now men shocked her at times with their description of friendship. Does this one have a best friend? "Why, of course, we see each other every February." Does that one call his most intimate pal long distance? "Why, certainly, whenever there's a real reason." Do those two old chums ever have dinner together? "You mean alone? Without our wives?"

18   Yet, things were changing. The ideal of intimacy wasn't this parallel playmate, this teammate, this trenchmate. Not even in Hollywood. In the double standard of friendship, for once the female version was becoming accepted as the general ideal.

19   After all, a buddy is a fine life-companion. But one's friends, as Santayana once wrote, "are that part of the race with which one can be human."

POST-READING QUESTIONS

Content

1. Whom is Goodman comparing in this essay? What relationships is she comparing?

2. According to Goodman, who make better friends, men or women? Who make better buddies? Why?

3. What are the differences between friends and buddies? Why are there these differences?

4. What kind of relationship does Goodman prefer? Why does she prefer it over the other? Is she critical of the other type of relationship?

Strategies and Structures

1. Goodman starts her essay by alluding to some films her friend had seen and how they signaled a change in her definition of friendship. Why do you think Goodman starts her essay this way? What are the advantages to starting your essay with a personal recollection?

2. What is Goodman's thesis statement? What is the purpose of the thesis? Why did she place the thesis after her personal recollection?

3. Which sentences act as topic sentences throughout her essay? How does she develop each topic sentence? Does she provide specific examples or generalizations based on her experience or both? What are the different effects?

4. In what way does Goodman's conclusion do more that summarize her ideas? How does quoting Santayana strengthen her argument? (Who is Santayana and what subjects were common topics for his books?)

Language and Vocabulary

1. Vocabulary: *fragility, resiliency, binge, atavistic, primal, claustrophobic, intimacy, acceptance.* Divide the vocabulary into two groups: adjectives and nouns. Then, look up the words in your dictionary, find the different forms of each word, and finally change nouns to adjectives and adjectives to nouns.

2. Many of the words and phrases in Goodman's essay come from the world of film-making. Identify some of them. Why are the allusions to Hollywood films effective? What is the purpose of the references to the different films and the world of Hollywood? Why might these be effective allusions?

GROUP ACTIVITIES

1. Goodman mentions several films in her essay. As a group watch two films: one that portrays male friendship and one that portrays female friendship. Goodman suggests some titles; your teacher can supply others. Before viewing the films, list the characteristics of friends and then those of buddies (see activity 2, below). As you watch the films, note how many of the characteristics on your lists are illustrated in the different relationships shared by men and women. Then your group should analyze the films using Goodman's description of "buddies" and "friends." Is Goodman's analysis correct? Are men "buddies" and women "friends?" Afterwards, write a collaborative position paper in which you either agree or disagree with Goodman's assessment of male vs. female friendships.

2. As a group, using your answers to Pre-Reading Question 2, you should come up with your own definition of friends and buddies. Then provide examples from your lives to illustrate your ideas. You may want to divide two pieces of paper in half. First on one sheet of paper, write the characteristics of friends in one column and then in the next column list your examples. Next, on the other piece of paper, write the characteristics of buddies in one column and then in the next column list your examples.

WRITING ASSIGNMENTS

1. Write a paper in which you contrast a buddy with a friend of yours. Be sure to follow a clear pattern of organization, either the block or point-by-point method. Provide specific examples to illustrate your thesis and supporting points.

2. Write an essay in which you compare and contrast the definition of "friendship" in your parents' or grandparents' generation with the definition of

"friendship" in your generation. Don't rely on stereotypes. If possible, interview your parents or grandparents, research writers' definitions of friendship in their generation, and gather examples from films that were popular during their youths.

Afghani and American Education
M. DAUD NASSERY

In the following piece, M. Daud Nassery uses the strategy of comparison and contrast to discuss his experiences with Afghani and American educational systems. Based on Al Santoli's interview of Nassery, this excerpt was taken from Santoli's book entitled *New Americans: An Oral History.*

PRE-READING QUESTIONS

1. Do a freewriting about American education. What associations, memories, opinions, and ideas do you have about American education?

2. Write a brief sketch of your previous educational experiences (1 to 2 pages of freewriting). You may want to answer some of the following questions as you write. What classes did you take? Which were easiest and which most difficult? What were the teachers like? What was expected of you? What kinds of tests did you take? What were the other students like? What were their expectations? What did they want to learn?

1   When I left high school in Afghanistan, I was in the middle of my junior year. At Nauset High, I was placed in the senior class. I was confident that I wouldn't have any difficulty with English, because I had taken language classes in Kabul. But

people were talking so fast, I couldn't understand the English accent. And my vocabulary was limited. For a few months, I had a terrible time. I forced myself to listen carefully.

2   In my country it was required to take seventeen different subjects during junior year. Every one was compulsory, including geography, history, geology, literature, chemistry, religion, trigonometry, and others. If you failed one, you failed the whole year.

3   I found the American school system to be much easier—only a few compulsory subjects like English, physical education, and American history. When I registered at Nauset High, I had to go through a list of subjects that my counselor gave me. I picked out fifteen or sixteen subjects. The principal was amazed. He thought that I was kidding. I said, "This is the way that we do it in my country. The schedule is staggered so that we can take many courses."

4   The principal said, "Even if you are capable of taking that many courses, our curriculum couldn't fit you into our time-table." So I cut it down to five or six subjects, including advanced biology. There were only four Americans in the class, and one of them dropped out. In calculus, also, there were only three of us.

5   The examinations system is easier here, too—the multiple-choice questions. Even if you read through the textbook once, it's easy to get a passing grade. Afghanistan's system is like that of the French. You have to memorize a thick book, and for the exam you write a long essay. If you were tired and missed a few pages of the text, or didn't have time to read them, you could fail the test and consequently the whole term.

6   My second semester here, after my English improved, I made the honor role. I became a member of the National Honor Society. The advanced biology course was a tough one—I got a C+ in the first semester. So the next semester, when they gave me the Honor Society membership card, I was surprised. I doubted myself and thought that I didn't deserve it. I learned that the American system is very fair. In Afghanistan, you can be an excellent student all through the year, but the final examination can break you. I liked school in America, because there wasn't that much pressure and students have a wider choice of subjects that they could enjoy.

POST-READING QUESTIONS

Content

1. Why did M. Daud Nassery feel he would have no problems with English once he reached America? What problems did he encounter? How did he deal with his problems?

2. How do American and Afghan educational practices differ? What practices do they have in common?

3. What does Nassery feel makes the American examination process easier? Why is it easy to answer these types of questions as compared to the type he had in Afghanistan? Do you agree with Nassery? Why or why not?

4. Why is he surprised to be admitted to the Honors Society? What were his initial reactions?

5. What does Nassery appreciate about the American system? Do you share his beliefs? If not, where do you differ and why?

Strategies and Structures

1. What strategy does Nassery use to contrast American vs. Afghan education: the point-by-point method or the block method? What are the advantages to his method?

2. How does he make his comparison/contrast vivid? What specifics and examples does he provide?

3. Where does Nassery gather his material to compare and contrast? What other sources might he have used?

4. In the last paragraph, Nassery makes an evaluation. Why is the concluding paragraph an appropriate place for an evaluation? What advantages are there to placing his opinion in the last paragraph?

Language and Vocabulary

1. Nassery uses many words relating to education: *compulsory, curriculum, multiple-choice questions, term,*

semester, Honor Society, geography, geology, chemistry, trigonometry, biology, history, religion, physical education. If you are unfamiliar with any of these terms, look them up in your dictionary and write your own definition of them. Otherwise, group as many of the words as you can into specific categories (e.g., types of classes).

2. Nassery uses relatively simple vocabulary words. Why do you imagine simple words dominate his essay? (Consider his past and his intended audience.) What are the advantages and disadvantages to using simple vocabulary?

GROUP ACTIVITIES

1. As a group, discuss the advantages and disadvantages of Afgahan educational practices. First, clearly establish what those practices are by carefully rereading Nassery's essay while taking notes. Next, make a list of the advantages, in your opinion, to those practices. Then, make a list of disadvantages, in your opinion, to those practices. Finally, as a group, write a paragraph stating which system you would prefer to be educated in. Be sure to give clear reasons for your choice.

2. Educational practices today differ from educational practices of the past. Your assignment is to explore the similarities and differences between the past and present. First each member of the group should interview either his or her parents or grandparents about educational practices in their day. (Before your interview, you may want to brainstorm a series of appropriate questions as a group.) Next you should do an individual freewriting on educational practices today; try to draw comparisons and contrasts with your parents' or grandparents' experiences. Finally, in groups, share your findings and then draw some general conclusions about the similarities and differences between the two different generations.

WRITING ACTIVITIES

1. Compose an essay in which you compare and/or contrast the American educational system with an educational system from another country. You may gather the needed information in several ways: interview someone who has been educated in another country, interview a teacher who has taught in another system, research another system in the library, and/or watch a documentary on another educational system. As you gather your information, take notes on the similarities and differences between the other system and the American educational system.

2. Write an essay in which you contrast high school with college, a city school with a country school, or a private school with a public school. What are the differences? What specific experiences have you had which illustrate these differences? Which educational system do you prefer and why do you prefer it?

The Myth of German Unity
MICHAEL MEYER

The year 1990 saw many political and economical changes in Eastern Europe. Besides free elections in many Eastern Block countries, the world witnessed East and West Germans tear down "the Wall" which had separated East and West Berlin for over three decades. In the following article written for and published in *Newsweek* on July 9, 1990, Michael Meyer offers a look at what we might expect from the reunification of East and West Germany.

PRE-READING QUESTIONS

1. How does a common name unite a group of people?
2. What cultural and political attitudes do you imagine you commonly share with people living in South

America, Central America, Mexico, or Canada? How
and why might your attitudes differ from theirs?

1   *"Wir sind ein Volk,"* they chanted in Dresden, Leipzig and
Berlin: we are one people. For more than a century, Germans
have subscribed to what George Kennan once called "romantic
linguistic nationalism"—a belief that a common tongue creates
a community. They have lived since the war in the conviction
that only an artificial border divides them. It is a myth. After
45 years, East and West Germans have grown apart. Now, as
they come together in pursuit of prosperity, the Germans are
ignoring a little secret. The new Germany will be one nation,
but two peoples.

2   The German Question has thus been reincarnated, in a new
form. The problem? The Federal Republic is prosperous, toler-
ant and solidly democratic. The German Democratic Republic
is impoverished, intolerant and undemocratic—a product of
oppression on the one hand and ideological conditioning on the
other. Now they will merge, but to become what? No one knows.
The new Germany will be as much an enigma for the Germans
as for the rest of us. An official at a prominent West German
think tank expresses a common sentiment. "I know the Americans, the British, the French," she says. "But the East Germans?
They are alien to me." A German diplomat in Berlin scoffs at
what he calls the Grand Illusion. "We've always talked of the
GDR as 'the other Germany'," he says. "But really, after so
many years of communism, [they] are more like Russians."

3   This is more than unification angst. Opinion surveys find
that a majority of West Germans think unification is going too
fast; many of the young and educated question whether it should
happen at all. Newspapers have launched "nationality" education
campaigns. Die Welt recently ran a series, "A Life in Germany:
How people in the GDR really live." Die Zeit notes that while
West German Deutsche is studded with trendy international
idioms, from "manager" to "high tech" to "bottom line," the German spoken across the Elbe is essentially unchanged from 50
years ago.

4   The soul-searching has a darker dimension. A Pakistani
businessman tells of twice being called a *Schwarze* on a short

visit to the East. An American reports being surrounded by East Berlin skinheads shouting *"Ausländer raus!"* "Xenophobia runs deep among East Germans," says Irene Runge, a sociologist in East Berlin. "We will not make very good democrats."

5   The East German longing for unity had more to do with economics than politics—with jobs and living standards. Cynics call it "Mercedes democracy." They have a point. For West Germans, the last 40 years have been a social as well as an economic miracle. Traditional "German" biases have broken down. "West Germans today are as European as they are German," says Elisabeth Noelle-Neuman, head of the Allensbach Research Institute. "We care about the Third World and the environment. We have a peace movement. We value opposing views." East Germany, by contrast, has seen no such evolution. "Decades of socialism have reinforced our worst traits," says Runge. "We East Germans are more respectful of authority, less flexible and less accepting of individual differences than we were before the war."

6   What does this mean? Possibly nothing. Perhaps Mercedes democracy will become genuine democracy under the weight of West German anschluss. But the Germans are more likely to create a hybrid—to try to mingle the "best" of both Germanys. Almost certainly, Germany will swing to the left. Three quarters of East Germans still believe the state should be responsible for their welfare. If their economic transition proves difficult, the social policies of a future Germany will surely reflect their views. The new Germany will remain within NATO. But is it coincidence that the soft diplomatic policies of East Berlin, with its emphasis on Pan-European security solutions, is suddenly finding a more forceful expression in Bonn?

7   That in itself might not be bad. More disturbing are the prospects for pluralism in a united Germany. The West German news magazine Der Spiegel recently devoted a cover to Helmut Kohl's *"Machtrausch"* (power drive). It pictured the chancellor hurtling down the autobahn in a sports car, his passenger (East German leader Lothan de Maizière) losing both his hat and his political equilibrium. The image sits uneasily with many West Germans, who feel as if unity were being conferred upon them from on high (in this case, Bonn) with little of the debate such a momentous event would ordinarily inspire. "Kohl tells us what

we must do, and we obey," says a sociologist in Bonn. "Suddenly, Germans are behaving as passively as we did in 1933."

8   No one contemplates the emergence of a Fourth Reich. But there is fear of a new cult of leadership. The concern is that unity will create a political vacuum. Bewildered by choices and the velocity of events, Germans may hanker for a commanding presence—especially before Western prosperity comes to the East. Democracy could deteriorate into a politics of personality as the driving force in the new Germany. That would be a step backward.

POST-READING QUESTIONS

Content

1. What is "The German Question"? How do the people living in East Germany differ significantly from those in West Germany? What conflicts could arise as a result of differences?

2. Explain Meyer's position regarding the real reason East Germany wanted to reunite with West Germany.

3. Why were some West Germans uncomfortable with Kohl's actions? Why should anyone care if Germans as a nation of people are behaving passively?

4. Though Meyer does not contemplate a "Fourth Reich," he expresses "fear of a new cult leadership." What is he ultimately afraid might happen?

Strategies and Structures

1. What is Meyer's thesis? Where does it appear in the essay? How do the topic sentences in each paragraph focus in on a particular aspect of his thesis: *"The new Germany will be one nation but two peoples"*?

2. What does the word unity suggest? How does the title of this essay, "The Myth of German Unity" prepare a reader for a discussion of contrasts?

3. Why is the strategy of comparison and contrast the most effective, natural rhetorical device for

developing this expository essay? Would it even be possible to write an essay with the same purpose (discussing the division between East and West Germany) without comparing and contrasting each group? Why? Why not?

4. In what order does Meyer structure examples as he compares and contrasts East and West Germans? (What does he talk about first? Second? Third?)

5. Why do you imagine Meyer begins his essay by quoting German citizens who said: *"Wir sind ein Volk"* (we are one people) if his intention is to disprove such a point?

Vocabulary

1. Vocabulary: *linguistic, nationalism, ideological, xenophobia, angst, socialism, pluralism, chancellor, enigma, equilibrium, Schwarze (black), Auslander (foreigner), raus, reich (rule), autobahn (freeway)*. Meyer uses many words which deal with government and society. Look for examples of each word in a newspaper or magazine this evening (e.g., an article about a socialist country), and with the help of your article, write about each word in your journal or writing log ("A good example of *nationalism* would be the move of Eastern Block countries towards independence and often democracy during 1990. . . .").

2. What is the effect of including German words in this essay? What does the author assume about his audience? What would this essay lose by removing the German words?

GROUP ACTIVITIES

1. German reunification occurred in 1990. In the years since this article first appeared in *Newsweek,* which of Meyer's concerns have become actual problems? As a group, spend an hour or so in the library and look through recent news magazines for any recent articles

dealing with the effects of a united Germany, and prepare an "update" for class discussion based on your findings.

2. Discuss personal instances of xenophobia (fear of outsiders/foreigners) with each other. *Why* did you fear other people? *What* exactly were you afraid of? *When* were your experiences with xenophobia most acute? *How* did those you feared react towards you; did they do things to strengthen your prejudices? As a result of readings and intense group discussion, what conclusions can you reach regarding those who have xenophobia?

WRITING ACTIVITIES

1. Write an essay comparing and contrasting two ethnic/cultural groups who share a common language in order to demonstrate a major point. Exactly what you have to say about the two cultures will provide you with a definite focus—a controlling idea— which will determine parts of your subject you need to compare and contrast to achieve your objective for writing your composition.

2. Contrast two generations of Americans who share a common government but have very different values or beliefs about what citizens owe the government and what the government owes its citizens. To narrow this topic a bit, limit your focus to a particular town or region in the United States. Make sure you qualify generalizations and support your observations with specific, representative examples.

Additional Topics and Issues for Comparison and Contrast Essays

1. Compare and contrast the most popular social activities in your parents' or grandparents' day to the most popular social activities of today.

2. Using the strategy of comparison and contrast, develop an essay in which you argue that one car, sport, movie star, sports hero (or team) is better than another.

3. Compare two very different magazines like *People* and *Time;* discuss their different characteristics (e.g., the sort of ads, amount of pictures, and choice of subjects). How does the intended audience for each magazine determine its characteristics?

4. Compare two places that you have visited (e.g., countries, restaurants, parks).

5. Contrast two likely candidates for public office in an upcoming election. Consider their qualifications for the office they seek. A variation of this assignment would be to compare dirty campaign tactics (which often ignore issues of public concern) to dignified ones.

6. Compare two characters in a novel, short story, or play you have read, or two people in a television show or movie you have seen.

7. Compare and contrast stereotypes between two cultures or between males and females for an ultimate purpose, determined by your thesis statement.

8. Write an essay in which you contrast the portrayal of a particular ethnic group on television and/or movies with your knowledge of and experiences with that particular culture.

9. Compare and contrast two sides of a current social issue in your community (e.g., banning some of the books in the library). Your strategy of comparison/contrast should ultimately lead your reader to a sound conclusion.

10. Compare and contrast countercultures or subcultures (surfers, hippies, beatniks, bikers, yuppies) in America from different eras. This topic may require a little bit of research, but most of your information can be gathered by talking to people who lived during different time periods.

8

DIVISION AND CLASSIFICATION

When we divide and classify, we take a large and complicated subject and break it into smaller parts more easily handled by the writer and more easily grasped by the reader. Sometimes the smaller parts, or categories, are readily apparent, but at other times, we must carefully analyze our larger subject in order to discover how it breaks apart. As with other strategies, division and classification can be seen and used in everyday life. For instance, your college is more than likely divided into schools, divisions, and/or departments. You probably have a School of Humanities which contains an art department, an English department, a humanities department, a speech and communication department, and a philosophy department.

When we write, we divide and classify in order to make a subject clear to the reader. We may hope that by clarifying an issue or subject like racism, our reader will be motivated to take some sort of action as Martin Luther King, Jr. does in his essay, "The Ways of Meeting Oppression." Or we may hope to bring to the forefront some forgotten points about a certain issue or subject as Gary Tewalestewa does in "American Indians: Homeless in Their Own Homeland." For whatever reason we divide and classify a subject, we usually follow a few basic steps.

When we start to divide and classify a subject, we need to clearly divide it into recognizable parts. We should analyze our subject from several points of view until we feel that we have found the clearest and most appropriate categories in which to break it. Obviously, Robertson Davies in his essay "A Few Kind Words About Superstition" carefully considered the many forms of superstition found in his community before he divided it into four forms: Vain Observances, Divination, Idolatry, and Improper Worship of a True God.

After you have carefully analyzed your subject and divided it into parts, it may help to create a rough outline or some other form of notes to help guide you as you write. A rough set of notes for Constance García-Barrio's essay "Creatures that Haunt the Americas" might look like this:

I. Creatures from Africa that stalk children

    Hairy Man

    guije

    Tunda

    deformed woman

II. Creatures from Africa that haunt adults

    Ciguapa

    Lobisón

    the ghost of the slave owner

As you write, you should feel free to revise or delete certain parts of your outline, but as a general rule, an outline will help keep you from wandering off the subject and into less important or irrelevant points.

As in most of your essays, use clear transitions to help guide your reader. Simple transitions such as *first, second,* and *third* can be very helpful. Often by simply keeping your points clearly separated (divided), you can write an essay that is easy to follow. For example, Norman Cousins in his essay "The Decline of Neatness" first discusses slovenly dress, then goes on to discuss crude speech, and finally discusses untidy emotions. He carefully separates one point from another until he unifies all three toward the end of his essay: *"Untidiness in dress, speech and emotions is readily connected to human relationships."*

After you have written your rough draft, you should go back over your essay and ask yourself if you have achieved your purpose. How do your categories help achieve your original goal—possibly to persuade your audience into a certain action or possibly to reveal a hidden truth about your subject? If a category does not ultimately contribute to your goal, you should delete it from your essay.

Tips on Writing Division and Classification Essays

1. Decide why you are classifying and dividing this subject. Keep this purpose in mind as you analyze your subject and compose your essay.

2. Carefully analyze your subject from many different points of view, looking for clear dividing lines.

3. Make some rough notes or an outline to help guide you during your writing. (Feel free to make alterations to your outline as necessary; it may be necessary to revise your outline several times.)

4. Use clear transitions to guide your reader and unify the parts of your essay.

5. Use controlling ideas and/or topic sentences to make your divisions clear. Then use specifics and details to help illustrate your divisions.

6. Carefully reread your rough draft looking for inappropriate and irrelevant points or categorizations and eliminate them.

The Ways of Meeting Oppression
MARTIN LUTHER KING, JR.

Martin Luther King, Jr. a Baptist minister and civil rights leader during the 1950s and 1960s, preached nonviolence when advocating civil disobedience. He was awarded the Nobel Peace Prize in 1964 and assassinated in Memphis, Tennessee, on April 14, 1968. The following extract was taken from his book *Stride Toward Freedom* (1958) and classifies ways people have historically reacted toward their oppressors.

PRE-READING QUESTIONS

1. What is oppression? What freedoms does an oppressor deny another person?
2. Have you ever been oppressed? What did you do to try and change the situation you were in? Was your method of overcoming oppression successful? How?

1   Oppressed people deal with their oppression in three characteristic ways. One way is acquiescence: the oppressed resign themselves to their doom. They tacitly adjust themselves to oppression, and thereby become conditioned to it. In every movement toward freedom some of the oppressed prefer to remain oppressed. Almost 2800 years ago Moses set out to lead the children of Israel from the slavery of Egypt to the freedom of the promised land. He soon discovered that slaves do not always welcome their deliverers. They become accustomed to being slaves. They would rather bear those ills they have, as Shakespeare pointed out, than flee to others that they know not of. They prefer the "fleshpots of Egypt" to the ordeals of emancipation.

2   There is such a thing as the freedom of exhaustion. Some people are so worn down by the yoke of oppression that they give up. A few years ago in the slum areas of Atlanta, a Negro guitarist used to sing almost daily: "Been down so long that down don't bother me." This is the type of negative freedom and resignation that often engulfs the life of the oppressed.

3   But this is not the way out. To accept passively an unjust system is to cooperate with that system; thereby the oppressed become as evil as the oppressor. Noncooperation with evil is as much a moral obligation as is cooperation with good. The oppressed must never allow the conscience of the oppressor to slumber. Religion reminds every man that he is his brother's keeper. To accept injustice or segregation passively is to say to the oppressor that his actions are morally right. It is a way of allowing his conscience to fall asleep. At this moment the oppressed fails to be his brother's keeper. So acquiescence—while often the easier way—is not the moral way. It is the way of the coward. The Negro cannot win the respect of his oppressor by acquiescing; he merely increases the oppressor's arrogance and contempt. Acquiescence is interpreted as proof of the Negro's inferiority. The Negro cannot win the respect of the white people of the South or the peoples of the world if he is willing to sell the future of his children for his personal and immediate comfort and safety.

4   A second way that oppressed people sometimes deal with oppression is to resort to physical violence and corroding hatred. Violence often brings about momentary results. Nations have frequently won their independence in battle. But in spite of temporary victories, violence never brings permanent peace. It solves no social problem; it merely creates new and more complicated ones.

5   Violence as a way of achieving racial justice is both impractical and immoral. It is impractical because it is a descending spiral ending in destruction for all. The old law of an eye for an eye leaves everybody blind. It is immoral because it seeks to humiliate the opponent rather than win his understanding; it seeks to annihilate rather than to convert. Violence is immoral because it thrives on hatred rather than love. It destroys community and makes brotherhood impossible. It leaves society in monologue rather than dialogue. Violence ends by defeating itself. It creates bitterness in the survivors and brutality in the destroyers. A voice echoes through time saying to every potential Peter, "Put up your sword."* History is cluttered with the wreckage of nations that failed to follow this command.

6   If the American Negro and other victims of oppression succumb to the temptation of using violence in the struggle

for freedom, future generations will be the recipients of a desolate night of bitterness, and our chief legacy to them will be an endless reign of meaningless chaos. Violence is not the way.

7   The third way open to oppressed people in their quest for freedom is the way of nonviolent resistance. Like the synthesis in Hegelian philosophy, the principle of nonviolent resistance seeks to reconcile the truths of two opposites—the acquiescence and violence—while avoiding the extremes and immoralities of both. The nonviolent resister agrees with the person who acquiesces that one should not be physically aggressive toward his opponent; but he balances the equation by agreeing with the person of violence that evil must be resisted. He avoids the nonresistance of the former and the violent resistance of the latter. With nonviolent resistance, no individual or group need submit to any wrong, nor need anyone resort to violence in order to right a wrong.

8   It seems to me that this is the method that must guide the actions of the Negro in the present crisis in race relations. Through nonviolent resistance the Negro will be able to rise to the noble height of opposing the unjust system while loving the perpetrators of the system. The Negro must work passionately and unrelentingly for full stature as a citizen, but he must not use inferior methods to gain it. He must never come to terms with falsehood, malice, hate, or destruction.

9   Nonviolent resistance makes it possible for the Negro to remain in the South and struggle for his rights. The Negro's problem will not be solved by running away. He cannot listen to the glib suggestion of those who would urge him to migrate en masse to other sections of the country. By grasping his great opportunity in the South he can make a lasting contribution to the moral strength of the nation and set a sublime example of courage for generations yet unborn.

10   By nonviolent resistance, the Negro can also enlist all men of good will in his struggle for equality. The problem is not a purely racial one, with Negroes set against whites. In the end, it is not a struggle between people at all, but a tension between justice and injustice. Nonviolent resistance is not aimed against oppressors but against oppression. Under its banner consciences, not racial groups, are enlisted.

POST-READING QUESTIONS

Content

1. What are the three ways "oppressed people deal with their oppression"?

2. Why does King say some people prefer to remain oppressed? How do such people undermine the quest for equality and reinforce injustice?

3. Explain why King says that *"Violence as a way of achieving racial justice is both impractical and immoral."*

4. What are the advantages of nonviolent resistance over doing nothing or violence in order to cause change? How does King argue this point?

Strategies and Structures

1. How does King strategically use historical instances of oppressed people to illustrate each of the three ways of oppression?

2. In what way does King's division/classification of material help a reader to read, comprehend, and evaluate the merit of each type of resistance to oppression?

3. King presents the three ways of dealing with oppression (acquiescence, violence and non-violence) in a particular order. What would have happened if he had reversed or mixed his present sequence of material? What does your conclusion point out about the importance of organizing the parts of an essay?

Language and Vocabulary

1. Vocabulary: *acquiescence, tacitly, corroding, annihilate, desolate, synthesis, sublime.* Denotation is the dictionary definition of a word; connotations are the associated meaning of the word (see glossary). Reread through the first two ways of dealing with oppression, acquiescence, and violence, noting King's choice of vocabulary. Make a list of the words you encounter which

have negative connotations (e.g., acquiescence suggests giving-in, laziness). Then read through the last part of King's essay where he discusses non-violence (peaceful resistance), making a list of words that have positive connotations. Overall, how does King use "connotations" to win his readers over to his point of view?

2. King refers to African-Americans as negroes several times in his essay. How do such references in and similar references in other compositions indicate the time period when something was written? Why might knowledge of when something was written be of interest to a reader?

GROUP ACTIVITIES

1. Divide into three groups, review all content and strategy questions, and then study one way King mentions of resisting oppression in greater detail. Each group will be responsible for a different strategy for overcoming oppression. Your group will ultimately *teach* the section of King's essay dealing with the type of resistance your group studied to the rest of the class.

2. Go to your learning resource center on campus and locate some recordings or videotapes of King. In particular, search for his famous "I Have a Dream" speech. (After listening to his speech, you may also want to get a copy of it from the library and reread it). Discuss the impact King's speech had on group members, and then re-evaluate each of the ways of fighting oppression in view of his ultimate goal.

WRITING ACTIVITIES

1. Write an essay wherein you classify and divide one of the following topics in order to explain it: ways of making friends, ways of reacting to aggressive people, ways of influencing people with the language

that you use (e.g., big or dirty words), or ways of dealing with fame, racism, or sexism.

2. Leaving the method you agree with until last—like King structured his discussion of nonviolence when writing about ways to overcome oppression—write an essay explaining the ways people deal with *stress* or *depression*.

Creatures that Haunt the Americas
CONSTANCE GARCÍA-BARRIO

Constance García-Barrio is a widely published author, with articles appearing in such magazines and newspapers as *Essence* and *The Philadelphia Inquirer*. She speaks English, Spanish, and Chinese and has received her doctorate in Romance Languages. Currently, García-Barrio is writing a novel and teaching at West Chester University, West Chester, Pennsylvania.

PRE-READING QUESTIONS

1. What are some of the scary creatures, ghosts, and/or monsters that are common in the stories of your culture? When did you hear about these creatures? What do they do that makes them frightening?

2. Brainstorm the word haunt. What do you associate with the word haunt? What is its dictionary definition? What kinds of creatures do you think García-Barrio will be describing?

1   When Africans were forced into slaving ships, the creatures, invisible, slipped in with them. A witch's brew of supernatural beings, these were creatures remembered from stories from the homeland. When Africans reached the New World, the creatures stepped ashore with them.

2   The supernatural beings made their homes in the mountains, rivers, and forests of the Americas, wherever the Africans went. The Hairy Man, for example, has the run of Georgia's woods, according to a story told by a former slave from that state. The Hairy Man is a fat, ugly little man with more hair all over than hell has devilment. Tricky as he is hairy, he can shrink or swell at will. He's afraid of dogs and is most at home near rivers. The Hairy Man spends his time capturing careless children.

3   The guije seems to be a Caribbean cousin of the Hairy Man, the way the late Cuban centenarian Esteban Montejo tells it in *The Autobiography of a Runaway Slave.* The guijes, or jigues, are mischievous little black men who wear no clothes and live near rivers. Their heads are like a frog's. Black people have a natural tendency to see them, according to Montejo. Guijes pop out of the river to admire a señorita as she bathes, especially during Holy Week. The guijes are also known to carry off children.

4   The Tunda looms large in the folklore of Esmeraldas, a predominantly black province on the northern coast of Ecuador, notes Afro-Ecuadorian writer Adalberto Ortiz. Local legend has it that in the 1530s a ship whose cargo included twenty-three enslaved blacks was traveling from Panama to Peru. As it skirted Ecuador's northern coast, the ship struck a reef. In the confusion that followed, the Blacks scrambled from the vessel, swam ashore, and fought with Indians occupying the land.

5   After one especially fierce battle, dying Blacks and Indians moaned so much that the noise reached hell and disturbed the devil. He decided he'd have to exterminate both sides if he wanted peace and quiet. So the devil went to Esmeraldas disguised as an African prince, Macumba. But before he could carry out his plan, a lively, buxom Esmeraldeña caught his fancy. He married her and settled down, as much as the Devil can ever settle.

6   One of the creatures born from their union is the Tunda, a deformed black woman with huge lips and clubfoot. As a child of the devil, the Tunda can't have children, so she's taken to carrying off those of black folk in Esmeraldas. The Tunda can make herself look like a member of the potential victim's family. She lures people into the forest, then stuns them by breaking wind in their faces. After this they lose their will power and are easily led to her lair, usually a place in or near water.

7   Adalberto Ortiz mentioned that there are similarities between the Tunda, character in Afro-Colombian stories and the Quimbungo from Bantu folklore.

8   If some creatures pursue black children, others stalk adults. The Afro-Dominican Ciguapa is a gorgeous but strange being who lives in the island's forests. She comes out at night to steal food but is never caught since she escapes by jumping from tree to tree. Her beauty has won many hearts, but she uses her magic to destroy men. Wise to her ways, they try to avoid her. But she can fool them. The Ciguapa's feet are on backward, so they think she's going when she's coming.

9   Tales of the Lobisón, or Wolfman, made many an Afro-Uruguayan peasant cringe. Legend has it that every Friday night at midnight the seventh consecutive son in a family turns into an animal. This animal has a wolf's body and a misshapen pig's head. It commits acts too horrible to tell. It has great supernatural powers, and only by wounding the Lobisón and drawing its blood can it be made to return to human form.

10   The old and new worlds blend in the Lobisón legend. The story shows the influence of Bantu, European, and certain South American Indian cultures.

11   Some tales of the supernatural arose from historic events in which Blacks took part. Such was the case with Spanish America's struggle for independence from Spain from 1810 to 1822. One Afro-Uruguayan story tells of a rich but miserly man who treated his slaves cruelly. Emancipated before the wars of independence, the newly freed Blacks demanded money with which to start a new life. They knew their former master had gold nuggets hidden in the house. When he refused to give them anything, they killed him.

12   The money remained hidden after the murder until a platoon of Black soldiers camped near the old house during the wars of independence. The location of the treasure was revealed to them by the ghost of a Black who had remained with the master even after emancipation. The soldiers divided the cache, each receiving a nice sum. The ghost had waited years but finally saw that his black countrymen got the money.

13   Like the ghost who showed the soldiers the treasure, black folk-tales bring to light sometimes forgotten cultural treasures Africans brought to the Americas.

POST-READING QUESTIONS

Content

1. Where do the creatures that García-Barrio describes originate? How did they get here?

2. García-Barrio describes the actions of these creatures. What are some actions or deeds common to them all? What do these common elements suggest about the creatures?

3. Why did the devil decide to exterminate the "Blacks and Indians"? What happened to him on his way to exterminate them? What creature was the end result of the devil's actions?

4. García-Barrio claims "*As a child of the devil, the Tunda can't have children . . . .*" What characteristics do you associate with the devil and his offspring? How might these characteristics prevent them from having children?

Strategies and Structures

1. What is the thesis of this essay? Is it stated directly or implied? What is the purpose of the opening paragraph?

2. García-Barrio writes vivid descriptions of the different creatures which "haunt the Americas." What are some of the images she uses to create vivid physical descriptions? What is the purpose of these vivid descriptions?

3. How is this essay organized? What general categories do the different creatures fit into? Why might García-Barrio divide the essay in such a way?

4. What is the purpose of the last paragraph? Outside of summarizing the essay, what might be some of its other purposes?

Language and Vocabulary

1. García-Barrio uses many unfamiliar geographical place names: *Georgia's woods, Caribbean, Esmeraldas,*

Ecuador, Panama, Peru, Colombian, Uruguayan. Where are these different places located? What are the unique geographical characteristics of these regions? What make them particularly suitable to tales about frightening creatures?

2. García-Barrio uses the prefix *Afro-* before many words: *Afro-Colombian, Afro-Dominican, Afro-Uruguayan.* (1) Write a definition for the prefix *Afro-*. (2) Write a definition for each of the root words. (3) Write a definition for the word made when the prefix and roots are combined.

GROUP ACTIVITIES

1. In groups, discuss the following questions: Who usually passes on the stories of creatures such as ghosts or monsters? Who are these stories often told to? When are they often told? What are the purposes of such frightening folk tales about creatures? What is the function of such imaginative creatures in our culture? What specifics in the stories García-Barrio retells illustrate your ideas?

2. It has been suggested that stories about creatures and monsters are really imaginative representations of our individual and cultural fears. (1) What do the creatures in García-Barrio's essay suggest about the fears of their creators? In other words, what might their fears be? (2) Create a list of some of the creatures and monsters in the different cultures your group represents and then, next to each creature's name, list the fears it represents. (3) According to your analysis, what fears do most cultures have common? Why do we have these common fears?

WRITING ACTIVITIES

1. García-Barrio divides and classifies the creatures of African-Americans: those that haunt children, those that haunt adults, those that came to America from

Africa, and those that are a hybrid of African and European culture. Write an essay in which you classify the creatures and monsters of your own culture. First, brainstorm a list of creatures. Second, divide these creatures into general categories (e.g., creatures associated with holidays, creatures associated with certain regions, creatures associated with certain historical events). Finally, write your essay to clearly illustrate your division, using transitions and vivid descriptions.

2. Write an essay in which you explain the origin of a specific folk tale, ghost story, or myth from your culture. It may be useful to divide your topic into smaller units (paragraphs) as you develop your ideas.

A Few Kind Words for Superstition
ROBERTSON DAVIES

A novelist, playwright, and scholar, Robertson Davies remains one of Canada's best known authors. Novels *Fifth Business* (1970), *The Manticore* (1972), *World of Wonders* (1975), and *What's Bred in the Bone* (1985) are among the more than two dozen books Davies has to his credit.

PRE-READING QUESTIONS

1. What is a superstitious person? Do you consider yourself superstitious? Why? Why not?

2. If superstition is folly, why don't airplanes have a row 13? Why don't most business buildings have a floor 13 indicated on the elevator panel?

3. What part does superstition play in your daily life? What cultural roots lie behind your superstitions?

1   In grave discussions of "the renaissance of the irrational" in our time, superstition does not figure largely as a serious challenge to reason or science. Parapsychology, UFOs, miracle cures, transcendental meditation, and all the paths to instant enlightenment are condemned, but superstition is merely deplored. Is it because it has an unacknowledged hold on so many of us?

2   Few people will admit to being superstitious; it implies naiveté or ignorance. But I live in the middle of a large university, and I see superstition in its four manifestations, alive and flourishing among people who are indisputably rational and learned.

3   You did not know that superstition takes four forms? Theologians assure us that it does. First is what they call Vain Observances, such as not walking under a ladder, and that kind of thing. Yet I saw a deeply learned professor of anthropology, who had spilled some salt, throwing a pinch of it over his left shoulder; when I asked him why, he replied, with a wink, that it was "to hit the Devil in the eye." I did not question him further about his belief in the Devil: But I noticed that he did not smile until I asked him what he was doing.

4   The second form is Divination, or consulting oracles. Another learned professor I know, who would scorn to settle a problem by tossing a coin (which is a humble appeal to Fate to declare itself), told me quite seriously that he has resolved a matter related to university affairs by consulting the *I Ching.* And why not? There are thousands of people on this continent who appeal to the *I Ching,* and their general level of education seems to absolve them of superstition. Almost, but not quite. The *I Ching,* to the embarrassment of rationalists, often gives excellent advice.

5   The third form is Idolatry, and universities can show plenty of that. If you have ever supervised a large examination room, you know how many jujus, lucky coins, and other bringers of luck are placed on the desks of the candidates. Modest idolatry, but what else can you call it?

6   The fourth form is Improper Worship of the True God. A while ago, I learned that every day, for several days, a $2 bill (in Canada we have $2 bills, regarded by some people as unlucky) had been tucked under a candlestick on the altar of a college chapel. Investigation revealed that an engineering

student, worried about a girl, thought that bribery of the Deity might help. When I talked with him, he did not think he was pricing God cheap because he could afford no more. A reasonable argument, but perhaps God was proud that week, for the scientific oracle went against him.

7   Superstition seems to run, a submerged river of crude religion, below the surface of human consciousness. It has done so for as long as we have any chronicle of human behavior, and although I cannot prove it, I doubt if it is more prevalent today than it has always been. Superstition, the theologians tell us, comes from the Latin *supersisto,* meaning to stand in terror of the Deity. Most people keep their terror within bounds, but they cannot root it out, nor do they seem to want to do so.

8   The more the teaching of formal religion declines, or takes a sociological form, the less God appears to great numbers of people as a God of Love, resuming his older form of a watchful, minatory power, to be placated and cajoled. Superstition makes its appearance, apparently unbidden, very early in life, when children fear that stepping on cracks in the sidewalk will bring ill fortune. It may persist even among the greatly learned and devout, as in the case of Dr. Samuel Johnson, who felt it necessary to touch posts that he passed in the street. The psychoanalysts have their explanation, but calling a superstition a compulsion neurosis does not banish it.

9   Many superstitions are so widespread and so old that they must have risen from a depth of the human mind that is indifferent to race or creed. Orthodox Jews place a charm on their doorposts; so do (or did) the Chinese. Some peoples of Middle Europe believe that when a man sneezes, his soul, for that moment, is absent from his body, and they hasten to bless him, lest the soul be seized by the Devil. How did the Melanesians come by the same idea? Superstition seems to have a link with some body of belief that far antedates the religions we know—religions which have no place for such comforting little ceremonies and charities.

10   People who like disagreeable historical ceremonies recall that when Rome was in decline, superstition proliferated wildly, and that something of the same sort is happening in our Western world today. They point to the popularity of astrology, and it is true that sober newspapers that would scorn to deal in love philters carry astrology columns and the fashion magazines

count them among their most popular features. But when has astrology not been popular? No use saying science discredits it. When has the heart of man given a damn for science?

11   Superstition in general is linked to man's yearning to know his fate, and to have some hand in deciding it. When my mother was a child, she innocently joined her Roman Catholic friends in killing spiders on July 11, until she learned that this was done to ensure heavy rain the day following, the anniversary of the Battle of Boyne, when the Orangemen would hold their parade. I knew an Italian, a good scientist, who watched every morning before leaving his house, so that the first person he met would not be a priest or a nun, as this would certainly bring bad luck.

12   I am not one to stand aloof from the rest of humanity in this matter, for when I was a university student, a gypsy woman with a child in her arms used to appear every year at examination time, and ask a shilling of anyone who touched the Lucky Baby; that swarthy infant cost me four shillings altogether, and I never failed an examination. Of course, I did it merely for the joke—or so I thought then. Now, I am humbler.

POST-READING QUESTIONS

Content

1. What is the ultimate point of this essay? Where does Davies stand on the topic of superstition?

2. Why is "Vain Observances" an appropriate title for the author's first category of superstition? Name a few examples of "Vain Observances" that you can remember from your childhood.

3. Why will few people admit it if they are superstitious? What is superstition generally associated with?

4. How would referring to the *I Ching* (a Chinese book offering general advice on how to act) be similar to consulting an oracle?

Strategies and Structures

1. What kind of superstition do you feel is most common? In what order does Davies divide and classify

superstition? What does he talk about first? Second? Third? Fourth?

2. According to Davies, what are the four divisions of superstition? Can you think of any other division he might have made?

3. In the final paragraph, Davies mentions how during examination week as a student, he'd spent a shilling to touch a Gypsy lady's lucky baby. Why?

4. Davies refers to the reaction of distinguished professors to exemplify the first two kinds of superstitions. Why might professors acting superstitiously be more effective and thought provoking than farmers acting superstitiously?

Language and Vocabulary

1. Vocabulary: *placated, cajoled, minatory, proliferated, philter.* One of the ways to better understand words and their meanings is to learn the origin of the word. Your dictionary is the first tool you should employ for this task. For instance, the word *expand,* which means to spread out or unfold, is listed as coming from Middle English *expanden,* which comes from the Latin word *expandere: ex-* out+*pandere* to spread. Trace the origins of the above words and use each in a sentence. If you can not find such explanations in your pocket dictionary, use an etymological dictionary (one that traces the origin and historical development of a word) that can be found in your school library.

2. List the words in your present vocabulary beginning with the prefix super-. What common meaning do all of these words share? How do the words on your list change meaning if you eliminate the prefix?

GROUP ACTIVITIES

1. Write down two superstitions that came to your mind while reading this essay. Now write down two other

superstitions which have their roots in your cultural origins. Next, break into groups and share your various superstitions. Which were most common? Did you find that many superstitions were universal? How? Finally, write a short collaborative essay whose thesis is based on your group's findings.

2. Interview several people one-on-one and as a group; your questions should focus on what the people say they believe and how they behave. You might also ask the people you interview for a sample of the kind of superstitions they grew up with. Have everyone who claims he or she does not believe in superstition to give you a definition of the word. What percentage of the people interviewed admitted they believed or reacted to some superstitions? Did group interviews differ significantly from one-on-one interviews? How? Why?

WRITING ACTIVITIES

1. Using some of the material gathered in group activity 2, write a thoroughly developed essay in which you divide and classify superstitious or folk beliefs.

2. Write an essay in which you defend the importance of superstition in American society. Make sure you cite several specific superstitions (other than the ones mentioned by Davies) and show how their presence often influences our actions.

American Indians: Homeless in Their Own Homeland
GARY TEWALESTEWA

Gary Tewalestewa, a member of the Alliance of Native Americans, wrote the
following article which originally appeared in *LE GENTE: DE AZTLAN* in
November of 1989. With the winter approaching, Tewalestewa takes a grim
look at what the changing seasons mean to thousands of Native Americans.

PRE-READING QUESTIONS

1. How do you feel about homeless people? What influences your attitudes? In your opinion, why are there so many homeless people in America?

2. In what way does independence differ from the confines of homelessness?

1   Where will the American Indian homeless go to avoid freezing to death this winter? Yes, that's right; it's hard for some people to believe, but it's true. There are a lot of American Indians who are homeless; as a matter of fact, 1 out of 18 homeless on skidrow is Indian (Testimony provided at the Los Angeles County Board of Supervisors Budget Hearings, June 5, 1988).

2   The American Indian Studies Center at the University of California at Los Angeles (UCLA) estimates that 90,000 of the country's American Indian population reside in Los Angeles. Through no fault of their own, more than half of those estimated 90,000 Indians living in Los Angeles are one paycheck away from becoming homeless—be it welfare, food rations, unemployment insurance, food stamps, Tribal benefits, or unemployment. Homelessness does not discriminate.

3   As programs continue to get cut and budgets of existing programs that target the general homeless population are slashed, groups of homeless Indians standing on street corners

grow. Many of these Indians are reluctant to take refuge from the elements mainly because they do not feel accepted.

4   Throughout history, the United States government has successfully isolated Indian people from the general population. Hence, a basic philosophical conflict exists between American Indians and the U.S. capitalist system. American Indian philosophy is based on a cooperative, spiritual, and communal way of life. The capitalist system, on the other hand, is based on accumulation of land wealth, mass profit, and individual competition. The goal of capitalist education for Indian people has always been that of total indoctrination into the American education system. American Indians have been taught that their communal ways are savage and anti-Christian. The worst lesson being taught to American Indians is to hate themselves. It becomes increasingly clear that the conflict existing between the two social systems is manifested in the classrooms, which can be said to have even more devastating results than struggles over land and resources. These two warring systems are the root of the increasing numbers of American Indians becoming homeless.

5   Despite all out efforts to destroy the identity and land base of the American Indian Population, Indian people have held on to their spiritual and cooperative cultural forms. A resurgence of Indian spirituality and sobriety is occurring throughout the land. But, Indian people maintain their "Walls of silence" and other cultural strategies in order to protect the little they have left.

6   Because there are so few service agencies for the homeless, this winter thousands of homeless people will be forced to compete against each other. A sort of "This is our turf! Keep away!" extortion atmosphere, comparable to the rival street gang dilemma, will intensify. Similar situations in the past have resulted in frustration and anger to those waiting in soup lines, and in many instances, fights break out and killings occur. Thus, battle lines are drawn and in many instances ethnic groupings are formed and intimidate other groups from entering "their territory" for a mere meal. Yet all have one condition in common, homelessness.

7   Despite the fact the American Indians are neglected in general and the condition worsens if they become homeless,

President Bush contends that he is taking care of the situation. The U.S. government has taken care of American Indians through the BIA relocation, forced sterilization, broken treaties, political isolation, and House and Senate bills which more often than not take away rights that protect them. Meanwhile, nuclear supplies are stockpiled and orbiting missiles are fueled which provide substantial profit.

8   American Indians are presently organizing throughout the United States. They see through the lies, tricks, and ploys of the capitalists. Their need for decent housing, education, nutritious food, real jobs, and programs that really work has steadily increased and the demand has not been met. The United States government and the Federal offices that oversee Indian affairs cannot afford to neglect the need of American Indians to live as they were meant to live. American Indians need to be Indian.

POST-READING QUESTIONS

Content

1. List some of the causes that contribute to the growing number of "homeless" Native-American Indians.

2. Explain the philosophical conflict between Native-American Indians and the capitalist system.

3. Why does Tewalestewa believe that many Native-American Indians feel like inferior members of American society? What Native-American "needs" have not been met by the United States Government?

4. Since this article was written, what headlines have you noticed in the news about the homeless population in America? What have you read about Native-Americans?

Strategies and Structures

1. What emotions does the author try to draw out of the reader with his essay's title: "American Indians: Homeless in Their Own Homeland"? What ultimate irony does Tewalestewa express?

2. How could we break down Tewalestewa's essay into four major parts?

3. How does the author use the word "capitalists" in his essay? Why does it create a sense of "us" and "them" (two categories of people).

Language and Vocabulary

1. Vocabulary: *reluctant, resurgence, relocation.* The prefix *re-* means back to; again. Jot down your understanding of each word's meaning. Then write down what you believe is the root of each word along with its meaning. Finally, write as many words as you can think of that use the prefix *re-,* bearing in mind its meaning.

2. In his second paragraph, Tewalestewa condenses the University of California at Los Angeles with an acronym: UCLA. Often, writers will use acronyms (a group of letters formed by taking the first letter of a compound term and writing them in succession) throughout their papers, but like Tewalestewa, by initially presenting what the capitalized letters represent—complete words—a writer is certain not to assume too much on the part of a reader. Write five sentences using references to businesses or schools followed by their acronyms in parenthesis (e.g., My mom attended the University of Santa Barbara (UCB).

GROUP ACTIVITIES

1. Compare your initial responses to the pre-reading questions with other members in your group. Then work through the post-reading questions together.

2. For a week, collect as many articles as you can find that deal with homeless people. In addition to weekly newspapers, have each group member responsible for looking up recent "Homeless People" articles in magazines like *Time, Newsweek,* and *U.S. News and*

World Report. You'll have 15 minutes in class to compare your materials. Then you will do a short individual writing assignment on the topic.

WRITING ACTIVITIES

1. Should Native-Americans expect and receive special privileges from the U.S. government? Construct a thesis based on your answer to this question, divide and classify your material, and develop it into a logically argued, well-supported essay.
2. Write an essay explaining how growing-up on a reservation—isolated from the rest of the real world— would be like aging in a concentration camp. (Consider the fact that after the American Indian tribes were conquered and placed on reservations, the U.S. government tried to "westernize" them, changing them *culturally* and *spiritually*.)

The Decline of Neatness
NORMAN COUSINS

A former executive editor for the *Saturday Review*, Norman Cousins wrote about important topics and issues affecting American Society and the world for over 45 years, including *Modern Man Is Obsolete* (1945) and *Anatomy of an Illness* (1979). He died in 1991.

PRE-READING QUESTIONS

1. Cluster the words *tidy* and *neat.* Do the two qualities have anything in common? If so, what?
2. What is the difference between individual expression and conformity? Are the two necessarily incompatible?

1   Anyone with a passion for hanging labels on people or things should have little difficulty in recognizing that an apt tag for our time is the Unkempt generation. I am not referring solely to college kids. The sloppiness virus has spread to all sectors of society. People go to all sorts of trouble and expense to look uncombed, unshaved, unpressed.

2   The symbol of the times is blue jeans—not just blue jeans in good condition but jeans that are frayed, torn, discolored. They don't get that way naturally. No one wants blue jeans that are crisply clean or spanking new. Manufacturers recognize a big market when they see it, and they compete with one another to offer jeans that are made to look as though they've just been discarded by clumsy house painters after ten years of wear. The more faded and seemingly ancient the garment, the higher the cost. Disheveled is in fashion; neatness is obsolete.

3   Nothing is wrong with comfortable clothing. It's just that current usage is more reflective of a slavish conformity than a desire for ease. No generation has strained harder than ours to affect a casual, relaxed, cool look; none has succeeded more spectacularly in looking as though it had been stamped out by cookie cutters. The attempt to avoid any appearance of being well groomed or even neat has a quality of desperation about it and suggests a calculated and phony deprivation. We shun conventionality, but we put on a uniform to do it. An appearance of alienation is the triumphant goal, to be pursued in oversize sweaters and muddy sneakers.

4   Slovenly speech comes off the same spool. Vocabulary, like blue jeans, is being drained of color and distinction. A complete sentence in everyday speech is as rare as a man's tie in the swank Polo Lounge of the Beverly Hills Hotel. People communicate in chopped-up phrases, relying on grunts and chants of "you know" or "I mean" to cover up a damnable incoherence. Neatness should be no less important in language than it is in dress. But spew and sprawl are taking over. The English language is one of the greatest sources of wealth in the world. In the midst of accessible riches, we are linguistic paupers.

5   Violence in language has become almost as casual as the possession of handguns. The curious notion has taken hold that emphasis in communicating is impossible without the incessant use of four-letter words. Some screenwriters openly admit that

they are careful not to turn in scripts that are devoid of foul language lest the classification office impose the curse of a G (general) rating. Motion-picture exhibitors have a strong preference for the R (restricted) rating, probably on the theory of forbidden fruit. Hence writers and producers have every incentive to employ tasteless language and gory scenes.

6   The effect is to foster attitudes of casualness toward violence and brutality not just in entertainment but in everyday life. People are not as uncomfortable as they ought to be about the glamorization of human hurt. The ability to react instinctively to suffering seems to be atrophying. Youngsters sit transfixed in front of television or motion-picture screens, munching popcorn while human beings are battered or mutilated. Nothing is more essential in education than respect for the frailty of human beings; nothing is more characteristic of the age than mindless violence.

7   Everything I have learned about the educational process convinces me that the notion that children can outgrow casual attitudes toward brutality is wrong. Count on it: if you saturate young minds with materials showing that human beings are fit subjects for debasement or dismembering, the result will be desensitization to everything that should produce revulsion or resistance. The first aim of education is to develop respect for life, just as the highest expression of civilization is the supreme tenderness that people are strong enough to feel and manifest toward one another. If society is breaking down, as it too often appears to be, it is not because we lack the brainpower to meet its demands but because our feelings are so dulled that we don't recognize we have a problem.

8   Untidiness in dress, speech and emotions is readily connected to human relationships. The problem with the casual sex so fashionable in films is not that it arouses lust but that it deadens feelings and annihilates privacy. The danger is not that sexual exploitation will create sex fiends but that it may spawn eunuchs. People who have the habit of seeing everything and doing anything run the risk of feeling nothing.

9   My purpose here is not to make a case for a Victorian decorum or for namby-pambyism. The argument is directed to bad dress, bad manners, bad speech, bad human relationships. The hope has to be that calculated sloppiness will run its course.

Who knows, perhaps some of the hip designers may discover they can make a fortune by creating fashions that are unfrayed and that grace the human form. Similarly, motion-picture and television producers and exhibitors may realize that a substantial audience exists for something more appealing to the human eye and spirit than the sight of a human being hurled through a storefront window or tossed off a penthouse terrace. There might even be a salutary response to films that dare to show people expressing genuine love and respect for one another in more convincing ways than anonymous clutching and thrashing about.

10   Finally, our schools might encourage the notion that few things are more rewarding than genuine creativity, whether in the clothes we wear, the way we communicate, the nurturing of human relationships, or how we locate the best in ourselves and put it to work.

POST-READING QUESTIONS

Content

1. What is Cousins concerned about? What is his thesis?

2. According to Cousins, what effects has the entertainment industry had on young children?

3. Why is the author alarmed by the "glamorization of human hurt?" What might this lead to?

4. What is an "untidy" relationship? Offer some examples from your own experience and discuss the extent to which your examples fit Cousins' definition.

5. The author concludes his assault on "untidiness" saying schools should encourage creativity in *"the clothes we wear, the way we communicate, the nurturing of human relationships, or how we locate the best in ourselves and put it to work."* While what he says seems to make sense, what are the implications of his call to action?

Strategies and Structures

1. How does Cousins divide and classify the different aspects of "untidiness" in this essay?

2. How does Cousins establish a relationship between neatness and language? What are the effects of slovenly language?

3. Why do you think Cousins waited until his ninth paragraph to point out that he is not saying people should dress and act like Victorians (overdress and be extremely formal)?

4. Is this essay directed at any particular audience? Does Cousins take steps to appeal to a broad range of readers? Explain.

Language and Vocabulary

1. Vocabulary: *unkempt, sector, untidy, disheveled, slavish, deprivation, slovenly, linguistic, incessant, atrophying, saturate, debasement, dismembering, desensitization, decline, revulsion, manifest, annihilates, eunuchs, decorum, namby-pambyism, unfrayed, hip, salutary, anonymous.* Which of the words above have a prefix meaning "not"? Why is the repetition of negative words appropriate to his essay? What type of meaning do most of the other vocabulary words carry?

2. Good writers are often good listeners. Spend ten minutes listening to the way people talk in the student union or cafeteria. What characteristics and patterns do you notice among your peers' speech? After listening to people talk, are you more or less inclined to agree with Cousins' view that we rely on "grunts and chants of 'you know' and 'I mean'" in place of colorful, expressive language?

GROUP ACTIVITIES

1. As a group, discuss the tone of "The Decline of Neatness." How does it differ from the tone of Suzanne Britt's essay, "Neat People vs. Sloppy People," on a related theme? Analyze how each author achieves his or her tone.

2. First, take an inventory of the clothes each group member is wearing. Then, compare notes on the sort of money everyone spent on movies last year. What type of films did most people see? Third, brainstorm the word "sensitivity" and put together a list of the five most important qualities in a sensitive person. How sensitive are individuals in your group? Finally, assess the validity of Cousins' essay based on your findings.

WRITING ACTIVITIES

1. Write an essay wherein you classify and divide your concept of sloppiness or "untidiness." Model your essay after Cousins', beginning with a catchy title. How you divide and classify your topic will largely depend on what you have to say about it. Therefore, spend some time prewriting and arrive at a specific controlling idea. Also, pull the divisions of your topic together in the final paragraph so your reader can consider everything you have said and supported in proper perspective.

2. Compare and contrast Norman Cousins' essay "The Decline of Neatness" to Suzanne Britt's essay called "Neat People vs. Sloppy People (p. 137). What is each author's attitude toward neatness and its ideal place in American Society?

Additional Topics and Issues for Division and Classification Essays

1. Divide and classify different kinds of relationships in order to gain a better insight into your own life.

2. Compose an essay in which you classify the different ways you have noticed yourself and have observed others deal with problems. (Some people, for instance, deal with problems by seeking solitude, others by confronting problems head-on, and still others by seeking advice from friends.)

3. After devising a thesis on the issue of racism, divide and classify the issue in order to develop each part of your topic thoroughly.

4. Compose an essay discussing the different types of fears a child might have which might affect his or her behavior. How do these fears change as one grows older—or do they?

5. Examine the different careers available to you, dividing them into distinct categories, and conclude your essay with the most likely profession you will pursue in your future.

6. Many people feel art is only decorative, but after careful analysis one can see that art serves many functions in American society. Write an essay in which you classify and divide the different uses of art in America.

7. We all speak and write in different ways, depending on the situation and audience. Write an essay examining a specific topic and discuss (1) how you would talk to your friends about your subject, (2) how you would inform a professor or government official about your topic, and (3) how you would compose a formal essay on it.

8. Discuss the subject majors available from your college or university. What are the characteristics of each major? What job opportunities can a student look forward to upon graduation?

9

CAUSE AND EFFECT

When we explain the causes and/or the effects of something, we are busy explaining *why* something occurs (cause) and/or *what* is the consequence of an action (effect). There are immediate and secondary (contributing) causes which lead to an effect, as well as immediate and long-range effects from an action. When our stomachs begin to make noises after going without food for two days, we can identify an immediate cause: hunger. However, more often than not, a string of causes leads to an ultimate effect. By the same token, a number of causes can lead to numerous effects—not just one.

Structuring Cause and Effect Essays

Usually, a writer will begin to develop a topic using the strategy of cause and effect by stating the effect(s) of something in a thesis paragraph and then examining the cause or multiple causes. For instance, in Carlos Bulosan's "Labor and Capital: the Coming Catastrophe," he cites the fattening of industrialists by profits, their investing profits in idle luxury, and quarrelling among themselves, and the causing of depression as reasons for discontent among the workers.

Sharon Curtin in her essay "Aging in the Land of the Young," demonstrates the second method of organizing a cause and effect essay. She focuses her discussion on the *effects* of growing old rather than the *causes*. For instance, she points out how "*The world becomes narrower as friends and family die or move away,*" and that she herself has "*A kind of cultural attitude,*" making her bigoted "*against old people.*" Similarly, Karen Ray structures her essay, "The Naked Face," by initially stating reasons why she does not wear make-up (her "nakedness is partly pragmatic and partly philosophical") and then explains the effects of wearing or not wearing make-up in society from a historical as well as a personal perspective.

In yet other instances, your essay may focus as much on the reasons why something occurs (the cause(s)) as the result (the effect(s)) of an action. For instance, Joaquin Murieta devotes as much time in "I Will Not Submit" explaining causes for his hatred of Americans as he spends on the results of it. Murieta and his family were mistreated by U.S. citizens, people he had formerly admired, and turning to crime is what he perceives as a justified response (effect) to the violence and injustice he encountered.

Regardless whether your essay moves from cause to effect(s), from effect to cause(s), or a fairly balanced combination of the two, your explanations should answer the question "why" something has happened.

Cause and Effect Fallacies

Post hoc ergo propter hoc: The post hoc fallacy deals with faulty cause and effect relationships, something you'll definitely want to avoid when writing any composition. Literally, the Latin phrase translates as: "It happened *after* this; therefore, it happened *because* of this." A good example of the post hoc fallacy would be a sentence like, "My sister won a million dollars last night because she found a lucky penny in the morning." In many instances, just because one event follows another does not produce a cause and effect relationship. Thus, in the case of the above sentence, the person could very well have found a penny and won a million dollars on the same day, but one (finding a penny) did not enable the other to occur (winning a million dollars).

Tips on Writing Cause and Effect Essays

1. While almost any essay may contain an element of causation, for the purpose of this essay, select a topic that can be best explained by focusing on causes and/or effects. A discussion of two cars, for instance, would be a poor choice for a cause and effect topic; this lends itself to comparison and contrast.

2. After you have selected a topic or issue, pre-write (cluster, freewrite, brainstorm, list) to determine the focus of your composition. Will you initially mention causes and devote the majority of your composition to a discussion of the short-term and long-range effects of your topic? Or will you move from mentioning the results of an action to a discussion of its causes?

3. Check your work carefully for faulty cause and effect relationships. Never mistake coincidence as evidence of a valid cause and effect relationship.

4. Ask yourself questions like: What sort of evidence have I offered to prove what I say? Are my examples specific and compelling? Would my examples convince even the most doubtful reader? How much do I rely on my reader simply agreeing with what I say? And, most importantly, have I thoroughly addressed the question *why?*

Aging in the Land of the Young
SHARON CURTIN

Born and raised in Wyoming, Sharon Curtin has lived in many parts of the United States from New York to California. A former nurse, Curtin now spends most of her time writing and maintaining her small farm in Virginia. Her books include *Nobody Ever Died of Old Age* (1972).

PRE-READING QUESTIONS

1. Cluster the words "old age" or "aging." What sort of things do you associate with growing old?

2. Take a look at some advertisements in popular magazines and commercials on television; what do many of them suggest about growing old?

1   Old men, old women, almost 20 million of them. They constitute 10 percent of the total population, and the percentage is steadily growing. Some of them, like conspirators, walk all bent over, as if hiding some precocious secret, filled with self-protection. The body seems to gather itself around those vital parts, folding shoulders, arms, pelvis, like a fading rose. Watch and you see how fragile old people come to think they are.

2   Aging paints every action gray, lies heavy on every movement, imprisons every thought. It governs each decision with a ruthless and single-minded perversity. To age is to learn the feeling of no longer growing, of struggling to do old tasks, to remember familiar actions. The cells of the brain are destroyed with thousands of unfelt tiny strokes, little pockets of clotted blood wiping out memories and abilities without warning. The body seems slowly to give up, randomly stopping, sometimes starting again as if to torture and tease with the memory of lost strength. Hands become clumsy, frail transparencies, held together with knotted blue veins.

3   Sometimes it seems as if the distance between your feet and the floor were constantly changing, as if you were walking on shifting and not quite solid ground. One foot down, slowly, carefully force the foot forward. Sometimes you are a shuffler, not daring to lift your feet from the uncertain earth but forced to slide hesitantly forward in little whispering movements. Sometimes you are able to "step out," but this effort—in fact the pure exhilaration of easy movement—soon exhausts you.

4   The world becomes narrower as friends and family die or move away. To climb stairs, to ride in a car, to walk to the corner, to talk on the telephone; each action seems to take away from the energy needed to stay alive. Everything is limited by

the strength you hoard greedily. Your needs decrease, you require less food, less sleep, and finally less human contact; yet this little bit becomes more and more difficult. You fear that one day you will be reduced to the simple acts of breathing and taking nourishment. This is the ultimate stage you dread, the period of helplessness and hopelessness, when independence will be over.

5   There is nothing to prepare you for the experience of growing old. Living is a process, an irreversible progression toward old age and eventual death. You see men of eighty still vital and straight as oaks; you see men of fifty reduced to gray shadows in the human landscape. The cellular clock differs for each one of us, and is profoundly affected by our own life experiences, our heredity, and perhaps most important, by the concepts of aging encountered in society and in oneself.

6   The aged live with enforced leisure, on fixed incomes, subject to many chronic illnesses, and most of their money goes to keep a roof over their heads. They also live in a culture that worships youth.

7   A kind of cultural attitude makes me bigoted against old people; it makes me think young is best; it makes me treat old people like outcasts.

Hate that gray? Wash it away!

Wrinkle cream.

Monkey glands.

Face-lifting.

Look like a bride again.

Don't trust anyone over thirty.

I fear growing old.

Feel young again!

I am afraid of growing old—we're all afraid. In fact, the fear of growing old is so great that every aged person is an insult and a threat to society. They remind us of our own death, that our body won't always remain smooth and responsive, but will someday betray us by aging, wrinkling, faltering, failing. The ideal way to age would be to grow slowly invisible, gradually disappearing, without causing worry or discomfort to the young. In some ways that does happen. Sitting in a small park across from a nursing home one day, I noticed that the young mothers and their children gathered on one side, and the old people from the home on the other. Whenever a youngster would run over to the "wrong" side, chasing a ball or just trying to cover all the available space, the old people would lean forward and smile. But before any communication could be established, the mother would come over, murmuring embarrassed apologies, and take her child back to the "young" side.

9   Now is seemed to me that the children didn't feel any particular fear and the old people didn't seem too threatened by the children. The division of space was drawn by the mothers. And the mothers never looked at the old people who lined the other side of the park like so many pigeons perched on the benches. These well-dressed young matrons had a way of sliding their eyes over, around, through the old people, they never looked at them directly. The old people may as well have been invisible; they had no reality for the youngsters, who were not permitted to speak with them, and they offended the aesthetic eye of the mothers.

10   My early experiences were somewhat different; since I grew up in a small town, my childhood had more of a nineteenth-century flavor. I knew a lot of old people, and considered some of them my friends. There was no culturally defined way for me to "relate" to old people, except the rules of courtesy which applied to all adults. My grandparents were an integral and important part of the family and of the community. I sometimes have a dreadful fear that mine will be the last generation to know old people as friends, to have a sense of what growing old means, to respect and understand man's mortality and his courage in the face of death. Mine may be the last generation to have a sense of living history, of stories passed from generation to generation, of identity established by family history.

POST-READING QUESTIONS

Content

1. According to Curtin, what does it mean to "grow old"?

2. What cultural attitude causes Curtin to feel "bigoted against old people"? Where does she suggest her biases originated?

3. Why does the author believe the ideal way to age in American society *"would be to slowly grow invisible, gradually disappearing, without causing discomfort to the young"*?

4. Review the final paragraph of this essay; Curtin expresses fears the future generations may not know or appreciate old people like she did. What evidence in the text proves that her fears are well-grounded?

Strategies and Structures

1. Curtin devotes the first part of her essay towards explaining what it is like to grow older, points out how America "worships youth," and concludes with paragraphs detailing her innermost fears. What do you think is particularly effective about her organization of material?

2. The author feels it is important to have the ability to visualize what it is like to grow old. Why?

3. In addition to descriptions, the author makes frequent comparisons as she writes. How does blending more than one strategy of development serve the purpose of her essay?

Language and Vocabulary

1. Vocabulary: *conspirators, precocious, perversity, shuffler, cellular, aesthetic, integral, transparencies.* Write five sentences using a pair of the vocabulary words (one following the other). The first word will function as an adjective and the second a noun. As always, check the meaning of the word you are not familiar with.

2. Curtin carefully uses adjectives (modifying words) to create vivid images. Find four or five instances where you feel she uses adjectives quite effectively.

Explain why you feel her adjective use enriches the sense of her composition.

GROUP ACTIVITIES

1. Gather in groups and re-evaluate what Curtin claims in view of our growing multi-cultural society where some ethnic groups still revere elderly people and live in extended families. You may want to collect representative data and materials which indicate that the emphasis on youth continues to grow. Regardless of your stance, you will have to come to some conclusions based upon your data. Which attitude is strongest in America, and do second- and third-generation ethnic people tend to still revere elderly people or do they adopt the "American" point of view? Write a group essay showing which view of aging is dominant and the causes for it.

2. Have each group member prepare a list of questions and interview at least five people over the age of 50. You might begin by asking them how they feel about getting older in America and whether they feel that the emphasis is totally on youth. Statistics show that by the year 2020 there will be more people over the age of 50 than teenagers. What do the people you interview think about this? Do they think that their status in society will change as a result of their being the majority. Discuss your findings in your group. Have your feelings about the elderly changed since you began this assignment? Why and in what ways?

WRITING ACTIVITIES

1. Based on personal observations, experience, findings from your interviews, and readings, write an essay describing what you believe it is like or will be like to grow old in America.

2. Compose an essay which shows how the media often influence and shape our cultural attitudes towards

aging in general and how they have changed specific segments of our population in particular. In your essay demonstrate how the media affect and even control our judgments of the elderly.

The Naked Face
KAREN RAY

Karen Ray is a full-time writer whose articles, columns, and essays have appeared in many magazines and periodicals throughout the nation: *Glamour, Science Digest, Working Woman,* the *Christian Science Monitor,* and the *New York Times.* Ray's novels include *The Proposal* (1981) and *Family Portrait* (1983). Her third novel, *Murder by Witness,* will be published during the fall of 1991.

PRE-READING QUESTIONS

1. When do you feel "naked" or incomplete in front of other people? Why?
2. Do you like "beauty aides" such as make-up? Who determines what is and what is not beautiful?
3. What is the relationship between fashion and beauty?

1   From the neck up, I am a nudist.

2   No mascara for me. No eyeliner, no lipstick, no blush, no powder, foundation, eye shadow, highlighter, lip pencil or concealing stick.

3   My nakedness is partly pragmatic and partly philosophical. Just getting my eyes open in the morning is a feat. I have neither the will nor the ability to apply makeup when I can hardly see straight. At night, the most I can manage is brushing my teeth. I'm afraid that removing makeup would go the same way as scrubbing the sink and cleaning the oven. Also I rub my eyes

occasionally, which doesn't help the makeup. Neither does my baby daughter.

4   My philosophical reasons are less defined. I don't like the idea of having to put cosmetics on my face to appear in public. Many women who wear makeup every day don't look "themselves" without it. I remember running home one long ago Saturday morning to tell my mother that a strange lady had come out of the Johnsons' house and picked up their newspaper. Turned out Mrs. Johnson just hadn't gotten her "face" on yet that morning.

5   My college roommate wouldn't step out the door without her makeup. I've heard sad stories of women who didn't want their husbands to see them as they really are and a pathetic one about a husband who forbade his wife to be seen without makeup. (The latter marriage is no longer intact.)

6   Most people don't go this far. Women use cosmetics to hide imperfections, to accentuate good points, to add drama and to feel polished. Many women in fact look "better" with makeup though, of course, our idea of beauty is tremendously affected by fashion. There are probably millions of men who would look "better" wearing makeup, but I've never met a man who did.

7   Recently a major women's magazine placed various amounts of makeup on a hypothetical job applicant, then asked managers and personnel directors which face they would hire. It should come as no surprise that in a magazine whose major advertisers are cosmetics companies the woman with the naked face was not awarded the job.

8   It has not always been so. During the 19th century, unadorned innocence was the height of fashion. Intricate hairstyles and colors were out of fashion and lip coloring was thought to be downright vulgar. The Roman poet, Ovid, in his famous poem *Ars Amatoria (Art of Love)*, criticized Roman women for their excessive use of artifice. At various times Christian leaders have taught that makeup was sinful. A ridiculous attitude, but the opposite stand is equally absurd. To say, in one's mind if not with one's mouth, that a woman is not fully dressed without a full facial complement is crazy.

9   My friend Mary is manager in a technical area at a Fortune 100 company. Not long ago, she was in a business meeting when—in the middle of arguing an especially sticky point—a

male superior leaned over and asked, "Why don't you wear makeup?" When she recovered, Mary asked her questioner why he didn't wear makeup? The response, "Because I'm not a girl." Focus on makeup, whether the right amount for the job, the profession or the company, often seems to be just one more excuse for not taking women seriously in the work world. Much of the worry about makeup is really a worry about being accepted.

10   According to Fenja Gunn's recent history of cosmetics, *The Artificial Face,* makeup has been used throughout history to help create an everchanging ideal of beauty. Prehistoric body painting and tattooing began as pagan ritual, in part to camouflage defenseless man and to help conjure up the fiercer qualities of animals.

11   Later, Egyptian eye paint also helped guard against eye diseases of the region and so children and men, as well as women, were encouraged to use kohl. Fashions changed with the time and geography, reaching a peak of ridiculousness in 18th century England. During that time the fashionable woman (and man, too) wore false eyebrows made of mouseskin. Natural beauty was usually destroyed by about age 30 from the use of lead-based cosmetics. The scarlet or black patch, or *mouche,* originated as a cover for smallpox scars but became a fashion symbol. Lipstick and rouge were popular. Perfume was fashionable, in part, because bathing was not.

12   Modern women, who are glad we have grown past such things, may be surprised to learn that, as in Elizabethan or Egyptian days, talc and rice are still the base of face powders. Waxes, oils and fats are still used as binding agents and as the primary ingredients in lipstick and complexion creams. Red ochre, used as a cosmetic coloring since civilized antiquity, is still used for that purpose. Women who favor pearlized lipstick, however, may be relieved to discover that there is now an artificial substance responsible for the silvery glitter, a role historically filled by fish scales.

13   On a recent dreary afternoon, I decided that a little lipstick might cheer me up. There wasn't much time to be cheered, however, because my baby daughter soon smeared it all over my

face, shirt and her clothes. My friend Debbie has two small boys and refuses to give it up: "The lady at the cosmetics counter gets positively gleeful whenever she sees me." Debbie's boys, two and four, have experimented generously with the use of cosmetics on themselves, the walls and furniture.

14   I wash my face with soap that costs $8.50 a bar, even though I am not convinced it's better than hand soap. Occasionally I use the cleansers, toners and scrubs that come along in the bonus package. But when it comes time for the colors and enhancers and concealers, I hesitate. In high-minded moments I like to think this is because my self-confidence comes from inside, not from a collection of products.

15   At the same time, I admit to being proud of my fingernails. They are naturally strong and hard. Even with housework and baby, it is easy to keep them long. I keep thinking it might be nice to show them off a little more. One of these days I'm going to have a manicure.

POST-READING QUESTIONS

Content

1. How does Ray explain that her decision not to wear make-up—and thereby remain naked—is "partly pragmatic and partly philosophical?"

2. Why does the author spend time discussing the history of cosmetic use? What were some of the historical reasons for wearing rouge and perfume?

3. When did human beings began to use make-up? In what way did prehistoric humans try to enhance their natural beauty? How do we know?

4. Ray claims that "our idea of beauty is tremendously affected by fashion." What evidence does she offer to support what she says? Do you agree with her? Why?

5. What might modern women be surprised to learn about cosmetics? What might they be "relieved to discover?"

Strategies and Structures

1. What does Ray's one-sentence opening paragraph accomplish? What effect did it have on you, the reader?

2. How does the author's use of specific examples strengthen her essay?

3. Paragraph 2 consists of what we recognize as fragmented sentence structures. However, in context, how do these fragments shed light on the essay's title and initial paragraph, clarifying the focus for the rest of the composition?

4. What is the tone or mood of this essay? Where does it become firmly established? How does the author feel about make-up use?

5. Explain the irony of Ray's final paragraph. Does it call the rest of Ray's attitudes towards make-up or artificial aids to beauty into question? Why? Why not?

Language and Vocabulary

1. Vocabulary: *mascara, foundation, highlighter, blush, concealing stick, lipstick, eyeliner, lip pencil, cosmetics, artiface, kohl, mouche.* All of these vocabulary words deal with make-up or are some type of make-up. If you are not familiar with the different sorts of make-up discussed, look up their definitions in your dictionary or ask your friends what they are used for. Then write both the make-up and its definition on a sheet of paper. Next, make a list of cosmetics and their uses which were not mentioned by the author of this paper.

2. This essay contains a very *personal* voice. What pronouns, phrases, and specifics contribute to this *personal* voice?

GROUP ACTIVITIES

1. For use in interviews get into groups and brainstorm at least *ten* questions about wearing or not wearing make-up. Next, individually interview friends and strangers, jotting down their responses to your questions. Interview people of all ages, of both genders, and from a wide range of socio, economic, and ethnic backgrounds; then write a brief essay on the topic of "beauty aids" in modern society. The next time your group assembles, pass out photocopies of each other's essays and read them. Then, categorize the common uses of cosmetics among men and women in America as a group. Note which categories men do not fall into. Finally, from the viewpoint of advertising executives, how would your group increase the male market for cosmetics? Write a five-point plan.

2. Go to the library after class and have each group member select three different popular magazines (e.g., *People, GO, Ms.*). Then go through your magazines page by page, noting the number of ads that deal with beauty aids ranging from eyeliner and lipstick to hair transplants and cologne. Then, get together with your group and make a master list of your findings. You may want to use statistics your group has gathered in one of the following writing assignments. Therefore, remember to write down the names and issue dates of the popular magazines you reviewed.

3. Over the weekend, participate in a small group activity that involves make-up. For instance, you might get together with three other people (male or female) who never wear make-up and go somewhere Saturday night outrageously painted like peacocks. Whatever you do, write a brief group summary of your activity, including your initial plans, and what you learned about yourself and others with regard to make-up.

WRITING ACTIVITIES

1. What is the relationship between cosmetic use and sexism in American society? Write an essay explaining how and why the media in America make women feel dependent upon "beauty aides" to be presentable or complete human beings.

2. Compose an essay entitled: "The Masked Face," wherein you argue that you have a strong philosophical and logical basis for wearing make-up. Illustrate your material with examples drawn from personal experience, observations, and readings.

I Will Not Submit
JOAQUIN MURIETA

Joaquin Murieta became a folk hero in California during the mid 1800s. A bandit and self-confessed murderer, Murieta began his violent lifestyle following numerous unethical, unlawful acts against him, and according to popular belief, after some Americans—whom he had formerly trusted and admired—raped and killed his wife. In the following paragraphs, Murieta explains the causes behind his eventual disregard for the law and disrespect for Americans. This account was originally published as "Joaquin's Confession" in the *San Francisco Herald* during the mid 1800s.

PRE-READING QUESTIONS

1. Answer the following questions (in your journal or writing log if you have one): What would you do if you were robbed and cheated by someone you trusted? What would you do if someone constantly insulted and annoyed your family, not letting them live in peace?

2. Use the library to investigate the history of Mexican-American relations. What happened in California and Texas? What is the treaty of Guadalupe Hildago? How were Mexican-Americans treated in the United States at the turn of the century?

1   I was once a great admirer of Americans. I thought them the noblest, most honorable and high-minded people in the world. I had met many in my own country and all forms of tyranny seemed as hateful to them as the rule of the *Gachupines* (foreigners, or Spaniards) to the Mexicans. I was sick of the constant wars and insurrections in my native land and I came here thinking to end my days in California as an American citizen.

2   I located first near Stockton. But I was constantly annoyed and insulted by my neighbors and was not permitted to live in peace. I went then to the placers (gold mines) and was driven from my mining claim. I went into business and was cheated by everyone in whom I trusted. At every turn I was swindled and robbed by the very men for whom I had the greatest friendship and admiration. I saw the Americans daily in act of the most outrageous and lawless injustice, or of cunning and mean duplicity hateful to every honorable mind.

3   I then said to myself, I will revenge my wrongs and take the law into my own hands. The Americans who have injured me I will kill, and those who have not, I will rob because they are Americans. My trail shall be red with blood and those who seek me shall die or I shall lose my own life in the struggle! I will not submit tamely to outrage any longer.

4   I have killed many; I have robbed many; and many more will suffer in the same way. I will continue to the end of my life to take vengeance on the race that has wronged me shamefully.

POST-READING QUESTIONS

Content

1. How did Murieta feel about the Americans at first? How does he define them?

2. How does Murieta feel about the Americans after he moves to Stockton? Why? What do they do to him?

3. How does Murieta react to the injustices done against him? Do you feel he had sufficient grounds for what he did?

4. Why do you think Murieta tells us his personal story? What does he hope to get the reader to do or see?

Strategies and Structures

1. What strategy does Murieta use to present his ideas? In other words, what is the purpose of each of the paragraphs in the essay?

2. How does the image of the Americans in the first paragraph compare to the image of the Americans in the second?

3. What examples does Murieta use to show how he was mistreated?

4. What vivid images does Murieta use to show the extent of his anger? What vivid images does he use to appeal to the reader's emotion?

5. Compare the image of Murieta in the first paragraph to the image of Murieta in the last. How has he changed? What does this suggest about the effects of racism on the victim?

Language and Vocabulary

1. Vocabulary: Look up the meanings of *tyranny, duplicity, insurrections, cunning,* and *swindled.* What do all these words have in common? How do they apply to *all* people of a particular race or social class? Find the opposite meanings of each of these words (such words are known as antonyms) and rewrite each sentence in which the original word appears, giving it a positive expression. What conclusion can you make about similar word groupings?

2. What kinds of problems do we have with *absolute* expressions? Write a paragraph in which you try to explain a person or a situation using either all positive or all negative words without using qualifiers like most or few.

GROUP ACTIVITIES

1. Murieta writes of the outrageous acts of injustice against him. Prepare an oral report for the class that catalogues the injustices done to social, economic, ethnic, or religious minorities today. Be sure to clearly explain each injustice and to offer solutions to the problems (e.g., join clubs or organizations).

2. As a group, examine the difference between justifiable causes for one's actions and rationalizing one's behavior *after* doing something.

WRITING ACTIVITIES

1. Write an essay explaining the causes and/or effects of an *injustice,* using a personal narrative the way Murieta did. You could write about social, economical, political, or ecological injustices as presented in the news.

2. Write an essay appealing to others to join you in a fight against an injustice. It will be important to establish the ultimate impact or effect the injustice could have on all members of society in order to successfully persuade your reader to act. Feel free to write about global, regional, or local injustices.

Elderly Refugees and Language Learning
ALLENE GUSS GROGNET

Allene Guss Grognet has been active in second language learning and immigrant services as Vice-President of the Center for Applied Linguistics in Washington, DC. Mary Schleppegrell and Brenda Bowmen assisted the author in this essay.

PRE-READING QUESTIONS

1. If you were a newcomer to a country that has a language different than yours, what problems would you expect to encounter and what factors would affect your ability to learn the new language?

2. What expectations or demands would be placed on you by your family? Would these expectations hinder or help you in the learning process?

1   Since 1975, approximately 1 million refugees have come to the U.S. from Vietnam, Cambodia and Laos. They range from highly educated, multilingual former cabinet ministers to non-literate hilltribe people who practiced slash and burn agriculture. Fleeing from one's homeland and starting over again in a strange country is traumatic for refugees of any age. For elderly Southeast Asian refugees, it has been particularly difficult. At a time in their lives when they should be looking forward to the respect and reverence that traditional Asian society affords elders, they find themselves transplanted to a culture which is focused on youth. They have lost their homes, probably many of their family members, and, most of all, their honored status.

2   Refugees have many adjustments to make, among them a new language, new culture, and new expectations. Americans expect to work until they are about 65; Southeast Asians are

more likely to consider their mid-forties rather than their mid-sixties as the beginning of "old age." In Asia, it is not expected that one would start learning new things in the elder years, but that is exactly what most refugees have had to do.

3   There is no research evidence which suggests that older adults cannot succeed in learning another language. Older adults who remain healthy do not show a decline in their ability to learn. However, we also know that it is easier for pre-pubescent children to acquire a language and to speak it without an accent. Researchers are not sure why this phenomenon occurs. One theory claims it is connected with cerebral elasticity; another theory attributes it to developmental differences in the brain pre- and post-puberty; while another theory highlights changes in self-perception and willingness to change one's identity that come with adolescence. Whatever the reason, more effort needs to go into language learning by adults than by children.

4   In some important aspects, though, adults may have superior language learning capabilities. Researchers have shown that neural cells responsible for higher order linguistic processes, such as understanding semantic relationships and grammatical sensitivity, develop with age. Especially in the area of vocabulary and language structure, adults are better language learners than children. While children may be better at mimicry, older learners are more able to make higher order associations and generalizations, and can integrate new language inputs into already substantial experience and learning. Instructional programs which capitalize on these strengths can succeed with older refugee learners.

5   **Physical health** is an important factor in learning at any age, and chronic disease may affect the ability of the elderly refugee to learn. Many have had little or no "professional" medical care throughout their lives and suffer the residual effects of illnesses that went untreated. This may affect physical mobility, or the converse, their ability to sit for long periods of time.

6   Life other elderly adults, refugees may be affected by hearing loss and vision problems. Their ability to understand oral English, especially in the presence of background noise, may be affected, and they may have difficulty deciphering written English displayed in small type, especially if their native language does not use a Roman alphabet.

7   The changes that have occurred in diet and climate sometimes affect refugees physically and are most often seen in elderly refugees who have been in the U.S. three years or less.
Finally, short-term memory loss which often occurs with aging
can adversely affect the older refugee's success.

8   **Mental health** is probably the single most decisive factor in
refugee language learning. Depression is very common in the
refugee elderly population, and it is often somaticized in such
forms as loss of appetite, short attention span, nightmares and
inability to sleep.

9   It is not surprising that refugee elders are depressed. They
have experienced war, disorder, uprooting, and in some cases
the horrors of torture, rape, and the bloody death of loved
ones. They may no longer be considered wise and due respect;
they do not speak English well enough to talk on the telephone,
shop or use public transportation; and they sense that they have
lost their traditional role as the purveyor of cultural values.
Refugees' depression does not permit them to concentrate well,
thus reinforcing the cycle of not being able to speak English and
deal with the demands of everyday life.

10   **Cultural expectations**, such as what old age should be, the
role and place of the teacher, or how a language should be
taught, also impinge on learning. Cultural beliefs, values and
patterns of a lifetime are not easily changed, even though new
circumstances and surroundings may not support old ways.

11   **Attitude and motivation** are key factors in any learning,
but especially in language learning. The greatest obstacle to
older adults' learning language is the doubt in the mind of the
learner that older adults *can* learn a language. Unfortunately,
this doubt is often shared by the language teacher as well.

12   Another barrier is the fact that there is often no real need for
older adults to learn English. Children, and especially grandchildren, become the negotiators in the new country. Though there
may be loss of status in letting younger family members become
one's voice, this is often preferable to attempting a learning task
which is perceived as hopeless. Many refugee adults fear failure,
because it often means loss of "face." They are reluctant to take
the risks needed in language learning.

13   Four major ways in which teachers can encourage the
older language learner are: eliminating affective barriers,

incorporating adult learning strategies into their teaching, making the learning situation and the learning materials relevant to the needs and desires of older refugees, and tapping into the goals of the refugee community.

14   **Eliminating affective barriers** means first and foremost a belief on the part of the teacher that older adult learners are not necessarily poor learners. This is key to reducing anxiety and building self-confidence in the learner. Teachers need to emphasize the positive, focus on the progress learners are making, and provide opportunities for them to be successful. Students must feel that they have learned something every time they leave a classroom. Such successes can then be reinforced with more of the same.

15   **Taking adult learning theory, or andragogy, seriously** can help build successes. Andragogy assumes that learning situations take into account the experiences of the learner, providing the opportunity for new learning to be related to previous experiences. Furthermore, the adult learner should be involved in analyzing both the new and old experiences.

16   Andragogy also assumes that for the adult, readiness to learn is decreasingly the product of biological development or academic pressure, and increasingly the product of the desire to accomplish tasks required in work and/or social roles.

17   Finally, andragogy assumes that children have more of a subject-centered orientation to learning, whereas adults tend to have a problem solving orientation to learning (e.g. The child wants to learn "arithmetic," while the adult may want to learn to add and subtract in order to keep a check book.) This means that language learning must incorporate strategies appropriate to adult learners. Learning situations which adults perceive as putting them in the position of being treated as children are bound to interfere with their learning.

18   **By making the learning situation, the curriculum and the teaching materials relevant** to the adult refugee, teachers demonstrate that they take andragogy seriously. What is taught, as well as the learning environment, should be based on what older learners want and need to learn. Needs analyses of the target populations in a given community should be carried out, and of course, adult learners should be consulted about what they want to learn. For older refugees particularly, the

learning situation needs to be viewed not only in terms of teaching a language, but in terms of the fulfillment of cultural and social needs as well.

19   The high drop-out rate of older refugees enrolled in many traditional adult education classes attests to the fact that adults are not willing to tolerate boring or irrelevant content, or lessons that stress the learning of grammar rules out of context. When grammar and vocabulary are embedded in the situations refugees will encounter (i.e., in conversations or readings about food, clothing or shelter), they not only come to class, but they seem more willing to risk using their new language outside of the classroom. Refugees understand that they are learning English for specific purposes, and they take it as a sign of respect when teachers acknowledge those purposes.

20   It is also important that the learning environment acknowledge age. Presentation of new material should have both listening and viewing components to compensate for auditory or visual impairments, and there should be good lighting and the elimination of as much outside noise as possible.

21   Activities which follow presentations should provide opportunities for learners to work together that are focused on helping them *to understand* English rather than on getting them to speak the language. Class activities which include large amounts of oral repetition or fast-paced drills, extensive pronunciation correction or competitive exercises will inhibit the older refugee's active participation.

22   Methodology should also knowledge age. Learning strategies that rely more on long-term memory rather than short-term memory, ones that integrate new concepts and materials with already existing cognitive structures tend to be best for older learners. This means that learning by rote, which relies on short-term memory may not be successful, even though many adult refugees believe that rote learning, which is widely used in Asia, is the best method. On the other hand, many Southeast Asians may be reluctant to engage in such learning activities as "role playing," because such methodology is not part of their culture. However, they may find that putting news words to familiar or everyday situations may be a satisfying experience. A balance needs to be struck between the teacher's beliefs about learning and the older refugee's beliefs.

23   Language teachers also need to encourage older learners to rely on those learning strategies which have served them well in other contexts. By allowing different approaches to the learning task inside the classroom, teachers can help students discover how they learn best. A visual learner may need to write things down, even though the teacher might prefer that students concentrate on listening. Non-literate refugees might rely on auditory and memory cues, even though teachers tell them to write in their notebooks. By paying attention to learning channels, be they auditory, visual, kinesthetic or tactile, teachers will reduce frustration and will help other learners to be comfortable in the learning situation.

24   Finally, by *tapping into the goals of the refugee community,* an essential bond is formed between the teacher and the older refugee. Language learning goals for older adults must mesh not only with individual goals, but with familial and community aspirations as well. For instance, refugee elders need to share and pass on their culture to younger refugees. The refugee community is also concerned with cultural preservation. Teachers might use these concerns to create language learning situations.

25   Language learning programs for elderly refugees have been sparse. Those that incorporate more than just language learning seem to be the most successful. In Philadelphia, Project LEIF (Learning English Through Intergenerational Friendship) utilizes college-age tutors to teach and learn from older adult refugees.

26   Tutoring takes place in a community learning center as well as in the students' homes. Retired Americans are also recruited as tutors for refugee youngsters.

27   In California, older Vietnamese refugees learned English as part of a training program for baby-sitters and day care workers. Among other new skills, these refugees are now not afraid to answer the telephone or to initiate emergency calls.

28   In the Washington, D.C. area, illiterate elderly Cambodian women learned English around a stove, a kitchen table and a sewing machine. Among their new skills is the ability to write their names and addresses and to recognize warning signs on household products.

29   A hopeful sign for more older language learning projects is the beginning of a dialogue between the aging and refugee

networks. There is much the two fields can learn from each other. Sharing what works is a first step, and demonstration projects which are effective can then be adapted and replicated.

30   The scene is not as hopeful in the case of research into language learning for the older adult. Few studies have been conducted which investigate the specific characteristics of the older adult language learner. Research into the interaction of memory and age in language learning, as well as into the *attitudinal* characteristics and learning strategies of older adults are needed to identify appropriate motivational techniques and teaching strategies for this population. Such research would benefit not only the older refugee, but the American population in general as we become an older nation.

POST-READING QUESTIONS

Content

1. What is the correlation between language learning and age? What are the advantages and disadvantages of learning a language as an adult?

2. According to Grognet, what are some of the factors that affect adult language learning?

3. What are the four major ways "teachers can encourage the older language learner?"

4. How does the author ultimately demonstrate the ways in which older refugees acquire language skills? What are some of the benefits Vietnamese and Cambodian refugees have received from learning a new language?

Strategies and Structure

1. Prior to presenting his thesis, Grognet gives us background material on Southeast-Asian refugees. Why? How does this prepare the reader for the rest of the essay?

2. Why does the author discuss factors that affect learning prior to discussing the strategy of learning itself?

Why is this organization of material the most logical pattern to follow? What would have happened if Grognet had talked about strategies before influential factors in successful language learning?

3. Grognet tends to use more of a *journalistic* approach to writing—including subheadings within the essay and glossed words—than standard expository style. How are such *journalistic* techniques effective? How might they be misused?

4. Rather than using a simple summary to pull this essay to a close, Grognet uses a "call to action." Why is "a call to action" the most appropriate way to end this composition?

Language and Vocabulary

1. Vocabulary: *non-literate, puberty, residual, deciphering, purveyor, affective, andragogy, orientation, components, auditory, methodology, aspirations, attitudinal.* The meaning of a word can be changed in several ways; one of those ways is to add a prefix (at the beginning of the word) or a suffix (at the end of the word). You can identify a prefix in the dictionary, for example, *un-* (the dash means more of the word follows) and a suffix, for example, *-ment* (the dash means the suffix is the end of the word). In the list above, first define each word and then point out all prefixes and suffixes. In what ways have the prefixes and suffixes changed the original meaning of the root word (see glossary).

2. Using the list of words below, add a prefix, suffix, or both to each, explaining how the meaning of the word has changed. (For example, *populate* can be changed to *repopulate* meaning to populate again and *population,* meaning the number of people in a specified area.) Write a paragraph in which you use all of the words. Also note that the addition of a suffix or prefix often changes the function of a word: for example, populate is a verb, population is a noun.

advantage	man
assist	child
take	achieve
rely	believe

GROUP ACTIVITIES

1. As a group, analyze Grognet's process for learning. Have each group member use his or her personal experience to prove or support the points Grognet makes.

2. Divide groups into subgroups and have one subgroup interview pre-college students and the other subgroup interview college students about what effective strategies they have found for learning their own or a second language. Bring your two groups together and, after presenting your ideas, come to a group consensus (an agreement) about the best method for learning a language.

WRITING ACTIVITIES

1. Write a paper that outlines and argues the positive effects of a learning technique you have found successful.

2. Write an essay where you discuss your own language-learning experiences as an adult (or a high-school student) and the effects they have had on your education as a whole.

Labor and Capital:
The Coming Catastrophe
CARLOS BULOSAN

Carlos Bulosan was born in Luzon in the Central Philippines and spent the first
17 years of his life working in fields with his father or selling fish at the public
market with his mother. Bulosan came to America in 1930 and worked as
a migrant worker, a union activist, and a writer. Bulosan published several
books, including *The Laughter of My Father* (1942), *America is in The Heart*
(1977), *If You Want to Know Who We Are: A Carlos Bulosan Reader* (1983).
In the following essay, Bulosan expresses his views on the need for unions to
protect the laborer from exploitation by an employer.

PRE-READING QUESTIONS

1. Cluster the word capitalism. What positive and negative associations do you relate with the word?

2. Who controls most of the money in America? Who is
responsible for producing our nation's wealth?

1   Labor is the issue of the day. It has always been the issue. It
is high time we should understand why thousands of workers'
lives are sacrificed; why millions of dollars' worth of property
are destroyed in the name of labor.

2   As in all industrial countries, America's wealth is concentrated in the hands of the few. This wealth is socially produced and privately appropriated. This precisely means that
the wealth of the United States is produced by the people, the
workers as a whole, and distributed by the industrialists. The
contradictions of the social production and the private distribution of wealth [brings about] all social problems.

3   Industrialists are fattened by profits. Profits are sucked
from the very blood of the workers. This profiteering scheme is
made possible by speed-ups, long hours and brutal methods. It
is by driving workers into a most intolerable condition that

the profiteers grow impregnable. There is a better term for this condition: barbarism. But do not think they spend their profits in philanthropic ventures. They invest it in the forces of production, machines, etc. They spend it in idle luxury. Have you seen a banker's daughter throwing away thousands of dollars for a sick dog? They pay more attention to animals than to us. Have you seen a manufacturer's machinery housed and guarded by a cordon of armed men? We are nearly [destroyed] in their riot for profits.

4   But the industrialists have also a quarrel among themselves. The bigger ones pool together and drive out the smaller ones. This struggle goes on until only one or two are left to dictate in the market. The bigger the combines they have, the more enormous profits they acquire, which means more exploitation. This goes on until society constricts and workers are thrown into the streets to starve. Do not believe that economic depressions are natural phenonema. All depressions are made, and inevitable when the markets are overflowing with surplus: Crisis is bound to come. The only solution that capitalism could give is war. This is why the coming war is more threatening and dangerous than the previous ones. All wars are fought for profit. That is why we must sacrifice everything for the prevention of war. For war is not only the slaughter of humanity but also the destruction of culture, the barbarization of man. We must die for peace and not for profit.

5   Labor and capital are sharp enemies. There never was any amnesty between them and there shall never be. One or the other stay[s]. The most disastrous proposal is compromise between them. This will never do: it only means the demoralization of the workers, the betrayal of these advanced groups working among the exploited and oppressed.

6   Unionism is one way of fighting for a better living condition. We are lucky to have in this country a considerable strong group which is fighting for us workers. But this is only a stepping-stone available in democracies. Unionism is a way to economic freedom. But we must have political freedom also. We could have this through unionisms. We must have everything or nothing.

POST-READING QUESTIONS

Content

1. What does Bulosan state are the causes of "labor exploitation"? What are the implied effects of such exploitation?

2. According to Bulosan, what are the causes of economic depression?

3 Why does Bulosan say that we must avoid war at all costs? Do you agree with him? Why or why not?

4. Although the author wrote this essay in 1937, much of what he says is true today. What issues discussed in his essay are relevant to our modern workforce? How? Why?

Strategies and Structures

1. Why does Bulosan take a commonly accepted notion like "wars are justified by noble ideals" and claim "wars are fought for profit"? Which idea about war do you believe? Why?

2. Reread the topic sentences in each of the body paragraphs of the essay; in what way does Bulosan break down his theme? How well does he build upon his previous points?

3. Bulosan concludes his essay talking about the need for unionism to achieve better living. Does his composition logically build up to his conclusion? How? Why?

Vocabulary

1. Vocabulary: *slaughter, amnesty, philanthropic, intolerable, profiteering, impregnable, cordon, exploitation, phenomena.* What do the majority of these words suggest to you? Which do you find more closely associated with labor?

2. The author is quite descriptive in this essay, and most of his descriptions produce a negative feeling in the reader (e.g., *"Profits are sucked from the very blood of the workers."*) Write two or three paragraphs in which you present "profits" in a positive way.

GROUP ACTIVITIES

1. Discuss capital or money. Is there anything positive that can be said about money other than it can "buy" people, places, and things? Would you change your present opinion about money or the capitalist system if you were a blue-collar worker picking fruits and vegetables for $4.00 an hour?

2. Break the class up into two groups—one group representing the interests of laborers and the other group representing the interests of big business—and prepare a class debate arguing which is more essential to the well-being of a capitalist society. Write a summary of the debate explaining which group presented the best argument (you need not be faithful to your group).

WRITING ASSIGNMENTS

1. If you were a top industrialist, how would you spend your profits? Would you go out of your way to improve working conditions for your laborers or invest your money in schemes to make you even greater profits? Focusing in on either the causes or the ultimate effects of your actions, write a composition explaining the rationale for what you would do with your money.

2. Write an essay comparing and contrasting the unions mentioned by Bulosan in his article written in 1937 and unions of today. Have people's attitudes changed regarding unions? Are the unions of today more, less, or equally as effective as those of 1937? Are unions necessary today? Why or why not? Make sure you support your statements with verifiable facts and not personal opinions.

Additional Topics and Issues for Cause and Effect Essays

1. Write an essay regarding the cause(s) and/or effect(s) of watching so much television in American society. You may want to limit your audience to adults, teenagers, or children.

2. Compose an essay explaining the effects that growing up in a one-parent family can have on a child. In developing your essay, try to avoid cliches.

3. Because they often looked so much like real weapons, a few years ago toy guns began to appear in stores in a variety of colors to indicate their nature (a toy versus a threatening weapon). Based on personal observation and readings, compose an essay discussing the effects of this action by toy makers. Has America's interest in firearms decreased? Has it had any effect on crime (formerly people used toy guns to commit robberies and other acts of violence)?

4. Compose a paper explaining how aging affects an animal's temperament, agility, eating habits, and character in general. A good place to begin this assignment is to freewrite about the pets you or your family have owned or have known over the years.

5. Write about the cause(s) and/or effect(s) of one of the following: role-playing, shoplifting, flirting, stereotyping.

6. What are the causes of pollution and what are the effects of unchecked pollution? Who are the main culprits, and why do they pollute? You will want to incorporate authoritative sources in your essay. (A good source of information would be an environmental studies department. If your college has such a department, consult with professors or majors in that field.)

7. Describe a person who irritates or frustrates you abnormally. What does this person do that frustrates you so. Does this person clean too much, watch television excessively, expect favors, or complain too much? Write an essay in which you concentrate on the causes or the effects of your irritation. Use specific details to demonstrate your point.

10

EXPOSITION: COMBINED STRATEGIES

We could also have labeled this section "additional essays;" however, there is one point we wanted to emphasize with the title: Essays rarely use only one rhetorical strategy for development—a point that is quite obvious from our selections here. In "The Libido for the Ugly," H. L. Mencken, for instance, blends illustration and example, and division/classification with argumentation to question why America seems to have a love affair with ugliness. N. Scott Momaday couples narration and description as he traces his trip to Rainy Mountain, making connections between the past and the present, the land, and his grandmother's life. Jeanne Wakatsuki Houston is also using more than one rhetorical strategy when she recalls her arrival at Manzanar, a Japanese internment camp, during World War II. Simple narration provides Wakatsuki Houston with a vehicle to chronologically tell her story while other strategies, cause and effect, are also at work in the essay.

It may be a good idea to determine the dominant rhetorical strategies at work in the following selections and review the introductory chapters dealing with each. For example, one would review narration and illustration/example after reading E. B. White's, "A Report in Spring." No new knowledge is required to blend two rhetorical techniques; in fact, it comes quite naturally. For instance, you may begin a process or illustrate something by first defining it or argue for a cause by narrating a story. Still other times in the act of classifying and dividing a subject, you may be using some other rhetorical strategy without being aware of it. Exposition means to expose or explain and is not limited to a single method of development.

Tips on Writing Expository Essays

After pre-writing to arrive at a specific focus, answer the following questions:

1. Have you sufficiently narrowed your thesis?
2. What is the point of this expository essay? What are you trying to explain and what rhetorical strategies lend themselves naturally to your objective?
3. Who is your audience? What tone or mood is most appropriate in addressing your audience and your occasion for writing?
4. Does your essay have an interesting introductory paragraph, a thoroughly supported thesis, and a satisfying conclusion?
5. Is there anything that you believe would make your essay more memorable?
6. Did you vary your sentence patterns to add variety and interest?
7. How often did you use transitions and linking devices to establish a relationship with words, phrases, clauses, and entire paragraphs?
8. Did you carefully proofread your work for careless spelling, verb, pronoun agreement, and subject/verb agreement errors?
9. Did you punctuate all complete ideas with a period, question mark, or exclamation point in order to avoid run-on sentences or comma splices?

10. Were all partial ideas combined with other sentences to avoid fragments?

11. Did you revise awkward, misleading sentences—sentences that forced your audience to read and reread your essay in order to understand what you meant?

12. Did you defend your discussion points or merely make a list of them?

Is There Really Such a Thing as Talent?
ANNIE DILLARD

Annie Dillard, a poet, essayist, and naturalist, is well-known for her nonfiction writing such as the Pulitzer Prize winning book *Pilgrim at Tinker Creek* (1974) and several collections of poems, including *Tickets for a Prayer Wheel* (1974), *Holy the Firm* (1977), and *Teaching a Stone to Talk* (1982).

PRE-READING QUESTIONS

1. What is your idea of talent? Whom do you know who is talented? Can you pick out a person with talent when he or she is walking down the street? How? Why?

2. Discipline is a key word in this essay. What are its different definitions—connotations and denotations? (see glossary) What is the value of discipline? How might discipline be misunderstood as talent?

1 It's hard work, doing something with your life. The very thought of hard work makes me queasy. I'd rather die in peace. Here we are, all equal and alike and none of us much to write home about—and some people choose to make themselves into

physicists or thinkers or major-league pitchers, knowing perfectly well that it will be nothing but hard work. But I want to tell you that it's not as bad as it sounds. Doing something does not require discipline; it creates its own discipline—with a little help from caffeine.

2   People often ask me if I discipline myself to write, if I work a certain number of hours a day on a schedule. They ask this question with envy in their voices and awe on their faces and a sense of alienation all over them, as if they were addressing an armored tank or a talking giraffe or Niagara Falls. We want to believe that other people are natural wonders; it gets us off the hook.

3   Now, it happens that when I wrote my first book of prose, I worked an hour or two a day for a while, and then in the last two months, I got excited and worked very hard, for many hours a day. People can lift cars when they want to. People can recite the Koran, too, and run in marathons. These things aren't ways of life; they are merely possibilities for everyone on certain occasions of life. You don't lift cars around the clock or write books every year. But when you do, it's not so hard. It's not superhuman. It's very human. You do it for love. You do it for love and respect for your own life; you do it for love and respect for the world; and you do it for love and respect for the task itself.

4   If I had a little baby, it would be hard for me to rise up and feed that little baby in the middle of the night. It would be hard, but certainly wouldn't be a discipline. It wouldn't be a regimen I imposed on myself out of masochism, nor would it be the flowering of some extraordinary internal impulse. I would do it, grumbling for love and because it has to be done.

5   Of course it has to be done. And something has to be done with your life too: something specific, something human. But don't wait around to be hit by love. Don't wait for anything. Learn something first. Then when you are getting to know it, you will get to love it, and that love will direct you in what to do. So many times when I was in college I used to say of a course like Seventeenth-Century Poetry or European History, "I didn't like it at first, but now I like it." All of life is like that—a sort of dreary course which gradually gets interesting if you work at it.

6   I used to live in perpetual dread that I would one day read all the books that I would ever be interested in and have nothing more to read. I always figured that when that time came I would force myself to learn wild flowers, just to keep awake. I dreaded it, because I was not very interested in wild flowers but thought I should be. But things kept cropping up and one book has led to another and I haven't had to learn wild flowers yet. I don't think there's much danger of coming to the end of the line. The line is endless. I urge you to get in it, to get in line. It's a long line—but it's the only show in town.

POST-READING QUESTIONS

Content

1. What is Dillard's opinion of hard work?
2. How did the author write her first book? Did it require discipline on her part?
3. What does Dillard feel one should do with his or her life? Why?
4. The author lived in dread that one day she would read all the books she was interested in and never have anything more to read. What happened instead?

Strategies and Structures

1. What is the purpose of the opening line of the essay? What effect does it have on the reader? What does it expose?
2. What is the controlling idea (thesis) in this essay? How is it presented?
3. How do Dillard's personal recollections strengthen the content of her essay?
4. What is the purpose of Dillard's hypothetical example (an imaginary yet representative example of a situation) of the little baby?

Language and Vocabulary

1. Vocabulary: *queasy, discipline, regimen, extraordinary, masochism, dreary, perpetual, marathon.* This essay deals with something Dillard learned about life. After looking up the definitions of these words in the dictionary, write a paragraph using them to explain something you have learned.

2. Dillard focuses on the word discipline throughout her essay. Using an unabridged dictionary, find all the different meanings and uses of the word, including various forms of the word. Make sure to record all the different definitions and usages of the word, writing sentences for each meaning and usage.

GROUP ACTIVITIES

1. Dillard asks if there is any such thing as talent. As a group, discuss whether she answers this question in her essay or whether her title is misleading. If she doesn't believe there is talent, what takes its place?

2. In small groups compare and contrast the role of discipline in Murray's article "How I Write—I Think" and the Dillard article which you just read. How are their attitudes similar and different?

WRITING ACTIVITIES

1. Write a short composition describing a talent that you have.

2. Imitating Dillard's style, write a paragraph or two answering the question "Is There Really Such a Thing as _____?" (i.e., Fashion, Love, Sex Appeal)

From *The Way to Rainy Mountain*
N. SCOTT MOMADAY

A member of the Kiowa tribe, N. Scott Momaday has spent his life telling the history and the tales of his people. He has published such books as the Pulitzer-Prize winning *The House made of Dawn* (1968), *The Way to Rainy Mountain* (1969), *The Gourd Dancer,* a volume of poetry (1976), and *The Ancient Child* (1989). The following excerpt is the introduction to *The Way to Rainy Mountain.*

PRE-READING QUESTIONS

1. What does the title suggest will be the topic of this essay? Make a list of some of the possible things you think the author will write about.

2. The name of the mountain—Rainy Mountain—has several connotations. What connotations (feelings and/or images) do you associate with the words "rainy" and "mountain"?

1   A single knoll rises out of the plain in Oklahoma, north and west of the Wichita Range. For my people, the Kiowas, it is an old landmark, and they gave it the name Rainy Mountain. The hardest weather in the world is there. Winter brings blizzards, hot tornadic winds arise in the spring, and in summer the prairie is an anvil's edge. The grass turns brittle and brown and it cracks beneath your feet. There are green belts along the rivers and creeks, linear groves of hickory and pecan, willow and witch hazel. At a distance in July or August the steaming foliage seems almost to writhe in fire. Great green and yellow grasshoppers are everywhere in the tall grass, popping up like corn to sting the flesh, and tortoises crawl about on the red earth, going nowhere in the plenty of time. Loneliness is an aspect of the land. All things in the plain are isolate; there is no confusion of objects in the eye, but *one* hill or *one* tree or *one* man. To look upon the landscape in the early morning, with the

sun at your back, is to lose the sense of proportion. Your imagination comes to life, and this, you think, is where Creation was begun.

2   I returned to Rainy Mountain in July. My grandmother had died in the spring, and I wanted to be at her grave. She had lived to be very old and at last infirm. Her only living daughter was with her when she died, and I was told that in death her face was that of a child.

3   I like to think of her as a child. When she was born, the Kiowas were living the last great moment of their history. For more than a hundred years they had controlled the open range from the Smoky Hill River to the Red, from the headwaters of the Canadian to the fork of the Arkansas and Cimarron. In alliance with the Comanches, they had ruled the whole of the southern Plains. War was their sacred business, and they were among the finest horsemen the world has ever known. But warfare for the Kiowas was preeminently a matter of disposition rather than a survival, and they never understood the grim, unrelenting advance of the U.S. Cavalry. When at last, divided and ill-provisioned, they were driven onto the Staked Plains in the cold rains of autumn, they fell into panic. In Palo Duro Canyon they abandoned their crucial stores to pillage and had nothing then but their lives. In order to save themselves, they surrendered to the soldiers at Fort Sill and were imprisoned in the old stone corral that now stands as a military museum. My grandmother was spared the humiliation of those high gray walls by eight or ten years, but she must have known from birth the affliction of defeat, the dark brooding of old warriors.

4   Her name was Aho, and she belonged to the last culture to evolve in North America. Her forebears came down from the high country in western Montana nearly three centuries ago. They were a mountain people, a mysterious tribe of hunters whose language has never been positively classified in any major group. In the late seventeenth century they began a long migration to the south and east. It was a journey toward the dawn, and it led to a golden age. Along the way the Kiowas were befriended by the Crows, who gave them the culture and religion of the Plains. They acquired horses, and their ancient nomadic spirit was suddenly free of the ground. They acquired Tai-me, the sacred Sun Dance doll, from that moment the

object and symbol of their worship, and so shared in the divinity of the sun. Not least, they acquired the sense of destiny, therefore courage and pride. When they entered upon the southern Plains they had been transformed. No longer were they slaves to the simple necessity of survival; they were a lordly and dangerous society of fighters and thieves, hunters and priests of the sun. According to their origin myth, they entered the world through a hollow log. From one point of view, their migration was the fruit of an old prophecy, for indeed they emerged from a sunless world.

5   Although my grandmother lived out her long life in the shadow of Rainy Mountain, the immense landscape of the continental interior lay like memory in her blood. She could tell of the Crows, whom she had never seen, and of the Black Hills, where she had never been. I wanted to see in reality what she had seen more perfectly in the mind's eye, and traveled fifteen hundred miles to begin my pilgrimage.

6   Yellowstone, it seemed to me, was the top of the world, a region of deep lakes and dark timber, canyons and waterfalls. But, beautiful as it is, one might have the sense of confinement there. The skyline in all directions is close at hand, the high wall of the woods and deep cleavages of shade. There is a perfect freedom in the mountains, but it belongs to the eagle and the elk, the badger and the bear. The Kiowas reckoned their statue by the distance they could see, and they were bent and blind in the wilderness.

7   Descending eastward, the highland meadows are a stairway to the plain. In July the inland slope of the Rockies is luxuriant with flax and buckwheat, stonecrop and larkspur. The earth unfolds and the limit of the land recedes. Clusters of trees, and animals grazing far in the distance, cause the vision to reach away and wonder to build upon the mind. The sun follows a longer course in the day, and the sky is immense beyond all comparison. The great billowing clouds that sail upon it are shadows that move upon the grain like water, dividing light. Farther down, in the land of the Crows and Blackfeet, the plain is yellow. Sweet clover takes hold of the hills and bends upon itself to cover and seal the soil. There the Kiowas paused on their way; they had come to the place where they must change their lives. The sun is at home on the plains. Precisely there

does it have the certain character of a god. When the Kiowas came to the land of the Crows, they could see the dark lees of the hills at dawn across the Bighorn River, the profusion of light on the grain shelves, the oldest deity ranging after the solstices. Not yet would they veer southward to the caldron of the land that lay below; they must wean their blood from the northern winter and hold the mountains a while longer in their view. They bore Tai-me in procession to the east.

8   A dark mist lay over the Black Hills, and the land was like iron. At the top of a ridge I caught sight of Devil's Tower upthrust against the gray sky as if in the birth of time the core of the earth had broken through its crust and the motion of the world has begun. There are things in nature that engender an awful quiet in the heart of man; Devil's Tower is one of them. Two centuries ago, because they could not do otherwise, the Kiowas made a legend at the base of the rock. My grandmother said:

> Eight children were there at play, seven sisters and their brother. Suddenly the boy was struck dumb; he trembled and began to run upon his hands and feet. His fingers became claws, and his body was covered with fur. Directly there was a bear where the boy had been. The sisters were terrified; they ran, and the bear after them. They came to the stump of a great tree, and the tree spoke to them. It bade them climb upon it, and as they did so it began to rise into the air. The bear came to kill them, but they were just beyond its reach. It reared against the tree and scored the bark all around with its claws. The seven sisters were borne into the sky, and they became the stars of the Big Dipper.

From that moment, and so long as the legend lives, the Kiowas have kinsmen in the night sky. Whatever they were in the mountains, they could be no more. However tenuous their well-being, however much they had suffered and would suffer again, they had found a way out of the wilderness.

9   My grandmother had a reverence for the sun, a holy regard that now is all but gone out of mankind. There was a wariness in her, and an ancient awe. She was a Christian in her later years, but she had come a long way about, and she never forgot her birthright. As a child she had been to the Sun Dances; she had taken part in those annual rites, and by them she had learned

the restoration of her people in the presence of Tai-me. She was about seven when the last Kiowa Sun Dance was held in 1887 on the Washita River above Rainy Mountain Creek. The buffalo were gone. In order to consummate the ancient sacrifice—to impale the head of a buffalo bull upon the medicine tree—a delegation of old men journeyed into Texas, there to beg and barter for an animal from the Goodnight herd. She was ten when the Kiowas came together for the last time as a living Sun Dance culture. They could find no buffalo; they had to hang an old hide from the sacred tree. Before the dance could begin, a company of soldiers rode out from Fort Sill under orders to disperse the tribe. Forbidden without cause the essential act of their faith, having seen the wild herds slaughtered and left to rot upon the ground, the Kiowas backed away forever from the medicine tree. That was July 20, 1890, at the great bend of the Washita. My grandmother was there. Without bitterness, and for as long as she lived, she bore a vision of deicide.

10   Now that I can have her only in memory, I see my grandmother in the several postures that were peculiar to her: standing at the wood stove on a winter morning and turning meat in a great iron skillet; sitting at the south window, bent above her beadwork, and afterwards, when her vision failed, looking down for a long time into the fold of her hands; going out upon a cane, very slowly as she did when the weight of age came upon her; praying. I remember her most often at prayer. She made long, rambling prayers out of suffering and hope, having seen many things. I was never sure that I had the right to hear, so exclusive were they of all mere custom and company. The last time I saw her she prayed standing by the side of her bed at night naked to the waist, the light of a kerosene lamp moving upon her dark skin. Her long, black hair, always drawn and braided in the day, lay upon her shoulders and against her breasts like a shawl. I do not speak Kiowa, and I never understood her prayers, but there was something inherently sad in the sound, some merest hesitation upon the syllables of sorrow. She began in a high and descending pitch, exhausting her breath to silence; then again and again—and always the same intensity of effort, of something that is, and is not, like urgency in the human voice. Transported so in the dancing light among the shadows of her room, she seemed beyond the reach of time.

But that was illusion; I think I knew then that I should not see her again.

11   Houses are like sentinels in the plain, old keepers of the weather watch. There, in a very little while, wood takes on the appearance of great age. All colors wear soon away in the wind and rain, and then the wood is burned gray and the grain appears and the nails turn red with rust. The windowpanes are black and opaque; you imagine there is nothing within, and indeed there are many ghosts, bones given up to the land. They stand here and there against the sky, and you approach them for a longer time than you expect. They belong in the distance; it is their domain.

12   Once there was a lot of sound in my grandmother's house, a lot of coming and going, feasting and talk. The summers there were full of excitement and reunion. The Kiowas are a summer people; they abide the cold and keep to themselves, but when the season turns and the land becomes warn and vital they cannot hold still; an old love of going returns upon them. The aged visitors who came to my grandmother's house when I was a child were made of lean and leather, and they bore themselves upright. They wore great black hats and bright ample shirts that shook in the wind. They rubbed fat upon their hair and wound their braids with strips of colored cloth. Some of them painted their faces and carried the scars of old and cherished enmities. They were an old council of warlords, come to remind and be reminded of who they were. Their wives and daughters served them well. The women might indulge themselves; gossip was at once the mark and compensation of their servitude. They made loud and elaborate talk among themselves, full of jest and gesture, fright and false alarm. They went abroad in fringed and flowered shawls, bright beadwork and German silver. They were at home in the kitchen, and they prepared meals that were banquets.

13   There were frequent prayer meetings, and great nocturnal feasts. When I was a child I played with my cousins outside, where the lamplight fell upon the ground and the singing of the old people rose up around us and carried away into the darkness. There were a lot of good things to eat, a lot of laughter and surprise. And afterwards, when the quiet returned, I lay down with my grandmother and could hear the frogs away by the river and feel the motion of the air.

14   Now there is funeral silence in the rooms, the endless wake of some final word. The walls have closed in upon my grandmother's house. When I returned to it in mourning, I saw for the first time in my life how small it was. It was late at night, and there was a white moon, nearly full. I sat for a long time on the stone steps by the kitchen door. From there I could see out across the land; I could see the long row of trees by the creek, the low light upon the rolling plains, and the stars of the Big Dipper. Once I looked at the moon and caught sight of a strange thing. A cricket had perched upon the handrail, only a few inches away from me. My line of vision was such that the creature filled the moon like a fossil. It had gone there, I thought, to live and die, for there, of all places, was its small definition made whole and eternal. A warm wind rose up and purled like the longing within me.

15   The next morning I awoke at dawn and went out on the dirt road to Rainy Mountain. It was already hot, and the grasshoppers began to fill the air. Still, it was early in the morning, and the birds sang out of the shadows. The long yellow grass on the mountain shone in the bright light, and a scissortail hied above the land. There, where it ought to be, at the end of a long and legendary way, was my grandmother's grave. Here and there on the dark stones were ancestral names. Looking back once, I saw the mountain and came away.

POST-READING QUESTIONS

Content

1. Why does Momaday return to Rainy Mountain? What effect does this trip have on him?

2. Who is the central character in Momaday's essay? What traits make up her character?

3. What is the history of the Kiowas? How do they come to reside below Rainy Mountain?

4. What journey does Momaday make? Where does he begin his essay? Where does he say he is going? Where does he end the essay?

Strategies and Structures

1. Momaday opens his essay with a description. What is the primary mood (see glossary) of this description? What images create this mood? What images are most vivid? How does this description set up the tone for the rest of the essay?

2. Why does Momaday tell the story of the Kiowas? How is their story similar to the story of his grandmother?

3. In paragraph 11, what senses—sight, sound, smell, taste, and touch—does he use to describe his grandmother?

4. Momaday writes two descriptions of his grandmother's house—paragraphs 13–14 and 15. What are the two distinct differences between the descriptions? What images does Momaday use to create the two distinct moods?

5. What is the mood of the final paragraph? Is it different from the opening paragraph? What images create the mood?

Language and Vocabulary

1. Vocabulary: *knoll, range, plain, fork, canyon, highland meadows, caldron.* All of these vocabulary words are used to specify or explain geographical areas or features. After you look up the dictionary definition of the words, go back and see where and how Momaday uses them to describe the area around Rainy Mountain. Then, write a paragraph or so describing a geographical area you are familiar with (or an imaginary place), using at least five of the eight vocabulary words.

2. Momaday enables the reader to "relive" his trip to Rainy Mountain because he connects the different parts of his journey. What sort of transitions and linking devices help the reader follow Momaday?

GROUP ACTIVITIES

1. As a group, take a walk around the campus. As you walk, write down all that you can see, smell, taste, touch, and hear. After you finish your walk, decide on a dominant impression the campus projects: old, friendly, traditional, modern, busy and so on. After you determine the dominant impression of the campus, decide which details from your notes illustrate this impression best.

2. Write a collaborative essay describing the classroom you are sitting in. Make sure everyone in your group contributes information and impressions. In addition to details which help a reader to visualize the room, your essay should create a dominant mood.

WRITING ACTIVITIES

1. Write a description of a close relative. Include the history of the relative's heritage, the relative's past, and the relative's present.

2. Write a description of your hometown or land. In the same manner as Momaday, try to create a mood by careful use of details and images.

A Report in Spring
E. B. WHITE

Born in 1899 in Mount Vernon, New York, E. B. White was a well-known essayist and contributing editor to *The New Yorker*. White's works include *Is Sex Necessary?* (1929), *Stuart Little* (1945), *Charlotte's Web* (1952), and *The Trumpet of the Swan* (1970). White also revised William Strunk's *The Elements of Style*. Though White died in 1985, his works are still widely read today.

PRE-READING QUESTIONS

1. Make a list of words you associate with spring. What does this list lead you to expect of White's topic?
2. What visual signs—both in people and in nature—indicate the coming of spring? Do people generally behave any differently at this time of year? Why?

1   I bought a puppy last week in the outskirts of Boston and drove him to Maine in a rented Ford that looked like a sculpin. There had been talk in our family of getting a "sensible" dog this time, and my wife and I had gone over the list of sensible dogs, and had even ventured once or twice into the company of sensible dogs. A friend had a litter of Labradors, and there were other opportunities. But after a period of uncertainty and waste motion my wife suddenly exclaimed one evening, "Oh, let's just get a dachshund!" She had had a glass of wine, and I could see that the truth was coming out. Her tone was one of exasperation laced with affection. So I engaged a black male without further ado.

2   For the long ordeal of owning another dachshund we prepared ourselves by putting up for a night at the Boston Ritz in a room overlooking the Public Garden, where from our window we could gaze, perhaps for the last time, on a world of order and peace. I say "for the last time" because it occurred to me early in the proceedings that this was our first adoption case in which there was a strong likelihood that the dog would survive the man. It had always been the other way round. The garden had never seemed so beautiful. We were both up early the next morning for a final look at the fresh, untroubled scene; then we checked out hastily, sped to the kennel, and claimed our prize, who is the grandson of an animal named Direct Stretch of the Walls. He turned out to be a good traveler, and except for an interruption caused by my wife's falling out of the car in Gardiner, the journey went very well. At present, I am a sojourner in the city again, but here in the green warmth of a city backyard I see only the countenance of spring in the country. No matter what changes take place in the world, or in me, nothing ever seems to disturb the face of spring.

3   The smelts are running in the brooks. We had a mess for Monday lunch, brought to us by our son, who was fishing at two in the morning. At this season, a smelt brook is the nightclub of the town, and when the tide is a late one, smelting is for the young, who like small hours and late society.

4   No rain has fallen in several weeks. The gardens are dry, the road to the shore is dusty. The ditches, which in May are usually swollen to bursting, are no more than a summer trickle. Trout fisherman are not allowed on the streams; pond fishing from a boat is still permissible. The landscape is lovely to behold, but the hot, dry wind carries the smell of trouble. The other day we saw the smoke of a fire over in the direction of the mountain.

5   Mice have eaten the crowns of the Canterbury bells, my whitefaced steer has warts on his neck (I'm told it's a virus, like everything else these days), and the dwarf pear has bark trouble. My puppy has no bark trouble. He arises at three, for tennis. The puppy's health, in fact, is exceptionally good. When my wife and I took him from the kennel, a week ago today, his mother kissed all three of us good-bye, and the lady who ran the establishment presented me with complete feeding instructions, which included a mineral supplement called Pervinal and some vitamin drops called Vi-syneral. But I knew that as soon as the puppy reached home and got his sea legs he would switch to the supplement *du jour*—a flake of well-rotted cow manure from my boot, a dead crocus bulb from the lawn, a shingle from the kindling box, a bloody feather from the execution block behind the barn. Time has borne me out; the puppy was not long in discovering the delicious supplements of the farm, and he now knows where every vitamin hides, under its stone, under its loose board. I even introduced him to the tonic smell of coon.

6   On Tuesday, in broad daylight, the coon arrived, heavy with young, to take possession of the hole in the tree, but she found another coon in possession, and there was a grim fight high in the branches. The new tenant won, or so it appeared to me, and our old coon came down the tree in defeat and hustled off into the woods to examine her wounds and make other plans for her confinement. I was sorry for her, as I am for any who are evicted from their haunts by the younger and stronger—always a sad occasion for man or beast.

7   The stalks of rhubarb show red, the asparagus has broken through. Peas and potatoes are in, but it is not much use putting seeds in the ground the way things are. The bittern spent a day at the pond, creeping slowly around the shores like a little round-shouldered peddler. A setting of goose eggs has arrived by parcel post from Vermont, my goose having been taken by the fox last fall. I carried the package into the barn and sat down to unpack the eggs. They came out of the box in perfect condition, each one wrapped in a page torn from the *New England Homestead.* Clustered around me on the floor, they looked as though I had been hard at it. There is no one to sit on them but me, and I had to return to New York, so I ordered a trio of Muscovies from a man in New Hampshire, in the hope of persuading a Muscovy duck to give me a Toulouse gosling. (The theme of my life is complexity-through-joy.) In reply to my order, the duck-farm man wrote saying there would be a slight delay in the shipment of Muscovies, as he was "in the midst of a forest-fire scare." I did not know from this whether he was too scared to drive to the post office with a duck or too worried to fit a duck into a crate.

8   By day the goldfinches dip in yellow flight, by night the frogs sing the song that never goes out of favor. We opened the lower sash of the window in the barn loft, and the swallows are already building, but mud for their nests is not so easy to come by as in most springtimes. One afternoon, I found my wife kneeling at the edge of her perennial border on the north side, trying to disengage Achillea-the-Pearl from Coral Bell. "If I could afford it," she said bitterly, "I would take every damn bit of Achillea out of this border." She is a woman in comfortable circumstances, arrived at through her own hard labor, and this sudden burst of poverty, and her inability to indulge herself in a horticultural purge, startled me. I was so moved by her plight and her unhappiness that I went to the barn and returned with an edger, and we spent a fine, peaceable hour in the pretty twilight, rapping Achillea over the knuckles and saving Coral Bell.

9   One never knows what images one is going to hold in memory, returning to the city after a brief orgy in the country. I find this morning that what I most vividly and longingly recall is the sight of my grandson and his little sunburnt sister returning to their kitchen door from an excursion, with trophies of the

meadow clutched in their hands—she with a couple of violets, and smiling, he serious and holding dandelions, strangling them in a responsible grip. Children hold spring so tightly in their brown fists—just as grownups, who are less sure of it, hold it in their hearts.

POST-READING QUESTIONS

Content

1. What signs of spring does White discuss in this essay?
2. How does White demonstrate spring is about a time of change—a season when the old must make way for the young?
3. White says, "No matter what changes take place in the world, or in me, nothing seems to disturb the face of spring." What sort of conflicts does spring overcome here?

Strategies and Structures

1. White opens his narrative explaining how he and his wife were going to get a new dog. What connection can you make between this episode and the conclusion of the essay?
2. Explain what White meant by "*Children hold spring so tightly in their brown grips —just as grown-ups, who are less sure of it, hold it in their hearts.*"
3. Go back over the list of words you associate with spring. Did the title of White's narrative fulfill your expectations of the essay? How?
4. How does the author use words and phrases to suggest his attitude towards spring? Does he seem moody or sentimental?

Language and Vocabulary

1. Vocabulary: *sculpin, ventured, exasperation, sojourner, bittern, rhubarb, Muscovies, horticulture, Canterbury*

bells, Achillea-the-Pearl, Coral Bell. Check the definitions for these words. Which words deal with flowers or gardening? Which words convey other information, and how do they help the author achieve his purpose in this essay? Begin a personal vocabulary list and add any words from above whose definition you did not know.

2. Write a paper explaining how you would landscape your own garden using the plants White mentions in his essay (half of the vocabulary words above). You will want to consider their size, shape, color, or purpose (e.g., shade). Feel free to include plants you are familiar with in your garden.

GROUP ACTIVITIES

1. One technique White uses here is personification: attributing human characteristics to nonhumans. For instance, in paragraph 2, he refers to "the face of spring," and in paragraph 5 he says the puppy's mother "kissed all three of us good-by." Find as many instances of personification as you can in this essay, and discuss what you like or dislike about White's figurative use of language.

2. As a group, choose a current event and write a collaborative essay about it using concrete nouns (specific references) and active verbs (verbs that show rather than tell). Include a few examples of personification.

WRITING ACTIVITIES

1. Freewrite for ten minutes (see Peter Elbow's essay, "Freewriting") on the topic of spring. What sort of themes tend to reoccur? Pick a sentence that focuses on a particular aspect of spring and develop it into a paragraph, using the sentence as your controlling idea (topic sentence).

2. Write a narrative titled: "A Report in Summer," "A Report in Fall," or "A Report in Winter." To generate

ideas, you might want to cluster the words summer, fall, and winter before you begin.

Arrival at Manzanar
JEANNE WAKATSUKI HOUSTON AND
JAMES D. HOUSTON

During World War II, Jeanne Wakatsuki Houston was moved to the Japanese-American internment camp in Manzanar, California, for four years. She was only seven years old at the time and the memories of her years there are recorded in *Farewell to Manzanar*, which she wrote with her husband James D. Houston, a well-known novelist.

PRE-READING QUESTIONS

1. Answer the following questions in your journal. What do you know of the Japanese-American internment in the United States during World War II? Who was confined in these camps? Why were they confined? What were the results of such internment? What were the conditions of these camps?

2. How would you react if suddenly your family and you were suddenly asked to move to an internment camp and to give up your possessions, property, and professions? As you write, think of all your possible actions and the advantages and disadvantages of each one.

1   In December of 1941 Papa's disappearance didn't bother me nearly so much as the world I soon found myself in.

2   He had been a jack-of-all-trades. When I was born he was farming near Inglewood. Later, when he started fishing, we moved to Ocean Park, near Santa Monica, and until they picked

him up, that's where we lived, in a big frame house with a brick fireplace, a block back from the beach. We were the only Japanese family in the neighborhood. Papa liked it that way. He didn't want to be labeled or grouped by anyone. But with him gone and no way of knowing what to expect, my mother moved all of us down to Terminal Island. Woody already lived there, and one of my older sisters had married a Terminal Island boy. Mama's first concern now was to keep the family together; and once the war began, she felt safer there than isolated racially in Ocean Park. But for me, at age seven, the island was a country as foreign as India or Arabia would have been. It was the first time I had lived among other Japanese, or gone to school with them, and I was terrified all the time.

3   This was partly Papa's fault. One of his threats to keep us younger kids in line was "I'm going to sell you to the China-man." When I had entered kindergarten two years earlier, I was the only Oriental in the class. They sat me next to a Cau-casian girl who happened to have very slanted eyes. I looked at her and began to scream, certain Papa had sold me out at last. My fear of her ran so deep I could not speak of it, even to Mama, couldn't explain why I was screaming. For two weeks I had nightmares about this girl, until the teachers finally moved me to the other side of the room. And it was still with me, this fear of Oriental faces, when we moved to Terminal Island.

4   In those days it was a company town, a ghetto owned and controlled by the canneries. The men went after fish, and when-ever the boats came back—day or night—the women would be called to process the catch while it was fresh. One in the after-noon or four in the morning, it made no difference. My mother had to go to work right after we moved there. I can still hear the whistle—two toots for French's, three for Van Camp's—and she and Chizu would be out of bed in the middle of the night, head-ing for the cannery.

5   The house we lived in was nothing more than a shack, a barracks with single plank walls and rough wooden floors, like the cheapest kind of migrant workers' housing. The people around us were hardworking, boisterous, a little proud of their nickname, *yo-go-re,* which meant literally *uncouth one,* or rough-neck, or dead-end kid. They not only spoke Japanese exclu-sively, they spoke a dialect peculiar to Kyushu, where their

families had come from in Japan, a rough, fisherman's language, full of oaths and insults. Instead of saying *ba-ka-ta-re,* a common insult meaning *stupid,* Terminal Islanders would say *ba-ka-ya-ro,* a coarser and exclusively masculine use of the word, which implies gross stupidity. They would swagger and pick on outsiders and persecute anyone who didn't speak as they did. That was what made my own time there so hateful. I had never spoken anything but English, and the other kids in the second grade despised me for it. They were tough and mean, like ghetto kids anywhere. Each day after school I dreaded their ambush. My brother Kiyo, three years older, would wait for me at the door, where we would decide whether to run straight home together, or split up, or try a new and unexpected route.

6   None of these kids ever actually attacked. It was the threat that frightened us, their fearful looks, and the noises they would make, like miniature Samurai, in a language we couldn't understand.

7   At the time it seemed we had been living under this reign of fear for years. In fact, we lived there about two months. Late in February the navy decided to clear Terminal Island completely. Even though most of us were American-born, it was dangerous having that many Orientals so close to the Long Beach Naval Station, on the opposite end of the island. We had known something like this was coming. But, like Papa's arrest, not much could be done ahead of time. There were four of us kids still young enough to be living with Mama, plus Granny, her mother, sixty-five then, speaking no English, and nearly blind. Mama didn't know where else she could get work, and we had nowhere else to move *to.* On February 25 the choice was made for us. We were given forty-eight hours to clear out.

8   The secondhand dealers had been prowling around for weeks, like wolves, offering humiliating prices for goods and furniture they knew many of us would have to sell sooner or later. Mama had left all but her most valuable possessions in Ocean Park, simply because she had nowhere to put them. She had brought along her pottery, her silver, heirlooms like the kimonos Granny had brought from Japan, tea sets, lacquered tables, and one fine old set of china, blue and white porcelain, almost translucent. On the day we were leaving, Woody's car

was so crammed with boxes and luggage and kids we had just run out of room. Mama had to sell this china.

9   One of the dealers offered her fifteen dollars for it. She said it was a full setting for twelve and worth at least two hundred. He said fifteen was his top price. Mama started to quiver. Her eyes blazed up at him. She had been packing all night and trying to calm down Granny, who didn't understand why we were moving again and what all the rush was about. Mama's nerves were shot, and now navy jeeps were patrolling the streets. She didn't say another word. She just glared at this man, all the rage and frustration channeled at him through her eyes.

10   He watched her for a moment and said he was sure he couldn't pay more than seventeen fifty for that china. She reached into the red velvet case, took out a dinner plate and hurled it at the floor right in front of his feet.

11   The man leaped back shouting, "Hey! Hey, don't do that! Those are valuable dishes!"

12   Mama took out another dinner plate and hurled it at the floor, then another and another, never moving, never opening her mouth, just quivering and glaring at the retreating dealer, with tears streaming down her cheeks. He finally turned and scuttled out the door, heading for the next house. When he was gone she stood there smashing cups and bowls and platters until the whole set lay in scattered blue and white fragments across the wooden floor.

13   The American Friends Service helped us find a small house in Boyle Heights, another minority ghetto, in downtown Los Angeles, now inhabited briefly by a few hundred Terminal Island refugees. Executive Order 9066 had been signed by President Roosevelt, giving the War Department authority to define military areas in the western states and to exclude from them anyone who might threaten the war effort. There was a lot of talk about internment, or moving inland, or something like that in store for all Japanese Americans. I remember my brothers sitting around the table talking very intently about what we were going to do, how we would keep the family together. They had seen how quickly Papa was removed, and they knew now that he would not be back for quite a while. Just before leaving Terminal Island Mama had received her first letter, from

Bismarck, North Dakota. He had been imprisoned at Fort Lincoln, in an all-male camp for enemy aliens.

14   Papa had been the patriarch. He had always decided everything in the family. With him gone, my brothers, like councilors in the absence of a chief, worried about what should be done. The ironic thing is, there wasn't much left to decide. These were mainly days of quiet, desperate waiting for what seemed at the time to be inevitable. There is a phrase the Japanese use in such situations, when something difficult must be endured. You would hear the older heads, the Issei, telling others very quietly, *"Shikata ga nai"* (It cannot be helped). *"Shikata ga nai"* (It must be done).

15   Mama and Woody went to work packing celery for a Japanese produce dealer. Kiyo and my sister May and I enrolled in the local school, and what sticks in my memory from those few weeks is the teacher—not her looks, her remoteness. In Ocean Park my teacher had been a kind, grandmotherly woman who used to sail with us in Papa's boat from time to time and who wept the day we had to leave. In Boyle Heights the teacher felt cold and distant. I was confused by all the moving and was having trouble with the classwork, but she would never help me out. She would have nothing to do with me.

16   This was the first time I had felt outright hostility from a Caucasian. Looking back, it is easy enough to explain. Public attitudes toward the Japanese in California were shifting rapidly. In the first few months of the Pacific war, America was on the run. Tolerance had turned to distrust and irrational fear. The hundred-year-old tradition of anti-Orientalism on the west coast soon resurfaced, more vicious than ever. Its result became clear about a month later, when we were told to make our third and final move.

17   The name Manzanar meant nothing to us when we left Boyle Heights. We didn't know where it was or what it was. We went because the government ordered us to. And, in the case of my older brothers and sisters, we went with a certain amount of relief. They had all heard stories of Japanese homes being attacked, of beatings in the streets of California towns. They were as frightened of the Caucasians as Caucasians were of us. Moving, under what appeared to be government protection, to an area less directly threatened by the war seemed not such

a bad idea at all. For some it actually sounded like a fine adventure.

18   Our pickup point was a Buddhist church in Los Angeles. It was very early, and misty, when we got there with our luggage. Mama had bought heavy coats for all of us. She grew up in eastern Washington and knew that anywhere inland in early April would be cold. I was proud of my new coat, and I remember sitting on a duffel bag trying to be friendly with the Greyhound driver. I smiled at him. He didn't smile back. He was befriending no one. Someone tied a numbered tag to my collar and to the duffel bag (each family was given a number, and that became our official designation until the camps were closed), someone else passed out box lunches for the trip, and we climbed aboard.

19   I had never been outside Los Angeles County, never traveled more than ten miles from the coast, had never even ridden on a bus. I was full of excitement, the way any kid would be, and wanted to look out the window. But for the first few hours the shades were drawn. Around me other people played cards, read magazines, dozed, waiting. I settled back, waiting too, and finally fell asleep. The bus felt very secure to me. Almost half its passengers were immediate relatives. Mama and my older brothers had succeeded in keeping most of us together, on the same bus, headed for the same camp. I didn't realize until much later what a job that was. The strategy had been, first, to have everyone living in the same district when the evacuation began, and then to get all of us included under the same family number, even though names had been changed by marriage. Many families weren't as lucky as ours and suffered months of anguish while trying to arrange transfers from one camp to another.

20   We rode all day. By the time we reached our destination, the shades were up. It was late afternoon. The first thing I saw was a yellow swirl across a blurred, reddish setting sun. The bus was being pelted by what sounded like splattering rain. It wasn't rain. This was my first look at something I would soon know very well, a billowing flurry of dust and sand churned up by the wind through Owens Valley.

21   We drove past a barbed-wire fence, through a gate, and into an open space where trunks and sacks and packages had been dumped from the baggage trucks that drove out ahead of us. I

could see a few tents set up, the first rows of black barracks, and beyond them, blurred by sand, rows of barracks that seemed to spread for miles across this plain. People were sitting on cartons or milling around, with their backs to the wind, waiting to see which friends or relatives might be on this bus. As we approached, they turned or stood up, and some moved toward us expectantly. But inside the bus no one stirred. No one waved or spoke. They just stared out the windows, ominously silent. I didn't understand this. Hadn't we finally arrived, our whole family intact? I opened a window, leaned out, and yelled happily. "Hey! This whole bus is full of Wakatsukis!"

22   Outside, the greeters smiled. Inside there was an explosion of laughter, hysterical, tension-breaking laughter that left my brothers choking and whacking each other across the shoulders.

23   We had pulled up just in time for dinner. The mess halls weren't completed yet. An outdoor chow line snaked around a half-finished building that broke a good part of the wind. They issued us army mess kits, the round metal kind that fold over, and plopped in scoops of canned Vienna sausage, canned string beans, steamed rice that had been cooked too long, and on top of the rice a serving of canned apricots. The Caucasian servers were thinking that the fruit poured over rice would make a good dessert. Among the Japanese, of course, rice is never eaten with sweet foods, only with salty or savory foods. Few of us could eat such a mixture. But at this point no one dared protest. It would have been impolite. I was horrified when I saw the apricot syrup seeping through my little mound of rice. I opened my mouth to complain. My mother jabbed me in the back to keep quiet. We moved on through the line and joined the others squatting in the lee of half-raised walls, dabbing courteously at what was, for almost everyone there, an inedible concoction.

24   After dinner we were taken to Block 16, a cluster of fifteen barracks that had just been finished a day or so earlier—although finished was hardly the word for it. The shacks were built of one thickness of pine planking covered with tarpaper. They sat on concrete footings, with about two feet of open space between the floorboards and the ground. Gaps showed

between the planks, and as the weeks passed and the green wood dried out, the gaps widened. Knotholes gaped in the uncovered floor.

25   Each barracks was divided into six units, sixteen by twenty feet, about the size of a living room, with one bare bulb hanging from the ceiling and an oil stove for heat. We were assigned two of these for the twelve people in our family group; and our official family "number" was enlarged by three digits—16 plus the number of this barracks. We were issued steel army cots, two brown army blankets each, and some mattress covers, which my brothers stuffed with straw.

26   The first task was to divide up what space we had for sleeping. Bill and Woody contributed a blanket each and partitioned off the first room: one side for Bill and Tomi, one side for Woody and Chizu and their baby girl. Woody also got the stove, for heating formulas.

27   The people who had it hardest during the first few months were young couples like these, many of whom had married just before the evacuation began, in order not to be separated and sent to different camps. Our two rooms were crowded, but at least it was all in the family. My oldest sister and her husband were shoved into one of those sixteen-by-twenty-foot compartments with six people they had never seen before—two other couples, one recently married like themselves, the other with two teenage boys. Partitioning off a room like that wasn't easy. It was bitter cold when we arrived, and the wind did not abate. All they had to use for room dividers were those army blankets, two of which were barely enough to keep one person warm. They argued over whose blanket should be sacrificed and later argued about noise at night—the parents wanted their boys asleep by 9:00 p.m.—and they continued arguing over matters like that for six months, until my sister and her husband left to harvest sugar beets in Idaho. It was grueling work up there, and wages were pitiful, but when the call came through camp for workers to alleviate the wartime labor shortage, it sounded better than their life at Manzanar. They knew they'd have, if nothing else, a room, perhaps a cabin of their own.

28   That first night in Block 16, the rest of us squeezed into the second room—Granny, Lillian, age fourteen, Ray, thirteen,

May, eleven, Kiyo, ten, Mama, and me. I didn't mind this at all at the time. Being youngest meant I got to sleep with Mama. And before we went to bed I had a great time jumping up and down on the mattress. The boys had stuffed so much straw into hers, we had to flatten it some so we wouldn't slide off. I slept with her every night after that until Papa came back.

POST-READING QUESTIONS

Content

1. Why does the mother move her family to Terminal Island? What are some of the results of the move?

2. What does the description of the town suggest about the people and their condition? What specific details give you these impressions?

3. What did the Navy decide to do to Terminal Island? How did second-hand dealers take advantage of the situation? Why did the narrator's mother react as she did, smashing her dishes and getting angry?

4. How did the narrator feel about moving to Manzanar? What are some of her initial feelings and reactions upon arriving at the camp? What details and specifics create the first impression of Manzanar?

5. What is the impression you have after reading the description of the camp and its activities? What problems would these Japanese-Americans encounter?

Strategies and Structures

1. Wakatsuki Houston's narration explains many causes and effects. What is the cause of her fear of other Asian children? What is the effect of being isolated from other Asians? How does she explain this cause and effect?

2. How does Wakatsuki Houston show the effects of being unable to speak the language of the community? What specifics make this passage so vivid and detailed?

3. What is the purpose of the episode about the second-hand dealer and the china set? Why is narration an effective means of achieving this purpose?

4. How does Wakatsuki Houston organize her material in order to make this essay easy to follow? What transitional devices and/or linking words does she use to make this organization apparent to the reader?

Vocabulary and Language

1. Often place names are used in narratives to suggest the journey a narrator of character takes; however, if we are unfamiliar with the region, these place names may confuse us. An excellent strategy for getting a sense of place is to consult a map and to try and follow the narrative journey. Wakatsuki Houston uses the following place names in her narrative: *Inglewood, Ocean Park, Santa Monica, Terminal Island, Long Beach, Manzanar, Boyle Heights, Los Angeles, Owens Valley.* Get a map of California and follow Wakatsuki Houston's journey using the above vocabulary words. Consult the essay as needed.

2. Wakatsuki Houston uses several Japanese words in paragraph 5. How does she explain the meaning of these words? Do you find this strategy effective? How might you be able to use such a strategy in your own essays?

GROUP ACTIVITIES

1. Many people have faced hardships because of the fear caused by the ignorance of another culture. Wakatsuki Houston explains the hardships encountered by Japanese-Americans because of the U.S. government's ignorance of Japanese-American culture. As a group, brainstorm and discuss other instances in which whole groups of people faced problems and hardships because of a lack of understanding. What groups have faced problems? What problems have

they faced? Why? Whose ignorance has caused these hardships? How have the persecuted people tried to deal with these problems?

2. Wakatsuki Houston explains how she felt about the camp as a child; however, she includes enough details about the reality of the camp to clearly show that it was not a pleasant place. First, freewrite about an experience which you either enjoyed or found unpleasant as a child but now feel differently about. Then share your freewriting with the rest of the group. As you listen to others, note why we change our feelings about an event.

WRITING ASSIGNMENTS

1. Write about an event in which you faced prejudice and/or hardship because of someone's lack of understanding about you or your culture. What were the causes of your problems and their lack of understanding? What were the effects of their misunderstanding?

2. Write an essay discussing the initial impression a person(s) had made upon you and how your first impression was subject to change once you got to know that person(s). Make sure you give plenty of representative examples to illustrate the validity of what you say.

The Libido for the Ugly
H. L. MENCKEN

Henry Louis Mencken (1880–1956) was a newspaper reporter, an editor and a columnist in Baltimore for over forty years. As illustrated in the following essay, Mencken was also a social critic who seemed to enjoy exposing the absurdities and hypocrisies of America's middle class. His works include *A Mencken Chrestomathy* (1949) and *A Choice of Days* (1980), the latter being a selection of his memoirs.

PRE-READING QUESTIONS

1. What does beauty look like? What sort of houses, buildings, or monuments do you consider ugly?

2. Though the word libido has been commonly associated with one's sex drive in the 20th century, its primary definition is: "emotional or psychic energy derived from primitive biological urges . . . ." Bearing this definition in mind, what sense can you make out of the title of this essay? What does it prepare you for? What expectations does it build?

1   On a Winter day some years ago, coming out of Pittsburgh on one of the expresses of the Pennsylvania Railroad, I rolled eastward for an hour through the coal and steel towns of Westmoreland county. It was familiar ground; boy and man, I had been through it often before. But somehow I had never quite sensed its appalling desolation. Here was the very heart of industrial America, the center of its most lucrative and characteristic activity, the boast and pride of the richest and grandest nation ever seen on earth—and here was a scene so dreadfully hideous, so intolerably bleak and forlorn that it reduced the whole aspiration of man to a macabre and depressing joke. Here was wealth beyond computation, almost beyond imagination—and here was human habitations so abominable that they would have disgraced a race of alley cats.

2   I am not speaking of mere filth. One expects steel towns to be dirty. What I allude to is the unbroken and agonizing ugliness, the sheer revolting monstrousness, of every house in sight. From East Liberty to Greensburg, a distance of twenty-five miles, there was not one in sight from the train that did not insult and lacerate the eye. Some were so bad, and they were among the most pretentious—churches, stores, warehouses, and the like—that they were downright startling; one blinked before them as one blinks before a man with his face shot away.

A few linger in memory, horrible even there: a crazy little church just west of Jeannette, set like a dormer-window on the side of a bare, leprous hill; the headquarters of the Veterans of Foreign Wars at another forlorn town, a steel stadium like a huge rat-trap somewhere further down the line. But most of all I recall the general effect—of hideousness without a break. There was not a single decent house within eye-range from the Pittsburgh suburbs to the Greensburg yards. There was not one that was not misshapen, and there was not one that was not shabby.

3   The country itself is not uncomely, despite the grime of the endless mills. It is, in form, a narrow river valley, with deep gullies running up into the hills. It is thickly settled, but not noticeably overcrowded. There is still plenty of room for building, even in the larger towns, and there are very few solid blocks. Nearly every house, big and little, has space on all four sides. Obviously, if there were architects of any professional sense or dignity in the region, they would have perfected a chalet to hug the hillsides—a chalet with a high-pitched roof, to throw off the heavy Winter snows, but still essentially a low and clinging building, wider than it was tall. But what have they done? They have taken as their model a brick set on end. This they have converted into a thing of dingy clapboards, with a narrow, low-pitched roof. And the whole they have set upon thin, preposterous brick piers. By the hundreds and thousands these abominable houses cover the bare hillsides, like gravestones in some gigantic and decaying cemetery. On their deep sides they are three, four and even five stories high; on their low sides they bury themselves swinishly in the mud. Not a fifth of them are perpendicular. They lean this way and that, hanging on to their bases precariously. And one and all they are streaked in grime, with dead and eczematous patches of paint peeping through the streaks.

4   Now and then there is a house of brick. But what brick! When it is new it is the color of a fried egg. When it has taken on the patina of the mills it is the color of an egg long past all hope or caring. Was it necessary to adopt that shocking color? No more than it was necessary to set all of the houses on end. Red brick, even in a steel town, ages with some dignity. Let it become downright black, and it is still sightly, especially if its

trimmings are of white stone, with soot in the depths and the high spots washed by the rain. But in Westmoreland they prefer that uremic yellow, and so they have the most loathsome towns and villages ever seen by mortal eye.

5   I award this championship only after laborious research and incessant prayer. I have seen, I believe, all of the most unlovely towns of the world; they are all to be found in the United States. I have seen the mill towns of decomposing New England and the desert towns of Utah, Arizona and Texas. I am familiar with the back streets of Newark, Brooklyn, and Chicago, and have made scientific explorations to Camden, N.J. and Newport News, Va. Safe in a Pullman, I have whirled through the gloomy, God-forsaken villages of Iowa and Kansas, and the malarious tide-water hamlets of Georgia. I have been to Bridgeport, Conn., and to Los Angeles. But nowhere on this earth, at home or abroad, have I seen anything to compare to the villages that huddle along the line of the Pennsylvania from the Pittsburgh yards to Greensburg. They are incomparable in color, and they are incomparable in design. It is as if some titanic and aberrant genius, uncompromisingly inimical to man, had devoted all the ingenuity of Hell to the making of them. They show grotesqueries of ugliness that, in retrospect, become almost diabolical. One cannot imagine mere human beings concocting such dreadful things, and one can scarcely imagine human beings bearing life in them.

6   Are they so frightful because the valley is full of foreigners—dull, insensate brutes, with no love of beauty in them? Then why didn't these foreigners set up similar abominations in the countries that they came from? You will, in fact, find nothing of the sort in Europe—save perhaps in the more putrid parts of England. There is scarcely an ugly village on the whole Continent. The peasants, however poor, somehow manage to make themselves graceful and charming habitations, even in Spain. But in the American village and small town the pull is always toward ugliness, and in that Westmoreland valley it has been yielded to with an eagerness bordering upon passion. It is incredible that mere ignorance should have achieved such masterpieces of horror.

7   On certain levels of the American race, indeed, there seems to be a positive libido for the ugly, as on other and less Christian

levels there is a libido for the beautiful. It is impossible to put down the wallpaper that defaces the average American home of the lower middle class to mere inadvertence, or to the obscene humor of the manufacturers. Such ghastly designs, it must be obvious, give a genuine delight to a certain type of mind. They meet, in some unfathomable way, its obscure and unintelligible demands. They caress it as "The Palms" caresses it, or the art of the movie, or jazz. The taste for them is as enigmatical and yet as common as the taste for dogmatic theology and the poetry of Edgar A. Guest.

8   Thus I suspect (though confessedly without knowing) that the vast majority of the honest folk of Westmoreland county, and especially the 100% Americans among them, actually admire the houses they live in, and are proud of them. For the same money they could get vastly better ones, but they prefer what they have got. Certainly there was no pressure upon the Veterans of Foreign Wars to choose the dreadful edifice that bears their banner, for there are plenty of vacant buildings along the track-side, and some of them are appreciably better. They might, indeed, have built a better one of their own. But they chose that clapboarded horror with their eyes open, and having chosen it, they let it mellow into its present shocking depravity. They like it as it is: beside it, the Parthenon would no doubt offend them. In precisely the same way the authors of the rat-trap stadium that I have mentioned made a deliberate choice. After painfully designing and erecting it, they made it perfect in their own sight by putting a completely impossible pent-house, painted a staring yellow, on top of it. The effect is that of a fat woman with a black eye. It is that of a Presbyterian grinning. But they like it.

9   Here is something that the psychologists have so far neglected: the love of ugliness for its own sake, the lust to make the world intolerable. Its habitat is the United States. Out of the melting pot emerges a race which hates beauty as it hates truth. The etiology of this madness deserves a great deal more study than it has got. There must be causes behind it; it arises and flourishes in obedience to biological laws, and not as a mere act of God. What, precisely, are the terms of those laws? And why do they run stronger in America than elsewhere? Let some honest *Privat Dozent* in pathological sociology apply himself to the problem.

POST-READING QUESTIONS

Content

1. What is the controlling idea of thesis in this essay?

2. What does Mencken think of American architects? Why?

3. Why does the author suspect "the vast majority of the honest folk of Westmoreland county, and especially the 100% Americans among them, actually admire the houses they live in, and are proud of them"?

4. Though Mencken refers to the United States and its citizens in general, where does he focus the better part of his essay in particular? Why?

Strategies and Structures

1. How does Mencken support his claim that the ugliest towns in the world "are to be found in the United States"? What strategies of development does he use? How convincing is his evidence?

2. Reread the introductory paragraph. What does Mencken initially do here to interest his reader in his topic?

3. How does he pull all the parts of his essay together in his concluding paragraph? What is the purpose of his final sentence?

4. Explain the function of paragraph 6 where Mencken talks about foreigners. How does it strengthen his claim that "in the American village and small town the pull is always toward ugliness"?

Language and Vocabulary

1. Vocabulary: This essay provides the basis for an ideal group exercise in vocabulary. See Group Activity 1.

2. What is the tone or mood of this composition, and how does Mencken's word choice reflect his attitude

towards Americans and ugliness? If he lowered his diction (used smaller words), would the mood of his essay change? Explain your point of view.

GROUP ACTIVITIES

1. Divide "The Libido for the Ugly" into three or four sections. Each group will then be responsible for locating vocabulary words in its section, looking-up definitions, and, finally, typing a lexicon (words and their definitions) of the vocabulary words for the rest of the class. Xerox or ditto enough copies of your lexicon for everyone in class.

2. Make a survey of the visible buildings/houses where you live—especially the newer constructions. Then, based on the results of your survey, determine if Mencken's assessment of Americans and their love of ugliness is justified. Begin by having your group decide what qualities make a building ugly or beautiful. Then either brainstorm the idea of "ugly/beautiful buildings" in the classroom—coming up with specific examples of each—or drive around town taking note of the same thing: the pull towards ugliness in building design rather than beauty.

WRITING ACTIVITIES

1. Is beauty really only in the eye of the beholder? To what extent do you think Mencken is being fair? Write an essay explaining why you think America (or a town in America) has or does not have a libido for the ugly or grotesque. Make sure your reasoning is clear and your examples are representative of your topic. You will want to mention exceptions to your thesis early in your essay to seem honest and fair.

2. Write an essay in which you prove or disprove Mencken's statement that: "Out of the melting pot emerges a race which hates beauty as it hates truth."

Additional Topics and Issues for Expository Essays

1. Compose and develop an original thesis that says something specific about visual pollution. In doing so, you may want to answer such questions as: "What is visual pollution? Where is one likely to encounter visual pollution?" and "What can or should be done about it?"

2. Write an expository essay wherein you explain a solution to the overpopulation problem without eliminating any of the people already alive.

3. Analyze the parking problem at your college. What is the cause of it? How does it affect your daily routine, particularly the time you get up and whether or not the solution cuts into your study time? Make sure you show your reader what goes on by offering him or her a glimpse into your life.

4. Explain how economics influence and often dictate our political and social relationships with countries around the world by comparing and contrasting an economic boom to a recession. If you draw information from outside sources, make sure that you acknowledge them correctly.

5. Explain why it is important to wear all the latest fashions in order to attract a love interest. Begin with a brief discussion of the process of keeping up with the fads. How much money do you have to spend? With whom is it important to be seen? Why? Are there any long-range effects of being a slave to fashion? You will want to conclude your essay with a thoughtful analysis of your topic.

6. Write an essay wherein you demonstrate how stockpiling nuclear weapons is a deterrence or an invitation to war.

7. After attracting your reader's interest by using a clever anecdote in your thesis, write an essay exposing how and why pets fulfill an emotional void in many people's lives.

8. There has been much written about the effects of television on today's generation. Write an original, insightful essay wherein you explain (1) why you think people spend so many hours in front of their television sets, and (2) the results of watching too much television.

11

ARGUMENTATION: THE LOGICAL APPEAL

Argumentative essays should be based on sound logic. The most elemental forms of reasoning stem from induction and deduction. When preparing to write an argumentative paper, imagine you are a detective, perhaps Sherlock Holmes, the famous fictional sleuth, renowned for his powers of observation that led to his deductive reasoning. Through this deductive reasoning, he was able to solve the most baffling cases. In a similar manner, by carefully observing all aspects of an argument, you may successfully draw conclusions from them, conclusions that are reasonable, logical, and verifiable.

Inductive Logic

Induction moves from the particular to the general. This is when you take several representative examples of a person, place, or thing and make a general observation of it. What general observation, for instance, could you make about the following three facts?

- Sixty-four people lost their lives due to California's earthquake last fall.

308

- Fifty-two people died during a flash-flood in Ohio last month.
- Hurricane Hugo claimed thirty-nine lives in South Carolina.

No doubt you noticed that each fact had two things in common with the others: multiple human deaths and a natural disaster. What can we conclude by considering the three facts? *Natural disasters can be dangerous.*

The greater number of representative examples (facts) you can offer your reader, the better. Why? Inductive arguments require a *leap in logic,* a leap from specific points to one believable general point, and the more examples you can offer, the smaller the inductive leap. When you check your argumentative essays for weak points, you frequently are searching for places where the connection between your specific points and generalizations requires your reader to place more "faith" in your word than concrete evidence. Whenever this occurs, your inductive leap—getting from your specific points to a general, logical conclusion—is too broad and thereby unconvincing. Furthermore, since one exception to a claim like "all men like to play golf on weekends" would disprove your point, you often will want to qualify what you say using words like "most, usually, often."

Deduction

The opposite of induction, deduction, moves from general points—evidence—and leads to a specific conclusion. A valid deductive conclusion, however, depends on the truth of its evidence (this evidence can be either of major or minor importance). The following logical statement illustrates this point. If I say *All show dogs have pedigrees* (major evidence) and that *My dog Grendel has a pedigree* (minor evidence), I could deduce that *Grendel is a show dog.* What is wrong with my reasoning? We all know that *not* every dog with a pedigree appears in dog shows; therefore, it cannot be concluded that every dog with a pedigree is automatically a show dog. Evidence that is not true can lead to untrue conclusions. To insure that your deduction is logical and valid, qualify your major evidence with a word like "many"—*Many pedigree dogs are show dogs.* Deductive reasoning, therefore, should be seen as an aid in leading the reader to the conclusion you want him or her to reach. Mark Fissel uses deductive logic in just such a way in "Distance Learning and American Society" to arrive at the conclusion that most segments of American society can or already do benefit from "distance learning" without threatening cultural diversity.

Types of Argumentation

Are there different types of argumentation? Yes. At times, one will argue for an entire essay that something like censorship is or is not constitutional. Here, an author argues to establish what he or she believes is a convincing fact, a fact worthy of a reader's attention. A good example of an argument of fact would be "Peyote, Wine, and the First Amendment." Laycock argues that governmental bodies in the United States—local or federal—should not regulate religious rituals and ceremonies of minor religions, particularly those of Native-American Indians who use peyote as part of a "substantial tradition" and that their use of peyote is limited to a "structured worship service." In arguing his case, Laycock points out that the First Amendment guarantees "the free exercise of religion."

Another way, though a bit more difficult, to write an argument of fact is through negation, which is explaining what something is *not*. This sometimes proves useful in developing an argumentative essay. By clearly stating what qualities, characteristics, or concepts something does not contain, a writer can create a clear picture of what something is. Often writers will disprove a popular definition, notion, or myth about something as they set up a different definition of their own. For example, in "Does America Still Exist?," Richard Rodriguez argues that the "ideal" America is *not* what Americans believe it is.

At times, however, writing a factual argument is only the starting point of an essay. In such an essay, a problem or issue will be identified and defined in the first few paragraphs. Then, an author will propose a logical course of action, convincing the reader of the merit of his or her solution. Arguments containing a *call to action* demand that an author impress his or her readers that a situation exists which needs to be addressed and changed. If your neighbor told you that your best friend was a terrorist and should be turned over to the police or the Federal Bureau of Investigation, what are the chances of your doing so? Without specific evidence, you are unlikely to embark upon any plan of action. Reacting to hearsay and unsubstantiated reason makes an act impulsive, not rational or ethical. In short, provide your reader with sufficient reason to "act."

Still another form of argumentation is the argument of refutation. In such an essay, an author strives to disprove an opposing viewpoint on a topic. To do so, writers attack generalizations and faulty logic used by their counterparts. In "Soul Food," for instance, Bakara refutes (argues) that those who claim African-Americans lack a distinct cuisine do not know what they are talking about. To tear apart his oppositions' argument, he shows through illustration and example that foods like *grits, fried porgie,* and *black-eyed peas* are definite African-American contributions to our country's varied cultural cuisines.

Clearly Stated Thesis

Though the type of argument may be determined by your objective for writing the essay, all types of argumentation usually have one thing in common: *a strong, clearly stated thesis.* As in most compositions, a specific thesis statement will help you keep your essay focused when developing the composition, avoiding digressions and superfluous facts. Such a thesis will unquestionably lead your reader to your opinion and help frame the supporting points of the argument. An uncertain thesis is bound to result in reader as well as writer confusion.

Avoiding Fallacies

A fallacy is an incorrect or falsely reasoned fact. We could devote an entire course in logic discussing them, but for our purposes, we'll only mention a few fallacies by name—the ones most likely to occur and weaken an argument.

1. *Ad Hominem* (To the Person): This is when you twist the focus of an argument by attacking the person who made it rather than arguing the issue at hand. In other words, a person guilty of *ad hominem* might spend time attempting to persuade readers that an opponent is disreputable rather than refute an argument that animals have rights.

2. *Stereotyping:* Since stereotyping inaccurately presents people, places, and things (e.g., all Californians have suntans, only Yuppies drive BMW cars, or anyone who lives in Florida is retired), using stereotypes to support an argument will weaken rather than strengthen it.

3. *Faulty Sampling:* When you support an argument with specific examples, you must make certain that your examples are truly representative of your topic. Suppose that you argue that Americans no longer like house pets and say that recently 90 percent of the Americans surveyed said they don't own or plan to own a pet. If, however, you surveyed only 10 people (9 of whom disliked animals), your examples can only be inaccurate. This points to one of the major problems in using statistics: you can make them say what you want.

4. *Sweeping Generalizations:* To avoid sweeping generalizations, make the use of qualifying word and phrases such as: usually, often, most, some, several, and avoid the use of absolute phrases like, "Everybody enjoys swimming." One person who dislikes or fears swimming makes your entire statement untrue!

Tips on Writing Argumentative Essays

1. Pre-write to determine what you wish to say about your topic. As mentioned earlier, a very clear thesis is essential, for if you have a fuzzy, unclear thesis, your reader won't know precisely what you are arguing for or against. A seemingly uncertain writer is not too trustworthy or convincing.

2. Don't apologize for your viewpoint; justify it! This is particularly important to remember when you take an unpopular stance on a topic or issue. After all, popular opinion does not depend on ethical or logical reasoning.

3. Make sure you can defend what you claim. Have a firm basis for what you are contending. Do not assume your reader will agree with your social, political, or religious viewpoints. Avoid "leap-of-faith" arguments.

4. Present all sides of your topic/issue; otherwise, your paper is not an argument. If your opponent makes or has a good point, don't ignore it. Place it early in your essay. By acknowledging that no issue is black or white, you will seem ethical and reasonable.

5. Present your material in emphatic order (move from your weakest to your strongest argument). Otherwise, your supporting argument may seem anticlimatic or weak by comparison. Step-by-step, lead your reader to the conclusion.

6. Use authoritative evidence for technical information whenever you can to make what you claim believable.

7. In arguments of action, show how and why your plan of action is the most logical one to adopt. By taking time to explain who or what will benefit from your proposal, you will not only appear a logical person but also an ethical person.

8. Check your work for faulty logic and generalizations; do so in all stages of the writing process to avoid building an entire argument on a faulty premise, one that you will only have to rethink and rewrite in order to make rational sense.

Who is Your Mother? Red Roots of White Feminism
PAULA GUNN ALLEN

A well-known Laguna (Sioux)/Lebanese poet, novelist, and essayist, Paula Gunn Allen's works include *The Scared Hoop: Recovering The Femine In American Indian Traditions* (1986), the source of the following excerpt, and *The Women Who Owned The Shadows* (1983).

PRE-READING QUESTIONS

1. Most Americans have immigrant origins. An old American saying is "we've all come from somewhere else." What are your family origins? What traditions and customs—holidays, foods, beliefs—does your family still observe?

2. What are some traditions of the Native-American people? Which of these traditions can you speculate have been lost? Which of their lost traditions could enrich American society today?

1   At Laguna Pueblo in New Mexico, "Who is your mother?" is an important question. At Laguna, one of several of the ancient Keres gynocratic societies of the region, your mother's identity is the key to your own identity. Among the Keres, every individual has a place within the universe—human and nonhuman—and that place is defined by clan membership. In turn, clan membership is dependent on matrilineal descent. Of course, your mother is not only that woman whose womb formed and released you—the term refers in every individual case to an entire generation of women whose psychic, and consequently physical, "shape" made the psychic existence of the following generation possible. But naming your own mother (or her equivalent) enables people to place you precisely within the universal web of your life, in each of its dimensions: cultural, spiritual, personal, and historical.

2   Among the Keres, "context" and "matrix" are equivalent terms, and both refer to approximately the same thing as knowing your derivation and place. Failure to know your mother, that is, your position and its attendant traditions, history, and place in the scheme of things, is failure to remember your significance, your reality, your right relationship to earth and society. It is the same as being lost—isolated, abandoned, self-estranged, and alienated from your own life. This importance of tradition in the life of every member of the community is not confined to Keres Indians; all American Indian Nations place great value on traditionalism.

3   The Native American sense of the importance of continuity with one's cultural origins runs counter to contemporary

American ideas: in many instances, the immigrants to America have been eager to cast off cultural ties, often seeing their antecedents as backward, restrictive, even shameful. Rejection of tradition constitutes one of the major features of American life, an attitude that reaches far back into American colonial history and that now is validated by virtually every cultural institution in the country. Feminist practice, at least in the cultural artifacts the community values most, follows this cultural trend as well.

4   The American idea that the best and the brightest should willingly reject and repudiate their origins leads to an allied idea—that history, like everything in the past, is of little value and should be forgotten as quickly as possible. This all too often causes us to reinvent the wheel continually. We find ourselves discovering our collective pasts over and over, having to retake ground already covered by women in the preceding decades and centuries. The Native American view, which highly values maintenance of traditional customs, values, and perspectives, might result in slower societal change and in quite a bit less social upheaval, but it has the advantage of providing a solid sense of identity and lowered levels of psychological and interpersonal conflict.

5   Contemporary Indian communities value individual members who are deeply connected to the traditional ways of their people, even after centuries of concerted and brutal effort on the part of the American government, the churches, and the corporate system to break the connections between individuals and their tribal world. In fact, in the view of the traditionals, rejection of one's culture—one's traditions, language, people— is the result of colonial oppression and is hardly to be applauded. They believe that the roots of oppression are to be found in the loss of tradition and memory because that loss is always accompanied by a loss of a positive sense of self. In short, Indians think it is important to remember, while Americans believe it is important to forget.

6   The traditional Indians' view can have a significant impact if it is expanded to mean that the sources of social, political, and philosophical thought in the Americas not only should be recognized and honored by Native Americans but should be embraced by American society. If American society judiciously

modeled the traditions of the various Native Nations, the place of women in society would become central, the distribution of goods and power would be egalitarian, the elderly would be respected, honored, and protected as a primary social and cultural resource, the ideals of physical beauty would be considerably enlarged (to include "fat," strong-featured women, gray-haired, and wrinkled individuals, and others who in contemporary American culture are viewed as "ugly"). Additionally, the destruction of the biota, the life sphere, and the natural resources of the planet would be curtailed, and the spiritual nature of human and nonhuman life would become a primary organizing principle of human society. And if the traditional tribal systems that are emulated included pacifist ones, war would cease to be a major method of human problem solving.

POST-READING QUESTIONS

Content

1. In the Laguna tribe, how does one establish his or her identity? What benefits does this form of identity have?

2. What are the disadvantages to not knowing your mother? What is important to the Native-American way of life?

3. Have contemporary Americans held onto their cultural origins? What forces does Allen suggest have promoted this cultural alienation?

4. What would be the results if contemporary American culture adopted traditional views of Native-Americans? Why would American culture change? How would it change?

5. What are the contrasting values of contemporary American and Native-American culture? What results from the contemporary American way of life? What are the results of Native-American cultural values?

Strategies and Structures

1. How does Allen start her essay? Why does she begin her essay this way?

2. Where does Allen present her thesis? How does it help the reader to focus on the controlling idea of her essay?

3. How does Allen use comparison and contrast to support her argument that we must not reject our traditions? And how does she use this strategy to develop her argument that we should adopt Native-American values?

4. In the final paragraph, Allen suggests the benefits of adopting Native-American values. Why does she present all of the benefits in one paragraph? What is the result of structuring the essay this way?

Language and Vocabulary

1. Vocabulary: *matrilineal, psychic, context, matrix, self-estranged, alienated, antecedents, interpersonal.* Most of these words cause the reader to lose track of what Allen is trying to say. Look up the definitions of the words and rewrite the sentences in which they appear using simple language. Does this in any way change the effect? How? Why?

2. Allen repeats key terms throughout the essay. What are they? How do they help unify the essay and keep it focused?

GROUP ACTIVITIES

1. Form multicultural groups and compare your different beliefs. How have the different cultures retained or rejected their traditions? Who is the traditional head of the household in the different cultures? What are the different relationships between humanity and nature? What are the different religious

beliefs? What are the different political beliefs and institutions present in the history of each culture? You may want to create a chart in which you list the different cultural beliefs under different headings such as religion, politics, assimilation.

2. As a group, do a short research project in which you compare three different world cultures and their traditions. What are their political histories? Who have been their leaders? What are their different religious beliefs and how have they developed over time? What have been their different beliefs about the relationship between humanity and nature? What are the different scientific discoveries that have shaped their cultures?

WRITING ACTIVITIES

1. Do some research on your cultural origins. You may want to interview relatives, do research in the library, and/or watch some films on your culture in the audiovisual center. After researching, write a paper in which you argue for the inclusion of one your culture's traditions into mainstream, contemporary American culture.

2. Write a paper in which you argue for or against assimilation or the "melting-pot" theory. Explain the different benefits and disadvantages of assimilation. Explain why immigrants should or should not abandon their original culture's traditions in favor of contemporary American culture.

Soul Food
IMAMU AMIRI BARAKA

An essayist, poet, novelist, and playwright, Imamu Amiri Baraka is best known
for his play *The Dutchman* (1964). Other works include: *Black Magic: Poetry
1961–1967* (1967), and *Selected Poetry of Imamu Amiri Baraka/LeRoi
Jones* (1979).

PRE-READING QUESTIONS

1. What does the essay's title suggest to the reader?
   Have you any idea what soul food is? What?

2. What do you think about when you hear the term
   soul linked with food or music? Have you any idea
   where the meaning you associate with such terms
   originated? Briefly write about your own "word history" for *soul* in your thesis notebook, writing log, or
   class journal.

1   Recently, a young Negro novelist writing in *Esquire* about
the beauties of America mentioned that one of the things wrong
with Negroes was that, unlike the Chinese, boots have neither a
language of their own nor a characteristic cuisine. And this to
me is the deepest stroke, the unkindest cut, of oppression, especially as it has distorted Black Americans. America, where
the suppliant, far from rebelling or even disagreeing with the
forces that have caused him to suffer, readily backs them up
and finally tries to become an honorary oppressor himself.

2   No language? No characteristic food? Oh, man, come on.

3   Maws are things ofays seldom get to peck, nor are you likely
ever to hear about Charlie eating a chitterling. Sweet potato
pies, a good friend of mine asked recently, "Do they taste anything like pumpkin?" Negative. They taste more like memory, if
you're not uptown.

4   All those different kinds of greens (now quick frozen for
anyone) once were all Sam got to eat. (Plus the potlikker, into

which one slipped some throwed away meat.) Collards and turnips and kale and mustards were not fit for anybody but the woogies. So they found a way to make them taste like something somebody would want to freeze and sell to a Negro going to Harvard as exotic European spinach.

5   The watermelon, friend, was imported from Africa (by whom?) where it had been growing many centuries before it was necessary for some people to deny that they had ever tasted one.

6   Did you ever hear of a black-eyed pea? (Whitey used it for forage, but some folks couldn't.) And all those weird parts of the hog? (After the pig was stripped of its choicest parts, the feet, snout, tail, intestines, stomach, etc., were all left for the "members," who treated them mercilessly.) Is it mere myth that shades are death on chickens? (Deep fat frying, the Dutch found out in 17th century New Amsterdam was an African specialty: and if you can get hold of a fried chicken leg, or a fried porgie, you can find out what happened to that tradition.)

7   I had to go to Rutgers before I found people who thought grits were meant to be eaten with milk and sugar, instead of gravy and pork sausage . . . and that's one of the reasons I left.

8   Away from home, you must make the trip uptown to get really straight as far as a good grease is concerned. People kill chickens all over the world, but chasing them though the dark on somebody else's property would probably insure, once they went in the big bag, that you'd find some really beautiful way to eat them. I mean, after all the risk involved. The fruit of that tradition unfolds everywhere above 100th Street. There are probably more restaurants in Harlem whose staple is fried chicken, or chicken in the basket, than any other place in the world. Ditto, barbecued ribs—also straight out of the South with the West Indians, *i.e.*, Africans from farther south in the West, having developed the best sauce for roasting whole oxen and hogs, spicy and extremely hot.

9   Hoppin' John (black-eyed peas and rice), hushpuppies (crusty cornmeal bread cooked in fish grease and best with fried fish, especially fried salt fish, which ought to soak overnight unless you're over fifty and can take all that salt), hoecake (pan bread), buttermilk biscuits and pancakes, fatback,

i.e., streak'alean-streak'afat, dumplings, neck bones, knuckles (both good for seasoning limas or string beans), okra (another African importation, other name gumbo), pork chops—some more staples of the Harlem cuisine. Most of the food came North when the people did.

10   There are hundreds of tiny restaurants, food shops, rib joints, shrimp shacks, chicken shacks, "rotisseries" throughout Harlem that serve "soul food"—say, a breakfast of grits, eggs and sausage, pancakes and Alaga syrup—and even tiny booths where it's at least possible to get a good piece of barbecue, hot enough to make you whistle, or a chicken wing on a piece of greasy bread. You can *always* find a fish sandwich: a fish sandwich is something you walk with, or "Two of those small sweet potato pies to go." The Muslim temple serves bean pies which are really separate. It is never necessary to go to some big expensive place to get a good filling grease. You *can* go to the Red Rooster, or Wells, or Joch's, and get a good meal, but Jennylin's, a little place on 135th near Lenox, is more filling, or some place like the A&A food shop in a basement up in the 140's, and you can really get away. I guess a square is somebody who's in Harlem and eats at Nedicks.

POST-READING QUESTIONS

Content

1. What argument of fact does Baraka seek to establish in this essay? Does the author accomplish his purpose? Why or why not?

2. What methods does the author use to illustrate that African-Americans, indeed, have a cuisine of their own?

3. What is the author attempting to express by his constant reference to "uptown?" Is this a reference meaningful only to African-Americans? Provide several examples to illustrate your reasoning.

4. Baraka concludes his essay by saying, "I guess a square is somebody who's in Harlem and eats at Nedicks." (Nedicks is a typical American fast-food

restaurant that does not serve soul food.) Why is it appropriate that he ends his essay in such a manner? How does his comment re-inforce his argument about African-Americans?

Strategies and Structures

1. Why does the author first *use* African-American terms for food and later define these food terms? Does this suggest a two-part argument? In what way?

2. What is the value of slang in this composition? Do slang terms serve a strategical purpose in Baraka's argument? Explain.

3. How well does the subject of food work as a unifying device in Baraka's essay? Cite some specific examples that support your claim.

Language and Vocabulary

1. *Vocabulary: chitterling, potlikker, collards, fried porgie, grits.* How many of these words can you find in a pocket dictionary? If you are unable to find all of the words, try using an unabridged dictionary. Next, try to locate the recipes for some of the above. Choose one recipe that particularly appeals to you and either cook it yourself or go to a *soul food* restaurant and order the food. Then write an essay persuading your reader to try the food.

2. Does the use of slang add an exotic nature to your conception of *soul food?* How? Why?

GROUP ACTIVITIES

1. Get into diverse groups and discuss foods that are typical in each represented culture. Argue for their uniqueness. Are there any slang terms that have developed for the foods your group considers? If so, are they in common use in America today? What would be lost without the slang terms?

2. Visit a restaurant—other than fast food restaurants like McDonalds—that serves a cuisine other than your own. Order a food you never have tasted and also sample those foods ordered by members of your group. Then write an essay in which you defend your own food or promote the new food that you have tried.

WRITING ACTIVITIES

1. Compose an essay based on a cultural issue (food, clothing, habits), arguing for your topic's uniqueness to your culture. Carefully consider any opposing arguments, addressing them as necessary, in order to be convincing.

2. Write an essay arguing how and why America needs to become a multilingual society (one that speaks several languages) in order to preserve cultural differences and enrich society as a whole.

This Land Was Your Land
JUDY CHRISTRUP

Judy Christrup contributed the following argument of fact and need for action in the September/October, 1990 edition of *Greenpeace,* a magazine devoted to discussing important issues about our immediate environment and the ecosystem of the world.

PRE-READING QUESTIONS

1. Cluster the words *forest* and *logging.* Outside of trees, what do they have in common? How might the relationship between environmentalists and loggers be positive? How might it be negative?

2. What do you believe is the primary objective of a business or industry? How many businesses can you think of where employing workers is more important than making profits? Jot down a brief list of such businesses/industries and then read the following essay.

1   Nearly all of the ancient trees have been cut down. Less than 5 percent of the virgin forests that once blanketed the United States remain, most in the Pacific Northwest. Known as "the west side" by foresters, the Pacific Northwest is hosting a showdown of sorts for the campaign to save the last shreds of ancient forest.

2   A citizen initiative on the California ballot in November would use eminent domain to buy out 3,000 acres of privately owned (and rapidly falling) old-growth redwoods. Because the owner, Maxxam Corporation, will try to cut as many trees as possible before the ballot, hundreds of activists are streaming into Northern California for a "Redwood Summer" of civil disobedience and demonstrations.

3   Casual readers of the mainstream press may come away harboring some sympathy for the timber magnates. Since the northern spotted owl was listed as a "threatened" species under the Endangered Species Act, articles in *The Washington Post* and *The New York Times* have drawn the battle lines between loggers on one side and environmentalists and owls on the other. Even *Time,* which correctly admitted that "It isn't that simple," still titled its feature story "Owl vs. Man." In fact, a more accurate description of the problem is "man vs. man."

4   "Since when has industry been worried about jobs?" asks Bob Freimark, Assistant Regional Director of the Wilderness Society's Oregon office. More than 26,000 timber-related jobs were lost to mill efficiency, mill automation and exports between 1979 and 1989 in Oregon and Washington states alone. Even if no habitat is set aside for the spotted owl, 20,800 more jobs directly and indirectly related to the timber industry will be lost over the next decade. In fact, Freimark's office has calculated that if we stopped exporting whole and split logs to the Orient, enough domestic jobs would be saved to offset those "lost" by protecting the spotted owl.

5   The economy of the Northwest depends little on the health of the logging industry. Oregon and Washington, which each have more spotted owl habitat than California, experienced an increase of 320,000 jobs in just two years (1987–1989). Dr. William Conerly, economist and vice president of the First Interstate Bank of Oregon (the state with the most timber jobs per capita, amounting to six percent of employment) issued a fact sheet that says, "The statewide effects of the owl plan will be relatively mild. The estimate of 150,000 jobs lost should be put in context. The state of Oregon has seen 200,000 jobs created in the last five years, and with normal growth would create another 150,000 new jobs in the next five years."

6   The industry's ill-created timber workers provide a convenient lobbying army for their management. Louisiana Pacific (LP), one of the largest timber companies bussed workers to Redding, California in August of 1989 to testify against the spotted owl, just one week before local newspapers revealed that the company was planning to open a huge mill in Mexico, where it can pay laborers under $2.00 an hour. In 1984 LP busted its union. While steadily trimming its American work force, LP has recorded its greatest-ever sales—$2 billion in 1989. That same year, its highest stock price rose 15 percent over the previous year, from $37.50 to $43.25 per share.

7   The logging crisis, and the record profits, are driven by the takeover fever that has gripped the timber industry over the last few years. To name a few: Sir James Goldsmith slowly devoured Diamond International from 1982 to 1988 and moved on to Crown Zellerbach in 1984; Georgia Pacific bought out Great Northern Nekoosa and Great Northern Paper; and Maxxam Corporation's notorious Charles Hurwitz swallowed Pacific Lumber and tripled its felling of old-growth redwoods to pay off the junk bond debt.

8   To keep corporate raiders at bay or to pay off debts accumulated in a raid, the only "rational" thing for timber companies to do is liquidate (read: clear-cut) their assets. Says Jeff DeBonus, president of the Association of Forest Service Employees for Environmental Ethics, "If you're a CPA in Chicago, and you are looking at timber land that is only giving you 3–5 percent on your investment, it's undervalued capital. So the big industries are clear-cutting, liquidating all of their forest land

as fast as possible, converting it into capital and reinvesting in other sectors of the economy at a much higher rate of return."

9   The U.S. Forest Service is party to this high stakes game. It makes Forest Service land available to logging companies. In fact, each regional Forest Service office is rewarded for selling standing timber (known as "stumpage" in the trade), due to the Knutson-Vandenberg Act, which allows each forest to keep an unlimited share of timber receipts for its own budget. But there is a catch. The Forest Service doesn't have to make a profit on the sales. In fact, over two-thirds of national forests lose money on their timber sales, contributing to an annual Forest Service deficit of about a billion dollars. The net result: American tax-payers are actually subsidizing the cutting of our national forests.

10   As the remaining old-growth forests continue to disappear under the chain saws, opposition to logging has increased in intensity. More established groups such as the Sierra Club and the Wilderness Society have found themselves outflanked by new cadres of tree protectors such as Earth First! and the Ancient Forest Alliance, who are less inclined to compromise with the timber industry and the Forest Service.

11   Other grassroots groups have sprung up across the country to oppose below-cost timber sales and clear-cutting in second- and third-growth national forests. Organizations like Protect Our Woods, Western North Carolina Alliance, Mark Twain Forest Watchers, and RACE (Regional Association of Concerned Environmentalists) are trying to protect trees in their own backyards. RACE has been quietly fighting an administrative and judicial battle to save hardwoods in Illinois' Shawnee National Forest. After losing an attempt to save an area called Fairview, Jan Thomas of RACE wrote, "The songbirds who depend on unbroken canopy are declining as more and more edge is created. Fairview is the last large unbroken woodlands in Jackson County on public lands. We will move into the woods tonight to see what we can generate in the way of hassling the cutters to distraction."

12   While activists are blockading logging roads, other environmentalists are planning for top-down reform. Forest economist Randall O'Toole has critiqued dozens of Forest Service plans, from New Mexico to Alaska, and has reduced timber sales by

millions of acres. O'Toole knew that national reform was necessary when he looked over his work in 1986. "I sat down and figured out what we'd done so far and how much further we have to go. I realized it was going to take 490 years more to finish the job. Well, I believe in medical miracles. But even if I live 490 more years, I wasn't convinced that the forests were going to last 490 more years."

13   The imperatives for ancient forest destruction—the "stumpage" funding arrangement in the Forest Service and the coalition between the industry and a few Congressmen to protect profits—must be changed. O'Toole advocates rearranging the funding for the Forest Service, charging user fees for recreation and other uses of public lands, and allowing people to buy timber and NOT cut it down.

14   While other activists are uneasy about charging for use of public lands, all agree that the cutting must stop. A new coalition called Save America's Forests is planning an assault on Capitol Hill. It has adopted a platform that calls for ending clear-cutting in public forests; aiding displaced workers, their families and communities; and creating new conservation incentives for forest managers.

POST-READING QUESTIONS

Content

1. What does the author claim is the real cause for vanishing jobs in the logging industry? To what extent is the Spotted Owl or any other animal responsible?

2. What is one of the main causes of the "logging crisis"?

3. According to Christrup, what is the role of the U.S. Forest Service in today's logging industry?

4. What are some of the organizations which oppose logging "old growth forests," and what strategies do they employ to further their cause?

Strategies and Structures

1. How is the tone of this essay immediately established by its title: "This Land was Your Land"?

2. To whom does the author seem to be appealing? How does she structure her composition in order to effectively argue her position on logging?

3. How does Christrup establish her point of view in the first two sentences of the essay? Which sentence serves as the controlling idea for her entire composition?

4. Christrup cites several authorities, facts, and statistics as she presents her argument. Which supporting information do you find most and least convincing? Why?

5. At what point in the essay is Christrup's "call to action" made clear? Why do you find this an effective place for it? Would the "call to action" have been as effective if it had been placed at the beginning of the essay? Why? Why not?

Language and Vocabulary

1. Vocabulary: *initiative, eminent, magnates, efficiency, habitat, liquidate, environmentalist, imperatives, coalition, advocates.* Write a one-page summary of Christrup's essay using the above vocabulary words. If you do not know the definition of each of the words, either look them up in the dictionary or figure out their meanings from the context of the passage.

2. Make a list of some specific instances in this essay where the author's language indicates her attitude towards her subject. Then, do the same thing to a recent composition you have written.

GROUP ACTIVITIES

1. Divide into two major groups, one pro and one con, and prepare to debate the need to continue logging. Your group will want to spend some time doing some library research to gain an in-depth understanding of *both* sides of this issue. If possible, visit a national park containing an "old growth forest." Finally, videotape the class debate; then, go back over the videotape and critique the persuasive merit of both arguments.

2. When this article first appeared in *Greenpeace* in September/October of 1990, the author provided a list of the following organizations' addresses:

Association of Forest Service
Employees for Environmental
   Ethics
P.O. Box 11615
Eugene, OR 97440

Forests Forever
2410 K Street, Suite C
Sacramento, CA 95816

LightHawk: The Wings
   of Conservation
Box 8163
Sante Fe, NM 87504

Forest Reform Network
5934 Royal Lane, Suite 223
Dallas, TX 95230

Native Forest Council
P.O. Box 2171
Eugene, OR 97402

Save America's Forest
1742 18th Street, NW
Washington, DC 20009

Have each group select one of these organizations and write a collaborative letter to it requesting specific information about the organization's formation, supporters, activities, and cause. After your materials arrive, analyze them in a group meeting and prepare to present your critique of your organization to the rest of the class. Regardless of your findings, the last thing your group will do on this assignment is to write a letter of appreciation back to the organization which sent you information. If your initial letter was ignored or returned, your group may write a letter to one of the other groups mentioned in the essay such as the Sierra Club or Protect Our Forest.

WRITING ACTIVITIES

1. Write a letter to a local or federal government official using argumentation to illustrate how and why he or she is doing a good job fighting for issues that affect the world around us (e.g., promoting bills encouraging practices to decrease the greenhouse

effect) or to point out a clear need for immediate action(s).

2. Refute the argument that: *"To keep corporate raiders at bay or to pay off debts accumulated in a raid, the only 'rational' thing for timber companies [or any other company at conflict with environmentalists] to do is liquidate . . . their assets . . . in other sectors of the economy at a much higher rate of return."*

Does America Still Exist?
RICHARD RODRIGUEZ

A San Francisco native, Richard Rodriguez was the son of Mexican immigrants. His articles frequently appear in *Change, The American Scholar,* and *The Saturday Review.* His works include *Hunger of Memory* (1982) which relates the conflict of ethnic identification and American cultural assimilation.

PRE-READING QUESTIONS

1. What are some traditional symbols and words associated with America? What do they stand for?

2. Who are Americans? Is America a common culture or a diverse culture? Are all its citizens truly equal in the eyes of society?

3. Is there a common *American Dream?* If so, what is it?

1   For the children of immigrant parents the knowledge comes easier. America exists everywhere in the city—on billboards, frankly in the smell of French fries and popcorn. It exists in the pace: traffic lights, the assertions of neon, the mysterious bong-bong-bong through the atriums of department stores. America exists as the voice of the crowd, a menacing sound—the high nasal accent of American English.

2   When I was a boy in Sacramento (California, the fifties), people would ask me, "Where you from?" I was born in this country, but I knew the question meant to decipher my darkness, my looks.

3   My mother once instructed me to say, " I am an American of American descent." By the time I was nine or ten, I wanted to say, but dared not reply, "I am an American."

4   Immigrants come to America and, against hostility or mere loneliness, they recreate a homeland in the parlor, tacking up postcards or calendars of some impossible blue—lake or sea or sky. Children of immigrant parents are supposed to perch on a hyphen between two countries. Relatives assume the achievement as much as anyone. Relatives are, in any case, surprised when the child begins losing old ways. One day at the family picnic the boy wanders away from their spiced food and faceless stories to watch other boys play baseball in the distance.

5   There is sorrow in the American memory, guilty sorrow for having left something behind—Portugal, China, Norway. The American story is the story of immigrant children and of their children—children no longer able to speak to grandparents. The memory of exile becomes inarticulate as it passes from generation to generation, along with wedding rings and pocket watches—like some mute stone in a wad of old lace. Europe. Asia. Eden.

6   But, it needs to be said, if this is a country where one stops being Vietnamese or Italian, this is a country where one begins to be an American. America exists as a culture and a grin, a faith and a shrug. It is clasped in a handshake, called by a first name.

7   As much as the country is joined in a common culture, however, Americans are reluctant to celebrate the process of assimilation. We pledge allegiance to diversity. America was born Protestant and bred Puritan, and the notion of community we share is derived from a seventeenth-century faith. Presidents and the pages of ninth-grade civics readers yet proclaim the orthodoxy: We are gathered together—but as individuals, with separate pasts, distinct destinies. Our society is as paradoxical as a Puritan congregation: We stand together, alone.

8   Americans have traditionally defined themselves by what they refused to include. As often, however, Americans have

struggled, turned in good conscience at last to assert the great Protestant virtue of tolerance. Despite outbreaks of nativist frenzy, America has remained an immigrant country, open and true to itself.

9　Against pious emblems of rural America—soda fountain, Elks hall, Protestant church, and now shopping mall—stands the cold-hearted city, crowded with races and ambitions, curious laughter, much that is odd. Nevertheless, it is the city that has most truly represented America. In the city, however, the millions of singular lives have had no richer notion of wholeness to describe them than the idea of pluralism.

10　*"Where you from?" the American asks the immigrant child. "Mexico," the boy learns to say.*

11　Mexico, the country of my blood ancestors, offers formal contrast to the American achievement. If the United States was formed by Protestant individualism, Mexico was shaped by a medieval Catholic dream of one world. The Spanish journeyed to Mexico to plunder, and they may have gone, in God's name, with an arrogance peculiar to those who intend to convert. But through the conversion, the Indian converted the Spaniard. A new race was born, the *mestizo,* wedding European to Indian. José Vasconcelos, the Mexican philosopher, has celebrated this New World creation, proclaiming it the "cosmic race."

12　Centuries later, in a San Francisco restaurant, a Mexican-American lawyer of my acquaintance says, in English, over *salade niçoise,* that he does not intend to assimilate into gringo society. His claim is echoed by a chorus of others (Italian-Americans, Greeks, Asians) in this era of ethnic pride. The melting pot has been retired, clanking, into the museum of quaint disgrace, alongside Aunt Jemima and the Katzenjammer Kids. But resistance to assimilation is characteristically American. It only makes clear how inevitable the process of assimilation actually is.

13　For generations, this has been the pattern. Immigrant parents have sent their children to school (simply, they thought) to acquire the "skills" to survive in the city. The child returned home with a voice his parents barely recognized or understood, couldn't trust, and didn't like.

14　In Eastern cities—Philadelphia, New York, Boston, Baltimore—class after class gathered immigrant children to women (usually women) who stood in front of rooms full of children, changing children. So also for me in the 1950s. Irish-Catholic nuns. California. The old story. The hyphen tipped to the right, away from Mexico and toward a confusing but true American identity.

15   I speak now in the chromium American accent of my grammar school classmates—Billy Reckers, Mike Bradley, Carol Schmidt, Kathy O'Grady. . . . I believe I became like my classmates, became German, Polish, and (like my teachers) Irish. And because assimilation is always reciprocal, my classmates got something of me. (I mean sad eyes; belief in the Indian Virgin; a taste for sugar skulls on the Feast of the Dead.) In the blending, we became what our parents could never have been, and we carried America one revolution further.

16   "Does America still exist?" Americans have been asking the question for so long that to ask it again only proves our continuous link. But perhaps the question deserves to be asked with urgency—now. Since the black civil rights movement of the 1960s, our tenuous notion of a shared public life has deteriorated notably.

17   The struggle of black men and women did not eradicate racism, but it became the great moment in the life of America's conscience. Water hoses, bulldogs, blood—the images, rendered black, white, rectangular, passed into living rooms.

18   It is hard to look at a photograph of a crowd taken, say, in 1890 or in 1930 and not notice the absence of blacks. (It becomes an impertinence to wonder if America *still* exists.)

19   In the sixties, other groups of Americans learned to champion their rights by analogy to the black civil rights movement. But the heroic vision faded. Dr. Martin Luther King Jr. had spoken with Pauline eloquence of a nation that would unite Christian and Jew, old and young, rich and poor. Within a decade, the struggles of the 1960s were reduced to a bureaucratic competition for little more than pieces of a representational pie. The quest for a portion of power became an end in itself. The metaphor for the American city of the 1970s was a committee: one black, one woman, one person under thirty. . . .

20   If the small town had sinned against America by too neatly defining who could be an American, the city's sin was a romantic secession. One noticed the romanticism in the antiwar movement—certain demonstrators who demonstrated a lack

of tact or desire to persuade and seemed content to play secular protestants. One noticed the romanticism in the competition among members of "minority groups" to claim the status of Primary Victim. To Americans unconfident of their common identity, minority standing became a way of asserting individuality. Middle-class Americans—men and women clearly not the primary victims of social oppression—brandished their suffering with exuberance.

21   The dream of a single society probably died with *The Ed Sullivan Show.* The reality of America persists. Teenagers pass through big-city high schools banded in racial groups, their collars turned up to a uniform shrug. But then they graduate to jobs at the phone company or in banks, where they end up working alongside people unlike themselves. Typists and tellers walk out together at lunchtime.

22   It is easier for us as Americans to believe the obvious fact of our separateness—easier to imagine the black and white Americas prophesied by the Kerner report (broken glass, street fires)—than to recognize the reality of a city street at lunchtime. Americans are wedded by proximity to a common culture. The panhandler at one corner is related to the pamphleteer at the next who is related to the banker who is kin to the Chinese old man wearing an MIT sweatshirt. In any true national history, Thomas Jefferson begets Martin Luther King Jr. who begets the Gray Panthers. It is because we lack a vision of ourselves entire—the city street is crowded and we are each preoccupied with finding our own way home—that we lack an appropriate hymn.

23   Under my window now passes a little white girl softly rehearsing to herself a Motown obbligato.

POST-READING QUESTIONS

Content

1. Where does Rodriguez claim America exists? What does he feel symbolizes America?

2. What is more important in America, individuality or membership? According to Rodriguez, where do we stand in relationship to each other?

3. Why does Rodriguez feel the 1960s were so important to American history? What has happened since that era?

4. According to Rodriguez, does the dream of a single society still exist? What proof does he offer?

Strategies and Structures

1. Rodriguez develops his definition of America by stating what it is *not* (arguing through negation). How effective is this strategy? If the author had reversed his strategy and told us what America is, would this have inspired any creative or critical thinking on the part of the reader? Why? Why not?

2. How does Rodriguez explain his definition of America? Through abstract discussion or concrete examples? Why does he choose one over the other?

3. In what other ways does the author develop his definition?

Language and Vocabulary

1. Vocabulary: *assimilation, reciprocal, inarticulate, congregation, gringo, chromium, bureaucratic, metaphor, exuberance.* Read the sentences in which these words are found and try to determine their definitions. Then look up each one in the dictionary and see how accurate your determinations were. What does this exercise show you about reading words in context? What did you discover about dictionary use?

2. Without looking up their definitions, use the following words in a paragraph: *conscience, secession, secular, beget, pamphleteer, allegiance, plunder.* As you did in the previous exercise, check your usage in the dictionary after you draft out your paragraph, noting how context assisted you in using words you were not too familiar with. Then, rewrite your paragraph making changes to improve the sense, and to eliminate faulty usage.

GROUP ACTIVITIES

1. If possible, get into culturally diverse groups and discuss what you have in common. For instance, do you eat foods, listen to music, or enjoy the sports of another culture? What are the greatest differences among the members of your group? Have you ever wanted to attend social functions of a different culture but were afraid to? What information have you always wanted to ask about another culture?

2. What is America or American? In a group forum analyze precisely what America is. What is and is not American? What historical facts can your group brainstorm supporting your position? Do people have a tendency to stereotype Americans? Why? You may want to save the information that you've collected for Writing Activity 2 below.

WRITING ACTIVITIES

1. Compose an original essay wherein you define a concept, a country, or a person through *negation*. That is, focus your attention on arguing what someone or something *is not* to define your topic. Make sure you use specific examples to illustrate what you claim.

2. Write an argument of fact, defining and defending your concept of America. Consider what you were taught since you were little about the United States (land of the free where everyone has an equal opportunity to achieve—where everything is fair). Does your personal experience support what you were told? How? Why?

Distance Learning and American Society
MARK CHARLES FISSEL

Mark Charles Fissel teaches Western Civilization via interactive television and fiber-optic video information systems. His publications include *The Bishops' Wars: Charles I's Campaigns against Scotland, 1638–1640* (Cambridge) and *War and Enforcement in Britain, 1598–1650* (Manchester).

PRE-READING QUESTIONS

1. In groups, consider the following: What would be the benefits and problems of learning by television? Who would benefit? What communities might it serve best? How would such a service work? When would such a service be most beneficial? Where might such a service become popular? Why might such a service become popular? Why might such a service receive criticism?

2. Have you ever taken a video course? What were your impressions of the course? Was it effective? What did you like and/or dislike about the course?

1   America created television; television altered social relationships through the rapid dispersal of information. The commercial impact of television is self-evident. But video's potential to educate has not yet been fully understood nor realized. Distance learning goes far beyond the limited functions of advertisement and entertainment and promises to facilitate the delivery of educational services in an increasingly service-oriented American economy and transmit benefits to those in America who have not had ready access to higher education. The creature, television, is now re-making its creator, America.

2   Distance learning via interactive video instruction makes teaching student-oriented and decentralized as opposed to

instructor-oriented, centralized instruction in the traditional classroom. As Jason Ohler points out, it "brings school to the students" not vice versa (Ohler 63). To a great extent, distance learning democratizes education by opening the classroom to people who cannot, or choose not, to matriculate in a traditional residential college program. In Britain, for example, the Open University commenced in a society where fewer than five percent of the total population enjoyed the benefits of university education. Through video and correspondence distance learning programs, there are now 200,000 "new" students in Britain utilizing the Open University's programs (Shane 26). Distance learning has achieved similar results in Third World and emerging countries such as Indonesia and Korea.

3   Precisely how does video distance learning work in the U.S.? A multitude of distance learning systems flourish in this country, such as the TI-IN network of Texas which provides tele-instruction to high schools and the Black College Satellite Network which links 105 college campuses. The Indiana Higher Education Telecommunications System embraces both high school and university curricula, sending via microwave interactive video courses from universities to local hospitals, corporations, military bases, and even prisons. Through a "teleresponse unit," distant learners telephone from the sites and speak directly to the instructor through an audio amplifier. The teacher responds "over the air." Examinations are proctored by site supervisors.

4   Who are these "distant learners?" Most are working people who contribute to the tax base which sustains universities but whose work schedule denies them the opportunity to attend college. Professional and familiar obligations, for example, in the case of nurses, deprive these would-be students of access to education. Distance learning opens new doors, quite literally, to a new educational clientele. This also includes military personnel whose service responsibilities require a flexible educational format. Recently, an Air Force enlisted man enrolled in my IHETS Western Civilization course found himself ordered to Alaska for a month. He kept up with the lectures through mailed VHS video cassette until his return to Grissom Air Force Base, where he made up his exams under the supervision of a site proctor. He completed the course in spite of career commitments. Currently, two distance learners at

Camp Atterbury will interrupt their course work for several weeks service in Germany. The missed lectures will await their return, recorded on videotape.

5   That very flexibility can provide inservice training for a number of occupations, benefitting employers as well as employees. For example in health care and medicine, distance learning, supplemented by teleconferencing, can enable professionals to keep abreast of recent developments in their fields without removing them from the workplace or expending large sums on conferences and seminars in far-off locales. In professions in which there is a high degree of technical change, such as in microelectronics, distance learning and teleconferencing allow workers to change areas of technical expertise in response to changing employment and market conditions (Shane 25-7). Most businesses, in fact, can include a distance learning component in their employment package as an incentive and reward for employees. Blue collar workers, such as those in the automotive industry, take courses which help them get a sampling of the college curriculum, or even in some cases complete secondary education long delayed. Interactive video can benefit both labor and management.

6   What effect will distance learning have upon our society in cultural terms? A paradox exists. On one hand, television tends to homogenize culture. Jason Ohler has warned that distance learning can threaten "cultural diversity" (Ohler 65). Yet distance learning can serve constituencies determined to preserve a high degree of their own cultural or social identity. Native Americans, it has been argued, can draw from distance learning the advantages of higher education while remaining within a given community, and quoting Ohler "keep one foot in mainstream culture and another in their own" (Bruder 31). Religious groups who are put off by the secularism of the modern university environment can circumvent that situation yet still obtain an education through distance learning. Of the estimated 500,000 individuals taking advantage of distance learning in America, the federal government suggests that roughly half do so "to avoid secular content" (Bruder 31). The disabled may assert their right to education more conveniently and more successfully by choosing courses from a variety of interactive broadcasts. Communities too impoverished to build schools or

hire teachers can share the curriculum of a major university equipped for distance learning. Clearly, then, distance learning has the potential to preserve and accomodate cultures as well as "standardize" them.

Works Cited

Bruder, Isabelle. "Distance Learning: What's Holding Back this Boundless Delivery System?" Electronic Learning April 1989: 30–35.

Ohler, Jason. "Techtrends Interview: Jason Ohler." Techtrends October 1989: 62–67.

Shane, Harold G. "Britain's University of the Air: On the Interview with Lord Walter Perry of the Open University." The Futurist July–August 1989: 25–27.

POST-READING QUESTIONS

Content

1. What is Fissel's thesis (what does he argue for)? Where is it located?
2. How does video distance learning work? How does the student participate in the course? How is the integrity of evaluation maintained?
3. Who will benefit from distance learning? How will they benefit?
4. Which occupations have the most to gain from distance learning? Why?
5. How will distance learning affect our society in cultural terms? What could be the advantages? What could be the disadvantages?

Strategies and Structures

1. Fissel presents his thesis in the first paragraph. How does this aid the reader and focus the essay on the controlling idea?

2. How does Fissel effectively use five of the journalistic questions (who, what, when, where, and why) to organize his essay and to support his argument? Why is such a strategy effective?

3. How does he begin each section of the essay? How does the repetition of this strategy aid the reader?

4. How does Fissel develop each section of the essay? In what way does he illustrate the different benefits of distance learning?

5. In what way does Fissel use outside sources in his essay? What does the use of outside sources suggest about the author? Do you find the use of outside sources effective?

Language and Vocabulary

1. Vocabulary: *dispersal, facilitate, interactive, matriculate, tele-instruction*. After looking up these words in your dictionary, go back to sections in Fissel's essay where he uses them. Then, replace the word he uses with their meaning (a group of words rather than a single term). In addition to making his sentences longer, what effect does wordiness have on the flow of his ideas? What does this suggest about the importance of building a strong vocabulary?

2. What linking words does Fissel use in the essay? What does he use them for? How do they aid the reader?

GROUP ACTIVITIES

1. Visit your campus audio visual center and interview either the director or one of the staff members. What services do they offer? Who uses these services the most, students or instructors? Which services are used the most? How might you use these services to become a better student? How might these services be put to better use?

2. Watch and critique an hour of instructional television. First summarize what you saw. Then write a section on the advantages and strengths of such television and a section on the disadvantages and weaknesses of such television.

WRITING ASSIGNMENTS

1. Write an essay in which you argue either for or against distance learning. Arrange your essay according to the five "w" journalistic questions. For example, if you are against instructional television, explain whom it will injure and what negative effects it will have on society.

2. There are many debates over educational practice, such as home versus public education, heterogeneous versus homogeneous classrooms, and large versus small classrooms. Research one of these debates in your library by reading newspapers, magazines, and books, by interviewing your instructors and the school administrators, and by soliciting the opinions of your fellow students. Then write an essay in which you argue for one instructional method over another.

Peyote, Wine and the First Amendment
DOUGLAS LAYCOCK

Essayist Douglas Laycock presently serves as the Alice McKean Young Regents Chair in Law at the University of Texas, Austin. He is currently working on a book with the tentative title *A Centrist Theory of Religious Liberty.*

PRE-READING QUESTIONS

1. Make a list of freedoms and practices you feel are guaranteed by the First Amendment. If you are uncertain what the First Amendment is, get a copy of the U.S. Bill of Rights, and look it up. Where does freedom of religion fit into our inalienable rights?

2. To your knowledge, is the continuance or growth of non-Christian religions, rituals, and ceremonies (excluding Satanism and death cults) discouraged in America? How many non-Christian religious shows have you seen on television?

3. What is your attitude towards the use of drugs (wine and other alcoholic beverages are drugs) in religious ceremonies? Does it matter that these drugs have been in use for centuries?

1   This fall the U.S. Supreme Court will consider arguments in a case that goes to the very heart of the constitutional guarantee of free exercise of religion. The court will decide whether the state can prohibit a religious ritual, and if so, what kinds of dangers justify such an extraordinary prohibition. This litigation involves not a practice of a mainstream faith but the peyote ritual of the Native American Church.

2   Peyote, or mescal, is a small cactus that grows in the southwest U.S. and in northern Mexico. It produces buds or tubers, called buttons, that have hallucinogenic properties. Peyote is an illegal drug, but the federal government and 23 states permit its use in at least some religious ceremonies. Federal drug authorities issue licenses to grow and sell peyote to religious users. But the case before the court comes from Oregon, which has no such exemption.

3   If the Supreme Court focuses too narrowly on drugs in this case and misses the larger issue of religious ritual, it could create a devastating precedent for religious liberty. For the Native American use of peyote has substantial parallels to Christian and Jewish uses of wine. If the peyote ritual is allowed only by legislative grace and not by constitutional right, the right to

participate in communion, the Passover Seder and sabbath rituals may rest on no firmer footing.

4   The Oregon case is an odd vehicle for addressing such an issue. It is not a criminal prosecution; questions about criminal prohibitions are involved only because the court reached out for them. Alfred Smith and Galen Black were drug- and alcohol-abuse counselors at a nonprofit agency. When their supervisor learned that they had consumed peyote at a religious service, he discharged them for violating the agency's absolute rule against drug or alcohol use. The supervisor later testified that "we would have taken the same action had the claimant consumed wine at a Catholic ceremony." But he offered no evidence that anyone had actually been discharged for drinking communion wine, and he did not claim to have inquired about which of the churches his employees attended used wine and which only grape juice.

5   Smith and Black first complained that their employer had discriminated against them based on their religion. Without admitting the charge, the employer changed its absolute rule against religious use of drugs, and it paid Smith and Black some of their lost pay. They agreed not to insist on being reinstated to their jobs.

6   Smith and Black also filed claims for unemployment compensation. A long line of Supreme Court cases holds that states must pay unemployment compensation to employees who lose their jobs because of their religious beliefs. Employees who refuse to work on their sabbath have been the principal beneficiaries of this rule (in another case a worker lost his job in a brass mill because he refused to help manufacture tank turrets). The Oregon courts followed these cases and awarded unemployment compensation to Smith and Black.

7   The U.S. Supreme Court vacated the judgment, deciding that if Oregon could send Smith and Black to prison for chewing peyote, it could surely refuse to pay them unemployment compensation. Therefore, the court reasoned, the constitutional status of Oregon's criminal prohibition of peyote was logically prior to the unemployment-compensation issue. It sent the case back to the state courts to ask whether Oregon would recognize a religious exception to its criminal laws against possession or consumption of peyote.

8   Oregon's Supreme Court, which had already concluded that this question was irrelevant, dutifully answered that in its judgment criminal prosecution of Smith and Black would violate the federal Constitution. Their consumption of peyote was a constitutionally protected exercise of religion; therefore, Oregon could not send them to prison or refuse to pay them unemployment compensation.

9   The U.S. Supreme Court has agreed to hear the case again. Presumably it intends to decide whether Smith and Black could be sent to prison, even though no one has shown the slightest interest in sending them there. If it has second thoughts about this exercise in judicial activism, it may retreat to the narrower issue and decide only whether Smith and Black are entitled to keep their unemployment compensation.

10   The opinions of the Oregon courts provide few details about exactly what Smith and Black did with peyote. Opinions in other cases provide more information about the peyote ritual, based on the testimony of witnesses and of anthropologists who have studied it. The peyote ritual is no modern innovation designed to evade the drug laws. Native Americans have practiced it at least since 1560, when it was first described in Spanish records. Today the ritual is practiced in substantially similar form from northern Mexico to Saskatchewan. Believers come from many Native American tribes, although it is not the major religion of any tribe. The faith has absorbed some Christian teachings as well, but peyote remains at the heart of its theology and practice.

11   To the believer, peyote is a sacramental substance, an object of worship and a source of divine protection. Peyote is the focus of the worship service, much as the consecrated bread and wine are the focus of mass and communion. The cases speak of prayers being directed to peyote; I suspect that the believer thinks of himself as praying to the holy spirit who is present in the peyote.

12   The believer may wear peyote on his person for protection; soldiers have worn a large peyote button in a beaded pouch suspended from their necks. While there is no parallel in Christian theology, there is ample parallel in Christian folk-belief—a consecrated communion wafer worn around the neck has been thought to be the best defense against Dracula,

and crosses and medals are put to similar use against modern dangers.

13   Finally, and most important for the question before the court, participants in the ritual believe that peyote intoxication enables them to experience God directly. Peyote is consumed for this purpose only at a "meeting," convened and controlled by a leader. It is a sacrilege to use peyote for a nonreligious purpose. A meeting is a solemn and somewhat infrequent occasion. Participants wear their finest clothing. They pray, sing and perform ceremonies with drums, fans, eagle bones and other symbolic instruments.

14   The central event is the consumption of peyote in quantities sufficient to produce intoxication. At the appointed time, the leader distributes up to four buttons to each adult participant. There is an opportunity for participants to take additional buttons at a later point in the ceremony. The buttons are extremely bitter, and difficult to chew and swallow. Some groups use a tea brewed from the buttons, but chewing the buttons appears to be the norm.

15   The meeting lasts from sundown Saturday to sunrise Sunday. In the morning, the leader serves breakfast. By then all effects of the peyote have worn off, and the participants leave in a sober state. Smith and Black were fired for participating in a service that, apparently, went according to this generic description.

16   The first amendment guarantees the free exercise of religion and forbids the governmental establishment of religion. One of the amendment's central purposes is to ensure that religious belief and practice be as free as possible from government regulation. There are limits to this freedom when serious and immediate harm is threatened; hardly anyone believes in a constitutional right to practice human sacrifice. But the Supreme Court has repeatedly said that government can limit religious liberty only for compelling reasons that cannot be served in any other way.

17   Another central function of the First Amendment is to ensure that small, unfamiliar and unpopular religions get equal treatment with larger, well-known and politically influential religions. In those compelling cases in which religious liberty must be restricted, the restrictions must be applied neutrally.

18   This principle of neutrality requires us to compare the peyote ritual to the rituals of mainstream faiths. Peyote is not the only mind-altering drug used in a religious ritual. Many Christians drink wine at communion. For Jews, a prayer over wine is part of the sabbath service, sabbath meals, all religious holidays and special religious events such as weddings and circumcisions.

19   Wine was once illegal in the U.S., just as peyote is now. But the National Prohibition Act, passed after ratification of the 18th Amendment, exempted wine "for sacramental purposes, or like religious rites." State prohibition laws, some of which survived into the 1960s, either had similar exemptions or at least were not enforced against religious users. (Contemporary local prohibition laws rarely require exemptions; they generally restrict the sale of alcohol, but permit private consumption of alcohol purchased elsewhere.)

20   Why is it that the religious use of wine was exempt everywhere during Prohibition, but the religious use of peyote is exempt in only half the states today? If Oregon may constitutionally punish the religious use of peyote, may it not also punish the religious use of wine? Could Oregon ban communion wine and require that all Christians use grape juice instead? The Supreme Court does not have to answer these questions formally; no case about wine is before it. But it should think hard about these questions, to make sure it is not suppressing a small and unfamiliar religion on the basis of principles it would not apply to a mainstream faith.

21   Oregon may respond that peyote is simply more dangerous than wine. I do not know whether that is true; I am sure that wine is more widely abused. But the court will assume that the legislature had good reason for its ban. It should inquire into dangerousness only in the narrow context of religious use. The judicial question is this: if the Constitution protects the religious use of wine when legislatures believe that wine is so dangerous it has to be banned, does the Constitution also protect religious use of peyote at a time when legislatures believe peyote must be banned? If sacramental uses of wine are protected and sacramental uses of peyote are not, it must be because of some compelling difference between the drugs or the rituals.

22   Each of the Christian and Jewish uses of wine is similar to the peyote ritual in some ways, and quite different in others.

Communion resembles the peyote ritual in the liturgical and theological centrality of the wine in the worship service. For many Christians, there are further similarities in the reverence and even adoration for the consecrated wine and the belief that the deity is present in the wine.

23   However, no one gets intoxicated on communion wine. Well, hardly anyone. In traditions that believe in the real presence of Christ, the priest or pastor may get tipsy from drinking the consecrated wine that is left over at the end of the service, since the blood of Christ cannot just be poured down the drain. This consequence could perhaps be avoided by recruiting enough helpers, but in some denominations only clergy and designated assistants are permitted to help.

24   Not even the matter of intoxication distinguishes Purim, the celebration of the Jews' deliverance from a genocidal plot during the Babylonian captivity. Some Jewish traditions teach a duty to celebrate Purim to the point of drunkenness. Jews drink four cups of wine at the Passover Seder, which commemorates the Exodus from Egypt. Prayer over a single cup of wine is part of the sabbath service and of sabbath meals.

25   But one important difference is that an essential part of the peyote ritual is to experience God through the mind-altering effects of the drug; that is not part of the communion service in any Christian tradition, and it is not part of any Jewish celebrations or rituals. Purim, the most intoxicating Jewish celebration, is only a minor festival. Because Purim is far less central theologically, a decision that Oregon could ban the peyote ritual would clearly imply that it could ban the use of intoxicating amounts of wine to celebrate Purim.

26   In an important sense it is a greater violation of religious liberty to ban a ritual that is at the theological heart of a faith than to ban a peripheral celebration. But either act limits religious liberty. We should be uncomfortable with governmental bans on minor religious festivals, or with judges deciding which festivals are important enough to deserve full constitutional protection and which are not. A court that starts down that path might eventually convince itself that wine is not central to the sabbath or to the celebration of Passover, or that the use of wine is not central to communion. The government could acquire a de facto power to review theology and liturgy.

27   If the court considers communion or the Passover Seder or the sabbath, its instinct will be to regard these as constitutionally protected. If it considers only peyotism, its instinct may be to consider it a weird and dangerous practice. Comparing familiar and presumptively protected faiths to an unfamiliar one is a way of guarding against unrecognized bias. But this cautionary device will not work if the court jumps at any possible distinction to rationalize its prejudices in favor of the familiar.

28   Thus, the ultimate question is whether Oregon's reasons for prohibiting the peyote ritual are compelling, and, if the peyote ritual is to be distinguished from Christian and Jewish rituals, whether the distinctions are compelling. The only plausible distinction is that Christian and Jewish uses are generally less intoxicating—but there are important exceptions even to that.

29   The distinction is further blurred by the mystical tradition in every major world religion, including Christianity and Judaism. The mystics often seek to experience God through altered states of consciousness, generally induced by trance or meditation instead of drugs. So neither the use of mind-altering drugs nor the achievement of altered consciousness distinguishes peyotism from mainstream faiths. It is only the combination of these two things that arguably distinguishes peyotism.

30   The most one can say without exceptions is that only in peyotism is drug-induced altered consciousness part of the central religious event. That difference is compelling only if peyote intoxication under the controlled conditions of a meeting poses a serious danger to the participants or others. To say only that Oregon disapproves of peyote intoxication is merely to restate Oregon's disapproval of this mode of worship. Oregon's disapproval does not provide a compelling reason to forbid a religious ritual . . . .

31   It may be that as a practical matter religious use of mind-altering drugs will be limited to groups that can point to some substantial tradition and that limit the use of drugs to structured worship service. Perhaps the practical difficulties of enforcing the drug laws will prevent any broader protection of religious liberty. But both familiar and unfamiliar groups can show a substantial tradition and a structured worship service. At least Christians, Jews and peyote worshipers fall into this

category. Peyote worship should be constitutionally protected, and Smith and Black should be allowed to keep their unemployment compensation.

POST-READING QUESTIONS

Content

1. What is Laycock's concern in this essay? Why does he claim that "peyote worship should be constitutionally protected"?

2. Did Smith and Black's supervisor treat them fairly when he discharged them for using peyote in a religious ceremony? Explain.

3. In what way is the Christian and Jewish use of wine similar and different to the Native-American use of peyote in religious rituals?

4. Why is it ironic that alcohol, a drug introduced by western society into Native-American culture, was "exempt" from prohibition when used for religious purposes, but the use of peyote, a Native-American drug used by American Indians in religious rituals for centuries, is allowed only in "half the states today"?

5. How does the reader know that Laycock is not advocating peyote use for the sake of a *high?*

Strategies and Structures

1. How does Laycock use the First Amendment to strengthen his argument in this essay?

2. This essay begins and concludes with references to U.S. governing bodies and laws. Why is the separation between the church and state an essential part of his argument?

3. How does Laycock demonstrate that peyote is a "sacramental substance, an object of worship and a source of divine protection"? What makes his argument logical?

4. Why does Laycock point out how Smith and Black are discriminated against by their employer, the Oregon Courts, and the Supreme Courts? Why does the employer make them agree not to ask for job reinstatement? Why does the Supreme Court decide to make no judgment? What does Laycock want us to conclude from all these points? Does his strategy work? Why or why not?

5. Why does Laycock want us to feel uncomfortable with the government and judges deciding which religions and religious rituals are important and which are not? What is his purpose for pointing out what these bans can lead to?

6. After reading this article, what deductions can you make about the legal attitude and treatment of minor religions by the U.S. courts and the government in general? What do you feel is more important to American society: the religious practices of many, the religious practices of a few, or both?

Language and Vocabulary

1. Vocabulary: *hallucinogenic, litigation, denomination, sacrilege, sacramental, consecrated.* Define the above words, choose one and write an extended definition incorporating your own views and/or observations on the subject.

2. Three of these words—sacrilege, sacramental, and consecrated—have the same root—*sacr, secr*—which comes from Latin and means holy or sacred. Words with this root deal with religion or ritual. Find at least five more words with the same root and compose two or three paragraphs in which you discuss something that is sacred or holy to you, using each of your chosen words at least two times.

GROUP ACTIVITIES

1. Does our constitution guarantee the rights of all or just a few? Are some religions better than others?

Divide the class into two groups, one assuming the role of a mainstream religion and the other a minority religion, and debate the issue. Following the debate, each student should write a summary of the opposing group's argument, noting its strengths and weaknesses.

2. When and where does censorship infringe on individual rights? Get in small groups and discuss how prohibiting traditions and rituals is censorship. (You first will have to have a clear idea of what censorship involves.) What examples of censorship in America today does your group agree with? Why? Now discuss what this censorship might lead to in the future? Finally, write a collaborative essay in which you argue for or against censorship of an ideal, a practice, or a privilege.

WRITING ACTIVITIES

1. Compose an essay arguing that all drug use in religious ceremonies or rituals should be outlawed, including the use of alcohol. Anticipate your reader's reaction to your proposal and defend your thesis with clear reasoning and concrete examples.

2. Write an essay arguing that our freedom of worship in America is in jeopardy if the U.S. government does not stop tampering with the mystical, religious traditions and legality of rituals in practice today.

Additional Topics and Issues for Argumentative Essays

1. Write an essay arguing that experience is or is not the best teacher. Make sure you provide several representative examples to convince your reader.

2. Argue for one of the two following positions: Money is a basic necessity to happiness or money creates a feeling of happiness but not true contentment. What observations or experiences lead you to your conclusion?

3. In an argumentative essay, disprove the popular idea that video games deteriorate reading abilities. In fact, you might want to show that video games enhance reading abilities.

4. Select a popular television show and argue that it does or does not reflect the values of the average American. For example, do the characters in *Roseanne, The Cosby Show,* or *The Simpsons* resemble the sorts of people who are your neighbors?

5. To what extent could one's eating habits indicate something about his or her personality? One variation of this topic might be to argue that being a vegetarian is healthier than being a meat eater or vice versa.

6. Sexually violent crimes are on the rise. Many lawmakers feel that to reduce such violations we must extend the death penalty to include rapists, child molesters, and those guilty of incest. Take a position on this issue and support it.

7. Some people claim that technology has made Americans lazy. For example, we use calculators to figure out math problems and spell checkers rather than learning to use a dictionary. Argue either in favor of or against the use of this technology and indicate where the line must be drawn between practicality and convenience.

8. Euthanasia, the killing of terminally ill or clinically brain dead people (those kept alive by machines), has been an issue of debate for the past three decades. In this overcrowded world is it either logical or moral to keep these people alive at a great expense and burden to society?

12

PERSUASION: THE EMOTIONAL APPEAL

Like formal argumentative essays, persuasive essays attempt to convince readers of a point or issue. However, while authors tend to stick solely to logic and facts (induction and deduction in particular) in formal argumentative essays, they often appeal to a reader's emotions—which frequently are not logical—in persuasive essays. Some common emotional responses would be indignation, joy, fear, love, hatred, compassion, greed, lust, disgust, and jealousy.

How much do our personal values and prejudices toward different words, issues, or situations influence our judgment? Quite a bit! In the past few years, the word democracy has stirred people's emotions, often uniting them in a cause, for they associate democracy with positive issues and inalienable rights, especially equality. Note how often leaders will preface their remarks with something like, "In the spirit of democracy," suggesting a group consensus rather than an individual opinion. Now, take the same phrase and picture a recent U.S. President saying, "In the spirit of communism, I offer you the following resolution . . . ." In America where communism has been a dirty word for decades, the President's resolution—no matter how logical, fair, and humanitarian—would probably not have received any serious consideration because of the negativity associated with communism. Authors make use of words that elicit emotions in persuasive essays to assist their arguments; authors count on emotional responses to influence readers where logic alone may not impress, motivate, or convince them.

We target different emotional responses for different situations. Jonathan Alter uses an appeal to an emotionally charged issue, "prejudice," in his essay, "Degrees of Discomfort: Is Homophobia Equivalent to Racism?" Similarly, Robert Keith Miller engages reader interest in his composition by appealing to an emotionally charged word, "discrimination," in "Discrimination Is a Virtue." In "The Female Has the Power," we see another type of emotional appeal—the appeal to desires. Though the focus of the essay is specifically on Native-American women, Bonita Wa Wa Calachaw Nuñez appeals to women the world over to put their desires into action and to seek the sort of jobs formerly held only by men. In "Racism and Militarism: The Nuclear Connection," we see yet another example of emotional appeal: an appeal to fear. Ron Glass capitalizes on our paranoia of nuclear disaster and danger to engage our emotions, using his thesis to persuade us that there is a clear and ever-present connection between racism and militarism.

Organizing Persuasive Compositions

Persuasive essays are organized like any argument. Initially, you will want to focus in on the topic or issue of discussion, state your thesis, define terms, and present your argument in emphatic order. For instance, in the essay entitled "Drugs," Gore Vidal clearly states his argument on how to stop most American drug addiction in his first paragraph: "Simply make all drugs available and sell them at cost." He then goes on to clarify and define some of the key issues like *freedom of choice* in this issue, and making parallels with an emotionally charged historical event (prohibition and its failures), Vidal argues his thesis. Though chances are Vidal has not made us all *believers* of his thesis, he has at least made us consider the merit of his argument by the end of the essay, possibly giving us reason to evaluate and re-evaluate our own positions on the issue.

Dealing with emotions can be very tricky. While, appealing to a person's feelings may be the most direct way you have of convincing someone of your point of view, uncontrolled emotional appeals can also make you seem like an excitable author, one who is led by the passion of the moment. Just bear in mind that it is difficult for a reader to maintain a high level of emotional intensity in a composition, so you need to keep focused on your argument and limit your emotional appeal only to those responses that further your ultimate objective. For instance, don't be sentimental if you are hoping to enrage your reader.

Tips on Writing Persuasive Essays

1. Target your audience. That is, become acquainted with the values of those you address and use your knowledge of their likes, dislikes, fears, and prejudices when selecting words. Your objective here is to get your reader involved emotionally as well as intellectually in your topic.
2. Determine your reason(s) for bringing your reader around to your point of view. Do you want to convince him or her that a problem exists? Do you want your reader to support a plan of action you have devised? Or do you want to disprove something another person has said?
3. When you develop the body of your essay, stay focused. Check your thesis occasionally to keep the controlling idea of your composition fresh in your mind. Make sure the facts and details in your body paragraphs have not wandered from your argument.
4. Integrate verifiable facts with information that is geared more to emotional responses than logical reasoning. This will give your composition a sense of balance and not appear like an argument based on illogical conclusions founded on emotional reactions to your topic.

Drugs
GORE VIDAL

Born in 1925, Gore Vidal has been a controversial essayist, novelist, and social critic for the past three decades. He has successfully written all major forms of literature and is well-known for novels like *City and The Pillar* (1948), *Julian* (1964), *Myra Breckenridge* (1968), *1876* (1976), *Burr* (1981), and *Lincoln* (1984).

PRE-READING QUESTIONS

1. Examine your present attitude toward drugs. When you hear the word *drugs* what is the first thing that pops into your mind?

2. What is the current attitude toward drug use in American society? When and where is drug use socially acceptable?

1   It is possible to stop most drug addiction in the United States within a very short time. Simply make all drugs available and sell them at cost. Label each drug with a precise description of what effect—good and bad—the drug will have on the taker. This will require heroic honesty. Don't say that marijuana is addictive or dangerous when it is neither, as millions of people know—unlike "speed," which kills most unpleasantly, or heroin, which is addictive and difficult to kick.

2   For the record, I have tried—once—almost every drug and liked none, disproving the popular Fu Manchu theory that a single sniff of opium will enslave the mind. Nevertheless many drugs are bad for certain people to take and they should be told why in a sensible way.

3   Along with exhortation and warning, it might be good for our citizens to recall (or learn for the first time) that the United States was the creation of men who believed that each man has the right to do what he wants with his own life as long as he does

not interfere with his neighbor's pursuit of happiness (that his neighbor's idea of happiness is persecuting others does confuse matters a bit).

4   This is a startling notion to the current generation of Americans. They reflect a system of public education which has made the Bill of Rights, literally, unacceptable to a majority of high school graduates (see the annual Purdue reports) who now form the "silent majority"—a phrase which that underestimated wit Richard Nixon took from Homer who used it to describe the dead.

5   Now one can hear the warning rumble begin: if everyone is allowed to take drugs everyone will and the GNP will decrease, the Commies will stop us from making everyone free, and we shall end up a race of Zombies, passively murmuring "groovie" to one another. Alarming thought. Yet it seems most unlikely that any reasonably sane person will become a drug addict if he knows in advance what addiction is going to be like.

6   Is everyone reasonably sane? No. Some people will always become drug addicts just as some people will always become alcoholics, and it is just too bad. Every man, however, has the power (and should have the legal right) to kill himself if he chooses. But since most men don't, they won't be mainliners either. Nevertheless, forbidding people things they like or think they might enjoy only makes them want those things all the more. This psychological insight is, for some mysterious reason, perennially denied our governors.

7   It is a lucky thing for the American moralist that our country has always existed in a kind of time-vacuum: we have no public memory of anything that happened before last Tuesday. No one in Washington today recalls what happened during the years alcohol was forbidden to the people by a Congress that thought it had a divine mission to stamp out Demon Rum— launching, in the process, the greatest crime wave in the country's history, causing thousands of deaths from bad alcohol, and creating a general (and persisting) contempt among the citizenry for the laws of the United States.

8   The same thing is happening today. But the government has learned nothing from past attempts at prohibition, not to mention repression.

9   Last year when the supply of Mexican marijuana was slightly curtailed by the Feds, the pushers got the kids hooked on heroin and deaths increased dramatically, particularly in New York. Whose fault? Evil men like the Mafiosi? Permissive Dr. Spock? Wild-eyed Dr. Leary? No.

10   The Government of the United States was responsible for those deaths. The bureaucratic machine has a vested interest in playing cops and robbers. Both the Bureau of Narcotics and the Mafia want strong laws against the sale and use of drugs because if drugs are sold at cost there would be no money in it for anyone.

11   If there was no money in it for the Mafia, there would be no friendly playground pushers, and addicts would not commit crimes to pay for the next fix. Finally, if there was no money in it, the Bureau of Narcotics would wither away, something they are not about to do without a struggle.

12   Will anything sensible be done? Of course not. The American people are as devoted to the idea of sin and its punishment as they are to making money—and fighting drugs is nearly as big a business as pushing them. Since the combination of sin and money is irresistible (particularly to the professional politician), the situation will only grow worse.

POST-READING QUESTIONS

Content

1. Vidal states that it is possible to "stop drug addiction in the United States in a very short time." What is the basis of his argument? Do you find it convincing or weak? Support your position.

2. How does Vidal establish himself as an authority on drug use? How would his argument have been less persuasive if he had omitted his background on the issue?

3. What parallel do you see between Congress's mission to "stamp out the Demon Rum" earlier this century and its present mission to punish drug users?

4. How persuasive is Vidal's claim that the American moralist "has always existed in a kind of time-vacuum?"

5. Some readers of this essay have taken offense at Vidal's use of masculine nouns and pronouns in the 3rd and 6th paragraphs. What is your opinion of this? Do his references imply that only men will become drug users? How? Why?

Strategies and Structures

1. Vidal balances logic and emotion in this essay to accomplish his objective. Where are some examples of sound reasoning (logic)? How does the author appeal to his reader's emotional prejudices toward drug use and drug users?

2. How well does Vidal address your concerns regarding drug use in American society? Does he seem to consider both sides of the issue carefully? How? What does he omit in his argument?

3. What is the effect of Vidal's final paragraph? How does it relate to his thesis? Why does he conclude a "reasonable" solution to America's drug problem is unrealistic?

Language and Vocabulary

1. How is Vidal's thesis echoed by his simple word choice?

2. What words in this essay did you respond to emotionally? Were such words used to support his position on drugs or present the opposing point of view?

3. Check a *Who's Who in America* at your library for background information on Dr. Spock and Dr. Leary. What were they famous for doing? Why do you imagine Vidal refers to them?

GROUP ACTIVITIES

1. Have each member of your group collect articles relating to drug use from different newspapers, magazines, and journals for a week. When you meet

again with your group, compare your findings. Were most of the articles you collected extremely biased? How? Were minorities unfairly associated with drug use?

2. Collect articles on alcohol abuse, alcohol consumption, and alcohol related deaths in America for one week. Based on your findings, develop sound ethical reasons for re-advocating prohibition, and present your material in a group forum.

WRITING ACTIVITIES

1. Write an essay refuting Vidal's conclusion that a reasonable solution to drug addiction will never be reached because, *"The American people are as devoted to the idea of sin and its punishment as they are to making money—and fighting drugs is nearly as big a business as punishing them."* Appeal to your reader on a logical and emotional level.

2. Develop an argument which persuades your reader that legalizing drugs and drug paraphernalia would decrease crime as well as disease. Consider both sides of the issue and address opposing points of view.

The Female Has the Power
BONITA WA WA CALACHAW NUÑEZ

In addition to being a writer, painter, and healer, Nuñez (1888–1972) was a strong social activist, devoted to such issues as women's rights and the plight of the Native-American in her lifetime. The following excerpt from *Spirit Woman: The Diaries and Paintings of Bonita Wa Wa Calachaw Nuñez* mentions a bit of both issues.

PRE-READING QUESTIONS

1. What are some of the traditional attitudes society has had about the role of women, their position in relation to men, and their place in education and politics?

2. Examine the women in your life. What characteristics have they had? What roles have they played: educator, mother, doctor, lover, wife, bread-winner, counselor, and/or friend?

1   A Woman's touch is the same the World over (give our girls a chance to choose their own career). The originality of an Idea as an identity forms in the Mind of a female. Man has sought to control the female (let Me tell you, they do not). The female has the *Power,* and Knowledge of complete Creativeness of the Being she carries.

2   Some day we are going to have a Woman of Indian Blood as the Commissioner of Indian Affairs; regardless whether there is an Interior Department.

3   Yes, the intellectual Mind of an Indian Woman can become the Dean of our Indian College. Women of Indian Blood, everywhere, will in the future hold the degrees required. We will demand this Right to higher education.

4   Let Me hear from our youthful females who think as I do. For a brighter tomorrow. At the age of 82 I can think, and have the Creative ability to help and encourage our people to get the opportunity [that] can only be ours so long as we are interested in Knowledge.

5   If a change is desired the Ideas are the basis for a balance. A Woman can bring this about. Woman has been Humanly neglected. Man has got to change his inferior lack of common sense.

6   A Nation is recognized by the intelligence of its Citizens. We [Women] are not lost. What we need most is to understand self-motivation.

POST-READING QUESTIONS

Content

1. In the first paragraph, what does Nuñez suggest all women have in common? What do you think she

means by "A Woman's touch" and "complete Creativeness?"

2. Where does Nuñez argue that women are capable of participating in politics, and what specific positions does she feel women should hold?

3. Who stands in the way of women achieving these goals?

4. Who holds the power to change a woman's role in society? What do women need most? What help does Nuñez offer?

Strategies and Structures

1. Nuñez establishes "a common bond" between all women in paragraph 1. Why do you think she does this? Why does she want all women to see themselves as part of a special membership?

2. Nuñez suggests specific positions that she feels women should hold: Commissioner of Indian Affairs and Dean of an Indian College. Why does she refer to specific positions? What do these positions have in common? And what do they suggest women are capable of?

3. Why does Nuñez tell the reader her age? Why does she explain that she is willing to help? What does she hope this will encourage other women to do? In what way does her own willingness to help act as an example to others?

4. Why does Nuñez make the last sentence in her essay *"What we need most is to understand self-motivation?"* Why would she put this sentence last?

Language and Vocabulary

1. Nuñez's capitalization is unorthodox. What words does she capitalize? Why do you think she capitalizes these words? Does her strategy work or does it interfere with your reading?

2. The author states that we need to understand *self-motivation*. What is your definition of this word? Write a paragraph in which you not only define the word, but also show us what a person needs to become motivated.

GROUP ACTIVITIES

1. Divide the class into two parts—men and women. Have men argue that women should assume positions of power traditionally held by men and have women argue that women should remain in traditional roles.

2. Bring in several advertisements from different women's magazines. On the back of each ad, attach a piece of binder paper on which you list the advertisement's suggestions about the role of women in society and how these roles may be changing.

WRITING ACTIVITIES

1. Using specific examples, write an essay wherein you illustrate the problems women have had attaining positions of power in society. Ultimately, persuade your audience that such problems are inexcusable in a democratic society.

2. Argue either for or against Nuñez's idea that women should hold positions of power and esteem.

Discrimination Is a Virtue
ROBERT KEITH MILLER

A professor at the University of Wisconsin, Stevens Point, Robert Keith Miller's essays have appeared in numerous anthologies, newspapers, journals, and magazines such as *Newsweek*. His works include *Oscar Wilde* (1982),

Mark Twain (1983), and *The Informal Argument: A Multidisciplinary Reader and Guide.*

PRE-READING QUESTIONS

1. What is the meaning of discrimination? Cluster the denotations and connotations of the word.
2. Do a freewriting exercise explaining when and where discrimination might be useful.

1   When I was a child, my grandmother used to tell me a story about a king who had three daughters and decided to test their love. He asked each of them "How much do you love me?" The first replied that she loved him as much as all the diamonds and pearls in the world. The second said that she loved him more than life itself. The third replied, "I love you as much as fresh meat loves salt."

2   This answer enraged the king; he was convinced that his youngest daughter was making fun of him. So he banished her from his realm and left all of his property to her elder sisters.

3   As the story unfolded it became clear, even to a 6-year-old, that the king had made a terrible mistake. The two older girls were hypocrites, and as soon as they had profited from their father's generosity, they began to treat him very badly. A wiser man would have realized that the youngest daughter was the truest. Without attempting to flatter, she had said, in effect, "We go together naturally; we are a perfect team."

4   Years later, when I came to read Shakespeare, I realized that my grandmother's story was loosely based upon the story of King Lear, who put his daughters to a similar test and did not know how to judge the results. Attempting to save the king from the consequences of his foolishness, a loyal friend pleads, "Come, sir, arise, away! I'll teach you differences." Unfortunately, the lesson comes too late. Because Lear could not tell the difference between true love and false, he loses his kingdom and eventually his life.

5   We have a word in English which means "the ability to tell differences." That word is *discrimination*. But within the last thirty years, this word has been so frequently misused that an

entire generation has grown up believing that "discrimination" means "racism." People are always proclaiming that "discrimination" is something that should be done away with. Should that ever happen, it would prove to be our undoing.

6   Discrimination means discernment; it means the ability to perceive the truth, to use good judgment and to profit accordingly. The *Oxford English Dictionary* traces this understanding of the word back to 1648 and demonstrates that for the next 300 years, "discrimination" was a virtue, not a vice. Thus, when a character in a nineteenth-century novel makes a happy marriage, Dickens has another character remark, "It does credit to your discrimination that you should have found such a very excellent young woman."

7   Of course, "the ability to tell differences" assumes that differences exist, and this is unsettling for a culture obsessed with the notion of equality. The contemporary belief that discrimination is a vice stems from the compound "discriminate against." What we need to remember, however, is that some things deserve to be judged harshly: we should not leave our kingdoms to the selfish and the wicked.

8   Discrimination is wrong only when someone or something is discriminated against because of prejudice. But to use the word in this sense, as so many people do, is to destroy its true meaning. If you discriminate against something because of general preconceptions rather than particular insights, then you are not discriminating—bias has clouded the clarity of vision which discrimination demands.

9   One of the great ironies of American life is that we manage to discriminate in the practical decisions of daily life, but usually fail to discriminate when we make public policies. Most people are very discriminating when it comes to buying a car, for example, because they realize that cars have differences. Similarly, an increasing number of people have learned to discriminate in what they eat. Some foods are better than others—and indiscriminate eating can undermine one's health.

10   Yet in public affairs, good judgment is depressingly rare. In many areas which involve the common good, we see a failure to tell differences.

11   Consider, for example, some of the thinking behind modern education. On the one hand, there is a refreshing realization that there are differences among children, and some

children—be they gifted or handicapped—require special education. On the other hand, we are politically unable to accept the consequences of this perception. The trend in recent years has been to group together students of radically different ability. We call this process "mainstreaming," and it strikes me as a characteristically American response to the discovery of differences: we try to pretend that differences do not matter.

12   Similarly, we try to pretend that there is little difference between the sane and the insane. A fashionable line of argument has it that "everybody is a little mad" and that few mental patients deserve long term hospitalization. As a consequence of such reasoning, thousands of seriously ill men and women have been evicted from their hospital beds and returned to what is euphemistically called "the community"—which often means being left to sleep on city streets, where confused and helpless people now live out of paper bags as the direct result of our refusal to discriminate.

13   Or to choose a final example from a different area: how many recent elections reflect thoughtful consideration of the genuine differences among candidates? Benumbed by television commercials that market aspiring office-holders as if they were a new brand of toothpaste or hairspray, too many Americans vote with only a fuzzy understanding of the issues in question. Like Lear, we seem too eager to leave the responsibility of government to others and too ready to trust those who tell us whatever we want to hear.

14   So as we look around us, we should recognize that "discrimination" is a virtue which we desperately need. We must try to avoid making unfair and arbitrary distinctions, but we must not go to the other extreme and pretend that there are no distinctions to be made. The ability to make intelligent judgments is essential both for the success of one's personal life and for the functioning of society as a whole. Let us be open-minded by all means, but not so open-minded that our brains fall out.

POST-READING QUESTIONS

Content

1. What is Miller's definition of discrimination, and how does he feel this word has been misused?

368 Persuasion: The Emotional Appeal

2. Why is the idea of differences "unsettling" to American culture? What is one effect of our discomfort with "the realization that there are differences among children"?

3. When does Miller suggest discrimination might be useful—if not virtuous? How and why do you agree or disagree with his point of view?

4. What has been the effect of our lack of our ability to discriminate in American society? When and where do Americans fail to discriminate?

Strategies and Structures

1. How do Miller's opening paragraphs tie in with his concluding remarks about discrimination in our society? (How did Lear fail to discriminate and what parallels exist between his actions and our own?)

2. What evidence or reasoning does Miller use to sway us to his way of thinking? What specific examples support his argument?

3. Why does Miller provide both the popular and his own definition for the word "discrimination"? Where do his definitions occur in the essay? Why would they have been less effective anywhere else in the composition?

4. In its simplest sense, we might conclude that Miller's essay is an argument "against" a definition. What is his first strategy for challenging the popular definition for discrimination. What is his second strategy? Why does he place his *call for action* in the final paragraph?

Language and Vocabulary

1. Vocabulary: *hypocrites, discernment, bias, preconceptions, euphemistically, indiscriminate, mainstreaming, arbitrary*. Each person should pick one of these words and come to class prepared to discuss Miller's essay, assuming the personality and characteristics

dictated by the meaning of the word he or she has chosen.

2. After the above activity, decide which person best presented characteristics associated with his or her word, and write a paragraph wherein you justify your opinion referring specifically to ways this person succeeded in bringing his or her word to life.

GROUP ACTIVITIES

1. For the day, practice *discrimination:* when you go to the store, when you choose your words for conversation, when you create your schedule for the day, and so on. Record your discriminatory actions. For example, if you went shopping and one bar of soap was cheaper than another, you'd discriminate prices in making your decision. Bring your journal entries to class the following day and as a group, make one list of "discriminate" behavior.

2. Get the position papers of two candidates in a recent election and reflect on "the genuine differences" between the candidates. As a group, determine for whom you would vote by discriminating between the candidates' stands on the real issues surrounding the election. Also, have a critical eye toward how and why politicians try to appeal to us emotionally first and intellectually last. What techniques do they use to obscure the issues and win our hearts rather than minds?

WRITING ASSIGNMENTS

1. Pick a word like *prejudice* and write a persuasive essay, convincing your reader that the popular definition of the word is misleading and that your definition is more appropriate or useful. Support your claims with a clear definition of terms and examples drawn from authoritative references and personal observations.

2. Summarize the differences between two opposing points of view (e.g., we should or should not allow people who have tested positive for the AIDS virus to immigrate to America), and then argue for one of the positions.

Racism and Militarism: The Nuclear Connection
RON GLASS

The former director of the Adult Education Development Project, Ron Glass now teaches philosophy and philosophy of education at Stanford University. His article, "Racism and Militarism: The Nuclear Connection," was excerpted in 1985 in *Freedom Notes,* Dennis Banks Defense Committee, San Francisco, from "By Our Own Lives: Moving the Foundation Stone of Racism."

PRE-READING QUESTIONS

1. Go to the library and do research on nuclear weapons and their production. Why do we produce nuclear weapons? What are the advantages and disadvantages/dangers of their production and proliferation?

2. In your journal answer the following questions. How do you feel about nuclear weapons and their production? What are the philosophical and moral advantages of these "peace keepers?" What are the disadvantages?

3. A great deal of money is spent on nuclear weapons; do you believe your tax dollars should be spent supporting their production? Why or why not? Would you allow a nuclear weapons plant to be built in your neighborhood? Share your responses in small groups.

1   The nuclear industry, in alliance with major U.S. corporations, has blatantly disregarded and disrespected people of color in the search for profits. The greedy effort to maintain a global military superiority threatens the health of vast populations, and already ravages Native Americans and other non-white indigenous peoples.

2   The heart of nuclear weapons and energy plants is radioactive material. The first step in getting this material is mining uranium ore. The uranium used by the U.S. government and corporations is mined in the Western United States, Canada, Australia and South Africa. The vast majority of the land under which the uranium is mined belongs to Native peoples. An October 1979 conference in Copenhagen concerning the uranium mining threat to the peoples of the Third and Fourth Worlds found that 72% of the known worldwide uranium reserves are on lands of these peoples. The U.S. nuclear industry continues to exploit Native Americans and Native Canadians, as well as supporting the apartheid government of South Africa. In Australia, the Aborigines have been severely impacted by uranium exploitation, which now threatens their most sacred grounds. In the continental U.S. alone, 55% of uranium deposits are on land recognized as belonging to Native Americans. If contested treaties are honored, the figure jumps to over 90%. Almost 100% of current mining occurs on Indian territory. Most of the profit from the extraction of this deadly material goes into the hands of a few gigantic multinational corporations. According to a 1977 study by the Oil, Chemical and Atomic Workers Union, a mere seven firms control 81.5% of all uranium reserves.

3   As Native Americans struggle to regain their sovereignty rights, the U.S.'s relationships with its other suppliers of nuclear materials becomes critical. Thus we find the U.S. in alliance with exploitative governments and the attacks on Native lands around the world. Sovereignty status for Native Americans and the honoring of Indian treaties could lead to keeping the U.S. uranium underground and undisturbed. This possibility is part of the reason for the government's unwarranted Navajo relocation at Big Mountain and violation of treaty agreements in the Black Hills. Uranium mining has already had an extremely negative impact on many residents of the Navajo,

Laguna Pueblo, Spokane, Ute, Lakota, and Chippewa Nations. One out of five working Laguna Pueblo Indians, and one of four working Spokane Indians, are employed at mines. The largest uranium strip mine in the world is Anaconda Corporation's abandoned and still radioactive Jackpile Mine on the lands of the Laguna Pueblo Nation. Many of these Nations have also been adversely affected by coal mining and coal fired power production, as have members of the Crow, Cheyenne, and Hopi Nations. Coal is included as a radiation danger, for burning it emits "sizable quantities of low level radioactivity" according to scientific studies.

4   In the U.S. Southwest, uranium mining began in 1946 as the U.S. launched the effort to build up a nuclear arsenal following the bombing of the desert in tests and Hiroshima and Nagasaki in warfare. Any kind of mining has dangers associated with it, but uranium mining is more hazardous because of the intense radioactivity. LaVerne Husen, Director of the Public Health Service in Shiprock, New Mexico, on the Navajo Nation says:

5   These mines had 100 times the level of radioactivity allowed today. They weren't really mines, just holes and tunnels dug into the cliffs. Inside, the mines were like radiation chambers, giving off unmeasured and unregulated amounts of radon. The problem was that back in the 1950's nobody was riding herd on the companies. It was a get rich quick scheme that took advantage of the Navajo miners who didn't know what radioactivity was or anything about its hazards.

6   It wasn't until 1972 that Federal radiation standards were enforced in the uranium mines. Not surprisingly, the result of such long neglect has been disastrous for the miners. A study by the National Institute of Occupational Health and Safety notes that lung cancer among uranium miners is now occurring "in what can only be classified as epidemic proportions." A 1975 study at Brandeis University found miners dying from lung cancer at six times the predicted rate. Because of other life style factors, such as low socio-economic status and close ties to food sources directly linked to contaminated land, Indian miners and families are even more susceptible to radiation induced cancers. Dr. Gerald Buker reported in a monograph entitled

"Uranium Mining and Lung Cancer Among Navajo Indians" that the "risk of lung cancer increases by a factor of at least 85 among Navajo uranium miners." These chilling statistics are borne out by findings at Shiprock Indian Hospital, where it is estimated that 70 of the original 100 Navajo uranium miners at a Kerr-McGee mining and milling operation at Red Rock Cover will die of lung cancer. The United Mine Workers estimate that 80-90% of those doing shaft mining for uranium will die of lung cancer.

7   Mining uranium exposes the miners to dangerous radioactivity from the uranium and from other radioactive elements into which it decays, one of which is radon gas. When the ore is mined and milled and left in tailings piles, the radon gas is free to mix with the air and be inhaled. The miners are obviously in danger from this, but so also are the surrounding communities of women and children. The danger to others should not be underestimated. Los Alamos Scientific Laboratory in New Mexico, one of two U.S. nuclear weapon design laboratories, stated in a 1978 study that "perhaps the solution to the radon emission problem is to zone the land into uranium mining and milling districts so as to forbid human habitation." Even if this were done, it is far too late for the countless Native Americans already exposed to this indiscriminate poisoning.

8   Uranium mining contaminates the water as well as the air, again threatening all that lives in the environment served by local water supplies. Radioactivity can leach into both aquifer and non-aquifer waters. Depending on the underground deposit formations, contamination of an aquifer can spread over large areas and poison waters for vast periods of time. Water contamination has a disproportionately high effect on rural peoples such as Native Americans. Federal regulations cover contamination of water supplies serving more than 25 people, and so most reservation wells are not even monitored. Yet according to a 1979 Interagency Task Force on the Health Effects of Ionizing Radiation, studies have indicated that "potable ground waters contain measurable quantities of radiation . . . and that high, and in some cases extremely high, concentrations exist in some waters used for domestic purposes." The poisonous water supplies on reservations where there are uranium mining and milling operations may account for some of the high

rates of birth defects and other reproductive anomalies which have been reported.

9   The problems for Native Americans and others do not end when the uranium ore has been mined. It then undergoes a milling process to turn the ore into "yellowcake." Each ton of ore contains only about six pounds of uranium, and to get rid of the other materials the ore is finely crushed and treated with acid. This process produces 70% pure uranium which then must be further "enriched" to be used in power plants and bombs. What is left over from the milling process is a sand-like residue called "tailings" and the liquid acid. The acid is dumped after dilution into settling ponds, and the tailings are discarded in huge piles. Over 1990 pounds of tailings are created for every six pounds of uranium.

10   The more than 150 million tons of tailings in the U.S. retain 60–80% of their original radioactivity. The sandy residues can blow away as dust, be dissolved by water and contaminate water supplies, or decay to radon gas and escape to the atmosphere. The Department of Energy estimates a risk of cancer 100% greater than the general population for people who live within one mile of tailing sites, and concluded that "none of the sites can be considered in satisfactory condition from the long term standpoint." The short term solution of covering the thousands of acres of tailings with six feet of soil, even if it were actually done, is obviously inadequate in light of the 80,000 year hazard life of the piles. And meanwhile, Indians suffer daily from the wastes left in the midst of their homelands. For example, after two decades of small scale uranium mining near Edgemont, South Dakota, the state with the highest percentage of Native Americans in the U.S., over three million pounds of tailing were produced. These were casually left within 100 yards of the Cheyenne River. Now cancer rates in the county that uses that water are 50% higher than in any other South Dakota county.

11   Even more alarmingly, these sandy tailings piled near where people live have been used as children's playgrounds, and when mixed with cement and mortar, to build schools and houses. The "dark, rich-looking stuff" has been mixed into countless gardens. Oscar Sloan, a former miner living in an isolated Indian community near Monument Valley, Arizona, says that:

12   All the people have used the uranium wastes to build our houses. The company never told us they were dangerous. Some white men came here a couple of years ago and said we shouldn't live in our houses. They said the government would get us new houses because our homes are radioactive, but they never did. I don't want to live in this house any more, but I have no place else to stay, no place else to go.

13   It is unknown how many Native Americans live in houses that are hastening their and their children's deaths. The scale of the problem can be imagined by considering the case of Grand Junction, Colorado, site of an early mine. Tailings were given away to contractors. Years later, researchers discovered high rates of birth defects, as well as cancer occurring twenty years earlier than in the rest of the population. According to the U.S. General Accounting Office, geiger counters have indicated contamination of more than one-third of the 15,126 buildings checked through 1976. Tailings had been used in building fifteen schools.

14   The tailings and acid ponds have also accounted for the worst radiation accident in U.S. history. This catastrophe occurred on July 16, 1979, near Church Rock, New Mexico, and contaminated vast tracts of rural and Indian lands, yet the accident received less publicity than the less severe earlier accident at Three Mile Island. Near Church Rock, a dam broke by a United Nuclear Corporation mill, and tons of radioactive debris and water rushed downstream. "Extremely high" levels of radioactivity spread more than 75 miles, poisoning large areas of land and many more miles of streams and rivers, including the Puerca, Little Colorado, and Colorado Rivers. Three months after the accident, radiation in the water over 200 miles downstream was still 60 times greater than the Environmental Protection Agency's "maximum containment level." No fines were levied against United Nuclear Corporation, and the Church Rock mill has been permitted to go back into operation. The surrounding Navajo land has become virtually uninhabitable and the water remains deadly.

15   Thus far nothing has been done about millions of tons of tailings, and they remain largely on Navajo, Laguna Pueblo, and Lakota territory, blowing in the wind and leaching into the soil and water supplies. The wastes continue to pile up at alarming

rates, and the Secretary of the Interior waives regulations to facilitate leases for the multinational energy companies to dispose
of more of their poisons on Indian lands.

16   Native Americans face additional problems than those faced
by other groups living near nuclear dangers. These additional
problems are related to socioeconomic status, population size,
and relationship to the land and food supplies. Native Americans live at the lowest socioeconomic level of any group in the
U.S., and all studies have shown heightened impact of disease
on groups living at such levels. Poor non-whites have also been
shown to have almost four times the rate of increase in cancer
than poor whites. For Indians, these disadvantages are multi-
plied by dependence on food supplies closely tied to the land
and in which radioactive materials related to uranium mining
have been shown to accumulate. Finally, the increased risks to
Indians are based in genetic damage that could be manifest as
late as ten generations from now due to radiation exposure.
These effects will be greatest in genetically more homogeneous
Indian populations that are stable and isolated on reservations.
Experts predict, due to Native Americans' high exposure to
radiation, an increase in the incidence of club foot, subluxated
hips, mental retardation, diabetes, heart disease, rheumatic
fever, sterility, and cancers.

17   The overall result of the policies and actions of the nuclear
industry is genocide for Native Americans.

POST-READING QUESTIONS

Content

1. Glass presents his thesis in the first paragraph. What
is it?
2. What do the government and corporations need to
create nuclear weapons? Where is this material
found? What problems does this present?
3. What health hazards do Native-Americans and others face when uranium is mined near their homes?
4. What additional problems do Native-Americans face?

Strategies and Structures

1. Why does Glass start his essay with an immediate presentation of his thesis?

2 How does Glass develop his argument? How does he try to persuade the reader that his argument is valid? Is his mix of scientific data, historical events, and statistics effective?

3. Glass uses many statistics. What does he hope to achieve by using so many statistics? What effect did reading so many statistics have on you as a reader?

4. In paragraph 16 Glass presents many more problems faced by Native-Americans exposed to "nuclear dangers." Why does he present all of these additional problems in one paragraph? What linking words does he use to unify this paragraph?

Language and Vocabulary

1. Vocabulary: *blatant, radioactive, Aborigines, radon emission, "yellowcake", tailings, homogeneous, anomalies.* Many of these words—*radioactive, radon, "yellowcake,"* and *tailings*—deal with the mining of uranium. After defining these words, write one or two paragraphs explaining the hazards of mining the ore, using each word several times.

2. The author mixes rather "plain" language with many scientific terms. How does he keep the reader from becoming confused by the scientific terms?

GROUP ACTIVITIES

1. Explore in your group the difference between conventional and nuclear weapons. Is there any advantage in employing nuclear weapons in place of conventional arms? Are there any moral differences in the use of the two? If so, what are they? If you view the two types of weapons as similar, explain.

2. Discuss any nuclear arms or power films you have seen, books or magazine articles you have read, or lectures you have heard that are against nuclear arms. What do they suggest are the problems of nuclear production? Do they concur with Glass's findings? What kind of world do they believe we live in because of nuclear weapons?

3. Discuss the following questions in groups. What if these films, books, and so on, had been produced by pro-nuclear arms persons? How would they differ? What arguments missing in the original films would be present if pro-nuclear arms people had produced them? How might a pro-nuclear person have tried to persuade the audience that we need nuclear weapons and power?

WRITING ACTIVITY

1. Using specific examples, statistics, and quotes from a variety of sources, write an essay in which you argue for either the abolition of nuclear arms production or the further production of them.

2. Write an essay in which you argue that nuclear arms production has positive or negative effects on the world community.

Degrees of Discomfort: Is Homophobia Equivalent to Racism?
JONATHAN ALTER

Jonathan Alter is a contributor to several popular magazines. His following critical analysis of homophobia first appeared in the March 12 issue of *Newsweek*, 1990.

PRE-READING QUESTIONS

1. How do you feel about homosexuality? Should homosexuals hold prominent positions in medicine, education, government, and the community (e.g., Boy and
   Girl Scout Leaders). Are you homophobic? Do you
   feel you have logical reasons for your fear(s)?

2. Do you feel uncomfortable around people who practice alternate lifestyles? Why? Why not? Do you believe that people who adamantly voice their objections
   to homosexuality are racist? Why or why not?

1   When Andy Rooney got in trouble last month, gay activists
complained he was being publicly rebuked for his allegedly
racist remarks and not for his gay-bashing. They wanted to
know why homophobia was viewed as less serious than racism.
The case of Martin Luther King III last week brought the comparison into even sharper relief. After a speech in Poughkeep-
sie, N.Y., in which he said "something must be wrong" with
homosexuals, the young Atlanta politician met with angry gay
leaders and quickly apologized. His father's legacy, King said,
was "the struggle to free this country of bigotry and discrimination." In that light, he added, he needed to examine his own
attitudes toward homosexuals.

2   King will need to ask himself this question: is homophobia
the moral equivalent of racism? To answer yes sounds right; it
conforms to commendable ideals of tolerance. But it doesn't
take account of valid distinctions between the two forms of
prejudice. On the other hand, to answer no—to say, homophobia is not like racism for this reason or that—risks rationalizing
anti-gay bias.

3   Discrimination against homosex*uals* is not the same as personal distaste for homosex*uality*. The former is clearly akin to
racism. There is no way to explain away the prejudice in this
country against gays. People lose jobs, promotions, homes and
friends because of it. Incidents of violence against gays are up
sharply in some areas. Hundreds of anti-sodomy laws remain on
the books, and gays are shamelessly discriminated against in
insurance and inheritance. The fact is, a lot of people are pig-
headed enough to judge a person entirely on the basis of his or

her sexuality. Rooney's mail—and that of practically everyone else commenting publicly on this issue—is full of ugly anti-gay invective.

4   But does that mean that anyone who considers the homosexual sex act sinful or repulsive is the equivalent of a racist? The answer is no. Objecting to it may be narrow-minded and invasive of privacy, but it does not convey the same complete moral vacuity as, say, arguing that blacks are born inferior. There is a defensive middle position. Recall Mario Cuomo's carefully articulated view of abortion: personally opposed, but deeply supportive of a woman's right to choose. That tracks quite closely to polls that show how the majority of Americans approach the subject of homosexuality.

5   Like all straddles, this one offends people on both sides: straights who consider all homosexuality sinful, and gays who consider a hate-the-sin-but-not-the-sinner argument merely another form of homophobia. Moreover, the "personal opposition" idea rings more hollow on homosexuality than on abortion; after all, there is no third-party fetus—just consenting adults whose private behavior should not be judged by outsiders. Of course there are times when squeamishness is understandable. In coming of age, many gays have made a point of flaunting their sexuality, moving, as one joke puts it, from "the love that won't shut up." Exhibitionism and promiscuity (less common in the age of AIDS) are behavioral choices that, unlike innate sexual preference, can be controlled. It's perfectly legitimate to condemn such behavior—assuming heterosexuals are held to the same standard.

6   Simply put, identity and behavior are not synonymous. A bigot hates blacks for what they *are;* a reasonable person can justifiably object to some things homosexuals *do.* The distinction between objecting to who someone is (unfair) and objecting to what someone does (less unfair) must be maintained. The worst comment about gays allegedly made by Rooney was that he would not like to be locked in a room with them. That would be a tolerable sentiment only if the homosexuals were *having sex* in the room. Otherwise it's a form of bigotry. Who would object to being locked in a room with cigarette smokers if they weren't smoking?

7   "Acting gay" often involves more than sexual behavior itself. Much of the dislike for homosexuals centers not on who they are

or what they do in private, but on so-called affectations—"swishiness" in men, the "butch" look for women—not directly related to the more private sex act. Heterosexuals tend to argue that gays can downplay these characteristics and "pass" more easily in the straight world than blacks can in a white world.

8   This may be true, but it's also irrelevant. For many gays those traits aren't affectations but part of their identities; attacking the swishiness is the same as attacking *them*. Why the visceral vehemence, particularly among straight men? Richard Isay, a psychiatrist and author of the 1989 book "Being Homosexual," suggests that homophobia actually has little to do with the sex act itself. "This hatred of homosexuals appears to be secondary in our society to the fear and hatred of what is perceived as being 'feminine' in other men and in oneself."

9   Such fears, buried deep, are reminiscent of the emotional charge of racial feelings. At its most virulent, this emotion leads to blaming the victim—for AIDS, for instance, or for poverty. In its more modest form, the fear, when recognized, can be helpful in understanding the complexities of both homosexuality and race.

10   That consciousness is sometimes about language—avoiding "fag" and "nigger." But the interest groups that expend energy insisting that one use "African-American" instead of "black" or "gay and lesbian" instead of "homosexual" are missing the point. Likewise, the distinctions between racism and homophobia eventually shrivel before the larger task at hand, which is simply to look harder at ourselves.

POST-READING QUESTIONS

Content

1. Does Alter advocate a homosexual lifestyle? Do you feel he is trying to convert his audience to thinking as he does, or is he merely trying to make you a creative thinker, one who sets aside personal biases and looks at an issue from a rational point of view? Explain what he advocates.

2. What does Alter consider *bigotry*? How does he explain or illustrate it?

3. What does Alter consider objectionable and what does he consider acceptable behavior? How would he enforce common values or public sexual practices?

Strategies and Structures

1. Does Alter have an explicit thesis statement or is it inferred? How is this effective?

2. What is the function of rhetorical questions in this essay? How do they lead the reader to conclusions that the writer has not explicitly stated? Why is this strategy more effective than simply stating facts?

3. How does Alter use examples to set the tone and introduce the theme of his essay? What is ironic about Martin Luther King III expressing homophobic feelings?

4. How does the author's use of comparison between homophobia and racism help develop his implied thesis?

Language and Vocabulary

1. Vocabulary: *homosexual, heterosexual, rebuked, sodomy, exhibitionism, promiscuity, synonymous, affectation, swishiness, visceral, vehemence, virulent.* The above words have both prefixes and suffixes underlined, which change the meanings of the root words. Find the definition of each prefix and suffix and explain how they have altered the word's original meaning.

2. A *phobia* is a fear of something and is often used as a suffix in a word. Jot down as many phobias as you can think of and bring your list to class for use in a group activity.

GROUP ACTIVITIES

1. Get together in small groups and discuss the persuasive merit of Alter's argument that *"Discrimination against homosexuals is not the same as personal distaste*

for homosexuality." How and why is the former racist and the latter not?

2. Using the list of phobias written for the vocabulary section, write one group list of the most common phobias on your lists. Next, go through each *phobia* and analyze the logic behind the fear. Finally, determine which of your *phobias* are actually personal distaste for person, place or thing as opposed to well-founded fears. Submit your group list to the instructor at the end of class.

WRITING ACTIVITIES

1. Write an argumentative essay showing how any society that promotes the concept that men are superior to women is a homosexual society and needs to re-evaluate its stance on homosexual individuals.

2. Develop an original thesis on one of the following topics/issues, and thoroughly argue your thesis in a well-supported composition: homosexuality, bisexuality, heterosexuality. To avoid *leap-of-faith* arguments, use strict reasoning (deductive and inductive logic) here, omitting your religious beliefs and/or any holy book which might bias or distort clear, rational thinking.

I Want to Live Without Trouble
A North Chinese/Vietnamese Elder
As Told to JAMES M. FREEMAN

James M. Freeman, Professor of Anthropology, has focused his teaching, research, and community service on India and Indochinese refugees. His most significant publications are *Untouchables: An Indian Life History* (1979) and *Hearts of Sorrow: Vietnamese-American Lives* (1989) which won a 1990 American Book Award, and the Outstanding Book Award of the Association for Asian-American Studies. In the following excerpt from *Hearts of Sorrow: Vietnamese-American Lives,* the speaker, identified as a "North Chinese/Vietnamese Elder," lived under communist rule for over twenty years before, unwillingly, he immigrated to America. This, in part, may explain his rather critical attitude towards American society and Vietnamese refugees in particular.

PRE-READING QUESTIONS

1. How do you feel about America? Would you die for it? Why? Why not?

2. Is it more important to be an individual or a part of a group in American society? Why?

3. What do you believe makes living in America desirable? How can a person be considerate towards others if he or she is preoccupied with making money?

1   During the time of French rule, those of us who were Chinese were set apart from others. People were afraid that when the Chinese gained wealth, they'd send it back to China. As a Chinese, I was considered a foreigner, and I carried Chinese papers. Because of this, when I was in high school, I was exempt from entrance exams and could enter the high school.

2   When the Communists took over, our position at first was good because China was considered close friends with North Vietnam. They praised China, and so the Chinese participated in all activities from 1954 to around 1960 or 1962. As a minority group, the Chinese had privileges reserved for them, such as entrance into the university without high grades.

3   The treatment of the Chinese depended on how friendly Vietnam and China were at any moment. When war broke out between China and Vietnam, we were asked to leave. I was expelled because I allowed a relative to stay in my house illegally, that is, I failed to report to the proper authorities that someone had come to live in my house. For this, my neighbors distrusted me. Actually, I was not expelled by any official document. Rather, they used my relative's visit as a pretext to put

pressure on me, with veiled and indirect threats. The Administrative Committee of the Ward invited me to meet with them. The Public Security Agent explained, "For your protection against the Chinese aggression, we have to bring you to another place in the countryside." When I came back home, the Public Security Agent came to my house and asked, "Do you have any relatives in Hong King? You should leave."

4 After that, I understood that I could no longer stay on in Hanoi. I said, "I am poor; I have no relatives in Hong Kong."

5 The Public Security Agent said, "See if you can sell anything, even the door, but not the house, to give you the money to go."

6 The house was very big; that's why they didn't want to let us sell it. We were very bewildered. We were now old. I had no career except my government job. How could we survive? I didn't actually want to go, but so many of our relatives had left already, and that gave me a very good impetus, urged me to go.

7 I had lived all my life around Hanoi; 'I had never been to other provinces, never to South Vietnam. Many of my friends and relatives never thought I would go; they were quite surprised when I left for Hong Kong. My wife's sister, resident in America for six months, sponsored us, and three months later, we arrived in the United States.

8 When I lived in North Vietnam, even though I was not hungry, the food was meager. Even though I had money, I couldn't buy much food. My entire monthly salary was not enough to cover our food needs. For a North Vietnamese arriving in America, it is really paradise; we can buy food so easily, so cheaply! I live on public assistance. President Reagan wants to cut our aid. I don't think his cuts will affect us much, and I accept them because of his big efforts to resist the Communists. That's on the physical life, the material life.

9 I have talked with many Vietnamese, and they say that even though they have a good material life, their sentimental life is not good, not relaxed, not at ease. Those Vietnamese who are less than 30 years of age will be integrated into American society. Those people who are 30 to 50 years old and those over 50 still miss their old society; they cannot fully integrate. If 50 years later the two cultures can be integrated, then the people will feel more at home. Once people live here, they must have

an American soul. When people think of becoming a United States citizen, they think of the benefits, the jobs, the travel abroad. They never think, for example, of patriotism, of attachment or devotion to their adopted country. But if they think only of benefits, what will they do if there is aggression against the United States? Will they stand and fight for their country, or will they run away?

10   If you don't have a good foundation, no ideals, no attachment, then you won't die for your country. The majority of Vietnamese are like that now. They are not devoted to America. I think that America should create those kinds of people who will fight for their country. That should be the criterion for education in America.

11   The bad thing about America is that there is too much freedom. Americans think only about the maximization of profit, what they can do that will benefit themselves. There is too much individualism and freedom of one group at the expense of others, with little concern for the common good. Every community thinks of itself too much, not of the country, so people can sell secrets to the Russians just for money, for profit.

12   Some U.S. Congressmen proposed measures to lessen accidents on the highways, but other Congressmen and lobbyists opposed this because it affects capitalists. If a proposal for the good of everybody affects their profits, companies lobby or buy off the Congressmen.

13   Because of the division between legislative, judicial, and executive branches, the president is always affected. Every time he wants to make a decision he is controlled and hindered; he has to consult with the legislative branch and he cannot make quick and good decisions. The presidential term is only four years. How can all of the projects or plans be carried out in such a short time? Leaders can have a long-range view on many matters, maybe 20 years, but their term is too short to carry it out.

14   Because of too much freedom, Americans are so *careless* about so many things. When they go out on the streets, they do not wear shirts, or dresses; some use the flag for shorts and for trousers. But the flag is symbolic of the country.

15   Many people who stretch their legs on the bus don't leave room for other people. Some women put handbags on the seats

and don't let others sit down. I use the bus often; I see such disregard for people.

16   On American Independence Day, not many houses hang out flags. People are individualistic, and even neighbors do not know one another's names. One night, an old American man was robbed near my house; his wallet was taken, but no one seemed to care. Passersby watched as the man was dragged into the bushes and robbed. They did nothing.

17   Another point of too much freedom: Americans do not have many children, and the trend to remain single is on the rise. In my view, a superpower should have as many people as possible to be strong. Compare the populations of other superpowers; many are populous; many countries are really scared about the population of China.

18   If the Constitution could be changed and not too much freedom were allowed, I think America would be better off. For example, freedom of the press is excessive. If they would try to help and say something good about the government instead of criticizing it, they could not be exploited by the Russians, who use these negatives in their propaganda.

19   In the American educational system, both technology and human relations and values should be given equal emphasis. Family values, such as relationships between grandparents, parents, and children, should be introduced into the educational system. Too much emphasis is put on technology to the neglect of humans, so that when people grow up, they only think of money and profits at the expense of everything else. That's all they know.

20   I have tried to be humble. I've been here only a short time, but the things I've told you are really big. People think too much about themselves. They are too selfish, too individualistic.

21   There's much that's good in America. In their deeds, Americans are energetic and great; they do great things. When I came here to live, I found in my contacts with Americans that they were honest. If a teacher doesn't know something, he doesn't pretend; instead, he says he doesn't know. When I was in high school, I took a philosophy class in which the teacher made a mistake. He stated the wrong century in which Auguste Compte was born. A student discovered that. The teacher, in trying to cover this up, said, "There are two

August Comptes." What I like about Americans is that they admit they don't know.

22   Vietnamese refugees in the United States are very much anti-Communist. They try to identify those who show some sympathy with Communism. It is not accidental that in the last two years (1982–1984) two people (elsewhere in America) have been murdered, for they openly praised the Communist regime. When a respected professor wrote an article in which he referred to Ho Chi Minh as "Uncle Ho," people got very angry: "He's not our uncle; he destroyed the country."

23   Once I met some South Vietnamese military officers who said, "I hate Americans. Because of American policy we lost and have to suffer here."

24   I replied, "You should not complain about this because America should put the interests of its own 200 million people first, above those of South Vietnam's 20 million. All Vietnamese suffered, not just you." They became quite angry at my remarks. Because I come from the North, people believe I sympathize with the Communists. This makes it difficult to live, and now I'm very cautious. I'm old now; I don't want to have trouble, just to live in peace. My family heredity is that people do not live long. I don't want to do anything to affect my life. I just want to live a few more years.

POST-READING QUESTIONS

Content

1. Throughout this essay, the author expresses a fear of strangers. What are some of the more effective examples of this? How does this fear or distrust of strangers serve the purpose of his essay?

2. How does the author's discussion of Americans as careless, inconsiderate people relate to his theme of a society with too much freedom?

3. What parallels does the Chinese/Vietnamese Elder draw between the perils of the Vietnamese society he grew up in and those faced in the United States? Do you think his earlier experiences in Vietnam influenced his later critical view of America? Why?

4. According to the author, what dangers to American society are brought about by too much individualism?

Strategies and Structures

1. Why does the author begin his essay by recounting his experiences as a Chinese minority in Vietnam? What foundation does this lay for the rest of the essay?

2. Why does the author conclude his essay on a positive note? What purpose does this serve? What impressions are you left with in regard to the author?

3. The author constantly reminds us that he is an ethnic minority, no matter where he has lived. How has this fact influenced the way he observes the world around him? In what way does this repetition provide a "cohesive" (linking) device for the essay as a whole?

4. To what extent does the author support the arguments he presents to the reader? Why, in some instances, does his method of writing evoke an emotional response from you? Cite specific examples that particularly inflamed you.

Language and Vocabulary

1. Vocabulary: *aggression, capitalism, communism, criterion, individualistic.* Write down your personal definitions for each of these words. Then, on a separate piece of paper titled "Dictionary Definitions," write down the literal (dictionary) definitions of the words. (*Note:* Some of these words are concepts and require a lengthy explanation; to do justice to this assignment, avoid attempting short-cuts.) Compare the differences between what you associate with the words and what their real definitions are. Finally, after considering the literal and your personal definitions, write a short persuasive essay in which you develop a thesis and argue an issue about one of the words (e.g., aggression is healthy, capitalism is bad).

2. Chose six words from the essay that evoke an emotional response in you and write a paragraph in which you use those words to refute the argument that there is too much freedom in America.

GROUP ACTIVITIES

1. Assemble the class into two groups: one advocating complete freedom and the other advocating totalitarianism and prepare for a two-round debate. For round 1, appeal primarily to your audience's emotions (pathos). Then, during round 2, rationally argue and defend your group's point of view. Follow-up the class debate with an evaluation of the most effective methods of persuasion.

2. Write a collaborative, persuasive essay on one of the themes in this essay (e.g., Americans lack devotion to their country) wherein your group attempts to achieve an ideal balance among logics, ethics, and emotions.

WRITING ACTIVITIES

1. Do you believe that the individual's obsession with money has driven him or her to ignore his or her brothers and sisters? Is less personal concern about freedom and money the only way for people to care about fellow human beings? Write a persuasive essay based on your point of view.

2. Is blind allegiance to one's country the only way to demonstrate loyalty or patriotism, or in this highly technical age, is the "one world" concept more important? Integrating fact with emotion, write a persuasive argument based on this issue.

Additional Topics and Issues for Persuasive Essays

1. Write an essay in which you persuade the school to give you a scholarship. You will want to consider why you are a worthy beneficiary, and how your scholarship will further your education.

2. Devise an original thesis about the current position of men, women, children, and elderly people in American society. Then write a persuasive essay calling for a change in our present treatment of them.

3. Write an essay in which you persuade your audience that general education courses are useless. How do you expect college to prepare you for your major? In what way do general education courses assist you in achieving your goals? Avoid arguments like, "I could get my college degree a lot sooner if I did not have to have a general education."

4. Write an essay persuading your classmates and families to discontinue the use of plastics and/or Styrofoam (petroleum-based products).

5. Persuade your audience in a well-developed essay that all international boundaries should be dissolved and that we all become citizens of one world and one governing body, a government that includes the best of all existing political ideologies.

6. Write an essay defending a society which respects an individual's right to an alternate lifestyle.

7. Write a persuasive essay calling for drastic yet fitting punishment for those who sexually, psychologically, and physically abuse others.

8. Compose an essay wherein you defend two or three vices you have. Attempt to convince your reader that what society commonly views as a vice (e.g., smoking, drinking, gambling) is—in your case at least—a virtue.

GLOSSARY OF LITERARY AND RHETORICAL TERMS

Acronym   A word formed from the first letter of letters of subsequent parts of a compound term. For instance, International Business Machines becomes IBM, the Equal Rights Amendment becomes the ERA, the Central Intelligence Agency becomes the CIA, and the Bureau of Indian Affairs becomes the BIA.

Active Verbs   Verbs that show rather than just tell your reader what you are talking about. For instance, write *David practices law* instead of *David is a lawyer.* (See **Voice**)

Adjectives   Words that can indicate the quality of a noun or its equivalent (e.g., the *slippery* pavement, the *rocky* soil, the *blue* sky). Typically, adjectives answer questions like "which kind?" and "which one?"

Adverbs   Words that modify verbs, adjectives, other adverbs, and complete sentences:

Verbs:	Ngan drove *swiftly.*
Adjectives:	The cat was *extremely* frisky.
Adverbs:	Deborah spoke *very* slowly.
Sentences:	*Desperately,* Kevin pleaded his case to the jury.

Alliteration   The repetition of the same letters or sounds at the beginning of two or more words that are next or close to each other (e.g., My mother, makes mashed potatoes on Mondays.)

Allusion   A term used when making reference to a famous literary, historical, or social figure or event. For instance, reference to Watergate refers to political corruption.

Analogy   An extended comparison where an unfamiliar topic is explained by noting its similarity to something familiar.

Analysis   To closely inspect and come to a conclusion on something by separating the topic or issue into parts in order to better understand the whole.

Anecdote   A short story that illustrates a point.

Antonym   A word that has an opposite meaning to another word (e.g., Happy is the antonym of sad, and young is the antonym of old).

Argumentation   One of the four major forms of writing, the others being narration, exposition, and description. In an argument, you prove your point by establishing the truth about a topic or issue. In doing so, revealing the fallacies of another's argument may prove invaluable. For a detailed discussion of argumentation, see Chapter 11.

Audience   Those you address when you write (e.g., friends, professors, public servants). You must consider whether your audience knows nothing or a lot about your topic.

Brainstorming   Individually or collectively solving a problem by considering and/or rejecting ideas. A writer brainstorms to generate ideas on a topic, and then focuses on a specific controlling idea which will lead to a topic sentence or a thesis statement.

Cause and Effect   See Chapter 9.

Classification   See Chapter 8.

Cliché   A trite or worn-out expression that either becomes a stereotype or meaningless in its original context. Example: *I'm as hungry as a horse! It's raining cats and dogs!* (How often have you pictured a hungry horse eating or dogs and cats falling falling from the sky when someone makes either of those remarks?)

Clustering   A type of brainstorming where all the ideas one has about a topic or an issue are written down, circled, and related. Clustering words creates a visual picture of the relationships between ideas which are associated with a topic. For further discussion on this method of "prewriting," see Chapter 1.

Coherence   A term used to refer to the clear, logical relationship between words, phrases, clauses, and paragraphs. In writing, we use traditional devices and linking words to achieve coherence.

Colloquial Expressions   Informal expressions, somewhere between slang and formal language. Colloquialisms are acceptable in speech but not formal writing.

Comparison and Contrast   See Chapter 7.

Concrete/Abstract Concrete words may stand by themselves and be understood because they are perceived through the five senses: touch, taste, sight, smell, and sound. For instance, we can touch, see, and hear a small child; thus the word child is concrete. However, the child's *anger* would be abstract since it is perceived only through its relationship with another word. Abstract words define ideas, concepts, and attitudes (love, hate, ethical, indifference, honesty, pride) and tend to be subjective in their interpretation.

Concrete Nouns (See **Concrete/Abstract**)

Connotation The meanings or implications associated with a particular word beyond its literal definition. For instance, while a hospital denotes an institution which provides medical care for people, the word also suggests (connotes) fear, pain, misery, and possibly death. (See **Denotation**)

Context Words that occur before and after a specified word or words and determine its/their meaning.

Controlling Idea The main idea expressed in a paragraph or an essay.

Deduction A form of reasoning which moves from general points to a specific conclusion. See Chapter 11 of this text for a detailed discussion of deductive logic. (See **Induction**)

Definition See Chapter 5.

Denotation The literal or dictionary definition of a word. (See **Connotation**)

Description See Chapter 3.

Diction An author's word choice. Diction also deals with word usage (e.g., concrete/abstract expressions, denotation/connotation, colloquialisms).

Essay Map An essay map is using three or more ideas which are attached to your thesis statement, providing you with the controlling ideas for your body paragraphs. In essence, an essay map tells you where to go by providing a specific direction.

Euphemism The substitution of a mild expression for a harsh one. For example, it is common practice in today's business world to state that one is *terminated* or *laid off* instead of *fired*.

Evidence Facts and examples which prove what you claim.

Exposition   A form of writing where the author's main purpose is to explain or expose a topic or an issue.

Fallacy   Faulty logic (see Chapter 11).

Figures of Speech   Terms which are used to add variety to your essay where points are discussed *figuratively* instead of literally. Some of the common forms of figures of speech include the use of metaphor, simile, hyperbole, and personification (listed elsewhere in this glossary).

Freewriting   Spontaneous writing in which one does not stop to edit material, the objective being merely to generate ideas for one unified paragraph or essay. (See Peter Elbow's Essay, "Freewriting," in Chapter 1).

Generalization   A statement made without a foundation in fact.

Hyperbole   A figure of speech wherein one greatly exaggerates to emphasize a point. Example: Tom went through hell to get a yellow rose for his mother.

Idiom   The use of words unique to a particular group or language.

Illustration and Example   See Chapter 4.

Imagery   Concrete expressions which appeal to the senses, often employing the use of figurative speech to produce mental pictures.

Induction   A form of reasoning which takes several specific points and leads to a generalization about them. See the Introduction to the Argumentation Chapter for a more detailed discussion of inductive logic. (Compare to **Deduction**)

Introduction   In a short essay, the introduction acquaints the reader with the theme or topic which will be explored in depth within the body. Traditionally, one's thesis statement appears in the latter part of an introductory paragraph and provides a focus or direction for developing the remainder of the paper.

Irony   Irony is a figure of speech wherein the author states his or her intention in words that carry an opposite meaning. Irony can also be situational.

Jargon   Like slang, jargon consists of words or phrases particular to a specific profession or social group. Computer operators, for instance, use terms such as "interfacing" or "networking."

The problem is that many people do not know the definitions of these words, and if you use them in an essay, it will be necessary to define them.

Lexicon   A list of words or a wordbook such as a dictionary.

Linking Words   Basically, linking words are connectors, and refer to transitions and subordinating, coordinating, and adverbial conjunctions.

Metaphor   A comparison without the use of "like" or "as." For instance, a simile would state: My professor is like a prison warden. A metaphor would simply state: My professor is a prison warden.

Mood   The mood is the emotional tone of a work (e.g., gloomy, optimistic, pessimistic, cheerful).

Myth   Tales and stories about supernatural heroes, heroines, gods, goddesses, and monsters which originated before written language and were passed on to succeeding generations through the oral tradition of storytelling. The purpose of many primitive myths—just as modern myths—is to interpret natural phenomena such as creation and the seasons.

Narration   One of the major forms of writing. Narration is used to relate what happened at an event or a number of events. In essence, a narrative tells a story. (See Chapter 2 for further discussion on Narration.)

Paradox   A situation or statement which, although it is contradictory to what reason dictates, is nevertheless true. Example: The starving people at the edge of town were the happiest people I have ever met.

Parallelism   Constructing word groups into consistent and balanced patterns using the same grammatical forms. For example nouns should be combined with similar nouns (Doctors, lawyers, and accountants were in the room.), adjectives with like adjectives (The gardener planted yellow, white and red roses.), verbs with similar verbs (We studied, ate, and then slept for ten hours.).

Paraphrase   To put someone else's ideas or written material into your own words.

Parody   A device whereby an author employs humor to make fun of a particular situation or another piece of literature.

Persona   A character or voice used as the speaker of an essay or short story. The attitudes of the persona frequently differ from those of the author.

Personification   A form of figurative speech, personification is the treatment of animals or inanimate objects as if they were human. Example: The rose breathed a sigh of relief as the morning sun touched her, bringing warmth and life to her cold petals.

Persuasion   Like argumentation, persuasion is a form of writing where an author attempts to convince his/her reader of something. In contrast to argumentation, however, persuasion includes words that elicit an **emotional** rather than a rational, logical response from a reader to achieve the writer's ultimate objective. That is, the author appeals to one's emotions (pathos) and ethics (ethos) in addition to logic (logos). See Chapter 12.

Point of View   The perspective from which an essay or story is written. In formal writing, point of view is expressed in: first person, wherein the author uses the pronoun "I," and third person, which is a more subjective form of writing, wherein the writer uses "he," "she," or "it" as the narrator. Point of view may also refer to an author's attitude towards his or her subject matter.

Prefix   Something added to the beginning of a word to change its meaning or give it a new meaning (e.g., un+wanted= unwanted; re+united=reunited).

Prewriting   A spontaneous listing of thoughts to aid in the composition of your essay or paragraph. Prewriting techniques include: clustering, freewriting, listing, and mapping.

Purpose   The objective or reason for writing.

Rhetorical Question   A question which the author offers the reader, with the intention of promoting thought. Often, an author will answer his or her own question within the body of an essay.

Root word   A base word to which prefixes and suffixes are added.

Sarcasm   Heavy-handed verbal irony where a person expresses dislike or disapproval in a caustic, demeaning, jeering manner. Sarcasm is intended to ridicule and hurt by taunting an individual in a snide manner.

Satire   A form of writing which pokes fun at social conventions or attacks the follies of the human race, with the hope of getting the reader to reconsider the issue and thus improve the human condition.

Simile   A comparison with the use of *like* or *as*. Examples: Andrea's hands were as cold as frost. Chris's pants look like shreds of tissue paper.

Slang   While slang is often colorful and descriptive, such language is considered vulgar and/or informal and never should be employed in a formal essay.

Strategy   The method for approaching, analyzing, and writing about a topic.

Stereotype   Giving qualities to a particular person, race of people or situation which are overly generalized and are not a fair representation of the person, place or thing to which they refer.

Style   How a writer expresses what he or she wants to say. Important factors in style are word use, sentence structure, and voice.

Suffix   A syllable(s) added to the end of a word or root word to give the word a new meaning, a different grammatical function, or form a new word (e.g., wise+est=superlative form of the adjective wise).

Summary   Condensing your own or someone else's work into a shorter composition. Summaries are useful for a writer to get a good sense of a larger work, but they are only a starting point for analysis.

Support   Facts, details and examples which illustrate the validity of your points.

Syllogism   A three-part form of reasoning consisting of a major premise, a minor premise, and a conclusion. See the introduction to Chapter 11 for examples.

Symbol   Something which stands for or represents something other than itself. (e.g., A flag, just a piece of cloth, can represent a country and thus is a symbol for it.)

Synonym Synonyms are words with similar meanings (e.g., skinny/thin, desire/want). Synonyms should be used with care because no two words mean precisely the same thing. (See **Connotation**)

Syntax Syntax refers to the arrangement of words in a sentence.

Theme Subject or topic on which a person writes or speaks. (Note: A theme may also refer to a short essay.)

Thesis The main or controlling idea that a writer seeks to prove in his or her essay.

Tone The expressing of a writer's mood or attitude toward his or her subject through the use of carefully chosen words.

Topic Sentence Much like a thesis, a topic sentence is the controlling idea of a paragraph. Stated usually at the beginning of a paragraph, the sentences which follow must support the topic in order to provide unity for the paragraph.

Transitions Transitions are words or word groups which aid the writer in moving from one point to the next. Some common transitions include: *before, after, thus, therefore, however, moreover, nevertheless.*

Understatement Intentionally down playing an important point or a serious situation. Consider the following sentence: After losing her car, house, and every cent to her name, Colleen was a bit annoyed. To say Colleen was *a bit annoyed* underscores or understates the true gravity of the situation. (See **Irony**)

Unity To provide unity in a composition, the writer must stick to the controlling idea he or she has established without digressing from that major discussion point.

Voice There are two voices—active and passive. In the active voice, the subject _does_ the acting, (e.g., The hunter shot the wolf.), and in the passive voice the subject _receives_ the action of the verb (e.g., The wolf was shot by the hunter.).

ACKNOWLEDGMENTS

Chapter 1: P. 4, "Writers Together" by Toni Morrison, from the October 24, 1981, issue of *The Nation*. Reprinted by permission of *The Nation* Magazine/ The Nation Co., Inc., copyright © 1981. P. 16, "Sharing Tradition" by Frank LaPeña from *News from Native California*, Vol. 4, No. 1, © 1989. Reprinted by permission. P. 21, "My Mothers English" by Amy Tan, reprinted by permission of the author and the Sandra Dijkstra Literary Agency, copyright © 1989 by Amy Tan. P. 28, "Freewriting" by Peter Elbow, from *Writing Without Teachers* by Peter Elbow. Copyright © 1973 by Oxford University Press, Inc. Reprinted by permission. P. 33, "How I Write an Article—I Think" by Donald Murry, reprinted by permission of the author and Roberta Pryor Inc. Copyright © 1982 by Donald M. Murray.

Chapter 2: P. 42, "Ghosts" by Maxine Hong Kingston, from *The Woman Warrior: Memoirs of a Girlhood among Ghosts* by Maxine Hong Kingston. Copyright © 1975, 1976 by Maxine Hong Kingston. Reprinted by permission of Alfred A. Knopf Inc. P. 47, Black Elk: "The Offering of the Pipe" as told to John G. Neihardt (Flaming Rainbow), reprinted from *Black Elk Speaks*, by John G. Neihardt, by permission of University of Nebraska Press. Copyright © 1959, 1972 by John G. Neihardt. Copyright © 1961 by the John G. Neihardt Trust. P. 52, "Journey to Nine Miles" by Alice Walker, from *Living by the Word*, copyright © 1986 by Alice Walker, reprinted by permission of Harcourt Brace Jovanovich, Inc. P. 59, "Saigon, April 1975" from *The Will of Heaven* by Nguyen Ngoc Ngan, reprinted by permission of the author.

Chapter 3: P. 72, "The Woman Who Makes Swell Doughnuts" by Toshio Mori, from *Yokohama, California* by Toshio Mori—The Caxton Printers, Ltd., Caldwell, Idaho. P. 77, "Perimeter" by Barry Lopez, used with permission of Universal Press Syndicate, Kansas City, Missouri. P. 83, "Champion of the World" by Maya Angelou, from *I Know Why the Caged Bird Sings* by Maya Angelou. Copyright © 1969 by Maya Angelou. Reprinted by permission of Random House, Inc. P. 89, "Notes from a Son to His Father" by Russell Leong, from "Rough Notes for Mantos" as found in *Aiiieeeee! An Anthology of Asian-American Writers*, copyright © 1974 by Wallace Lin. P. 94, "Old Before Her Time" by Katherine Barrett, copyright © 1983, Meredith Corporation. All rights reserved. Reprinted from "Ladies Home Journal" magazine.

Chapter 4: P. 109, "My Own Style" by Nikki Giovanni, copyright © 1988 Nikki Giovanni from *Sacred Cows . . . and other Edibles*, William Morrow & Co., 1988. Reprinted by permission of the author. P. 113, "The Myth of the Model Minority" by Philip K. Chiu, reprinted from the May 16, 1988, issue of "U.S. News and World Report." P. 118, "A Young Polish American Speaks Up: The Myth of the Melting Pot" by Barbara Mikulski, from *Poles in the Americas: 1608–1972*. Copyright © 1973, Oceana Publications, Dobbs Ferry, N.Y. P. 122, "Artificial Intelligence" by R. Colin Johnson, copyright © 1990 by Omni Publications Intl., reprinted by permission.

Aging, HHS. Reprinted by permission. P. 265, "Labor and Capital: The Coming Catastrophe" by Carlos Bulosan, from *If You Want to Know What We Are: A Crolos Bulosan Reader,* copyright © 1983 by Aurelio Bulosan. Reprinted by permission of West End Press and Aurelio Bulosan.

Chapter 10: P. 272, "Is There Really Such a Thing as Talent?" by Annie Dillard, from *Seventeen* © Magazine, June 1979, copyright © 1979 by Annie Dillard and Triangle Communications Inc. Reprinted by permission of Annie Dillard and her agent, Blanche C. Gregory Inc. P. 276, from *The Way to Rainy Mountain* by N. Scott Momaday. Copyright © 1969 by the University of New Mexico Press. Reprinted by permission. P. 284, "A Report in Spring" by E. B. White, from *Essays of E. B. White.* Copyright © 1957 by E. B. White. Reprinted by permission of HarperCollins Publishers. P. 290, "Arrival at Manzanar" by Jeanne Wakatsuki Houston and James D. Houston. From *Farewell to Manzanar* by Jeanne Wakasuki and James D. Houston. Copyright © 1973 by James D. Houston. Reprinted by permission of Houghton Mifflin Co. P. 300, "The Libido for the Ugly" by H. L. Mencken. Copyright © 1927 by Alfred A. Knopf Inc. and renewed 1955 by H. L. Mencken. Reprinted from *A Mencken Chrestomathy* by H. L. Mencken. Reprinted by permission of Alfred A. Knopf Inc.

Chapter 11: P. 313, "Who Is Your Mother? Red Roots of White Feminism" by Paula Gunn Allen, from *The Sacred Hoop* by Paula Gunn Allen. Copyright © 1986 by Paula Gunn Allen. Reprinted by permission of Beacon Press. P. 319, "Soul Food" by Imamu Amiri Baraka, from *Home: Social Essays* by Amiri Baraka, copyright © 1966 by Amiri Baraka. Reprinted by permission of William Morrow and Co., Inc. P. 323, "This Land Was Your Land" by Judy Christrup, from the September/October 1990 edition of *Greenpeace* Magazine. Reprinted by permission of Judy Christrup. P. 330, "Does America Still Exist" by Richard Rodriguez. Copyright © 1984 by Richard Rodriguez. Reprinted by permission of Georges Borchardt, Inc. for the author. P. 337, "Distance Learning and American Society" by Mark Charles Fissel, copyright © 1989 by M. C. Fissel. Reprinted by permission of M. C. Fissel. P. 342, "Peyote, Wine and the First Amendment" by Douglas Laycock. Copyright © 1989 by Christian Century Foundation. Reprinted by permission from the October 4, 1989 issue of The Christian Century.

Chapter 12: P. 357, "Drugs" by Gore Vidal. Copyright © 1970 by Gore Vidal. Reprinted from *Homage to Daniel Shays: Collected Essays 1952–1972* by Gore Vidal. Reprinted by permission of Random House, Inc. P. 361, "The Female Has the Power" by Bonita Wa Wa Calachaw Nuñez, excerpt from *Spirit Woman: The Diaries and Paintings of Bonita Wa Wa Calachaw Nuñez,* edited by Stan Steiner. Copyright © 1980 by Stan Steiner. Reprinted by permission of HarperCollins Publishers. P. 364, "Discrimination Is a Virtue" by Robert Keith Miller, from *Newsweek,* July 1980. Reprinted by permission of the author. P. 370, "Racism and Militarism: The Nuclear Connection" by Ron Glass, excerpted in 1985 in *Freedom Notes,* Dennis Banks Defense Committee, San Francisco, from "By Our Own Lives: Moving the Foundation Stone of Racism," 1983 by Ron Glass. Reprinted by permission of the author. P. 378, "Degrees of Discomfort: Is Homophobia Equivalent to Racism?" by Jonathan Alter. From *Newsweek,* V115, March 12, 1990, copyright © 1990 Newsweek, Inc. All rights reserved. Reprinted by permission. P. 383, North Chinese/Vietnamese Elder: "I Want to Live Without Trouble" as told to James M. Freeman. Reprinted from *Hearts of Sorrow: Vietnamese-American Lives* by James M. Freeman with the permission of the publishers, Stanford University Press, © 1989 by the Board of Trustees of the Leland Stanford Junior University.

INDEX